Where There Are Mountains

Donald Edward Davis

Where There

AN ENVIRONMENTAL HISTORY

DONALD EDWARD DAVIS

Are Mountains

OF THE SOUTHERN APPALACHIANS

The University of Georgia Press | *Athens and London*

© 2000 by the University of Georgia Press
Athens, Georgia 30602
All rights reserved
Designed by Kathi Dailey Morgan
Set in 10.5 on 14 New Caledonia by G & S Typesetters
Printed and bound by Maple-Vail
The paper in this book meets the guidelines for
permanence and durability of the Committee on
Production Guidelines for Book Longevity of the
Council on Library Resources.

Printed in the United States of America

04 03 02 01 00 C 5 4 3 2 1

Library of Congress Cataloging in Publication Data

Davis, Donald Edward.
    Where there are mountains : an environmental history
of the southern Appalachians / Donald Edward Davis.
        p.   cm.
    Includes bibliographical references and index.
    ISBN 0-8203-2125-7 (alk. paper)
    1. Human ecology—Appalachian Region, Southern—History.
    2. Nature—Effect of human beings on—Appalachian Region,
Southern—History.   I. Title.
    GF504.A5D38   2000
    304.2'0975—dc21   99-23869
                                CIP

British Library Cataloging in Publication Data available

For my grandmother Janie Ross Davis

CONTENTS

PREFACE

HEN I WAS four years old my mother left me alone for a short time in the backyard, where I somehow discovered a book of matches. Within minutes, I had set fire to an adjoining field, and within an hour, firemen and three fire trucks as well as several bulldozer crews were attempting to put out the blaze. Fortunately, the fire was quickly contained after burning only two or three acres of pasture and woodland.

The year after the fire, hundreds of trees sprouted in the burned-over field, and as I grew older, those seedlings slowly matured into a small woods. By the time I entered college in the late 1970s, the recovering forests surrounding my childhood home were giving way to factories, subdivisions, and strip-development malls. Within a few years, the drone of highway traffic had replaced the once frequent song of the meadowlark and whippoorwill. Gone too were the flocks of evening grosbeaks and cedar waxwings that annually visited our rural community. By the late 1980s, there was little recognizable about my boyhood home.

In part as a result of these environmental changes, I embarked on a personal and intellectual journey that continues to this day. In the summer of 1984, after completing four years of undergraduate training in religious studies, I began working with environmental activist Jeremy Rifkin at the Foundation on Economic Trends in Washington, D.C., doing research that ultimately led to the publication of his *Biosphere Politics,* a book about humanity's changing relationship with the natural world. A year later, I enrolled in a master's program at Goddard College in Plainfield, Vermont, where I had the privilege of studying with the internationally renowned

Murray Bookchin at the Institute for Social Ecology. The major outcome of the Goddard degree was also my first book, *Ecophilosophy: A Field Guide to the Literature,* an annotated bibliography surveying major philosophical trends in contemporary environmental thought.

In 1987, after returning to the mountain region to live full-time, I joined Save Our Cumberland Mountains, a grass-roots environmental organization that was active in stopping strip-mining abuses in the southern Appalachian coalfields. I also became an organizer trainee for the Southern Empowerment Project, a nonprofit organization that continues to provide professional training for community organizers in the mountain region. As a trainee, I spent several weeks in eastern Kentucky, where I met, among others, Denise Giardina, Burt Lauderdale, Verna Mae Sloan, and Hazel King. At that time, my thinking was that if academia did not pan out as a career, there would always be a community group in the region that could use my services. After agonizing over which career path to take, community organizing or college teaching, I chose the latter.

In the fall of 1988 I entered a doctoral program in sociology at the University of Tennessee. From the very beginning, my goal was to work on a dissertation that would examine the evolution of human-environmental relationships in the region of my birthplace, the southern Appalachian Mountains. After receiving formal approval from several sympathetic faculty members, I began reading the works of leading environmental historians—scholars such as William Cronon, Alfred Crosby, Donald Worster, and Carolyn Merchant. I assumed, of course, that their basic analytical approaches could be applied to my study of the mountain region. In the fall of 1988, however, I was largely unaware of the vast literature available within the Appalachian studies field and the many methodological problems and theoretical complexities that such a project would present.

Finally, in 1992, with a deeper knowledge of Appalachian studies scholarship and a more intimate knowledge of the mountain landscape and its history, I began the enormous task of writing *Where There Are Mountains.* To my knowledge, no one had done an extensive environmental history of the southern Appalachian region, so the idea seemed challenging and timely.[1] Two years later, after completing the dissertation, I began working on revising the manuscript for publication as a book. Bringing the study into the twentieth century was an important goal of mine, even though I knew that adding an entire century to the project time-line would require many additional years of writing and research.

In 1995 I formally introduced the project and the work of several other Appalachian scholars to the American Society for Environmental History at its Eighth Biennial Conference in Las Vegas, Nevada. In a session I both organized and convened, the participants spoke not only of the importance of the mountain region to the field of environmental history but also of the importance of environmental change in understanding the history and social development of the southern Appalachians. All participants agreed that the region provided numerous opportunities for further study and research, and several committed themselves to doing book-length studies of the mountains.

One of the first problems I encountered in my own research was when to begin the study. More precisely, at what historical period should I begin the analysis of cultural and environmental change in the southern mountains? Other environmental historians have started by examining the great influx of Anglo-American settlers into the region, avoiding detailed discussions about the impact Native Americans had on the environment prior to Anglo-European contact. In the case of southern Appalachia, I found this approach problematic. This area has been home to a number of native peoples, many of whom altered the landscape prior to contact with northern Europeans during the eighteenth century. Equally important, Spanish exploration, more than a century before the first permanent European settlers arrived, had already put into motion important environmental and cultural changes. The Mississippians, first encountered by the Spanish in the 1500s, were virtually extinguished from the region by the spread of disease and warfare. A systematic examination of Native American subsistence patterns prior to initial contact was therefore essential to understanding the full impact of these changes on the lives of the Mississippians and those who came after them. By beginning the study at 1500, it was possible to provide a more detailed discussion of the precontact environment as well as document the social and environmental effects of Spanish presence in the mountain region.

After firmly fixing the starting point, I was then saddled with another important question: what are the geographical boundaries of the southern Appalachians? Because there has been considerable discussion surrounding the "correct" definition of the mountain region, I felt it necessary to give a more detailed explanation for the boundaries chosen in this study. Chapter 1 provides a brief geographic history of the region that includes my own reasons for defining the area as I do. The geographic area chosen

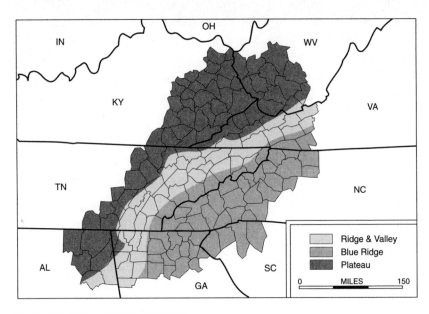

THE SOUTHERN APPALACHIANS

for this study includes the Cumberland Plateau, the Ridge and Valley, and the Blue Ridge Mountains, areas that extend roughly from the New River in southwestern Virginia southward to northern Georgia and northwestern Alabama.

Chapter 2 focuses specifically on the cultural and ecological landscape of the native peoples living in the mountain region during the precontact era. My primary goal is to try to reconstruct what the southern mountains must have looked like prior to European settlement. Here, as in later chapters, I use "Mississippians" or "Cherokees" to designate specific Indian groups and "Native Americans" or "Indians" when discussing native peoples in general. This chapter provides sketches of Mississippian settlement patterns, material culture, agriculture practices, hunting and gathering techniques, exchange networks, and relevant religious beliefs.

Chapter 3 addresses the effects of Spanish exploration of the region, the conquest and eventual demise of Mississippian culture. Cultural exchanges between the two groups are also closely examined, particularly those that had significant impacts on the mountain landscape. Horses, cattle, peaches, and other agricultural crops were first brought to the Southeast by the Spanish, and these cultural artifacts were widely adopted by the Mississippians and, later, their Cherokee descendants. Also important is the extent to which the introduction of disease facilitated the demise and subsequent migration of the Mississippians to areas outside the region. The effect of Spanish conquest on the location, size, and subsistence patterns of these first peoples is critical, providing a historical backdrop for the next stage of cultural and environmental change.

Chapter 4 examines the cultural ecology of the Cherokees over the course of the eighteenth and early nineteenth centuries. By the middle of the 1700s, the fur trade and European fur traders were having an enormous impact on both the mountain environment and Cherokee culture. Using deerskins as currency, Cherokees could purchase large quantities of iron tools, cloth, and even apple trees. Trade in furs hastened the Cherokees' use of guns and horses, which ultimately led to visible declines in deer, elk, and beaver populations. Along with the Europeans came domestic livestock. As game became harder to locate, the raising of hogs, cattle, and horses became more appealing to the Cherokees. In turn, European men married into Cherokee families and borrowed from them many native subsistence techniques and cultural practices. As a result, southern Appalachia today abounds with Cherokee place-names, and a large percentage of the "Anglo" population claims Cherokee ancestry.[2]

Chapter 5 looks at the effects of the European pioneers on the mountain landscape. The Scots-Irish, Germans, English, and Swedes all contributed to the settling of the frontier, and each group left an indelible mark on the mountain landscape. By 1780 pioneer settlements were dispersed throughout the entire region and, in some instances, even far away from the largest streams and rivers. In all of these areas, virgin timber was cleared for homes, gardens, and pastures. Water-powered grain and lumber mills were also erected, changing water levels and stream flows. The largest mammals of the southern Appalachians—buffalo, elk, and deer— were hunted to the point of extinction during the frontier period. Cattle and hogs were fed on the open range, grazing on the vegetation and clearing additional lands for human settlement. By 1810 the frontier had effectively ended in many parts of the mountain South.

Chapter 6 examines the effects of industrial development and the expanding agricultural economy in the region before 1865. Many scholars of the southern Appalachians have portrayed industrialization as a post–Civil War phenomenon. However, iron furnaces and saltworks played an important role in the region's economy as early as 1780.[3] Nevertheless, agriculture remained the dominant mode of subsistence for most of the region until the late nineteenth century. Prior to the Civil War, there were still important subregional differences in terms of crops grown, livestock herding styles, land-use patterns, and cultural practices related to agricultural production. A central concern of this chapter is the effects of land use on the natural environment and the impact of growing urban populations on agricultural production. Another important concern is the question of "self-sufficiency," that is, the extent to which farmers in the region produced surpluses for local or external markets.

Chapter 7 surveys the impact of industrial logging and dam building on the region's landscape and people. During this period, roughly 1870–1936, commercial timbering dramatically transformed the mountain landscape, leaving large tracts virtually devoid of timber. By 1935 the chestnut blight had decimated thousands of additional acres of southern Appalachian forests, continuing the decline of natural resource availability in the mountains. The chapter also looks at the multi-million-dollar pearl industry, which provided an important livelihood for mountain residents living along the region's major rivers. The pearl industry also ended during the 1930s, shortly after the Tennessee Valley Authority began its assault on the native river ecosystem, flooding thousands of acres of prime farmland and ultimately forcing the removal of thousands of mountain residents. A discussion of the environmental ravages of strip-mining was deliberately avoided in this chapter, since most of the destruction occurred solely atop the Cumberland Plateau well after 1936.[4]

Chapter 8 summarizes the process of environmental and cultural change in the southern Appalachians. After studying the four-hundred-year ecological history of the region, I was able to see the full impact of human settlement on the mountain landscape. While environmental degradation has been a relative constant in the region since before European settlement, it increased almost exponentially with the arrival of industrial logging and hydroelectric dam construction in the early twentieth century. Because culture in the southern Appalachians is the product of both social and environmental forces, environmental preservation and cultural preservation are closely linked. When the mountains are preserved, so is Appalachian culture.

ACKNOWLEDGMENTS

I OWE MANY THANKS to many people who helped me complete this project. Charles Cleland of the University of Tennessee kindly encouraged me to explore major themes in agricultural history. Donald Clelland introduced me to the world-systems theory of Immanuel Wallerstein, and John Gaventa was helpful in directing me in the field of Appalachian studies. Sam Wallace added to my knowledge of social ecology and even found time to share his expertise in organic gardening.

Brett Riggs helped me to understand the scope and evolution of Cherokee subsistence patterns throughout the eighteenth and early nineteenth centuries. His knowledge of the material culture of the Cherokees is perhaps without equal. Timothy Silver's book *A New Face on the Countryside* also deserves special mention. Not only was his book a valuable historical resource, but it also motivated me to study environmental and cultural change in post-nineteenth-century Appalachia.[5] Carolyn Merchant's *Ecological Revolutions* was also influential, especially her discussions of self-sufficiency and agrarian capitalism. Alfred Crosby's seminal work, *The Columbian Exchange: The Biological and Cultural Consequences of 1492*, forced me to address early Spanish influences upon the Appalachian landscape. Equally important was the work of Charles Hudson and Marvin Smith, which gave me the inspiration to address Spanish and Native American cultural exchanges that occurred in the mountains during the sixteenth and seventeenth centuries.

Chris Baker and Jeffrey Stotik provided stimulating discussions concerning the influence of external markets on southern Appalachian subsistence patterns. Ongoing conversations with independent scholar Lucy Gump helped me to better understand the material culture of frontier and antebellum Appalachia. Knowledge of changes in the modern Appalachian environment derives from many sources, and so I am indebted to a number of scholars. Two frequently consulted texts were Ronald Eller's *Miners, Millhands, and Mountaineers* and Karl Raitz and Richard Ulack's *Appalachia: A Regional Geography*. I also owe many thanks to Margaret Lynn Brown for sharing her knowledge of mountain culture and settlement patterns in what is now the Great Smoky Mountains National Park.

I am also immensely indebted to the Interlibrary Loan Services staff at the University of Tennessee John C. Hodges Library. Their courteous and efficient service is directly reflected in the rather extensive bibliography. The Special Collections staff of the University of Tennessee McClung Collection were equally helpful in granting my requests to peruse and photocopy portions of rare books and manuscripts. Kathleen Manscill, archivist, and Annette Hartigan, librarian of the Great Smoky Mountains National Park, provided important materials concerning the history and settlement of the Blue Ridge Mountains. Barbara Durham of the library staff at Dalton State College, my new campus home, also showed incredible patience and professionalism in granting my numerous manuscript and interlibrary loan requests. Dudd Dempsey is owed very special thanks for computer wizardry and for her many heroic efforts in preparing the final version of the manuscript.

Lastly, I must give special gratitude to my family members and close friends who have shared with me the ecological and spiritual virtues of mountain living. Tommy and Judy Touchstone, folk artists and ginseng diggers extraordinaire, are true friends and compatriots. Paul Shoffner provided photographic consultation and remained an important sounding board throughout the publication process. Mike Edmondson, a best man on more than one occasion, was always a good friend and confidant. Historian Dave Kimbrough always responded to my occasional requests for good corn liquor and was kind enough to read a final draft of the manuscript. My late grandmother Janie Ross Davis and my now deceased aunt Virginia Dailey also remain important inspirations to this day. They, perhaps more than all others, were my closest companions during the writing of *Where There Are Mountains*.

Where There Are Mountains

Poised between faith and doubt, we must make our way through the world of maps.—DENIS WOOD, *The Power of Maps*

Apalatchi

NAMING THE MOUNTAINS

*A*PPALACHIA. The word itself comes from a Native American tribe, the Apalachees, who did not actually live in the southern mountains. By all historical accounts, the Apalachee Indians lived within a forty-square-mile area of the central Florida panhandle, from the western bank of the Aucilla River to the lands just west of the Ochlockonee River. How, then, did the province of the Apalachees become associated with a mountain region four hundred miles to the north? Scholar David Walls credits French artist Jacques Le Moyne, traveling with a Huguenot expedition to Florida in 1564, with first designating the mountain region as the "Montes Apalatchi."[1] Le Moyne's map, "The Province of Florida in America," first published in 1565, does locate a village called Apalatchi near the headwaters of the Chattooga and Tugaloo Rivers in northeastern Georgia. The map's legend also describes the general area as "a place of great mountains" where, as the map shows, "arise three great rivers."[2]

Le Moyne's Montes Apalatchi is more accurately a reference to the Blue Ridge Mountains of northeastern Georgia near an improbable Apalachee town site and not to the larger mountain chain that we today refer to as the Appalachians. It is highly unlikely that the Apalachees lived near the mountains at that time since it took another century of Spanish colonization and tribal warfare to disperse them from their home on Florida's gulf coast. The citation is, nevertheless, the first referring to any group of mountains as "Appalachia."

Despite Le Moyne's influence on later mapmaking, it was Gerard Mercator's 1569 map that first showed the Appalachians "as a continuous mountain range stretching parallel to the coast in a southwest-northeasterly direction."[3] Only then, according to historical geographer William Cumming, is the term "Apalatchi" or "Apalachen" used consistently by geographers and explorers to describe the mountain region. For nearly two centuries afterward, the term "Apalachen" or "Appalachian" is commonly used to designate almost any part of the mountain region comprising the Eastern Continental Divide or to denote generically the Indian country "back of the foreign settlements."[4] Sir William Talbot used a slight derivation of the term in his translation of John Lederer's travels of 1670, stating that the "Apalatean Mountains—like the prodigious Wall that divides China from Tartary—deny Virginia passage into the West Continent." Similarly, in 1685 Henry Woodward, an English explorer who had obtained a large commission from the Crown for inland exploration, wrote of the benefits of having "the Inlands of our Province of Carolina well discovered . . . and a passage over the Apalateans Mountaines found out."[5]

By the middle of the eighteenth century, however, the term and its various derivations were used with less frequency on most maps, and when it does appear, as in James Adair's "Map of the American Indian Nations," published in 1775, it generally refers only to the southern half of the mountain chain.[6] By the end of the eighteenth century, the area originally known as the Appalachian Mountains was more frequently referred to as Alleghenia or the Allegheny Mountains. It is also at this time that terms such as "Southwest Frontier" and "Trans-Allegheny" first appear as names for the general region west of the mountain chain. The French and English explorers who entered the region in the early 1700s in search of trading opportunities with the Cherokees were likely the first to substitute the term "Allegheny" for "Appalachia." James Adair, who lived among the Cherokees during the 1730s, refers to "the Allegeny, or 'great blue ridge,' commonly called the Apalahche-mountains . . . above a hundred miles broad." Similarly, William Bartram, in his travels through the Blue Ridge Mountains of North Carolina, made reference to the "Cherokee or Alegany mountains." André and François Michaux, who traveled through the region at various times between 1793 and 1803, both consistently referred to the mountain chain as "the Alleghanies."[7]

Not surprisingly, as an increasing number of chroniclers began describing the southern Appalachians to interested readers, uncertainty arose about the proper name for the mountain region. The English traveler G. W. Featherstonhaugh, who explored the mountains in the early 1800s, appeared so interested in discovering the proper name for the mountains that he asked Lewis Ross, the brother of Cherokee chief John Ross, if the local Indians had ever used a specific name for the mountains. "Being desirous of learning whether the Cherokees had any distinct name for the . . . Alleghany or Appalachian Mountains," wrote Featherstonhaugh, "[Ross] inter-rogated some very ancient Cherokee; but not one of them had ever heard of their having a distinct name. The warpath which their ancestors used in crossing them to fight the Mangwee of the Five Nations [the Iroquois], had a particular name; but they knew of no other, neither did they know any-thing of the words Alleghany or Appalachy." [8]

By the first decade of the nineteenth century, the term "Allegheny" replaced "Appalachia" as the most commonly used toponym for the moun-tain region, remaining in common usage until well after the Civil War. A host of writers traveling through the mountains, including Thaddeus Mason Harris, Charles Lanham, and James W. Taylor, used the term when describing the area to the larger public. In his widely read *Excursion through the Slave States,* published in 1844, Featherstonhaugh wrote that the mountain chain, "which is called the Blue Ridge in the Northeastern Parts of Virginia, and which is the most advanced towards the Atlantic, is by many persons in this quarter called the Allegheny Ridge." [9] In 1883 Wilbur Zeigler, the author of one of the earliest histories of the west-ern North Carolina mountains, identified the area as "the Heart of the Alleghenies." [10]

In truth, Appalachia did not again become the most frequently used term for designating the southern mountain area until the first decade of the twentieth century. The individual most commonly given credit for reintroducing the term was the Swiss professor Arnold Henry Guyot, who first explored the southern mountains during the mid–nineteenth century in order to record their proper altitudes. In a paper published in the *American Journal of Science and Arts* in 1861, Guyot attempted to estab-lish the first "scientific and popular usage for the entire mountain range." The paper, entitled "On the Appalachian Mountain System," divided the Appalachian chain into eastern and western divisions, separated by what Guyot calls the Great Appalachian Valley. [11] Interestingly, on the legend of an accompanying map that purportedly was prepared earlier, Guyot iden-tifies the Appalachian range as the Allegheny Mountains, which clearly shows his own ambivalence about which term to use for the region.

Guyot's direct influence on popular opinion is questionable since the term "Appalachia" for the mountain region was not fully adopted by the American populace for another half-century. Traveling through the south-ern mountains in 1867, a young John Muir does not use the term "Appa-lachia" in his brief but descriptive account of the region, referring instead to the "Allegheny mountains" of eastern Tennessee and northern Georgia. Outdoor writer Horace Kephart claimed that as late as 1900 the residents of western North Carolina used the term "the Alleghenies" to identify their collective mountain home.[12]

The return of Appalachia as the principal geographic term for the mountain region was, in part, the result of its persistent use by physical geographers who, around the turn of the twentieth century, chose to use the terms "Appalachia" to designate the larger mountain range and "Allegheny" to designate a smaller subregion within the mountain chain. One of these individuals was John Wesley Powell, who in 1895 enlarged the boundaries of the Appalachian region to include both the Cumberland and Allegheny Plateau provinces to the west. For Powell, Appalachia was a much larger physiographic region: it included the towering mountain slopes of the Blue Ridge Mountains, the narrow hollows and steep knobs of eastern Kentucky, and the fertile river bottoms of the Tennessee Valley. Powell's specific use of "Allegheny" to designate the plateau regions of Kentucky and Tennessee suggests that he still thought the term important but no longer favored it for defining the larger mountain region.[13]

Equally important to this discussion were the sociologists, local-color writers, and Christian missionaries who also "discovered" the southern Appalachians during the late nineteenth century. Their maps of Appalachia were based not only on physiographic landforms but on more subjective criteria such as the culture and ethnic background of the local residents.[14] To these well-meaning reformers, Appalachia was not just a region of mountains; it was also, in the oft-quoted words of writer Will Wallace Harney, "a strange land inhabited by a peculiar people." Their exaggerated and often stereotypical accounts of the mountain populace helped to give the region its reputation as a place of extreme poverty, isolation, and cultural atavism. To these reformers, the mountain region was more than a geographic area; it was also a social and cultural region where pioneer life ways were practiced by a homogeneous population of self-sufficient farmers.[15]

In the twentieth century, the first widely sanctioned definition of southern Appalachia appeared in John C. Campbell's highly influential book *The Southern Highlander and His Homeland,* published in 1921. Campbell defined the region as a 9-state, 254-county area, comprising the peripheral corners of Alabama, Georgia, Tennessee, South Carolina, North Carolina,

Virginia, Kentucky, West Virginia, and Maryland. Campbell did not regularly use the term "Appalachia," however, preferring instead the designation "Southern Highlands." Though he certainly recognized the use of the phrase "southern Appalachians" in the geographic literature, Campbell thought its use restricted the region's boundaries to the area "lying south of the New River Divide" in southern Virginia. Campbell drew his northern boundary at the Mason-Dixon Line, declaring that it first originated from "a boundary dispute of long standing, growing out of claims of [William] Penn and Lord Baltimore."[16]

No serious challenge to Campbell's delineation of the mountain South surfaced until 1962, when sociologist Thomas R. Ford and other scholars reported on the social, economic, political, and cultural characteristics of the region in the well-known study *The Southern Appalachian Region: A Survey.*[17] Although Ford's region is visibly smaller, his boundaries differ only slightly from Campbell's: he simply moved the eastern and western boundaries inward by a single row of counties and shortened the southern end of the region by eliminating a dozen or so counties in northwestern Alabama. Ford's Appalachia, one of the more concise delimitations of Appalachia to date, includes 190 counties in 7 states. In many respects, Ford's Appalachia represents the core of the mountain region, or what sociologist Bruce Ergood has called the "heartland of Appalachia."[18]

In 1964, just two years after the publication of Ford's important study, the Appalachian Regional Commission (ARC) was formed as part of the War on Poverty's efforts in the mountains. Influenced heavily by the political gerrymandering on the part of congressmen who aggressively fought to include their home counties on the final map, the ARC defined Appalachia as an area stretching from New York to Mississippi. The ARC map also contained three geographic subregions: northern, central, and southern Appalachia. The ARC's definition of Appalachia is still widely held, although the national media generally focus attention on the coalfields of central Appalachia when doing stories about the social and economic ills of the mountain region.

In contrast, the study area chosen for *Where There Are Mountains* encompasses the southern core of Appalachia, which nearly all other definitions of the mountain region share. This designation is also much more faithful to the mountain region John Wesley Powell referred to as the southern Appalachians, the mountainous area south of the New River divide. It is made up of 152 counties located in 8 states, including a significant portion of central Appalachia as defined by the ARC in 1964. The boundaries are also closely aligned with the core of "cognitive" Appalachia, meaning that residents living in this area would today be more likely to use the term "Appalachia" when asked to identify the geographic region where they live.[19] Except for a few counties in eastern Kentucky and southern West Virginia, this area is drained almost exclusively by the Tennessee and Cumberland Rivers, which help to unify the region ecologically. It is also much more geographically inclusive than the Southern Appalachian Man and the Biosphere Cooperative's *Southern Appalachian Assessment*, a five-volume study of the region that, regrettably, excluded any treatment of eastern Kentucky or West Virginia.[20]

Topographically, *this Appalachia contains mountains.* In the east rise the Blue Ridge Mountains, the highest in the eastern United States. To the west is the Ridge and Valley physiographic province, an area comprised of parallel ridges lower in elevation than the lofty peaks of the Blue Ridge but often stretching more than a hundred miles in length. Continuing westward is the Cumberland Plateau, a series of high mountain plateaus deeply dissected by numerous streams and rivers that further subdivide the mountain range into hundreds of smaller plateaus and "knobs."[21] Through the heart of this mountain region flow the Tennessee River and its major tributaries. Collectively, these rivers and streams drain about 65,000 square miles of territory, an area representing the true heart of the southern mountains.

Since the late eighteenth century, the southern Appalachians have been the political domain of the Cherokee Nation, eight southern states, the independent State of Franklin, the Tennessee Valley Authority, and the ARC. Prior to that time, the region was home to a number of Native American peoples who, over a period of three centuries, relinquished political and economic sovereignty to the Spanish, French, and British before finally ceding all remaining territory to the Anglo-Americans in the 1830s. The social and political history of this region is without question a complicated and enigmatic one, perhaps as foreboding and precipitous as the southern mountains themselves. Our journey begins with an examination of the southern Appalachians as they appeared in 1500—a time when powerful Mississippian chiefdoms dominated the mountain landscape.

In *La Florida,* there are many walnuts, plums, mulberries and grapes.[1] The Indians sow and harvest the maize, each one cultivating his own. The fruits are common to all, for they grow very abundantly in the open fields, without it being necessary to plant or cultivate them. Where there are mountains, there are chestnuts. — THE GENTLEMAN OF ELVAS, *True Relation of the Hardships Suffered by Governor Hernando de Soto . . . ,* 1540

2 *Mississippia*
NATIVE APPALACHIA

WHEN SPANISH CONQUISTADOR Hernando de Soto and his army of six hundred men first arrived in the Appalachian Mountains in the spring of 1540, they encountered what to us would be an unimaginable landscape of old-growth timber, impenetrable canebrakes, and deep woodland meadows. They were also the first Europeans to cast their eyes upon the enormous stands of American chestnut trees that once comprised nearly a third of the mountain forest. In noting the great abundance of chestnut trees in the upland forest, a member of the De Soto expedition, the Gentleman of Elvas, provided the first recorded reference to the tree. "Where there are mountains," wrote Elvas, "there are chestnuts."[2]

Like other Spanish conquistadors exploring the New World, De Soto had come to the Appalachian Mountains to look for precious metals and to conquer the native people. In Latin America and in parts of the American Southwest, the Spanish Crown had already established a system of *encomienda,* forcing Indian villages to pay tribute in exchange for military protection and the "right" to practice Christianity.[3] In the spring of 1540, however, La Florida was the most remote territory of the Spanish empire, and the Appalachian Mountains were the most out of the way part of La Florida. Although the mountains would never be fully conquered by the Spanish, De Soto and his followers would leave an important mark on both the environment and the people of the southern Appalachian region.

De Soto and his four chroniclers—the Gentleman of Elvas, Hernandez de Biedma, Rodrigo Ranjel, and Garcilaso de la Vega—provide important documentation of one of southern Appalachia's first peoples, the Mississippian Indians. Equally important is the fact that they collectively furnish the first written record of the mountain landscape as it must have appeared before initial European contact.

By all accounts, the De Soto expedition entered the region from the east, arriving in western North Carolina toward the end of May. After ascending the first lofty ridge of the Blue Ridge Mountains around 25 May 1540, De Soto and his men entered a dense forest of mature chestnuts and oaks. The chestnut trees were probably in full bloom at this time, and the sweet aroma must have been intoxicating to De Soto and his men. Along major stream courses, rhododendron grew thick and tall in the forest understory, evoking a luxuriant and tropical clime. Occasionally the tall timber gave way to open clearings, revealing wild strawberries and pea vines in lush profusion. When passing over Swannanoa Gap above Asheville, North Carolina, the Gentleman of Elvas commented that they were crossing "very rough and lofty mountains."[4]

At the time of De Soto's visit to the region, the Blue Ridge Mountains contained large groves of American chestnut, red oak, chestnut oak, and eastern hemlock. In the higher elevations above 5,000 feet, mature stands of Fraser fir and red spruce towered over the upland forest. Sugar maples, many as large as 4 feet in diameter, grew plentifully in the mountain coves, providing shelter and habitat for a large variety of birds and mammals. Because of the great range of altitudes, soils, and temperatures, an enormous variety of herbaceous plants could also be found in the southern mountains, including more than 130 tree species and 200 kinds of herbaceous wildflowers.

To observers like De Soto, however, some plants were much more visible than others. River cane, a bamboolike plant only sporadically observed in the region after World War II, flourished in great abundance along the region's many mountain creeks and rivers. Its presence is confirmed by its extensive use by the Mississippians in both basket making and dwelling construction. The native plant was essential to the structural integrity of their dwellings, providing insulation and added protection from torrential rains. The Gentleman of Elvas noticed the increasing use of river cane as a building material as De Soto's expedition moved northward away from the Gulf Coast. In the Georgia town of Toa, he observed numerous houses quite different from those they had left behind. "[They] are roofed with cane after the fashion of tiles," he wrote. "They are kept clean; some have their sides so made of clay that they look like tapia."[5] River cane remained a dominant plant species in the southern Appalachians until well into the nineteenth century, lending its name to numerous creeks, branches, and local settlements, among them Cane Brake, an eighteenth-century settlement in Transylvania County, North Carolina.[6]

De Soto and his men may have also noted the presence of cranberries, a plant much more commonly found in the mountain region during the sixteenth century. According to ecologists who have studied the history of southern Appalachian plant communities, cranberries were originally found in the high altitude bogs created during the Ice Age, after sea levels rose and mountain valleys filled with rich soil deposits. Later, as glaciers moved southward (they never actually reached southern Appalachia), cranberries moved ahead of them, flourishing in the great beds of sphagnum moss that were found in isolated pockets of southwestern Virginia, eastern Tennessee, and western North Carolina. According to one report, Shady Valley, in upper eastern Tennessee, at one time contained no fewer than 10,000 acres of boreal cranberry bogs.[7]

De Soto's march was slowed considerably by the Blue Ridge Mountains, which forced the expeditionaries northward along the narrow valley of the French Broad River. It took over a week for the men to completely cross the mountains, as the rough terrain and weak condition of the men and horses greatly slowed travel. Food was a precious commodity, and the accounts of both Ranjel and the Gentleman of Elvas are quick to mention the great quantities of corn and fruit bestowed upon the men as they entered each Mississippian township. At Conasoga, a Mississippian village located in the vicinity of Hot Springs, North Carolina, the Gentleman of Elvas noted an abundant supply of native mulberries and walnuts, as well as the large trees on which these native fruits grew. As De Soto's army approached, the Gentleman of Elvas reported that "twenty Indians came out to meet him [De Soto] carrying baskets of mulberries which grow in abundance," adding that the trees "grow wild in the fields without being planted or manured and are as large and as vigorous as if they were cultivated in gardens."[8]

As historian and forest ecologist Tom Hatley has observed, mulberry and other fruit-bearing trees were extremely important to the precontact Indians of the Southeast. Such trees were likely cultivated in semidomesticated groves, which implies that as stands of these and other desired trees matured, competition from other species was probably suppressed by burning or cutting, thereby selectively removing them from the surrounding forest. In fact, the practice is corroborated by naturalist William Bartram, who observed fruit- and nut-bearing trees "cultivated by the ancients" at a former Mississippian township along the upper Savannah River. Drawing attention to their wide spacing and healthy appearance, Bartram added that "though these are natives of the forest . . . they thrive better, and are more fruitful in [their] cultivated plantations."[9]

On 3 June 1540 De Soto and his army reached the fast-moving Pigeon River, crossing it at its confluence near present-day Newport, Tennessee. The entourage followed the river closely downstream, arriving at the banks of the French Broad River. The following day they camped in a "pine forest," where they also encountered a small band of friendly Indians from the Mississippian town of Chiaha who, according to Ranjel, "came in peace and brought corn." Leaving the "rough and lofty mountains" must have been a momentous occasion for the men, who were undoubtedly weak and weary from a lack of familiar food and miles of travel in heavy armor. On 5 June, after officially entering Chiaha, a large village located near present-day Dandridge, Tennessee, the men saw a large open plain and across from it, at Zimmerman's Island, a thriving township. Seeking to restore both their provisions and spirits, the men decided to take rest at Chiaha, during which time their horses grew fat, says the Gentleman of Elvas, on "the luxuriance of the land."[10]

At Chiaha the De Soto party saw "many excellent fields" and in the village itself an abundance of "maize and beans," "butter in gourds," and "bee's honey." The "butter" was probably bear grease or possibly oil made from the pressed meats of butternuts or walnuts, and the "honey" most likely was maple syrup or possibly honey extracted from bumblebee nests. Honeybees, as explained in greater detail in chapter 4, did not inhabit the mountain region—indeed, the entire United States—until at least the beginning of the eighteenth century. The Gentleman of Elvas himself notes that after leaving Chiaha, honey or bees "were not seen in all the land."[11]

Having left the high mountain peaks of the Blue Ridge, De Soto and his men were now in the Ridge and Valley province of southern Appalachia, where, according to the Gentleman of Elvas, agricultural crops grew in noticeably greater abundance. As the conquistador and his men soon discovered, the rich, easily worked soils of southern Appalachia's Ridge and Valley province were especially suited for corn and beans, two important crops of the Mississippians. Upon their arrival at Chiaha, for example, De Soto and his men were given twenty granaries, all "full of choice maize." Similarly, at the northwestern Georgia chiefdom known as Coosa, the Gentleman of Elvas reported seeing great fields of "maize and beans," stretching, he added, "from one town to the other." [12]

Indeed, the fertile soils of the Tennessee and Cumberland River valleys were vital to the Mississippians, a largely agricultural people who located their permanent settlements almost exclusively along the floodplains of "meander-belt" river bottoms. They did so not only because of the easily tilled soils but also because of the proximity to an entire range of plant and animal life. Meander-belt river bottoms, as ecologist Eugene Odum has noted, are among the most productive ecological areas in all of North America. The Mississippians were thus able to make use of a vast range of fish and waterfowl species found in and around this lush river ecosystem. The proximity to water also provided water routes for dugout canoes, which were used to transport food and other goods to distant villages both up- and downstream. In sum, the river floodplain provided convenient access to three of the Mississippians' most important natural resources: river cane, used for dwelling construction, tools, and basketry; water, used for ceremonial bathing, transportation, cooking, and drinking; and rich tillable soil, the medium in which they grew their most important crops—maize, beans, and squash. [13]

Located within this lush river-bottom environment, Chiaha had grown to a sizable Mississippian town, providing important, if temporary, refuge for De Soto and his hungry men. The larger mission of the Spanish entourage—to seek out precious gold and treasure—loomed over them, however, forcing them to break camp in late June in order to continue their journey deeper into the southern Appalachian interior. After following the French Broad for a short distance, the men soon left the banks of the large stream, turning southward toward the oak-hickory forests of the southern Ridge and Valley province. As they made their way through the fertile valleys of eastern Tennessee, the men entered bottomland hardwood forests comprised of oak, hickory, and American sycamore. Growing extremely well in floodplain environments, American sycamore also served as important habitat for the Carolina parakeet, a now extinct bird species that once flew in large numbers among southern Appalachian swamp forests.

As the men pushed southward, the ancient hardwoods gave way to

occasional stands of pine, and in drier areas the woodlands became inter-
spersed with an assortment of native heath shrubs like huckleberry, mountain laurel, and wild azalea. On the higher ridges above the men, mountain
laurel replaced rhododendron as the dominant understory species. Despite the more level terrain, De Soto's march through the central Tennessee Valley was hardly without difficulty or incidence. At the chiefdom of
Tali, located along the Little Tennessee River near Tellico, the Spaniards
held the residents there hostage for several days, refusing to allow children
or women to leave the village. And as the *entrada* made its way toward
northern Georgia, De Soto took prisoner all Indians who refused to pay
tribute, and if none could be captured, he "destroyed their large maize
fields." [14]

Leaving Tali on 10 July, De Soto and his men pushed onward, whenever
possible marching along Indian trails and well-worn animal paths and
avoiding the large, dense canebrakes that surely dominated the riparian
environment along the banks of the Tellico River. Although De Soto and
his men never actually set foot atop the Cumberland Plateau (the third
major geographic subdivision in the southern Appalachians), they undoubtedly saw its rising escarpment along the far horizon to the west. Had
they visited the plateau in 1540, they would have found a mixed, or "mesophytic," hardwood forest of large mature chestnut, beech, poplar, hickory,
oak, blackgum, and sugar maple. Many of these trees, growing largely in
what today would be called primary or "old-growth" associations, grew to
diameters of 4–6 feet. Walnut and cherry trees also dominated particular
areas of the forest, since these were often the first species taken by early
frontier timbermen. Eastern red cedar was another prominent species
atop the plateau, particularly near limestone glades, or "barrens." "On the
hills, at the heads of rivers," Gilbert Imlay reported later, "were red cedars
four feet in diameter and forty feet clear of limbs." [15]

Although they were likely "not frequent nor large," the upland hardwood forests did have occasional open clearings, or what Imlay generally
referred to as "glades of rich land without timber." [16] The combination of
periodic small clearings and old-growth stands of timber provided ideal
habitat for both large and small mammals, including timber wolf, American elk, and eastern cougar. Black bears were also prevalent atop the plateau, as were smaller mammals such as fox squirrel, bobcat, otter, mink,

and gray fox. River cane was another important sixteenth-century endemic on the Cumberland Plateau, where it grew along almost all major creek and river bottoms. In fact, as one noted frontier historian explains it, when early pioneer settlers spoke of "Kain-tuck," they literally meant "the land of cane." [17]

Had they visited the Cumberland mountains, De Soto's party would have also likely come in contact with the Fort Ancient peoples who inhabited portions of eastern Kentucky and West Virginia at that time. According to Penelope Ballard Drooker, villages of these floodplain horticulturalists were found from southern Ohio southward, almost to the hydrological divides between the Cumberland and Tennessee river systems. Although recent archaeological evidence suggests that the vast majority of the Fort Ancient lived within 15 miles of the Ohio River, hunting parties routinely followed major tributaries upstream, well onto the Cumberland Plateau. Permanent Fort Ancient settlements included, among others, the well-excavated Sloan site, found today along the Levisa Fork River in eastern Kentucky, and Parker's Bottom, a Fort Ancient village located on the New River near Hinton, West Virginia.[18]

With the Cumberland Plateau in distant view to the west, De Soto and his army reached northern Georgia around 15 July, camping in the vicinity of Eton near the Conasauga River. The next day the men officially entered the township of Coosa, at that time the largest Mississippian village in the entire southern Appalachian region. According to Charles Hudson and several other noted scholars of the period, Coosa was situated along the headwaters of the Coosa River, near the confluence of the Coosawattee River and Talking Rock Creek. Like Chiaha, Coosa was a major agricultural center able to sustain large populations through the intensive cultivation of corn and beans. Expanses of open fields, many several miles in length, surrounded the village proper. The terrain was, in the Gentleman of Elvas's words, "a charming and fertile land, with good cultivated fields along the rivers." In the surrounding fields, he reported seeing many native persimmon and plum trees, as well as muscadine grapes "with large seeds." [19]

With the intense heat of summer bearing down on the men, Coosa was an oasis in the wilderness. De Soto decided to stay several weeks in the large town, taking advantage of the abundant food supply amassed by the powerful cacique. Almost immediately upon arrival, De Soto decided to enslave many of the men and women, placing them in chains and preventing them from working in the nearby bean and maize fields. After resting for twenty-five days and feeding on the area's abundant wild grapes, scuppernongs, plums, and crabapples, the men broke camp on 20 August. After taking several of the Coosa residents hostage, including the paramount chief and his sister, De Soto continued the march along the Etowah River to Itaba, a town known today as the Etowah archaeological site, and then a few days later on toward Ulibahali, a Mississippian town located near present-day Rome, Georgia. According to Ranjel, the De Soto expedition forded the Etowah River on 30 August before camping in an "oak wood" beyond the river's swollen banks. After spending a day in Ulibahali, De Soto and his men followed the Coosa River downstream, finally leaving the region on or around 4 September, thereby ending their four-month stay in the southern Appalachians.

First Culture

The four chroniclers of the De Soto expedition provide fascinating first glimpses into Mississippian life and the landscape they inhabited. Their accounts, along with historical documents gleaned from other Spanish expeditions into the region, are extremely important for reconstructing the sixteenth-century mountain landscape. As the De Soto narratives help to demonstrate, the mountain landscape of 1540 was notably different from that observed today. Their portrait is painted with a fairly broad brush, however, and when taken alone leaves much room for speculation about important details surrounding Mississippian life and culture. What is lacking in the historical record can, however, be augmented by the findings of anthropologists and archaeologists, who have amassed, in the last several decades, a great wealth of knowledge concerning the evolution and character of southern Appalachia's first peoples.

Most scholars now agree that Mississippian culture proper arose along the middle course of the Mississippi River around A.D. 700. From there Mississippian culture spread eastward, arriving in the southern Appalachian region around 900. The hearth of Mississippian culture was Cahokia, the largest and most densely populated city in North America during the pre-Columbian era. At the height of its development, Cahokia supported a population of more than forty thousand people, covering nearly 6 square miles on the eastern bank of the Mississippi River near St. Louis, Missouri.[20]

According to scholar Bruce Smith, Mississippian culture emerged in southern Appalachia at about the same time that Native Americans of the Late Woodland period began adopting new subsistence technologies, such as the use of pottery tempered with the crushed shells of freshwater mussels. Unlike their predecessors, the early Mississippian Indians depended almost entirely on the cultivation of maize and other crops such as beans and squash. They also built extremely large earthen mounds for use as ceremonial centers and constructed large wooden palisades for protection from enemies. It should be noted that Mississippian culture did not arrive in the region fully intact but evolved in the mountains over the course of several centuries. Both trade with Mississippian townships to the north, west, and south as well as the migration of people to the area doubtless influenced the development of Mississippian culture in the southern mountains. What social forces facilitated the spread of Mississippian culture into the region will perhaps never be fully known, but the general consensus among scholars is that it was the result of both migration into the region as well as the stimulation of already existing peoples to adopt new cultural forms.[21]

Between 900 and 1200, Mississippian society developed into a network of statelike chiefdoms that would reign supreme over the entire mountain region. What is generally called the Late Mississippian period began around 1200, with the introduction and development of northern flint corn, a greater yielding variety that replaced the lower yielding tropical varieties that had been used by the Indians of the Late Woodland and Early Mississippian eras. The cultivation of the common pole bean also appeared in southern Appalachia during this period, further increasing Mississippian dependence on the cultivation of domesticated crops. Anthropologist Richard Helkamp argues that it was the introduction of these new crops, along with rapidly increasing population, that forced the development of the centralized forms of political authority that are more characteristic of late Mississippian society. By 1300, Mississippian culture was at its apex in the southern Appalachians, reaching extraordinary levels of social and religious organization.[22]

At the time of De Soto's arrival to the mountains, Mississippian peoples were well established along the region's largest rivers and their major tributaries. A substantial population was found in the Blue Ridge Mountains in the area Alfred Kroeber has designated the "Appalachian Summit" region of the upland South.[23] Mississippian culture also extended, though to a more limited degree, onto the Cumberland Plateau along the broad valleys of the Cumberland, Big Sandy, and Kanawha Rivers. The largest populations of Mississippians were found along the slow-moving rivers of the Ridge and Valley province in eastern Tennessee and northwestern Georgia. For example, the Etowah metropolis, a major Mississippian village located on the Etowah River near present-day Dallas, Georgia, may have maintained a population of more than four thousand residents. Most Mississippian settlements in the southern mountain region were smaller in size, however, containing somewhere between three hundred and two thousand individuals at their peak. Although it is difficult to calculate precisely the population for the entire southern Appalachian region prior to European contact, it is quite possible that in 1500 more than sixty thousand residents lived in the southern mountain region.

Despite the fact that the native peoples of southern Appalachia had a great deal in common during the sixteenth century, the mountain area was not entirely culturally homogeneous. In 1300, for example, the peoples living on the upper Tennessee and French Broad Rivers possessed a material culture that most archaeologists refer to as Dallas, whereas those living in the Blue Ridge Mountains of western North Carolina exhibited a culture known as Pisgah. Those Mississippians inhabiting the Ridge and Valley areas of southeastern Tennessee and extreme northern Georgia possessed a Mouse Creek culture, named for the watershed inhabited by these people at approximately the same period. A fourth culture group known as Lamar existed in northwestern Georgia and northwestern Alabama after 1400. Occupying the northern reaches of the Cumberland Plateau in eastern Kentucky and West Virginia were, as noted above, the Fort Ancient peoples, who maintained few, if any, cultural ties with other Mississippian groups.[24]

It should be noted that for many archaeologists the only distinguishing feature of many of these culture groups is the type of pottery made by each group, a distinction based on a relatively minor detail of material culture. Despite important differences in pottery construction and perhaps language, all culture groups, with the possible exception of the Fort Ancient, shared a very similar way of life, establishing economic and social patterns that are still regarded as Mississippian.[25]

In addition to the Mississippians' large grain stores, what certainly impressed the Spanish about Mississippian settlements were the large earthen platform mounds they encountered in each major village. Centrally located above the town's main plaza, these earthworks often exceeded 30 feet in height, and the largest ones had been built in successive stages over a period of two or three centuries. The largest mound in the southern Appalachians was 60 feet high and was located along the Etowah River near Dallas, Georgia. The Indians directed almost all their public activity toward the central structure built atop these mounds, a sacred temple that also served as the residence of the principal ruler. The dimensions of some of the larger temples averaged 35 by 55 feet and could accommodate more than three hundred individuals without excessive crowding. In front of the structure were earthen stairs leading to a small platform outside the main entrance. Here the principal ruler, or cacique, who had descended from "the solar deity via a line of past rulers," addressed the village and presided over public ceremonies. Because the sun played such a central role in their religious beliefs, almost all temple mounds and the structures atop them were oriented toward the east.[26]

Surrounding the chiefly temple were the houses of the townspeople, smaller rectangular or circular structures carefully crafted from long slender saplings, cane lathing, and hardened clay. The Mississippians built these dwellings by placing small saplings firmly into the ground several inches apart. They then stabilized these structures by weaving additional poles perpendicular to the upright saplings. Next the entire dwelling was covered with a thick cane matting and then daubed with a tempered clay, or tapia, made from soft mud and the crushed mantles of freshwater mussels. On rectangular structures, the horizontal roofs were thatched with leaves of cane or covered with bark shingles, further protecting the interior from the elements. This particular method of house building—commonly referred to in the literature as wattle-and-daub construction—was used to construct nearly all Mississippian dwellings in the southern Appalachians.

Inside the dwelling were low couches or cots made with cane lathing and cedar posts. According to Hudson, these couches and other furniture were arranged according to a floor plan that duplicated the equal-armed cross motif found often in Mississippian ceremonial art. As each wall of the dwelling represented one of the four cardinal directions, the center of the armed cross, a small clay fire pit, symbolized the sun. There, at the center of the small room, a burning fire was used to provide warmth or to cook meals. The home was also divided along gender lines, with males generally occupying the western couches of the dwelling and females the northern or southern couches. Archaeological evidence tells us that the hard clay floors of the dwellings were generally kept free of debris, though in the corners could be found items such as clay vessels, tools, or food.[27]

Mississippians throughout southern Appalachia kept small garden plots outside their homes and larger fields for growing maize and beans outside the village proper. Their granaries, elevated corn cribs for storing maize and other important staples, were located on either side of the palisade walls. The Gentleman of Elvas described these structures as *barbacoas,* that is, "a house with wooden sides, like a room raised aloft on four posts."[28] Traveling through the Carolina backcountry a little more than a century later, the English naturalist John Lawson described similar granaries, providing important documentation of their intended use and appearance. According to Lawson, the barbacoas were made in a very curious manner, "supported with eight feet or posts, about seven feet high from the ground, well daub'd within and without upon laths, with loom or clay, which makes them tight, and fit to keep out the smallest insect, there being a small door at the gable end, which is made of the same composition."[29] The largest ones were often located near the residence of the principal ruler, so that subjects could bring together "the tribute of their people . . . maize, skins of deer, and blankets of the country." The existence of these barbacoas signifies a highly ranked form of social organization, in which allegiance was paid in the form of tribute, labor, or military service to one or more chiefs.[30]

Throughout the southern mountains, Mississippian chiefdoms were ruled by a paramount chief who resided in a regional town center and lower chiefs, or "micos," located at minor towns and outlying hamlets. Historical evidence suggests that at the turn of the sixteenth century only three or four caciques maintained political authority over most of the southern Appalachian region. The paramount chief of Coosa, for example, controlled the lower Tennessee Valley, although he probably extended his political authority as far north as the town of Chiaha in upper eastern Tennessee. Although his power was considerably less than that of the chief at

Coosa, the mico of Chiaha controlled much of the upper Tennessee Valley, possibly even towns along the headwaters of the Clinch and Powell Rivers in southwestern Virginia. Xuala, located near Marion, North Carolina, was the major town on the western side of the Blue Ridge Mountains and was also the site of Fort San Juan, built by the Spanish in 1566 in order to more fully secure the mountain region. The Fort Ancient Indians of Kentucky and West Virginia, who never achieved the level of social organization of other Mississippian culture groups, lived outside the influence of a single paramount chief or cacique and thus maintained a much more decentralized body politic.

The political structure of sixteenth-century southern Appalachia ensured social and economic interaction among villages, as each had to pay tribute to the central township. Of course, failure to pay this tribute could lead to warfare among villages, as has been well documented by Marvin Smith, Charles Hudson, and David Hally. In 1560, according to extant historical documents, fifty soldiers from a Spanish colony founded by Tristán de Luna joined with the chief of Coosa in an attack on the Napochies, a Mississippian township located near Chattanooga on the Tennessee River. The Napochies had rebelled against the chief of Coosa, refusing to pay their customary tribute of game, fruit, nuts, and chestnuts. After the warriors of Coosa and their Spanish allies defeated the Napochies, they promised to again pay tribute to Coosa, restoring their status as a subject people.

The presence of an economic system in which tribute was paid to a central regional township indicates that Mississippian chiefdoms operated much like primitive states. Those who refused to pay tribute to the paramount chief suffered dearly, sometimes in lost life. At the local level, however, minor chiefs did not dominate the lives of the common people to the same extent and probably possessed "no more than rudimentary means of sanctioning or repressing their people."[31] Local chiefs also acted as priests, possessing the necessary religious authority to perform the rites and sacred rituals of Mississippian religion. Randolph Widmer argues that paramount chiefs were controlled to a large extent by both religious custom and the needs of local kinsmen. For this reason, Widmer refers to Mississippian chiefdoms of the region as "intermediate" in political structure, meaning that they probably fell short of being despotic regimes.[32]

Another major component of Mississippian religion was the material goods used by individual members to pay for social services and debts, dowries, punitive fines, or funeral fees. In fact, the political power of the chief derived largely from his control over the trade and manufacture of these so-called prestige goods. Mississippian Indians traditionally made prestige goods out of materials found locally by artisans employed directly by the paramount chief. Prestige goods could also be precious stones, intricately carved animal effigies, or the skins of unusual birds or mammals. The large mussel shell gorget, commonly found by archaeologists in sixteenth-century ceremonial contexts, is one example of this type of religious artifact. Competition among elites eventually created a demand for more exotic prestige goods, including objects like conch shells that were certainly not indigenous to the southern mountains. As a result, the Mississippians of southern Appalachia had economic and social ties as far away as Mexico, the Rocky Mountains, and the Great Lakes region of North America.

Despite the hierarchical social structure of each community, the rank-and-file village members generally worked together, acting as a unified social entity for the purpose of the common good. Planting the soil was a communal event involving the participation of the entire township, men, women, and children. John Swanton observed that among the Creeks of the early Creek Confederacy, the care of the fields was under the charge of an elected overseer who called the men to the square "by going through the village blowing upon a conch shell and then marched in order to the field as if they were going into battle, headed by that overseer." According to Swanton, the women, whose participation was central to the successful completion of the planting, "followed in detached parties bearing the provisions of the day."[33]

Women and children took care of weeding the planted crops and were also likely responsible for protecting the fields from birds and other harmful vermin. According to Bruce Smith, temporary shelters, scattered in close proximity to outlying fields, provided "short-term shelter for families tending crops." James Adair similarly noted that Cherokees of the early Colonial era similarly erected high scaffolds in unattended fields upon which sat elderly women whose primary duty upon seeing crows was "to frighten them away with their screeches."[34] Weeding the fields was less a concern as crops matured, however. Commentators have often criticized the agricultural practices of North American Indian groups for this reason, stating that refusal to continually weed their crops stemmed from a "laziness and unskillfulness in planting." As forest ecologist Thomas Hatley has observed, this view of Native American horticulture is highly ethnocentric, because it fails to consider the important role of these so-called weeds in Native American agricultural practices. Not only did these weeds slow soil erosion and fix nitrogen in the soil, they also helped maintain in the surrounding fields "a favorable balance of predatory and pest insect species."[35] Weeds like maygrass, knotweed, pigweed, sumpweed, goosefoot, and native sunflowers were encouraged to grow since they were also eaten as supplemental food sources. In fact, archaeological evidence suggests that these and other high protein "weed" species made up a significant portion of the yearly Mississippian diet.[36]

For this reason, Mississippian agriculture was much more than the tending of a handful of individual crops. More accurately, it was a cultivation system embedded in a diverse and dynamic local ecology. Many edible foods grew in abandoned fields or along the disturbed edges of the upland forest. When in season, passion flower and morning glory roots as well as the fruits of the honey locust, persimmon, pawpaw, chickasaw plum, red mulberry, wild cherry, and scuppernong or muscadine grape might be gathered in large quantities. Likewise, the Mississippians prepared nutmeats of all kinds, including chestnuts, black walnuts, butternuts, hazelnuts, beechnuts, and chinkapins.[37]

In addition to practicing various forms of horticulture, Mississippians were also involved, to a limited degree, in animal husbandry. It is well known, for example, that they kept small dogs as both pets and hunting animals. Effigies of small dogs have been found in numerous burial sites, confirming their existence among the Mississippians. When De Soto first arrived in Gausali, a Mississippian village in the Blue Ridge Mountains of western North Carolina near present-day Marshall, "the Indians there made him service of three hundred dogs." The Gentleman of Elvas states that the Indians did not normally eat dogs, so their willingness to part with the animals seems beyond belief, unless of course De Soto coerced them to do so. The small dogs kept by the Mississippians could well be the ancestors of modern breeds such as the rat terrier and the treeing feist, a small dog still bred in the mountains for hunting squirrels. According to at least one source, the Spanish took those animals back to Europe, where they likely influenced the development of dogs in the Old World. It is also equally possible that European breeds arriving in the New World may have mixed with these Native American breeds, but what is most probable is that the intermixing of Indian and European dogs probably occurred randomly, as dogs and humans adapted to life on the early American frontier.[38]

Mississippians may have also been involved in the pen raising of wild turkeys. It is well known that turkeys were kept in a domesticated state in both Mesoamerica and the American Southwest as early as 300 B.C. Scattered reports of European explorers in Texas, Alabama, and Arkansas also confirm that the eastern wild turkey was sometimes kept by Indians of the Southeast. In 1681 the members of the La Salle expedition traveling through Arkansas saw large flocks of domesticated turkeys among the Indians, who offered them "many hens." When De Soto visited the province of Chalaque in the South Carolina upcountry, he was presented with no fewer than "seven hundred of them, and likewise in others they brought those they had and could get."[39] If this number is accurate and not bald exaggeration, a large proportion of these turkeys must have been kept in enclosed pens, since such a large number of wild birds could certainly not be supplied on immediate demand. According to ethnobotanist Gary Paul Nabhan, the young poults were probably captured in the wild and kept in large enclosed coops until they were fully grown. The wild turkey was certainly more plentiful during the pre-Columbian era due largely to the high mast production of the extensive oak, chestnut, and beech forests that dominated the mountain landscape. A. W. Schorger, a noted historian of this magnificent and shy bird, estimated their population in the United States at around ten million birds.[40]

Whatever the method by which the Mississippians obtained their daily food and sustenance (through domestication, horticulture, or by capture in the wild), the question concerning the relationship of the Mississippians to the mountain environment remains largely unanswered. Did the Mississippians of the southern Appalachians truly respect nature, imposing harsh self-restrictions on its use? Or were they more utilitarian, using nature as they saw fit and then confronting issues like resource depletion and sustainability only when their way of life was ultimately threatened? From amassed evidence it appears that both approaches to nature were certainly present within the Mississippian worldview. Nature held many sacred and religious attributes, a fact clearly reflected in their ceremonial art and culture. Yet as important as nature was to the Mississippians, historical and archeological evidence suggests that they were certainly capable of altering their local environment.

First Ecology

Although the diet and subsistence strategies of the native Mississippian mountaineers were extremely varied, involving the use of everything from mulberries and walnuts to deer and turkeys, it was corn or maize that remained the horticultural staple of the Mississippian people. In fact, corn contributed as much as 79 percent of the food intake of the Fort Ancient peoples inhabiting the wide terraces along eastern Kentucky's Levisa Fork River.[41] Corn required the cultivation of large areas of riparian bottomlands, particularly along the level floodplains surrounding each village. Several types of corn were grown, especially the northern flint variety, which had eight to ten rows of large white kernels. By today's standards, Mississippian flint corns were still exceptionally prolific, with some estimates placing yields at around 30 bushels per acre.[42]

Despite these exceptional yields, a large Mississippian village like Coosa, comprised of approximately five hundred to six hundred families, required a considerable amount of land to be cleared for cultivation. Anthropologist William Baden, in his study of Mississippian agricultural systems in eastern Tennessee, estimated that roughly nine tenths of an acre of corn were planted annually for each member of the village community. Using Baden's calculations for the Mississippian town of Coosa, for example, it is entirely possible that more than 2,000 acres of land were cleared for corn growing alone. As cultivated areas declined in productivity, additional lands would also have to be prepared for cultivation, so in any given year the total amount of cultivated and fallow lands would undoubtedly have exceeded that amount. Baden's formula is based on moderately conservative corn yields from sketchy historical data, however, which makes his land clearance estimates higher than they probably were in sixteenth-century southern Appalachia. Even so, the area cleared for cultivation would have stretched for several miles along river bottoms, creating, in effect, a wide treeless plain broken only by the occasional canebrake or wetland copse.[43]

Besides the extensive clearing of land for corn cultivation, the Mississippians also practiced the use of incendiary fire, which certainly had additional effects on the local mountain environment. Fire, which helped to control the growth of unwanted underbrush, was a cultural practice that provided additional habitat for birds and mammals as well as desirable plants like huckleberries, blackberries, and wild strawberries. Mississippians may have also set fires as a hunting technique: the approaching flames directed game toward waiting hunters. It is also possible that they set small fires over fallen chestnuts in order to expose them among the leaf litter and to kill the small weevils that persistently attacked the small nut. The most likely use of fire during the sixteenth century, however, was to clear land for cultivation. Periodic burning would have certainly helped fertilize the soil, increasing both nitrogen and potash levels on heavily used croplands. The clearing of land by fire not only provided a more convenient way of removing unwanted brush or saplings, it also helped villages keep pace with increasing food demands brought on by an ever growing population.

Because the use of incendiary fires by the Mississippians is extremely important for answering questions about the "original" ecological condition of the southern Appalachian mountains, the topic certainly warrants further discussion. Fires would have limited understory growth as well as changed forest composition in some areas. There is considerable evidence for the cultural use of fire east of the mountains during the sixteenth and seventeenth centuries, so the assumption can be made that at least some of the accounts from the early Colonial period might be "applicable to the practices of Indians living west of the Appalachian mountains."[44] In 1632 Thomas Morton described the use of fire among New England Indians as a long-standing custom that he said had "continued from the beginning," adding that the "[savages] are accustomed to set fire of the Country in all places where they come; and to burn it, twize a yeare . . . at the Spring and the fall of the leafe." Adriaen van der Donck wrote a similar description of Indian-set fires along the Hudson River in New York, not only outlining their principal reasons for doing so but telling us how the Dutch had also taken up the practice. "The Indians," wrote van der Donck, "have a yearly custom [which some of our Christians have also adopted] of burning the woods, plains and meadows in the fall of the year, when the leaves have fallen, and when the grass and vegetable substances are dry. Those places which are then passed over are fired in the spring in April."[45]

However suggestive, these frequently quoted accounts do not prove with complete certainty that fire was widely used in precontact southern Appalachia. None of the accounts of the De Soto or later Spanish *entradas* mention woods burning or the use of incendiary fire. The earliest ethno-historical documentation of fire burning in the region is recorded no earlier than 1756 by John de Brahm, who remarked in passing how the Cherokee Indians replenished the soil by "phlogiston," or annually burning their cultivated fields. In November 1799 Abraham Steiner and Christian de Schweinitz recorded burning at Great Tellico in southeastern Tennessee after seeing Cherokee women and children "setting fire to the grass in the woods." The pair also noted the existence of a large open meadow, a "beautiful plain, entirely clear of woods," that they believed was the result of past burnings by Cherokees or their "cultural ancestors"—the Mississippians.[46]

Additional evidence that fires were used by the Mississippians before European contact is the expansive stands of river cane seen by early travelers in the region. Since river cane was used in almost every aspect of Mississippian material culture and required annual harvests of tens of thousands of stalks, it is likely that they set periodic fires to encourage its continued growth. Because cane normally propagates itself via protected underground shoots, the periodic burning of the mature stalks would have caused the plant to quickly spread, choking out all other competing vegetation. Aided by the additional release of phosphorous, potash, and other essential nutrients from the accumulating ashes, river cane would have dominated riparian bottomlands, growing to remarkable heights and widths. F. A. Sondley reported that canebrakes along the French Broad River in North Carolina once extended "for miles," providing further testimony that large canebrakes of the pre-Columbian era were fire-induced.[47]

Another convincing argument for burning during the precontact period comes from evidence uncovered by paleobotanists and others who have laboriously analyzed pollen and other botanical remains uncovered at archaeological sites near Mississippian villages. In her study of human impacts on vegetation change in southeastern Tennessee, Patricia Cridlebaugh demonstrated the existence of large "fire-induced clearings" during the sixteenth century. Her meticulously amassed evidence shows a progressive increase in the distribution of ragweed and other disturbance-favored species from the Woodland period forward, challenging a widely held assumption that plants common to open fields increased only after eighteenth-century European settlement. Unfortunately, Cridlebaugh is unable to determine with any conclusive certainty what percentage of those clearings was the product of purposely set fires or other human disturbance activities like agriculture or tree felling. Moreover, because most of her evidence is also derived from highly localized samples, her findings are more applicable to Mississippian village sites near stream courses rather than to surrounding mountain uplands where human disturbance by fire is less likely to have occurred. As environmental historian Timothy Silver has argued, intentional woods burning in the pre-Colonial Southeast was probably an extremely confined practice with only occasional fires deforesting large, unintended areas. For that reason, pollen records do not, in the main, provide "objective evidence" of universal forest disturbance in the southern Appalachians prior to European contact, as some land-use planners have argued.[48] Like corn cultivation, woods or field burning was more likely restricted to level terraces along floodplains rather than higher elevation ridge tops or mountain slopes.

A final and equally important contribution of the Mississippians to environmental change in the southern Appalachians was the felling of trees for palisade and dwelling construction. Threat of warfare from rival communities required the Mississippians to erect high protective walls around their villages designed to stop the hostile approach of attacking invaders. The palisade surrounding the Mississippian town of Etowah, for example, stretched for more than half a mile along the edge of the Etowah River. At Toqua, a Mississippian town located on the Little Tennessee River in southeastern Tennessee, palisade walls extended around the entire length of the village, a distance of more than 5,000 feet. Archaeological excavations at the Toqua site tell us that the palisade poles were set at intervals ranging from 6 to 12 inches, so at least seven thousand trees had to be cut to make the finished structure. At Toqua a total of three different palisades were constructed during the entire Mississippian occupation there, which means that over several centuries, twenty thousand trees were removed from the surrounding forest. In addition to cutting trees for palisade walls, the Mississippians at Toqua used as many as 10,127 trees to construct the 133 roofed dwellings found within the village walls. And even though poles used for house construction were notably smaller than those used for palisade walls (averaging between 4 and 5 inches in diameter), an average-size Mississippian village required, over time, the removal of more than thirty thousand trees.[49]

In most cases, land disturbance due to palisade construction was significant, but, like burning and corn cultivation, it was highly localized, affecting the immediate village environs and only occasionally impacting the surrounding uplands. Many of the trees were also likely second growth due to their smaller diameter sizes, having sprouted in abandoned fields or on the edge of already cultivated croplands. Taking these trees would no doubt have served to clear additional lands for agriculture as well as eliminate the problem of carrying logs great distances over steep terrain. Trees were also cut as needed, so the observance of longer rotation cycles would have also minimized forest disturbance. On the other hand, the cutting would have encouraged the regeneration of pines and other shade-intolerant tree species that require full sunlight to grow and mature. This fact perhaps explains the occasional "pine forest" encountered by De Soto and his men as they made their way across the mountain region in 1540.[50]

The impact of Mississippian settlement and land clearance would certainly be noticeable, especially along river courses immediately up- or downstream from major town centers. This is not to imply that the Mississippians rarely ventured outside the village proper, beyond the borders of their large cultivated fields. As hunters of wild game they did take large numbers of birds and mammals from the surrounding forests, including passenger pigeons, white-tailed deer, and black bear. The American elk was also hunted, a giant of the mountain forest weighing more than 1,000 pounds with antlers spreading upward of 5 feet or more. A migratory animal, the American elk required an extended range that included both heavily wooded forests and occasional open clearings. During colder winter months, when browse was scarce, elk would have ventured close to Mississippian towns, where they were certain to find larger expanses of overgrown fields and grassy meadows. The earliest historical accounts recording the presence of American elk in the region is the 1670 account of John Lederer, who wrote that when his party first came to "the promontories or spurs of the Appalachian Mountains," they began to see vast herds of "red and fallow deer," referring to white-tailed deer and the American elk. Although the exact number of elk in the Appalachian Mountains will never be known, they undoubtedly had an important impact on the ecology of the region. Some of the grassy balds on the summits of the Blue Ridge Mountains were likely affected by the presence of elk if not maintained, in part, by them.[51]

Besides hunting large and small mammals in the nearby forest, the Mississippians also made frequent use of a great variety of aquatic life. In 1500, however, the major rivers of the southern Appalachians were largely unobstructed and free-flowing, resulting in a vastly different river ecology. For example, the average annual depth of the Tennessee River, the largest stream course in the southern Appalachian region, was less than 1.3 feet, and during high-water season, from January to June, its average water level rose only to 3 feet. Not only did freshwater eels swim in these shallow waters, but also large schools of paddlefish, quillback, gar, and American sturgeon. Numerous birds and mammals also inhabited the shoals and river shorelines, seeking out schools of small fish and reclusive crustaceans. During seasonal migrations, ducks, geese, sandhill cranes, and even whistling swans could be seen along major river courses in numbers that are unimaginable to us today.

Also extremely important to the subsistence base of the Mississippians were redhorse suckers, bass, mussels, and turtles, which in some areas of the mountain region composed a third of their annual protein intake. Excavations of individual townships dating from the sixteenth century revealed a similar inventory of fish and reptiles, including gar, drum, minnows, snapping turtles, and catfish. In fact, the freshwater catfish, one of the more common species taken by the Mississippians, has one of the highest calorie counts of any freshwater fish in North America. Fish were generally taken either by cane spears or ingeniously designed fish traps, the largest and most productive being the V-shaped weir dam. Weir dams were built by laying large boulders across major streams in such a way that the size and shape of the dam forced moving fish downstream toward its narrow end, where strategically placed cane baskets kept the fish from moving back upstream. The American freshwater eel, a fish weighing as much as 7 pounds and growing to 40 inches in length, was no doubt a frequent catch in these traps, particularly during annual spawning runs to waters on the Gulf Coast. Prior to the building of Tennessee Valley Authority dams, American eels were fairly common throughout the mountain region, where they were found as far upstream as the Caney Fork River on the Cumberland Plateau, the Clinch and Powell Rivers in southwestern Virginia, and the larger streams of the Blue Ridge Mountains.[52] Also found along the bottom of the cool and clear-running rivers of the mountains were hundreds of species of freshwater mussels, each acting as a living filter of silt and muddy debris. The Mississippians gathered and ate great quantities of these mollusks, preferring a variety known as the unio or quahog, a species that reaches more than 6 inches in length. Daniel Coxe, whose father was a trader in seventeenth-century America, observed that Indians of the early Southeast gathered quahogs in great quantities and then broiled them over fires until "they [were] fit to eat."[53] The heating process opened the tightly closed shells, revealing a lump of flesh not unlike a commercial clam in both taste and appearance. Small mounds of shell-midden refuse can still be observed around former Mississippian village sites in the region, the only remaining evidence of this once dominant subsistence practice.

An important Mississippian food source, mussels also produced freshwater pearls of varying degrees of smoothness and luster. In 1722 Coxe mentioned three places of "great pearl fishery" in the interior United States: Arkansas and the waters of the "Chiaha" (Tennessee) and "Coza" (Coosa) Rivers. As evidence of their importance to the Mississippians, at Chiaha De Soto was given "a string of beautiful and well-matched pearls as large as filberts." When De Soto asked to see how the pearls were extracted from the mollusks, the cacique ordered boats to fish the shallow pools of the French Broad River. After a night of successful fishing, the Indians placed the gathered mussels over a bed of hot coals to cook. When the shells were opened, they found among the roasted mantles ten or twelve pearls "the size of a pea." De Soto was quick to note that opening the shells in this manner damaged their luster, considerably reducing their value to the Spanish. The Mississippians harvested pearls of higher quality, but these were kept exclusively by the head cacique or lesser village chiefs. At Cofitachequi, located in the South Carolina upcountry, De Soto saw as many as 150 pounds of freshwater pearls stored inside a single village temple.[54]

Not only a source of freshwater pearls, mussels were also the source of another important commodity and sacred prestige good—the shell gorget. The shell gorget, which was generally worn around the neck of higher ranking Mississippians as a breastplate, was skillfully carved from the opulent mother-of-pearl shell of freshwater mussels. Other decorative items tooled from mussel shells included ear and body ornaments and cylindrical beads for necklaces. The survival of Mississippian material culture—at least as practiced during the sixteenth century—was therefore closely linked to the mussels' presence and availability. It is possible that the mussels' social and cultural importance may have actually precipitated their overuse, which would have increased Mississippian dependence on other staples such as flint corn and beans. It is more likely in the case of freshwater mussels, however, that overcollecting was socially discouraged or at least minimized to insure a continued harvest.

Without question, many of the plants and animals consumed by the Mississippians were central to their highly animistic nature cosmology. Nature was imbued with special mythical powers, so protocols and rituals would have regulated both the harvest and use of native flora and fauna. At the same time, corn growing and palisade construction contributed significantly to the deforestation of riparian bottomlands, encouraging the growth of river cane and other disturbance species such as ragweed and pine. Because their subsistence practices were narrowly prescribed around seasonal patterns, the Mississippians of southern Appalachia were largely restricted in their ability to radically alter the larger mountain landscape. The Mississippians had, in short, patterned their lives around the rhythms of a unique physical environment that for centuries remained relatively unchanged.

Living in North America and trying to develop a philosophy of place—a recognition of the spiritual and psychological dimensions of geography—inevitably brings us back to our beginnings here, to the Spanish incursion.—BARRY LOPEZ, *The Rediscovery of North America*

3 Apalachee

SPANISH APPALACHIA

PANISH INFLUENCE on the Mississippian way of life began early, as the conquistadors were the first to encourage trade in European goods. The Spanish added a variety of material elements to Mississippian culture, distributing among the Mississippians numerous trade items such as iron tools and broadcloth fabrics. As early as 1560, the de Luna expedition, comprised largely of starving Spanish settlers, traded "anything and everything" to the Mississippian peoples of northwestern Georgia. A decade later, the conquistador Juan Pardo was known to have given out more than sixty-one chisels, seventy-seven wedges, seventy-two hatchets, thirty knives, and numerous pieces of fabric to southeastern natives, with the majority of these items going to those Mississippians inhabiting the southern mountains. Archaeological evidence tells us an entire range of Spanish trade goods was distributed among the native population during the second half of the sixteenth century, including glass beads, brass bells, wrought-iron chisels, and iron hoes.[1]

At first, trade items had little cultural influence on the native population as a whole, remaining largely status items throughout much of the sixteenth century. Spanish tools and weapons initially remained in the hands of village elites, which meant they had little or no practical value to the rank-and-file members of Mississippian society. By the early 1600s, however, Spanish influence on cultural activities in the mountain area had increased substantially, particularly in the southern end of the region, where direct and indirect trade with Spanish Florida had been more fully established. Between 1597 and 1628, at least four Spanish military expeditions reached the Georgia interior, bringing weapons, horses, and other trade goods in direct contact with the native peoples.[2]

Prior to 1600, intercultural trade had been largely the result of the growing importance of Spanish missions and trading outposts in northern Florida and southern Georgia. The Spanish had built missions both inland and on coastal waters from the Apalachicola River to St. Augustine, the area geographers refer to as the Spanish culture core. After the founding of St. Augustine in 1565, Spain immediately took up the aborted French trade that had resulted from the destruction of the French colony of Fort Caroline.[3] Except for a brief two-year period between 1566 and 1568, when a series of five Spanish forts stretched northward into the Appalachian Mountains, the majority of sixteenth-century Spanish trade was with the many natives inhabiting the Atlantic Coast. The numerous Franciscan missions that were later established west of St. Augustine served as important Spanish trading centers, at first among Indians of the Gulf Coast and later with Indians of the southeastern interior.[4] Spanish influence on Indian culture in the mountains of Appalachia occurred at a more gradual pace, intensifying after 1639, when trade between the Spaniards and the Indians of northern Florida began occurring on a much larger scale. At that time trade became concentrated around the Gulf Coast, after Spanish packet boats began sailing between Havana and San Marcos, a seaport created by Colonial interests wanting to evade royal taxes levied on exports from St. Augustine.

According to extant historical records, deerskins, wild turkeys, maize, and beans obtained from the Indians were shipped in great quantities from these Gulf Coast ports.[5] At the various Franciscan missions, Spanish friars obtained pearls, skins of deer and elk, bison hides, blankets, and other native goods from the Indians in exchange for knives, axes, scissors, hoes, glass beads, brass bells, trinkets, blankets, and cloth. By the 1640s, a growing number of Indians from the southeastern interior were bringing items to the Spanish or trading with native middlemen living along the Gulf and Atlantic Coasts.[6]

By the middle of the seventeenth century, Indians from nearly all parts of southern Appalachia were actively engaged in Spanish trade. Indians from the mountains of Alabama, Georgia, North Carolina, and Tennessee were making periodic excursions to Spanish ports to trade furs and skins for beads, knives, tools, and assorted vegetable and fruit seeds. While historical evidence remains lacking on the scale and frequency of trade between mountain Indians and the Spanish, there are a number of documented accounts of encounters between the two groups. In 1673, for example, English explorer Gabriel Arthur, who was held captive by a group of Indians living on the site of a former Mississippian village near Rome, Georgia, reported that "[e]ight dayes jorny down this river lives a white people which have long beardes and whiskers and weares clothing." While staying with the Indians, Arthur learned that it had not been "many years since ye Tomahittans sent twenty men laden with beavor to ye white people." Although Arthur's account relates the unfortunate fate of the Indians (the Spanish "killed twenty of them and put ye other tenn in irons"), the incident did not stop the Tamahittans from entering the heart of mission territory. In October 1673 Arthur joined a fifty-member party of Tamahittan Indians that were en route "to rob the Spaniard" along the Gulf Coast of Florida. The raid ended only after the Tamahittans had killed a Spanish friar and an African slave. Afterward, the group returned to the Tamahittan village in northwestern Georgia with a bounty consisting of assorted neck bracelets, a Spanish musket, sword, pistol, powder, and various other things.[7]

As Arthur's fascinating account attests, the market for furs and skins was established in the Appalachian region well before the end of the seventeenth century. The trade in skins was of course initiated by the Spanish, who actively sought deer, bison, elk, and beaver skins for the burgeoning Dutch and Mexican leather industries. By 1681 the Spanish governor, Juan Marquez Cabrera, could make reference to trading outposts threatened by "mountain Indians," a sure sign they had penetrated the mountain interior.[8] The fact that Indians were trading furs at this time challenges conventional wisdom about the beginning of the deerskin trade in the southern Appalachians. To date, consensus among many scholars is that prior to 1670 "there was no regular trade in furs or deerskins with the interior of the Southeast." Indeed, most scholars assume the Cherokee trade in furs did not begin until 1690 and that European commerce with the Cherokees was insignificant until well after the turn of the eighteenth century. This view has been recently challenged by historical and archaeological evidence accumulated in the last few decades. Archaeologist Gregory Waselkov believes that enough evidence has now been amassed to assert that "the traditionally held view of American historians is incorrect regarding the origins of the southeastern deerskin trade. Trade did not begin with the founding of Charlestown in 1670. It started almost a half-century earlier, and even then probably drew on still older prehistoric exchange networks."[9]

Native American participation in Spanish trade also implies that re-source extraction was also occurring in the region at a much earlier date than previously proposed. If twenty Tamahittans were laden with beaver, and each man packed at least twenty skins (a conservative estimate), then more than four hundred skins could be taken south on a single trip to the Spanish missions. Beaver, deer, and elk populations were no doubt af-fected by Spanish commerce with the natives, although certainly not to the degree that occurred after the arrival of the British in the eighteenth cen-tury. The overhunting of beaver for the skin trade would have also, at least in the short term, allowed sloughs and marshes created by the beavers' industrious dam-building efforts to return to wooded forest and allowed stream courses to once again flow freely and unobstructed.

The primary impetus for the growing trade in the mountain region were Spanish merchants who had begun shipping deer, bison, and cattle skins from La Florida to Cuba. In Cuba, large quantities of hides and skins were being purchased by the Dutch, whose ships were now regularly calling at the growing port of Havana. There, hides not purchased by the Dutch, including *cueros al pelo* (deerskins with the hair left on), were shipped westward across the Caribbean to Mexico and then to Europe. The exact number and sources for these skins remain undocumented, but the pres-ence of numerous Spanish artifacts throughout the mountain area indi-cates that the Indians of southern Appalachia were actively involved in this trade. The exchange networks can be corroborated with existing historical documents, including Gabriel Arthur's observation that "not many years since ye Tomahittans sent twenty men laden with beavor to ye white people"—a clear sign that trade was occurring with the Spanish before contact with the English traders. Frontier historian Verner Crane noted that in 1680 the Chichimecos, Yuchis, and Cherokees attacked the Guale missions of Georgia, despite the fact that they had previously traded, he says, "in good friendship" with the Spaniards.[10] Additional evidence is a 1681 map drawn by Jean Baptiste Franquelin that clearly shows a path running directly from the Tennessee Valley to the coast of Florida, which, according to John Swanton, was the route "by which the Caskinampos and Shawnees came to the Spaniards to trade."[11]

Spanish missions not only served as important centers of trade and com-merce, but they may have also had an important impact on the native belief system. John Hann observed that as early as the beginning of the seventeenth century many native groups in the Georgia hinterland "began to express interest in giving obedience to Spain's monarch and in being Christianized." [12] While there is little historical evidence that large numbers of Indians of the southern Appalachians converted to Christianity at such an early date, there is reason to believe that their belief systems underwent some revision because of direct contact with the Spanish. In 1567 a Catholic priest who accompanied Juan Pardo on his expedition through the southern Appalachians was stationed at the Mississippian town of Guatri near present-day Salisbury, North Carolina. Charles Hudson notes that Spanish soldiers were also placed "at remote outposts to serve as lay catechists," so it is extremely likely that Indians in the nearby Blue Ridge Mountains were evangelized at this early date.[13] There is also some evidence that a number of Indians who migrated to the Gulf Coast during this period were former residents of the southern Appalachian region, and a few were even incorporated into the mission system. Because of frequent Indian migration to and from the area, it is conceivable that those Indians who did return to their former homelands would have taken back with them Christian ideas. Of course, not all native groups were equally impressed by the Catholicism of the Spanish. Around 1640, a group of Indians referred to only as the "Chisca" journeyed from the southern Appalachians to St. Augustine in order to "render obedience to the Spanish monarch." The Chisca eventually became antagonistic to the Spanish cause, however, and even enticed Christianized Indians in the area to actually revolt against them.[14]

It is also believed that Spanish soldiers of Portuguese descent created small permanent settlements in the mountain region and later married local native women or other exiled refugees from the Iberian peninsula. Several scholars now argue that the so-called Melungeons—a dark-skinned Appalachian people of debatable ethnic origin—are the direct descendants of the first inhabitants of those Spanish settlements. N. Brent Kennedy, as well as other members of the Melungeon Research Committee, have used a variety of historical and genealogical evidence to promote this view of Melungeon ethnic identity. Kennedy points out that common mountain surnames like Caudill, Collins, Goins, and Mullins are traceable directly to Spanish or Portuguese surnames such as Caudillo, Colina, Goinza, and Molina. He and others on the Melungeon Research Committee theorize that after Spanish colonists moved into the hinterlands from the Atlantic Coast, they "intermarried with various Carolina and Virginia Native Americans, and eventually became the reclusive Melungeons."[15]

Of course, the very presence of the Spanish in the Appalachian region insured the introduction of deadly microorganisms, resulting in fatal epidemics and the eventual demise of Mississippian culture. From historical accounts, it is clear that these epidemic diseases had an impact on Mississippian society even prior to the arrival of De Soto in the mountains of Appalachia. It is now believed that the Spanish introduced epidemic disease among the Indians of the Atlantic and Gulf Coasts as early as the second decade of the sixteenth century.[16] Fatal epidemics had also spread northward after Ponce de León and two hundred colonists attempted to settle Florida in 1521. Lucas Vázquez de Ayllón's attempt to colonize the Atlantic Coast south of Charleston in 1526 likewise resulted in the introduction of disease among the southeastern Indians. Because of their highly contagious nature, European diseases, especially smallpox and influenza, spread rapidly among native populations and within decades had, in all likelihood, reached the southern Appalachians.[17]

Historical evidence suggests that communicable diseases had, in fact, reached the South Carolina upcountry before 1540. Garcilaso de la Vega reported seeing numbers of dead bodies and depopulated townships along De Soto's route through the South Carolina uplands. As De Soto's army approached the Blue Ridge Mountains, the Gentleman of Elvas reported that maize was extremely scarce and that the Indians in the area were "very weak."[18] The people of the isolated townships deepest in the mountains appeared to have escaped the full blow of the earliest epidemics, a good fortune that came to an end in the summer of 1540. Individual contact with the Spanish meant almost certain death. As one missionary put it in the late seventeenth century, "the Indians die so easily that the bare look and smell of a Spaniard causes them to give up their ghost."[19] Unfortunately for the Mississippians, many of the Spanish were also in ill health as they traversed the mountain region. In the portion of the Gentleman of Elvas's narrative that details events in the southern Appalachians, there is recurrent mention of De Soto's Christians being "sick with fever."[20]

As primary carriers of fatal epidemic diseases, the Spanish were directly responsible for the decline and eventual demise of the Mississippians. According to one estimate, for every twenty Native Americans present in the southern United States at the time of De Soto's entrada, only one survived.

Charles Hudson places the mortality rate in the interior Southeast slightly lower, although his figure is still an astonishing 90 percent. Alfred Crosby reminds us that for populations with no natural immunity, diseases such as smallpox have at least a 30 percent mortality rate, and those who do survive such diseases are extremely weakened and prone to die later of other illnesses. In 1700 John Lawson remarked that smallpox destroyed entire towns on the North Carolina coast, estimating that only one sixth of the former Indian population remained after a fifty-year period. No doubt by the end of the sixteenth century, a dramatic demographic collapse had occurred in the southern Appalachians.[21]

For survivors of the demographic collapse, options were few. Most sought relocation in towns less affected by the epidemics, often in villages hundreds of miles away. Survivors banded with survivors, forming new and certainly less culturally homogeneous social groups. Cosmological and religious beliefs became quickly watered down or lost entirely to memory. And even if skilled artisans did outlive the epidemics, very few of the surviving chiefs could have supported their work. Because the production of prestige goods was partly subsidized by surplus corn, as grain surpluses declined, so did Mississippian material culture.[22] The epidemics, in effect, created a void in Mississippian life and culture that would never again be filled. Our knowledge of the local customs, religion, and art of the Mississippians is therefore a mere fragment of what existed prior to the time of De Soto's entry into the southern Appalachians.

Heavy loss of life also had a profound impact on settlement and land-use patterns. As a result of depopulation, the once centralized chiefdoms quickly devolved into smaller and much less powerful townships. When colonists from the Tristán de Luna expedition entered the chiefdom of Coosa in 1560, just twenty years after De Soto, they saw not an impressive Mississippian chiefdom but instead a small village. In fact, the members of the de Luna expedition were so bewildered by what they encountered that they mistakenly concluded "that they had not reached the same country that de Soto had explored." De Luna also reported that some of the outlying towns were refusing to pay tribute to the Coosa chiefdom, suggesting that its once powerful political authority was already in decline.[23]

By 1600, just half a century after initial contact, the mound-center/satellite-village settlement arrangement so characteristic of Mississippian society had given way to a much more decentralized pattern of settlement.

Roy Dickens, in his well-documented study of Mississippian settlements in the mountains of western North Carolina, concluded that by the early seventeenth century, Mississippian villages in the Blue Ridge Mountains were no longer clustered around a single mound but were spread out along the floodplains of the larger mountain streams.[24] A similar settlement dispersion also occurred along the Big Sandy and Kanawha Valleys of Kentucky and West Virginia after the social and political collapse of the Fort Ancient peoples.[25] Accompanying the loss of the centralized township was the raised temple mound, the central architectural focus of the Mississippian village. In the Mississippian belief system, the paramount chief was the primary religious medium and the temple mound the most sacred space. All important rituals and ceremonies were performed there. By the end of the sixteenth century, the raised temple mound no longer held the same religious and social importance, if any at all.[26] By the middle of the eighteenth century, the temple mound was little more than a cultural artifact, resulting in much conjecture on the part of both Europeans and Native Americans alike on its former origin and use. In 1776 William Bartram lamented that the Cherokees of North Carolina were "as ignorant as we are, by what people or for what purpose these artificial hills were raised," adding that they had found them in "much the same condition as they now appear, when their forefathers arrived from the West and possessed themselves of the country."[27]

The disruptions caused by the Spanish in sixteenth-century Appalachia had a profound influence on the social and cultural evolution of the mountain region. Within a century after Spanish contact, the Mississippian culture group formally known as Pisgah had been transformed into the culture group Qualla—the ancestral peoples of the modern Cherokees.[28] During the seventeenth century, the Qualla Cherokees continued many of the cultural practices of their Mississippian ancestors, including river cane basketry and the practice of wattle-and-daub building construction. Anthropologists tell us that the early Qualla Cherokees probably included survivors from the Spanish conquest as well as other Mississippian culture groups from the surrounding Blue Ridge Mountains and South Carolina piedmont.[29] Sometime during the early seventeenth century, smaller bands of these Indians migrated westward across the Blue Ridge and by 1700 had located permanent settlements among vacated Mississippian villages along the Tennessee and Little Tennessee Rivers. These later native peoples, generally referred to by historians as the Overhill Cherokees, were critical to the settlement and social development of the southern Appalachian frontier.[30]

In southeastern Tennessee, the surviving Dallas and Mouse Creek peoples probably migrated southward in order to join forces with fragmenting Indian groups in northern Georgia and Alabama.[31] By banding together, these Indians were able to withstand the effects of disease and defend themselves against invading tribes from the north. Eventually these southerly Indian migrations and the cultural coalescence they produced resulted in the development of the Creek Confederacy. Like the Cherokees, the Creeks also possessed many remnants of Mississippian culture; in fact, a great deal of what we know about Mississippian life comes from information gleaned from historical accounts of eighteenth-century Creek life.[32] And finally, most scholars now agree that the Fort Ancient peoples devolved into the Shawnee Indians of historical record, although it is still unclear exactly how and when the culture change process occurred. Gabriel Arthur, upon visiting the Shawnees along the Big Sandy River in 1673, remarked that they did not know "the use of guns" and had no iron instruments among them. Arthur does mention frequent trade between the Shawnees and the Tamahittans of northern Georgia, so they at least knew about the many iron tools, guns, and other cultural artifacts that were regularly entering the mountain region from Spanish Florida.[33]

The decline and eventual social demise of the Mississippians of southern Appalachia were swift in coming, taking less than a century after initial Spanish contact. By 1630 the surviving Mississippians had gone through a culture change process referred to as "deculturation."[34] Unlike acculturation, traditionally defined by anthropologists as "a type of culture change where one group becomes more like another group during a period of prolonged contact," deculturation implies that certain elements were also removed from the existing Mississippian culture.[35] After Spanish contact, Mississippians no longer sought out traditional prestige goods, paid religious homage to a paramount chief, or made intricately carved effigies from bone, shell, or stone.

After the collapse of their principal chiefdoms, the Mississippians of the southern Appalachians were left in a state of cultural impoverishment. Socially and politically weakened, the Indians were now in an even greater position to accept and utilize elements of Spanish culture that had first begun entering the region during the second half of the sixteenth century. Although it is not widely known by scholars writing today, the adoption of Spanish agricultural practices by the Native Americans during the seventeenth century played an extremely important role in the evolution and development of the southern Appalachians.

New World, New Crops

One of the more lasting contributions made by the Spanish to environmental and cultural change in the New World was their introduction of Old World subsistence crops and agricultural practices. After the Spanish settled the northern Florida and southern Georgia coasts in the early 1560s, Iberian plants and animals were quickly introduced among the working farms of the newly established Franciscan missions. By the late 1560s, a mutual agricultural exchange was taking place between Europe and the Americas. The Caribbean Islands played a major role in the exchange, as the Spanish would routinely transport crops cultivated in the Caribbean Islands by Indians and African slaves to their settlements along the coasts of southern Georgia, South Carolina, and northern Florida. Livestock was also involved in the cultural exchange. Iberian cattle, hogs, horses, mules, donkeys, burros, sheep, goats, and chickens were brought in large numbers to the Spanish missions.

Spanish colonists encouraged the introduction of more familiar and accepted foods, bringing peaches, oranges, grapes, figs, wheat, watermelons, muskmelons, barley, chickpeas, garlic, pears, medlars, and pomegranates to the New World. Yams, sorghum, okra, and castor beans were also brought to North America during the Spanish era, initially serving as foods for African slaves.[36] Although it is beyond the scope of this volume to discuss the introduction of all Old World cultigens, crops such as sorghum, okra, and castor beans may not have been introduced into North America directly by the Spanish. These crops are more closely associated with the slave trade and generally followed the Africans into North America. Even though the Spanish relied heavily on Native Americans for physical labor during the sixteenth century, Indians were also directly involved in slave trafficking and themselves owned slaves.

Among the first and arguably most important crops introduced by the Spanish to the southeastern United States were peaches, sweet potatoes, cowpeas, and watermelons. Plants cultivated in the New World were, in turn, taken back to the Europe, becoming dietary mainstays on that continent within decades. Tomatoes, sweet and "Irish" potatoes, tobacco, maize, beans, and peppers were among the many New World plants introduced to the Old World continent by the Spanish as a direct result of these trans-Atlantic exchange networks.[37]

Among the first of the Spanish foodstuffs to reach southern Appalachia were peaches. Spanish colonists brought peaches to northern Florida and southern Georgia, where they served as one of their primary food sources. Archaeologists have recovered peach pits dating from as early as the sixteenth century at the town of Santa Elena on the southern coast of Georgia. The earliest written record of peach trees growing in North America is 1602, at a Franciscan mission in St. Augustine. The Indians of the southeastern interior began growing peaches almost immediately after they were first introduced to the fruit; archaeological evidence suggests that by the early seventeenth century, the Indians of southern Appalachia were growing a Spanish variety of peach.[38]

The widespread use and acceptance of the peach in the southeastern United States were remarked upon by English colonists arriving in Jamestown in 1607, who observed that "the Indians of that region had already acquired them via trade routes extending back to Spanish Florida." By 1700, after naturalist John Lawson first arrived in the Carolinas, the Spanish peach was being dried, cooked, and used as medicine by the natives. In fact, the peach was so central to the culture of the Indians that Lawson and the other English colonists thought the Old World fruit was indigenous to North America, referring to it as the "Indian peach."[39]

The precise date when peaches were first brought to the southern Appalachians is not known. Peach pits have been uncovered at early-seventeenth-century archaeological sites in northern Georgia, southeastern Tennessee, and western North Carolina.[40] At the Joe Bell archaeological site located near Athens, Georgia, archaeologist Mark Williams found peach pits to be the second most common food remains.[41] These peaches, dating from the second quarter of the seventeenth century, may have been brought to the region by direct trade with the Guale missions on the Georgia coast or by Spanish missionaries who visited the Indian town of Ocute in 1596. If they hadn't already done so, it is very likely that the Indians of Ocute, who lived just south of the study area on the Oconee River, would have traded the seeds and/or plants to their northern neighbors. The Tristán de Luna expedition to Coosa in 1560 also may have taken peaches to the region, since there is little archaeological or historical evidence to support the claim that peaches were growing in northwestern Georgia earlier in the sixteenth century.[42]

However peaches were first obtained by the native inhabitants, they were quickly adopted as an important food source, becoming a major subsistence crop. The peach no doubt had a significant impact on the lives of the Indians, not only because the trees provided large yields but also because they ripened at a different time of year than do indigenous fruit trees like wild plums and persimmons. The high-yielding peach also required the subsequent adoption of certain pruning and horticultural skills by the Indians of the Southeast, including the art of grafting, which was by far the most efficient way to propagate the tree. The rapid adoption of the peach during the early seventeenth century does suggest, however, that fruit-tree horticulture was not entirely foreign to the native population. The Indians already had some rudimentary knowledge of fruit cultivation, since they had routinely harvested wild plums in what could be called a quasi-orchard context. In western North Carolina, William Bartram observed what he called an impressive "grove of Cassine yapon," which Cherokees commonly used to make a sacred Black Drink. According to Bartram, the Indians called it their "beloved tree" and so were "very careful to keep it pruned and cultivated."[43]

Within a century after their introduction into the region, peaches were an extremely important part of Native American culture. Not only was the fruit readily eaten, but the leaves, bark, and seeds of the peach were used as a remedy for skin diseases, fever, nausea, and internal parasites.[44] By the eighteenth century, the Cherokees grew peaches in such large orchards that the trees dominated the surrounding village landscape. In 1799, after arriving at the Tellico Blockhouse in southeastern Tennessee, Abraham Steiner and Frederick de Schweinitz commented on the view of the peach orchards in the Cherokee towns of Chota and Toqua: "One can see several miles up the Tennessee, with its charming islands covered with countless peach trees."[45] Peaches were so plentiful in the region during the Federal period that both the Cherokees and the early settlers fed bushels of them to their hogs and distilled the fermenting fruit into a profitable brandy. According to government records, among the personal property of Joseph Vann, the wealthy northern Georgia Cherokee planter, was a peach distillery and 1,133 peach trees.[46] By the early nineteenth century, peaches had spread as far north as West Virginia, lending their name to such places as Peachtree Creek, a tributary of the Coal River.[47]

Like the peach, the sweet potato is another important subsistence crop introduced to the southeastern United States by the Spanish. In the case of the sweet potato, the country of origin is not Spain but the West Indies. The Spanish prized the sweet potato for its sweetness and quickly took it into their gardens and kitchens in both the Old and New Worlds.[48] Commerce between Spanish Florida and the Caribbean certainly hastened the introduction of the tuber to North America, as the first sweet potatoes were brought to the Atlantic and Gulf Coasts around the time of the establishment of the first Spanish missions. Both sweet potatoes and yams were important crops of the Caribbean sugar plantations, although the latter is distinctly an Old World crop originally brought to the New World as a key provision on slave ships. High in essential vitamins and carbohydrates, both plants produce enormous yields on soils too poor for other crops.[49]

The sweet potato may have entered the southern Appalachians in the same manner as the peach, although reliable archaeological evidence is lacking. Agriculture historian Lewis Gray maintains that the sweet potato was probably cultivated by the Indians of northern Florida and coastal South Carolina by the early seventeenth century.[50] Natives of southern Appalachia could certainly have acquired sweet potatoes from trade with coastal populations during the early seventeenth century, but had they done so, particularly on a small scale, there would be little archaeological evidence since the soft skins of the tuber decay rapidly.[51] According to anthropologist Brett Riggs, sweet potatoes were probably introduced on a large scale to the southern Appalachian region after the onset in the early 1700s of trade with the British, who brought with them the tried and proven agricultural practices of the coastal plantations. Whatever the exact route or speed of sweet potato introduction into the southern Appalachians, the Cherokees were growing great quantities of the "Spanish potato" soon after Anglo-European contact. When Revolutionary War colonel William Christian's troops decimated Cherokee towns on the Little Tennessee River in 1776, they destroyed 50,000 bushels of corn and no fewer than 10,000 bushels of sweet potatoes.[52] James Mooney quotes an "old informant" who told him that before Removal, the Cherokees had virtually "lived on them."[53]

Because of the plant's important nutritional properties as well as its ability to thrive in soils too poor for other crops, the adoption of sweet potatoes had an overall positive effect on the lives of the native inhabitants, especially considering the disease, war, and social pressures suffered by them during the eighteenth century.[54] Of course, the Spanish sweet potato continued to be grown by the early white settlers of the region and became, in many frontier communities, one of the most important root crops. By the middle of the nineteenth century, the sweet potato was synonymous with southern eating, making up a significant portion of the mountaineers' diet. On the eve of the Civil War, the region boasted a number of varieties, including the Kentucky early red, Spanish Carolina, purple-skinned, and brimstone. Even as late as 1900 the sweet potato was still referred to by many in the southeastern United States as the "Spanish potato."[55]

Another important crop whose introduction must also be attributed to sixteenth-century Spanish trade is the field pea or cowpea. An Old World legume, the cowpea was an important provision on slave ships sailing from Africa. According to historian Lyman Carrier, the Spanish likely brought cowpeas to the New World shortly after 1500. Archaeologists have found cowpeas among mid-seventeenth-century Spanish artifacts in the lower Tallapoosa Valley of central Alabama, indicating that they first came with the friars who founded the missions of Spanish Florida.[56] Interestingly, the French botanist Le Page du Pratz, who observed them growing in western Mississippi and Louisiana in the early 1700s, referred to them as "Apalachean beans" because, he says, "we receive them from a nation of the natives of that name. They probably had them from the English of Carolina, whither they had been brought from Guinea. . . . They are like the other beans, but much smaller, and of a brown color, having a black ring around the eye, by which they are joined to the shell."[57]

Du Pratz was correct in identifying the cowpea with both the "Apalacheans" of northern Florida and the country of the plant's origination, Africa. He was probably wrong in saying that the British first brought the plant to the natives, although they could have certainly reintroduced the pea after the collapse of the Spanish missions in the early eighteenth century. Because the cowpea was central to slave culture it is doubtful that it would have needed a reintroduction. As Thomas Jefferson himself once observed, the cowpea is a "productive, excellent food for man and beast, awaits without loss our leisure for gathering, and shades the ground very closely through the hottest months of the year."[58] Many Indians preferred cowpeas over beans because they could be picked green or after they dried on the vine, and dried peas could be preserved for months. Peas that were harvested during the summer could be eaten as late as the following spring.

After its introduction by the Spanish, the cowpea apparently spread northward along the coast in much the same manner as the peach and sweet potato, arriving on the periphery of the southern Appalachians sometime around 1700. Cowpeas have been recovered from eighteenth-century Cherokee village sites, where the Indians grew the plant as a supplemental vegetable crop or as fodder for cattle.[59] A major problem in tracing the introduction of peas and beans into the southern Appalachian region is the obscurity of the available descriptions in the historical record. The words "pease," "pulses," "beans," and "calavances" are used almost interchangeably by the botanists, colonists, and early explorers who attempted to describe the various agricultural crops to interested readers living in the Old World. From archaeological evidence, however, it appears that prior to 1600 perhaps no more than two or three kinds of beans were cultivated in the southern Appalachian region. After that time, Spanish missionaries and British traders were responsible for introducing most of the varieties commonly grown in the region today.[60]

The watermelon is yet another Old World plant introduced into North America by the Spaniards during the sixteenth century. Lewis Gray claims that watermelons were growing in the settlements of Spanish Florida by 1579, but the initial introduction of the watermelon had likely happened several decades earlier.[61] In 1562 French explorer Jean Ribault found the Indians of Florida growing "beans, gourdes, cowekcumbers, citrons (watermelons), pease, and many other fruites." Colonial records reveal that members of the Raleigh expeditions to North Carolina in 1584 were served watermelon. Capt. John White, sent to Roanoke Island in 1587, saw among the overgrown fields of the abandoned fort "[m]elons of divers sortes, and Deere within them, feeding on those melons." Watermelons, like peaches, became so widely dispersed among Native American groups that the first English settlers to the continent regarded them as indigenous North American plants.[62]

Despite popular opinion to the contrary, watermelons of the size and form we know today were not native to North America. Their presence in the Appalachian region is due largely to the Spanish conquest of the New

World. The Spanish melons most likely reached southern Appalachia sometime during the early seventeenth century, although neither the Mississippians nor the Cherokees cultivated them in large quantities. The Cherokees did nevertheless grow them, making the watermelon another important marker in determining the influence of the Spanish on culture change in the southern mountains.

Watermelons, peaches, sweet potatoes, and cowpeas, as well as a host of other agricultural crops, including castor beans and okra, played a major role in shaping the subsistence practices of the inhabitants of the southern Appalachians. We know that prior to the founding of Spanish Florida, none of these crops was consumed by the residents of the southern mountains. Whether introduced directly by the Spanish or indirectly by the first European traders who obtained them at coastal settlements, these plants changed the diets of both the natives and the early white settlers. These plants not only added new foodstuffs to native diets but also made the cultivation and harvest of wild and semidomesticated mainstays such as chenopods and sunflowers less desirable. Most of these new plants were cultivated in the same fields as traditionally grown crops. Cowpeas, newly adopted bean varieties, and melons could be planted among cornfields with little or no alteration in traditional cultivation methods. The overall ecological impact of these various plants on the southern Appalachian environment was minimum, however. Only peach orchards caused any visible change to the surrounding mountain landscape.

Old Endings, New Beginnings

With the destruction of the Spanish missions by the English in the early 1700s, direct Spanish influence in the southern Appalachians began to subside. English and French traders quickly pushed their way inland across the mountains and by 1715 had completely captured the Northwest (Wisconsin and the Great Lakes) trade in furs and skins. Market forces quickly shifted from the Gulf Coast to the Atlantic ports of Williamsburg and Charleston, where buffalo hides, deerskins, and Indian slaves were regularly shipped to European and Caribbean ports. The push of English and French traders into the Appalachian mountain region exposed the Native Americans to a new range of trade goods, including clothing, guns, gunpowder, knives, glass beads, and assorted iron tools and implements. Political allegiances soon formed between the British and the Cherokees, making the Native Americans important players in world trade. Within decades hundreds of thousands of animal skins from the region were annually shipped across the Atlantic in order to clothe a growing European population.

Because the historical record is relatively sparse, the full extent of environmental change in the southern Appalachians for this period requires some informed guesswork and creative extrapolation. Evidence from paleobotanical records suggests that deforestation continued in the mountains, increasing throughout the seventeenth and early eighteenth centuries.[63] Pollen samples analyzed for the period do show a rise in the distribution of ragweed, a species indicative of abandoned fields and forest clearings. However, the increase in ragweed does not necessarily demonstrate an increase in Native American agricultural activities and overall land clearance but more likely reflects the plant's tendency to colonize already existing openings in the forest. Early successional tree species such as pine would have benefited from Mississippian population losses, gradually taking over many abandoned cornfields.

The seventeenth century was also, incidentally, the period of the first major buffalo migrations to the region. Without major predators and with larger expanses of land now uninhabited, these large animals could have entered the southern Appalachians in large numbers. The abandoned villages that resulted from the Spanish epidemics quite possibly created enough openings in the upland forest to allow bison to migrate, relatively unencumbered, into the southern Appalachians.[64] In fact, the gradual increase in open grasslands during the seventeenth century may indeed be explained by the migration of woodland bison herds to the mountains. According to several reputable sources, buffalo herds first arrived from the west after swelling populations there encouraged herds to seek food elsewhere.[65]

The very first buffalo herds—small wandering bands of a dozen or so individuals—likely entered the mountain region shortly after 1600, before Indian populations had recovered from the debilitating effects of Spanish-induced epidemics. There is some evidence for the presence of buffaloes in the mountain region prior to that time, however. In 1540 the Indians of a small Mississippian village in the Blue Ridge Mountains presented De Soto with a buffalo hide "as soft as the skin of a kid, with hair like that of the soft wool of sheep." Bison remains uncovered from a single specimen at the Garden Creek site in western North Carolina date to the seventeenth century, as do several specimens uncovered at Fort Ancient villages along the Kanawha River.[66]

Exceptional browsers, buffaloes would no doubt have assisted in the creation of more open woodlands, which may help to explain the numerous "fields, meadows and lawns" encountered by William Bartram during his eighteenth-century travels among the Blue Ridge Mountains.[67] Buffaloes would have had considerable impact on the growth of small plants and shrubs and would have created numerous wallows and trails among upland river valleys. Col. John Donelson, upon seeing the area surrounding the "French" mineral springs near the Cumberland River in Tennessee, felt compelled to comment on changes in the forest landscape that had been caused by bison herds. "The open space around and near the sulphur springs," wrote Donelson, "instead of being an 'old field,' as has been supposed by Mr. Mausker . . . was thus freed from trees and underbrush by the innumerable herds of buffaloes and elk that came to these waters." An English visitor to a salt lick in eastern Kentucky observed "fifty acres of land trodden by Buffaloes" that had, he noted, "not a blade of grass upon it." He added that "springs of this sort have large roads made to them, as large as most public roads in a populous country."[68]

Widespread environmental change due to buffalo herds during the seventeenth century was probably, at the same time, held in check by their relatively small numbers. Throughout most of the seventeenth and early eighteenth centuries, the largest herds in the region totaled fewer than two or three hundred individuals. The most sizable herds in the southern Appalachians were observed much later, during the late 1700s, and most of these were seen in eastern Kentucky around the Red and Licking Rivers.[69] Nevertheless, the presence of the buffaloes was felt for many years in the southern mountains, as buffalo paths often became the roadbeds of settlement trails and nineteenth-century transportation routes. As one noted historian of the mountain region put it: "Down to the outbreak of the Revolution herds of buffaloes grazed in the grassy prairie regions. And if the last of them disappeared beyond the mountains by 1775, their deep worn trails leading to favored licks and ranges persisted for many years afterwards, as was the case with the piles of bones of the slaughtered animals."[70] Environmental change caused by buffaloes was significant but highly localized, particularly around mineral springs and watering holes. In northwestern Georgia at historic Catoosa Springs, the water of one of several noted springs still has the appellation "buffalo water," a name attributed to the many woodland bison that were known to drink from that specific basin of water.

In retrospect, environmental change during the late sixteenth and seventeenth centuries may have involved as much ecological recovery as resource extraction due, in part, to the elimination of tens of thousands of Mississippians from the mountain environs. At the same time, the close proximity of the lower Tennessee Valley to coastal Georgia and Florida did precipitate the diffusion of Spanish agriculture into southern Appalachia, helping to explain the early cultivation of peaches, sweet potatoes, cowpeas, and other European foods in the mountains. Even though the introduction of these crops had a minor influence on the overall southern Appalachian landscape, village gardens and outfields underwent notable change after Spanish contact. After the devastation wrought by disease and famine, the surviving population dispersed linearly along river valleys and begin relying more heavily on corn and other high yielding species such as sweet potatoes and peaches. Within the context of this great social and cultural transformation, the remaining native population was quick to adopt new subsistence strategies that would help create, over the next two centuries, a cultural and physical landscape quite unlike anything seen before.

Their towns are still scattered wide of each other, because the land will not admit any other settlement: it is a rare thing to see a level tract of land of four hundred acres. [The Cherokee] are also strongly attached to rivers—all retaining the opinion of the ancients that rivers are necessary to constitute a paradise.

—JAMES ADAIR, *History of the American Indians*, 1775

4 *Kituah*

CHEROKEE APPALACHIA

$\mathcal{D}$ESPITE THE FACT that important elements of Mississippian life and culture persisted in the mountains for more than a century after initial Spanish contact, by the end of the seventeenth century the Cherokees could claim the vast majority of the southern mountains as their own. By 1700 the territorial boundaries of the Cherokees stretched from the mountains of northern Georgia to southwestern Virginia and from western North Carolina to central Tennessee, an area encompassing more than 70,000 square miles. The Cherokees also claimed much of the land that today comprises the state of Kentucky, although they shared those hunting grounds with the Chickasaws, Creeks, Iroquois, and Shawnees.[1] During the first decade of the eighteenth century, about four thousand families or approximately thirty thousand individuals resided in this vast mountain territory.[2] Concentrated in four main geographic areas, the towns of the Cherokees were located on both sides of the Appalachian Divide. The Lower Towns were located along the Chattooga, Tugaloo, and Keowee Rivers near the border of Georgia and South Carolina. To the north, in western North Carolina, were the Middle Towns, a group of villages scattered along the upper tributaries of the Little Tennessee River. The Valley Towns were located to the south and west of the Middle Towns along the upper Has and Knightly Rivers. And the Overhill Towns, in what is today eastern Tennessee, were found west of the Great Smoky Mountains along the narrow floodplain of the Tellico, Little Tennessee, and Hiwassee Rivers. Kituah, a Middle Town located near present-day Bryson City, North Carolina, was the "mother town" of the Cherokees where tribal leaders supposedly reigned over all Cherokee towns and their divisions.[3]

In all four settlement areas, the size and location of each village were greatly influenced by the topographical features of the surrounding mountain landscape. In the Middle and Lower Towns, where large level bottomlands were more readily available, Cherokees built smaller villages around a large central township. Keowee, a major town located in Pickens County, South Carolina, was a village of this type. In the Overhill area, where river valleys were narrower, a more linear settlement pattern was chosen, with longer distances between individual townships.[4] Henry Timberlake's map, a "Draught of the Cherokee Country," confirms this basic settlement pattern for the eighteenth century in the river valleys of eastern Tennessee. Throughout southern Appalachia, Cherokee settlements were oriented toward rivers, not only because of the necessity for daily bathing, a required ritual, but because of the availability of freshwater fish and waterfowl.[5]

Excluding hunting grounds, the land encompassing the major Cherokee settlements covered an area of approximately 40,000 square miles. This area was the cultural hearth of the Cherokees, encompassing the mountainous sections of Georgia, Tennessee, South Carolina, and North Carolina. The area's ecological diversity provided numerous game animals for hunting, insuring a bountiful harvest from the surrounding wooded forest. The Cherokees, like their Mississippian ancestors, knew the mountain environment well: in the spring they collected numerous herbs from the forest floor; in the summer they picked strawberries, blackberries, and blueberries; and in the autumn they gathered hickory nuts, walnuts, acorns, and chestnuts. Hunters acquired meat to be smoked or dried and stored for the winter. The men also collected fish, crayfish, and freshwater mussels from nearby rivers, and women raised communal gardens of beans, melons, and squash. Corn was the primary staple: by the early 1700s, the Cherokees grew at least three different varieties of corn.[6] They also depended heavily on river cane, which women wove into intricate baskets in which to gather and store the yearly harvest. Because many Cherokee dwellings were built using wattle-and-daub construction, river cane remained an extremely important plant to the Cherokees during the early eighteenth century.[7]

The environment of the southern Appalachians played a significant role in shaping the subsistence culture of the Cherokees. The region's vast mountain forests, replete with old-growth stands of oak and chestnut, as well as its large areas of early successional habitat along watercourses formed an ideal ecosystem for deer, elk, and buffaloes as well as rabbits, squirrels, turkeys, and beavers. Not only were all of these animals important food sources, they also provided pelts for clothing, blankets, and other leather goods. The black bear, a common mammal of the mountain environment, was second only to white-tailed deer in the Cherokee diet.[8] The Cherokees also hunted groundhogs, rabbits, frogs, birds, and turtles, all of which acquired an important place in Cherokee mythology. "Each animal had its appointed station and duty," wrote Cherokee ethnologist James Mooney. The frog was the marshal and leader in the town council, for example, while the rabbit was the messenger to carry all public announcements. The groundhog was emulated in the green corn dance, and, according to Mooney, "the bear figures as having been originally . . . a man, with human form and nature." Because of their important sacred powers, animals taken in the hunt were routinely asked for forgiveness, or, as one Cherokee myth stated it, "no hunter who has regard for his health ever fails to ask pardon of the Deer for killing it."[9]

The southern Appalachians were the acknowledged cornerstone of Cherokee existence, even though the Cherokees did not build permanent settlements among the highest ridges. In fact, at the time of first occupation, white settlers commonly referred to the hills of the Blue Ridge as the "Cherokee mountains."[10] The Cherokees frequently traveled mountain paths to trade, hunt, or conduct warfare, and the mountains themselves were incorporated into their worldview and religious cosmology. Clingman's Dome, in the Great Smoky Mountains, for example, was where the bears held council in several important Cherokee myths. Cherokee cosmology symbolically included the flora and fauna of the mountains, and the stories themselves often take place among the highest peaks. The mountains not only signified home to the Cherokees, they were also their spiritual center.[11]

Trading in Culture

Because of widespread Cherokee occupation, the Appalachian region remained an obstacle to permanent frontier settlement until well into the eighteenth century. But neither the lofty mountain peaks nor the Cherokees themselves could stop the white traders and trappers entering the region from the newly founded settlements on the East Coast. Europeans from the Carolinas and Virginia sought trade with the Cherokees as early as the 1670s, exchanging iron tools, knives, glass beads, cloth, and axes for skins and peltries. By 1716, regular trade was occurring between the Cherokees and the Europeans on the coast, so much so, in fact, that South Carolina had to appoint a superintendent of Indian trade to oversee trading activities.[12] Historical documents reveal that by 1740 as many as 150 traders were buying furs from the Cherokees of southern Appalachia, who, within a single decade, would fast become dependent on European goods. In fact, as early as 1745, Chief Skiagunsta wrote to the governor of South Carolina lamenting that his "people cannot live independently of the English. . . . The clothes we wear we cannot make ourselves. They are made for us. We use their ammunition with which to kill deer. We cannot make our own guns. Every necessary of life we must have from white people."[13]

The fur trade initiated by the British and French at the beginning of the eighteenth century signaled a new era of social and economic relations in the southern Appalachians. Even though Indians of the mountains had traded skins to the Spanish in previous decades, the British and French greatly intensified the practice. Moreover, with the founding of Charleston in 1670, the Cherokees acquired more ready access to an entire range of European goods.[14] Unlike the Spanish fur traders, English traders dealt directly with the Cherokees, often living among them for extended periods and regularly marrying Cherokee women to gain direct entrance into Cherokee society. These resident traders not only introduced new tools and weapons, but they also brought with them a variety of plants and animals that in turn helped to alter the mountain landscape.[15]

The impact of the fur trade on the Cherokees was significant, causing considerable ecological and cultural change even before the first permanent settlers arrived. The development of the southern frontier was therefore linked to the many economic and political changes brought about by the fur trade as well as the subsequent destruction of numerous Cherokee settlements by British and Colonial forces. At the close of the American Revolution, the Cherokees had ceded no fewer than 60,000 square miles of their original territory—including their principal hunting grounds in Kentucky—to the white man. Loss of essential game and hunting lands as well as the introduction of cattle, hogs, horses, and a variety of European plants into the region by English traders had a lasting and profound effect on Cherokee culture.

The first half of the eighteenth century was critical to the course and eventual development of Cherokee Appalachia. Even though the Cherokees began trading with the British and French as early as the 1670s, trading activities did not become a central feature of their lives until the second decade of the 1700s. The very first to settle in the region and live among the Cherokees were men who traded peltries for guns, knives, hatchets, broadcloth, steel traps, and iron hoes. Most of these traders were Scots-Irish, but some were French or English. Two of the very first traders to arrive in the southern Appalachians were Robert Hix and David Crawley; both are said to have visited western North Carolina as early as 1707. Four years later, Eleazor Wiggan, or "Old Rabbit," the first trader to visit the Overhill Cherokees of eastern Tennessee, brought his wares to the town of Tanasee along the Little Tennessee River.[16] Initial contacts with the Cherokees must have been somewhat disappointing to these entrepreneurs, however, since the Cherokees were still a people largely devoted to agriculture. An early government letter of reconnaissance dated 1708 describes them as being "but ordinary hunters and less warriors."[17]

The Cherokees eventually became fascinated by manufactured goods, however, and so their desire for guns, knives, and metal tools encouraged additional traders to settle in the region. Hunting for deer and trapping for beaver soon became a preoccupation of Cherokee men, who initially believed that European guns might give them an advantage over neighboring tribes. In the beginning traders were "kindly treated and watchfully guarded" by the Cherokees and were even occasionally allowed to live within the confines of the village.[18] In addition to guns and iron tools, the traders brought glass beads and various other items the Cherokees greatly desired, including fish hooks, eyeglasses, steel needles, and scissors. Because of their social and economic ties to the coastal settlements, the traders themselves did not depend entirely on the Cherokees for subsistence, bringing to the backcountry their own cattle, hogs, poultry, tea, sugar, salt, liquor, and European herbs and spices. In the gardens and orchards surrounding their settlements, traders planted fruits and vegetables more familiar to their own families and culture. Within decades after their first entry into the region, traders had introduced into the Cherokee country apples, onions, turnips, and cabbages—all common foodstuffs from the Old World.

The Cherokees did not immediately adopt the use of the English traders' new foods or farming methods, however. Nor were the traders particularly interested in transferring their culture directly to the Cherokees. For the first few decades of the eighteenth century, the primary task at hand was simply obtaining skins for the fur trade. Having depleted the deer and beaver populations of the Northeast, Europeans found in the southern mountains an incredible new source for leather and furs.[19] Deerskins stripped of their hair produced a chamoislike leather that could be fashioned into gloves or bookbindings—items that, on the European continent, were in considerable demand. Beaver skins, of considerably lesser value than buckskin, were used exclusively in the British hat-making trade, and the beaver hat, due largely to the availability of beaver skins in the New World, remained fashionable in Europe until at least the end of the nineteenth century.[20]

The increasing European demand for peltries can best be illustrated by the number of dressed and undressed animal skins shipped to England from Charleston, South Carolina, for the years 1700–1715. During that fifteen-year period, almost a million deer, beaver, elk, fox, otter, and raccoon skins found their way to the British leatherworks industry. As the fur trade grew larger, other southern ports became deeply involved in the exporting of skins and furs. From 1755 to 1772, more than 2.5 million pounds of deerskins, taken from approximately one million deer, were shipped from the port of Savannah.[21]

In Colonial days, fur transactions relied almost exclusively on credit, which placed both buyers and sellers in a financially tenuous position. Having been advanced goods from dealers in Charleston or Williamsburg, the traders could hardly afford a poor hunting season. As historian Mary Rothrock explained it, "The London merchant credited the Charles Town merchant, who in turn credited the trader for his season's stock of goods. When the trader sold to the Indians it was with the understanding that he was to be paid with the skins and furs to be obtained in the coming winter's hunt." Eventually this was less a problem for the trader since the Cherokees became highly skilled at obtaining large quantities of deer and beaver pelts. By 1725, explains Rothrock, "remote and small indeed was the Cherokee village . . . [that] could not boast of traders, white men of English, Spanish, or French, or even all three nationalities." Even by 1717 fur traders and the Cherokees had escalated their business so much that the colony formed the South Carolina Board of Indian Commissioners to regulate it.[22]

Initially, neither party had any problem agreeing to the open exchange of goods. The regulations drafted by the Board of Indian Commissioners and agreed upon by the principal Cherokee chief of the Lower Towns, for example, encouraged "a regular exchange of goods and peltries between Charleston and the [Cherokee] Nation." To help facilitate the exchanges, the board granted Theophilus Hastings, the chief Carolina agent for the Cherokees, the use of five assistants from the South Carolina government to oversee Indian trade in the territory. Each assisting agent was assigned one of five areas, which, at that time, consisted of the districts "Terrequa, Quanessee, Choty, Tougeloe, and One to the Northward."[23] Initially a schedule of values was agreed upon by all parties involved, for example, a gun was valued at thirty-five skins; a yard of stroud cloth, eight skins; one hatchet, three skins; a broad hoe, five skins; a calico petticoat, fourteen skins; an axe, five skins; and thirty bullets, one skin. Soon demand was so great for salt, gunpowder, tea kettles, and looking glasses that the board "fixed no price upon them, leaving the traders to exact as much as the savages were willing to pay for them."[24] A skilled hunter might kill fifty deer in one season, indicating both the availability of deer in the mountains and the hunter's desire to obtain European articles of trade. One of the earliest recorded purchases of Cherokee peltries was received at the village of Tugaloo, an important trading post located in the northeastern Georgia mountains. On 11 June 1717 the commissioners received there "nine hundred and one dressed deer-skins, fifty-six raw, thirty beaver skins, and twenty-one slaves."[25]

A year after the Cherokee trade agreement was made with South Carolina, merchants representing the Virginia Indian Company began arriving in the southern Appalachians. Formed in 1714 "to resuscitate the Cherokee trade," the Virginia Indian Company was initially prepared to bring a cargo of no fewer than "200 horseloads of goods under a guard of 40 men" into the Cherokee country.[26] According to Franklin, trade with the Cherokees had been at a low ebb for several years due to both competition from Carolina and the Tuscarora War. In direct competition with South Carolina, the Virginia Indian Company decided to send a company caravan deep into the mountains, where it remained for the summer and autumn of 1718. At the end of that year, traders brought back more than "seventy horses loaded with peltry," which clearly demonstrated the potential of the mountains to supply furs to the world market. Because of its perceived "monopolistic character," however, the Virginia Indian Company aroused powerful opposition in both England and the colonies and was immediately declared defunct by the British government. Despite the official ban, trade with Virginia and the Cherokees continued, so much so, in fact, that the amount of peltries exported from Virginia doubled after 1718. This increased trade greatly exacerbated tensions between the Old Dominion and South Carolina, even though the latter continued to receive the lion's share of Cherokee skins. The fact that both states could maintain a lucrative business in furs shows how plentiful deer and beaver remained in the southern mountains.[27]

By far the greatest trading in furs in the southern Appalachians took place between the years 1739 and 1761. In 1748 Charleston merchants are said to have exported to England 160,000 deerskins at an estimated value of 1.25 million dollars.[28] In 1751 alone it was estimated that 100,000 pounds of deer skins were obtained by no fewer than two thousand Cherokee hunters. Four years later, Cornelious Doherty believed that if the winter season was favorable for hunting, he would be able to obtain thirty-five hundred deerskins from his district alone. This would place the export figure for the entire Cherokee Nation at approximately twenty-five thousand skins.[29] Assuming that this rate held relatively constant between 1739 and 1761, it is conceivable that the Cherokees slaughtered well over half a million deer in this period alone. Goodwin places the figure for the same period much higher, at 1.25 million deer, but that number appears to be somewhat inflated. John Stuart, who kept yearly customs books for the Board of Trade, recorded a total of 5,239,350 pounds of deerskins leaving the port of Charleston from the years 1739 to 1761. Depending on their size and age (older skins weighed slightly less, since weight was lost in the curing process), buckskins could weigh anywhere from 1 to 4 pounds. Using the later estimate, the Cherokee deer kill for the southern mountains for those years could have been anywhere between one and five million deer. Verner Crane stated that skins exported to Great Britain "probably average about one and a half pounds" and so estimates the total deer kill in the Southeast at or near 3.5 million animals. Lawrence Gipson assumed that a buckskin weighed, on the average, 4 pounds, which would put the total deer kill at only slightly more than a million. Remembering that the number of animals dressed by the Cherokees was a fraction of the entire kill for the Southeast, it is perhaps safer to use the Doherty estimation of twenty-five thousand animals per year.[30]

Of course, deer kills for the entire southern Appalachian region would have far exceeded Doherty's figure, since the Creeks, who sold their pelts in New Orleans and St. Augustine, hunted regularly in sections of north-western Georgia and northeastern Alabama. Likewise, the Shawnees, who also shared hunting territory with the Cherokees, usually traded their skins with the Ohio Valley Company to the north. And sometimes the Cherokees themselves avoided traders based in Carolina or Virginia, where most Co-lonial export records were kept. By 1750, the long hunter was also taking his share of furs. To further complicate matters, after 1736 a considerable portion of Cherokee trade with Charleston and Savannah was diverted to Augusta, Georgia, where as many as two thousand packhorse loads of pel-tries were annually purchased. Since the *Georgia Gazette*, the first news-paper in Georgia and a major source of information on the fur trade, wasn't published until 1763, the full extent of the fur trade in the southern moun-tains may never be known.[31]

As uncertain as the deer kill in eighteenth-century Appalachia may be, we do know that the fur trade reached its apogee in the mountains during the 1750s. By this time, many of the smaller Cherokee villages had become entirely dependent on European goods, while still others resented that they were being neglected by those traders who dealt only with the largest townships. In 1751, to help remedy the situation, South Carolina divided the Cherokee Nation into thirteen hunting districts, each of which "should contain about two hundred gun men and three towns . . . in charge of one reputable trader."[32] The board's attempts to control trading activities were largely unsuccessful; in many instances, traders cheated Indians by ignor-ing ordinances that required the use of uniform weights and measures when receiving and distributing goods. An unjust trader might, for ex-ample, use a 30-inch yardstick to measure broadcloth. James Adair, who called such traders "idle, white savages," lamented that the Cherokees were too easily defrauded by the "enchanting force of liquor." Unfortu-nately, the government's separate hunting districts did little to keep dis-honest traders out of Cherokee territory. In 1751 sixteen traders made regular visits to the Cherokee Nation. By 1756, just four years later, more than 150 traders worked with the Cherokees.[33]

After more than three decades of intense hunting and trapping, game in the mountain region was becoming increasingly scarce. By 1760, buffaloes and elk, the largest and most valuable animals of the southern Appalachi-ans, began to disappear entirely from the mountain forests. Bear and deer populations also suffered greatly, not only due to indiscriminate hunting practices such as the killing of both sexes but also because of the increasing number of open-range hogs and cattle that competed with these animals for mast.[34] At the same time, wolves and mountain lions, the principal predators of deer and elk, still roamed the mountains. The only safe refuge for many of these predators became the area surrounding the Great Smoky Mountains in western North Carolina and the upper reaches of the Cumberland Plateau in eastern Kentucky and West Virginia. Outside these remote areas, large mammal populations declined dramatically in number, disappearing entirely near human settlements.

One of the more dramatic changes in forest and stream ecology resulted from the decline and eventual loss of beaver populations in the mountain region. For the period 1699–1715, roughly the first two decades of the British fur trade, nearly forty thousand beaver skins were exported to England from Virginia and Carolina ports. In 1711 alone eight thousand beaver pelts were sent from Virginia.[35] On 14 July 1716 Cherokee burdeners brought 416 beaver skins to Carolina traders; a year later, Theophilus Hastings, the Cherokee agent stationed in Tugaloo, reportedly sent 473 beaver skins to the port of Charleston.[36] Beavers not only provided skins for British hat makers, but they also supplied large amounts of castoreum, a musky oil used by Europeans to manufacture perfumes and medicines. Castoreum, extracted from the glands of beaver carcasses and sold abroad on the international market, was also applied by trappers to steel traps as a lure to attract the often wary animal. The Cherokees of southern Appalachia first acquired steel traps from white traders during the early part of the eighteenth century. Without them, it was extremely difficult to catch these extremely large rodents that, at maturity, weigh as much as 60 pounds.[37]

As more and more steel traps were obtained by Cherokee trappers, the trade in beaver skins became more lucrative. Not surprisingly, the impact of the traps on beaver populations was immediately felt. By 1740 beavers were becoming scarce in many parts of southern Appalachia. In 1747 the entire export of beaver skins from Charleston to England was a mere 200 pounds, or approximately six hundred pelts.[38] By the 1760s, they were valuable commodities indeed. Their importance is evidenced by Gavin Cochrane's letter to the British Crown, which tells of "repeated complaints from the Cherokees" against whites or "Crackers" who had encroached upon their hunting ground and "destroyed their beavers," which, he adds, meant "everything to them."[39] John Logan, an early historian of the Carolina backcountry, agreed that the rapid destruction of the animal was due largely to "the improved methods of hunting and trapping introduced by the whites" and predicted that the beaver would be "wholly extinct" in the upcountry by the "end of the eighteenth century." William Bartram saw only "a few beavers" on his visit to the region in 1776, and these, he noted, "abound most in the north of Georgia . . . near the mountains." By 1800 the industrious beaver had all but been eliminated from the southern mountains and could scarcely be found anywhere east of the Mississippi River.[40]

As important as the destruction of the beaver was the loss of beaver habitat. For centuries, beavers had been engaged in the business of creating floodplain meadows and wetlands along mountain stream courses. They used hundreds of small saplings in the construction of these dams and readily consumed the bark of larger nearby trees, which eventually died, leaving numerous ghostlike trunks to stand sentry along the edge of their slackwater ponds. Their tree-cutting activities created marshy meadows and shallow sloughs throughout the entire range of the southern Appalachians. Needless to say, this unique ecosystem also supported a diverse population of freshwater fish, ducks, herons, song and game birds, and countless reptiles and amphibians. Despite eliminating many acres of bottomland hardwoods from the mountain forest, beaver ponds and their network of channels and dams also helped prevent widespread flooding, equalizing stream flows during both spring freshets and summer droughts. In addition, this open habitat also provided feeding places for deer, bison, and elk, as meadow grasses and other plant species flourished in the moist alluvial soils of the creek and river bottoms surrounding each dam.[41]

The Roots of Dependency

The fur trade had a significant impact on mammal populations in the southern mountains. Similarly, several native plants like American ginseng also experienced dramatic declines in the eighteenth century, particularly after the full entry of the Cherokees into world trade. Ginseng, a valuable commodity on the global market since the mid–eighteenth century, grew abundantly in the rich deciduous forests of the southern Appalachians, particularly on northern-facing slopes above 2,000 feet. The

Cherokees were extremely familiar with the plant since they, like the Chinese, who readily purchased the root, believed it to have important medicinal qualities.

In fact, ginseng was used by the Cherokees for a variety of ailments, including headaches and "weakness of the womb and nervous infections" and as a general tonic.[42] Seneca snakeroot, another common plant of the southern mountains, was also gathered by the Cherokees, who found it to be an excellent remedy for snakebite. Snakeroot was purchased in great quantities by English and French apothecaries and, like ginseng, had become a significant trade item. The Moravians of North Carolina, who settled on the eastern border of the Appalachian frontier, reported that Indians routinely helped them gather hundreds of pounds of the plant, which they later shipped to European merchants.[43]

American ginseng was by far the most important plant of the mountain forest, though the trading of the root, like the trade in furs, got off to a slow start. In the mid-1740s ginseng was still bringing a relatively small price in the markets of Charleston and Williamsburg, partly because the Indians were not drying the root according to strict Chinese standards. In fact, a trader living in the upper Yadkin settlements of North Carolina sadly told James Adair that he "could not get from any of the South Carolina merchants, one shilling sterling a pound, though his people brought it from the Alegany, and Apalache mountains, two-hundred miles to Charles-Town." Adair, convinced of its importance to the region, wondered if some "public-spirited gentleman" might inform the region's inhabitants about "how to preserve the ginseng, so as to give it a proper colour; for could we once effect that, it must become a valuable branch of trade."[44]

Interestingly, ginseng did not become a significant commodity in the southern Appalachians until the 1750s, after the Chinese began to lose faith in Canadian suppliers. Jesuits living in Canada discovered the plant in 1716, and they were the first North Americans to regularly supply the Chinese with the root. Soon afterward tons of North American ginseng were being shipped to China, leading to its overharvesting. As Peter Kalm noted of the Iroquois in 1749,

> the trade which is carried on with here is brisk; for they gather great quantities of it, and send them to France, from whence they are brought to China . . . The Indians of this town were likewise so taken up by this business that the French

farmers were not able during that time to hire a single Indian to help in the harvest. Many people feared lest but continuing for several successive years to collect these plants without leaving one or two in each place to propagate their species.

So great was the demand for the root, adds Kalm, that it "obliged the Indians . . . to go far within the English boundaries to collect these roots."[45]

The growing demand and resulting scarcity of ginseng in the Northeast forced traders to look to the southern Appalachians as a new source for the plant. Moreover, in 1752 the Chinese discovered that an enormous amount of the root from Canada had been dug out of season (the highest grade ginseng is dug in the fall) and improperly dried in ovens. As a result, the Canadian export in ginseng dropped from about $100,000 to $6,500 in a single season before ceasing entirely in 1755.[46] The Chinese therefore turned to southern markets in order to fill the void, and the Cherokees immediately took advantage of the situation. Apparently, during the interim white traders or the Cherokees themselves received some instruction about proper methods of gathering the root, as "English merchants were soon shipping ginseng acquired from Cherokees halfway around the world." In 1761 Henry Timberlake saw it among the Overhill Cherokees, who sold large quantities to local traders, as well as used it in their native medical practice.[47] By the end of the eighteenth century, however, ginseng was so scarce in the Blue Ridge Mountains that John Drayton, the governor of South Carolina, commented that "ginseng had been so much sought by the Cherokee Indians for trade, that at this time it is by no means so plenty as it used to be in this state."[48]

The most conspicuous change to come about as a result of frontier settlement and trade on the native mountain landscape was in the region's many canebrakes, where Anglo traders and later the Cherokees ranged their cattle and hogs. River cane was extremely valuable as a livestock food source, since very few native grasses could survive year-round in the shaded understory of the upland forest. In fact, James Adair observed places in the southern Appalachians where the perennial reed was no longer growing abundantly as early as the 1750s. "On the level parts of the water-side, between the hills," wrote Adair, "there are plenty of reeds, [where] formerly, such places abounded with great brakes of winter canes." An evergreen plant, river cane made excellent fodder for livestock, so traders frequently used canebrakes to sustain their horses, cattle, and hogs. Adair himself once observed a herd of "one hundred and fifty horses" in a single Blue Ridge canebrake.[49] On the Cumberland Plateau, mountain canebrakes "were at once larders where people got their bear-hams and venison, pens for their pigs, sheds and mangers for their cattle . . . Kine [cattle] and swine ate the young stalks and leaves greedily, and there was no such beef, pork, milk and butter as that which came out of the brakes."[50]

Initially, river cane was not terribly affected by grazing cattle and hogs, because the roots of the hardy plant spread rapidly even after the parent stalk is eaten or destroyed. Eventually, however, the plant succumbs to intensive grazing, particularly when animals are returned every year to the same canebrake. This was certainly the case on the Cumberland Plateau, where, according to one Kentucky historian, "five years of foraging in a thicket ended it." A similar observation was made by the Moravians of western North Carolina, where cane grew scarce after "eleven years of continuous grazing."[51] Of course, the loss of river cane hastened the decline of other mammal species, including deer, which used the dense canebrakes for protection against predators, and the large swamp rabbit, or "cane-cutter," which relied heavily on the slender reed as its principal food source.[52]

After the Cherokees of the Lower Settlements widely adopted cattle herding, large canebrakes became harder and harder to find in many parts of the Blue Ridge Mountains. By the end of the century, after whites had pushed farther into the region, Governor Drayton reported that upper country canebrakes were "so closely cut down, by the continuous browsing of cattle, as to have nearly extirpated them."[53] Because the Overhill Cherokees generally had less to do with raising cattle than their counterparts elsewhere in the region, river cane still grew along many of the river bottoms of southeastern Tennessee well into the early part of the nineteenth century. Martin Schneider, who visited the region in 1783, observed several Cherokees pasturing horses in the canebrakes that bordered the Little Tennessee River. "If an Indian has a Horse," wrote Schneider, "he ties it in the Wood from one Place to the other, where the Reed is growing in great Plenty & is good Fodder for them."[54] Not surprisingly, as Overhill Cherokees began to adopt the practice of cattle herding, they too preferred the canebrakes as pasture. In 1799 "Frederici," an itinerant Anabaptist Dunker who lived near the Overhill Cherokees, knew of Indians who had fenced "a great place covered with cane as pasture for their cattle."[55] As late as 1816, Major John Norton reported seeing lush stands of the reed in the extreme southern end of the Tennessee Valley, "where the Cane, yet abounding, enables [the Cherokees] to raise cattle with less labour than where it has been eaten up."[56]

The very first range cattle in the mountains—many of them descendants of the Iberian cattle stocked in the Caribbean and Florida during the seventeenth century—were perceived as game animals by the Cherokees. Although the Cherokees initially had an aversion to beef as a food source, they could not tolerate the destruction of their crops by these wandering herds. Cattle also provided a source of leather, giving the pragmatic Indians an additional incentive for killing the large beasts. The first incidents of cattle killing by the Cherokees were largely isolated but gradually increased as more and more traders brought cattle to the region. By 1730 enough conflict had arisen among Indians and frontier traders over open-range cattle to prompt British authorities to draft an "article of friendship and commerce" to help remedy the situation:

> The Great King and the Cherokee Indians being thus fastened together by the Chain of Friendship . . . [the king] desires that the Indians and the English live together as the Children of one Family . . . so he now gives the Cherokee Indians the Privilege of living where they please; and he has ordered the Gov't. to forbid the English building houses or planting corn near our Indian town, for fear that your young people sho'd kill the Cattle and young Lambs & so quarrel with the English and Hurt them; and hereupon we give one
> Piece of Red Cloth.[57]

For several decades after their initial arrival, most encounters between Cherokees and cattle were not positive ones. Gradually, cattle gained more acceptance, however, particularly among Cherokees who had adopted the practice of fencing in their gardens and cornfields. Their slow acceptance was recorded by James Adair, who noted that "some of the natives are grown fond of horned cattle, both in the Cheerake and Muskohge countries, but most decline them, because the fields are not regularly fenced."[58] Prior to 1750, Cherokees could still find adequate supplies of traditional game such as deer, buffaloes, and turkey, and so most considered the cultivation of corn and beans more important than raising beef. By the middle 1760s, however, after Colonel Grant and his Carolina Volunteers destroyed the Lower and Middle Towns, decimating hundreds of acres of cornfields and numerous peach orchards, more and more Cherokees began adopting the practice of cattle herding. In 1776, when General Rutherford's troops destroyed thirty-six Cherokee towns along the Oconaluftee, Tuckasegee, Hiawassee, and Little Tennessee Rivers, they drove Cherokee cattle into cornfields in order to destroy the ripening corn and then later killed or carried off the remaining stock. The military defeat, famine, and social chaos experienced by the Cherokees over this period accelerated the rate of cattle adoption so that by the 1790s, cattle herding was a preferred activity, particularly among those Cherokees living among the Lower Towns of the Tennessee Valley.[59]

Interestingly, there is considerable historical evidence to suggest that the early cattle-herding practices of the Cherokees more closely resembled the Spanish cattle-herding tradition that had developed south of the mountains in northern Florida and southern Georgia. In fact, the Cherokee name for cattle—*wa'ka*—is actually a corruption of the Spanish term *vaca*, which means "cow." As cultural geographer Brad Alan Bays explains it, "The Spanish instituted an Iberian pattern of open range ranching in northern Florida during the second half of the seventeenth century. In the early eighteenth century this activity was adopted by Florida Indians. These, in turn, passed their experience to other tribes, including the Cherokee."[60]

The northward spread of Spanish cattle-herding practices from Florida into southern Appalachia is little known but certainly supported by the historical record. The Spanish originally brought cattle from Hispaniola to St. Augustine during the sixteenth century, and cattle from these original herds gradually spread westward across the entire Gulf Coast. Although their numbers were never very large there until 1650, cattle were extremely important to the economy of Spanish Florida, providing tallow for candle making, leather for export to Mexico and Europe, hides for wrapping bundles of tobacco, and draft oxen for plows. After 1675, cattle herding was done on a much larger scale as ranching became largely a civilian activity largely outside the control of Catholic missionaries.[61] Accordingly, the only significant white presence in north-central Florida during the second half of the seventeenth century was found at Spanish haciendas, where several thousand cattle could be found roaming freely on the open range.[62] The herds surrounding the haciendas were managed largely from horseback, a Moorish tradition rooted deeply in Iberian pastoralism.

As early as 1670, Indians in northern Florida began raising livestock in the same manner. Soon this cattle-herding method spread northward so that prior to the middle of the 1700s the Creeks, located in Georgia and Alabama, were ranching cattle on the open range. During most of the eighteenth century, the Spanish/Creek herding complex involved herdsmen who used horses during roundups and cattle drives. In 1799 the Moravians Abraham Steiner and Frederick de Schweinitz observed a Spanish/Creek cattle drive at its conclusion near the Tellico Blockhouse in eastern Tennessee and made the following entry in their journal:

> Early in the morning of the 10th we saw a number of Creek Indians, who had been driving cattle thither for the garrison. The cattle had been made to swim the river and were immediately shot . . . [The Creeks] were mostly young, with silver rings in their noses and slits in their ears. They wore short striped shorts, a strip of blue cloth about their loins, long, leatheren stockings laced at the side and Indian half-boots . . . The Creeks bring much cattle into this region, some of it very fine.[63]

According to Bays, the Cherokees most influenced by the Spanish herding tradition were those who had migrated from South Carolina after the Revolutionary War and settled in northeastern Alabama, southeastern Tennessee, and northwestern Georgia. The "Lower Cherokees" lived closest to the Creek Indians, who had adopted cattle herding earlier in the century. The Ridge and Valley also held abundant canebrakes and open, level land, an environment that allowed the cattle "to multiply prodigiously."[64]

Cherokees living in the Blue Ridge Mountains and upper Tennessee Valley, however, did not adopt large-scale, open-range herding until much later, instead free-ranging much smaller herds in the surrounding woodlands. In the more mountainous areas of southern Appalachia, cattle herding was largely associated with women, who oversaw the practice as an extension of their normal agricultural duties. William Bartram observed an Indian trader whose Cherokee wife had learned to make cheese and butter as early as 1775. Small-scale cattle herding did not become popular among traditional Cherokee women until at least 1776, when Nancy Ward, the noted Cherokee matriarch, is said to have learned to make butter and cheese from Mrs. Bean, a white prisoner from the Watauga settlements whom Ward reputedly saved from execution by Cherokee warriors. Afterward, Nancy Ward kept her own small herd and eventually introduced dairying to other Cherokee women, who quickly adopted the practice.[65]

The late adoption of cattle by the Cherokees was due in part to the early presence of hogs in the region, another animal introduced to the Americas by the Spanish. In 1539 De Soto brought into Florida thirteen sows, and by the time he entered the southern Appalachians a year later he had more than three hundred swine. These hogs were the offspring of domestic pigs Columbus brought to Cuba in 1493, which may be the progenitors of all the pigs that eventually populated the West Indies during the sixteenth and seventeenth centuries.[66] A few hogs from De Soto's swine herd probably escaped in the southern mountains, but most were killed by wolves, mountain lions, or the Mississippian Indians. Any hogs that survived such a fate would have multiplied quickly, however, causing some to believe that a few feral hog populations in the Southeast may have originated from the original Spanish herd.[67] Hogs constituted the principal livestock of Spanish Florida, so even if De Soto's hogs did not survive, the Indians of southern Appalachia could have seen them during the seventeenth century. Because raids on seventeenth-century Spanish settlements were fairly common, hogs could have also been obtained in this manner. In 1674 the English explorer Gabriel Arthur went with a Tamahittan hunting party from northwestern Georgia down the Coosa and Alabama Rivers to Mobile Bay, where they reportedly killed "swine, sturgin, and beavers."[68]

The Cherokees did not raise hogs for food until the early 1700s, after the first animals were brought into the settlements by British traders. Initially, it appears that the older generations of Indians did not think the hog was a desirable food source; in time, however, the Cherokees actually preferred hogs to cattle. Hogs could be penned during the growing season and subsequently allowed to forage during the fall and winter months. As Adair himself observed, the women would generally "confine the swine in convenient pens, from the time the provisions are planted to the time they are gathered in."[69] An abundant supply of chestnuts, acorns, hickory nuts, and fallen peaches insured an important food supply for the hogs, which meant less territory was needed for the free-ranging cattle. Pork could also be preserved by salting and smoking, which made its storage more convenient than beef, which had to be pickled in brine. In short, hogs were easier to manage in the mountains and so by the middle of the eighteenth century had become the most important domesticated animal of the Cherokees.[70]

Only decades after their initial introduction, free-ranging cattle and hogs of both the Cherokees and white traders were already competing with bear, white-tailed deer, and turkey populations for mast and browse. The growing shortage of available food, along with the overhunting promoted by the deerskin trade, meant that deer themselves were becoming harder and harder to find in the southern mountains. There is, in fact, ample evidence that as early as 1761 pigs and cattle "were beginning to displace the deer in the southern ecosystem." As deer became scarcer in the southern Appalachians, hunting parties were forced to go farther and farther from the village to secure game.[71] As noted earlier, the proliferation of cattle and hogs throughout the region also meant the ultimate destruction of large canebrakes, the signature plant species of riparian bottomlands in the mountains.

The introduction of large herds of livestock resulted in the clearing of not only canebrakes but other forest ground cover as well. Within decades of the first European settlement, wild pea-vines, hog-peanuts, and the wild strawberry were all but eliminated from vast areas of the forest floor. The pea-vine, which once grew "as high as a horse's back," was rarely seen in any great profusion after the American Revolution. The hog-peanut, a low twining vine that produces a small root eaten by livestock, was also eliminated from areas of the forest by advancing cattle herds. Wild strawberries, which had once carpeted large areas of the Blue Ridge Mountains, became scarce, making strawberry fields such as those witnessed by William Bartram, "in painted beds of many acres surface," no more than small scattered colonies or individual plants. Indeed, the ecological effects that resulted from the introduction of cattle, hogs, and horses were great enough to receive notice from the oldest generation of Cherokees.[72]

The reduction and sometimes elimination of understory plants by cattle and hogs were not the only important environmental changes to occur during the eighteenth century. "White man's fly," or the honeybee, was also introduced to the region at this time as a direct result of the honey and beeswax trade. Though such changes would be almost imperceptible to the modern eye, honeybees no doubt altered the pollination patterns and thus plant associations of some mountain flora.[73] According to several reputable accounts, the honeybee was first introduced to North America sometime during the late seventeenth century. By the time of the American Revolution, however, William Bartram found honeybees numerous "from Nova

Scotia to East Florida." During his tour of the Cherokee country in 1796, Benjamin Hawkins reported that the Cherokees already "had bees and honey" and were doing "a considerable trade in beeswax." Moreover, European plants such as apple trees were greatly dependent on the pollination of honeybees in order to consistently bear fruit. Certainly the honeybee also helped native plants, including Indian maize, to produce more prolifically.[74]

The changing composition of the mountain ecosystem no doubt had profound effects on Cherokee culture. Prior to the fur trade, the Cherokees had relied on the flesh of deer, elk, buffaloes, bears, and even beavers as dietary staples. Skins of these animals also provided essential clothing, as buckskin leather was the basic article of dress for the Cherokees prior to the fur trade. Formerly, the most common attire for Cherokee males was "a bit of skin about their middles, mockasons, a mantle of buffalo skin for the winter, and a lighter one of [turkey] feathers for the summer."[75] As these animals became more valuable in the fur trades and more scarce in the surrounding forests, the Cherokees began to adopt the use of European clothing. No longer dressed exclusively in animal skins or feathers, the Cherokees began to prefer smooth cotton broadcloths in various solid colors or calico prints. To make this clothing, Cherokee women gradually began to use steel needles, scissors, and cotton thread "rather than bone needles, sinew, and buckskin."[76] By 1800 the dress of a significant number of Cherokee men resembled more closely that of a southern gentleman squire. No longer self-sufficient natives, many Cherokees were now dependent on the European traders for putting clothes on their backs.

Style of dress is just one example of Cherokee culture change due, in large part, to changes in the local environment. The loss of ready access to river cane permanently altered the lives of the Cherokees, who had relied upon it for their homes, baskets, beds, arrow shafts, blowguns, and fishing spears.[77] Cherokee scholar Sarah Hill estimated that for domestic basketry alone, "a settlement of a hundred households . . . could harvest several thousand stalks of cane."[78] As large canebrakes became increasingly harder to find, the Cherokees resorted to finding new materials or European items as replacements for more traditional ones—metal fish hooks for cane fishing spears, for example. Wattle-and-daub huts gave way to log houses, guns replaced the locust bow and cane-shaft arrow, and steel traps supplanted the tension snare and log deadfall. As the environment changed around them, so did the Cherokee subsistence culture, making it increasingly difficult for them to return to an earlier way of life. In fact, John Stuart, Indian superintendent to the Cherokees, could write as early as 1762 that "a modern Indian cannot subsist without Europeans; and would handle a flint ax or any other rude utensil used by his ancestors very awkwardly; so what was only conveniency at first is now become necessity." One Cherokee remarked, only five years later, that "the deer, buffalo, and the turkeys are almost gone . . . the white people eat hogs, cattle, and other things which they have here, but our food is farther off." Adopting the ways of the European had, in fact, become necessary for survival.[79]

Prior to European contact, Cherokee subsistence culture had been largely congruent with the mountain environment. Agriculture, hunting, and food-gathering practices certainly changed throughout the period of Cherokee occupation, but these changes were generally guided by a framework of cultural values embedded in a diverse local ecology. For the Cherokees, cultural stability depended to a very large extent upon adaptation and attunement to the forces of the natural world. By 1740, with the onset of seemingly irreversible environmental change, Cherokee acculturation was well under way. By the end of the eighteenth century a majority of Cherokees had largely made the transformation from a gathering, hunting, and farming people to one almost entirely dependent on European goods and alliances.[80] Not only were they offered new material goods, but the very environment around them had grown unfamiliar. After losing their former relationship to the mountain landscape, a relationship held together by strong religious and mythological beliefs, the Cherokees were ready for even fuller participation in the market economy.

Cherokee Appalachia

From 1800 until their removal in 1838, the environment of southern Appalachia remained an integral part of Cherokee culture. At that time, however, many of their agricultural practices involved the use of domesticated plants and animals, the outcome of their adoption of European farming methods in general. Not all that was native was forgotten or lost, however. Just as they acquired European practices, the Cherokees also shared much of their knowledge of the mountain environment with the trappers, traders, and, later, mountain settlers. Even after removal, the remaining Cherokees of the Qualla Boundary and Snowbird Mountains in North

Carolina stayed in close communication with white mountain communities. Without question, their close contact with whites facilitated "exchanges in ecological knowledge between the two groups" and later helped to shape southern mountain culture.[81] In fact, upon their first arrival to the region, European settlers adopted many Cherokee ways, some out of sheer necessity, others simply due to their practical utility. In the mountains of North Carolina and southwestern Virginia, for example, ginseng was gathered from the eighteenth century on by settlers who must have learned of the plant's medicinal properties from the Cherokees. The Cherokees believed the plant to be a sentient being and so, upon digging it, dropped a single seed of the plant in the ground as repayment to the plant spirit. Even though most white settlers used it sparingly because of its high market value, ginseng was "reputed to cure anything from a cough to a boil to an internal disorder." In the northern Georgia mountains, frontier settlers generally boiled two or three roots in a pint of water before giving it to children as a cure for colic.[82]

The Cherokee practice of eating beaver flesh also was adopted by the first white traders, trappers, and long hunters until the first herds of cattle arrived in the mountain region. Those who regularly trapped the animal, however, did not entirely abandon the practice. The "old traders," observed Adair in 1775, "remember when they first began the custom of eating beavers: and to this day none of them eat them, except those who kill them."[83] Among native plants, the Cherokees gathered wild leeks, or "ramps," from late fall to early spring, and their abundance in the mountains helped to convince whites of their value as an important food source. Like the Cherokees, the settlers transplanted ramps near their homes to flourish in a semicultivated state.[84] Pokeweed, referred to on the frontier as "Cherokee sallet," became another green regularly eaten by frontiersmen. The young shoots of the green coneflower, or "sochan," were also eaten by the Cherokees as well as used for a variety of medicinal purposes. Sochan, whose name is a corruption of the Cherokee word for the plant, was cooked and consumed by mountain settlers, as were a number of other native greens.[85]

European settlers continued to grow numerous Cherokee crops throughout the frontier period. In fact, these crops can still be found in many gardens of the region today. Bottle gourds, for example, a plant commonly grown by the Cherokees, served as valuable storage containers for the early settlers. Whereas the Cherokees used them for holding water, garden seeds, or bear grease, the Anglo-Americans used them to store lard, sugar, or butter. The Cherokees also hung them horizontally on long poles to attract purple martins, a native bird that not only eats thousands of annoying mosquitoes but also drives crows from nearby cornfields. Frontier settlers, upon seeing the effectiveness of these native birdhouses, soon erected them in their own gardens.[86]

The Cherokee method of drying pumpkins by hanging them on long strings was also borrowed by European settlers. Before canning methods were developed, drying vegetables in this manner was the only way of preserving them. "Shuck-beans" and "leather-britches," two regional names for beans hung and dried in this manner, were eaten throughout the southern Appalachians well into the twentieth century. It is even possible that the frontier art of maple sugaring, a once common practice where large groves of sugar maples were found, was learned from the Cherokees. As evidence, Adair comments that "several Indians produce sugar out of the sweet maple-tree, by making an incision, draining the juice, and boiling it to a proper consistence."[87] Maple sugaring was taught to the French as early as 1684 by the Indians in Canada, and the practice apparently had spread from New England to the upper Shenandoah Valley before the end of the eighteenth century.[88] Even though settlers migrating down the Great Valley of Virginia may have already known how to make maple sugar, those arriving in the region from the Atlantic Coast or southern Piedmont may not have already acquired the skill and so either adopted the practice from observing other settlers or from closely watching the Cherokees.

One of the most enduring contributions to southern Appalachian culture from the Cherokees was apple cultivation. Although apple trees were first introduced to the region by British fur traders, it was the Cherokees who made them central to regional horticulture after 1750. The Cherokees' early adoption of the fruit is not surprising since the trees could be grown and harvested in much the same manner as the peach. The mountain environment was ideal for apple orchards because of plentiful rainfall and the presence of "thermal belts," a frostless and dewless zone on mountain slopes caused by an unusual meteorological phenomenon known as temperature inversion.[89] Although it is not widely known, the Cherokees were indirectly responsible for keeping apple growing alive in the southern Appalachians, as the practice among Anglo-Americans was, by the 1830s, in steady decline.[90] Apple trees, as Harriette Arnow has pointed out, were virtually nonexistent in the southern mountains until the early part of the nineteenth century. Because the trees mature slowly (eight years or more) and early settlers in southern Appalachia moved often, they generally did not bother to plant them. Peach trees, on the other hand, bear fruit within two or three years after transplanting, which helps to explain their greater popularity.[91]

In fact, by the early 1850s apple cultivation was so poor in the southern mountains that one northern Georgian complained that "we have only one peach . . . the Indian Peach; and one apple, the Horse Apple."[92] At that time, urban areas in the mountain region were supplied largely with apples from northern growers, who did not think that the fruit could be grown as a market crop in the mountains. In response to this skepticism, a handful of southern horticulturalists sought new cultivation methods and made improvements in crop selection. To promote apple growing in mountain communities, Jarvis Van Buren founded the Georgia Pomological Society in the 1850s, an organization that sought to locate, name, and classify desirable apple varieties.[93] Most of the varieties grafted and cataloged by Van Buren were found growing in northern Georgia, southeastern Tennessee, and western North Carolina in Cherokee apple orchards left behind after their removal. While collecting mountain apples, Van Buren renamed some according to his own liking; others he gave names of obvious Cherokee origin. One example is the Nantahalee, a Cherokee word meaning "maiden's bosom." Another was called the Junaluskee, after Chief Junaluska, a Cherokee who refused to sell the land on which this apple tree was growing but later sold the tree, and presumably the land, for fifty dollars. Other apples of certain Cherokee origin include the Mountaine Belle from Habersham County, Georgia; the Yahoola, found in Lumpkin County, Georgia; the Buckingham, a variety taken from Cass County, Georgia; the Toccoa, from an orchard near Toccoa Falls, Georgia; and the Tillaquah, an apple found growing in nearby Franklin, North Carolina. Other varieties originating from Cherokee northern Georgia include the Green Mountain Pippen, Nickajack, Julien, Golden Rustic, Vandiver, and Oconee Greening.[94]

With his impressive list of prolific varieties taken from Cherokee orchards, Van Buren was able to convince others of the profitability of apple growing. Soon apple cultivation, centered largely in Hall and Habersham

Counties in northern Georgia, became a profitable mountain industry. By the early 1860s, the South had completely lost its dependence on New York, New Jersey, and Pennsylvania for apples, due largely to the efforts of Van Buren—and, of course, native Cherokee farmers.

Besides apple trees, many place-names in the southern Appalachians are also of Cherokee origin, which further attests to the central role that the Cherokees played in the development of mountain culture. Although historian David Hackett Fischer has suggested that the greatest proportion of Appalachian place-names is drawn from the geography of Britain, a larger number of geographic toponyms can be directly attributed to the Cherokees.[95] Most of the mountains, creeks, and rivers of the region are derived from the names of former Cherokee settlements. The Hiwassee, Tuckasegee, Oconee, Chattooga, Tallula, Toccoa, Nantahala, Tellico, and Tuskaseegee Rivers, as well as Chickamauga and Watauga Creeks, to name only a few, are good examples. Cheoah Point, Chilhowee Mountain, Cowee Mountains, Stecoh Bald, Soco Gap, and Snowbird Mountains are also important Cherokee place-names. Admittedly, a goodly number of southern Appalachian place-names were anglicized after white settlement, but those toponyms could also be classified as Cherokee rather than Scots-Irish or English in origin. Fightingtown Creek, a translation of Unulstiyo, for example, derives its name from a myth that claims two giant frogs once battled there using the stems of a plant. Sugar Creek, also in northern Georgia, is a translation of Kulse Tsi, or "sweet place"—the former site of a large grove of honey locust trees. The Cherokee sport known as ball play, played on large level fields throughout the mountains, also lent its name to a number of roads, towns, and creeks throughout the mountains of southern Appalachia.

To be sure, groups of Cherokees persistently resisted white cultural encroachment and kept alive many of the old ways. Cherokee scholar Tom Hatley even goes so far as to suggest that as late as 1820, three quarters of the Cherokee population had chosen a route of self-isolation, as opposed to full-scale imitation of white cultural patterns. In these more conservative Cherokee households, he argues, traditional farming practices were "not radically altered," and "the reins of domestic economic authority were still held by women."[96] Historian Sarah Hill also notes that despite the relative scarcity of river cane in the mountains, most Cherokee women still insisted upon using the plant for making baskets until at least the third decade of the nineteenth century, underscoring the "extraordinary resilience of women's culture and values, even in the face of disastrous social upheaval."[97] No doubt many did avoid full-scale acculturation into white society by moving higher up into the mountains, where they farmed relatively independently of regional and global markets. Those Cherokees would no doubt retain their influence on the cultural development of the southern Appalachian frontier and on mountain culture in general. But even the most traditional of Cherokees could not stop the swell of white settlers who were determined to own every parcel of arable land in the mountains, individuals who would ultimately force the removal of the Cherokees from the mountain region in 1838.

Despite their noted influence on mountain life and culture, by the third decade of the nineteenth century many Cherokees utilized the southern Appalachian countryside in much the same way as the frontier settlers, particularly those Cherokees living in the more fertile river valleys of southeastern Tennessee and northwestern Georgia. In those areas, the surrounding landscape was valued more for its ability to grow corn, wheat, or cotton or to provide pasture for domestic livestock. Here they also made general use of the wheel, loom, and plow and even wore Anglo-style clothing. Many lived in log cabins; still others became Christianized.[98] As early as 1799 missionaries Abraham Steiner and Frederick de Schweinitz wrote that the Cherokees of the Tennessee Valley had "greatly increased in culture and civilization in the last few years; that in the course of the last summer 300 plows and as many pairs of cotton carding-combs had been sent to this nation and they have begun to devote themselves to agriculture and the raising of cotton; had several times brought cotton for sale and they had themselves begun to spin and weave."[99]

By 1809 the "civilized arts" of the whites prevailed to such an extent among the Cherokees that a government census found in the Cherokee Nation 19,165 "black" cattle, 6,519 horses, 19,778 swine, 1,037 sheep, 429 looms, 1,572 spinning wheels, 30 wagons, 567 plows, 13 grist mills, and 3 sawmills. In 1826, fifteen years later, there were no fewer than 22,000 cattle, 7,600 horses, 46,000 swine, 2,500 sheep, 762 looms, 2,488 spinning wheels, 172 wagons, 2,942 plows, 10 sawmills, 31 grist mills, 62 blacksmith shops, 8 cotton gins, 18 schools, 18 ferries, and numerous public roads in the Cherokee territory.[100] Taken together, these figures paint a vivid portrait of the change that had taken place in the cultural landscape of the Cherokees during the first three decades of the nineteenth century. For those now engaged in a life fully committed to European-style agriculture, untamed nature provided little reward.[101]

In retrospect, most Cherokees had little choice but to adopt, to some degree, the ways of the whites. A century of disease, war, and famine had taken an enormous toll on the Cherokees, hardly placing them in a bargaining position with European or Colonial governments. Needless to say, the Cherokees were ill-equipped to deal with the enormous social and political forces that would confront them during the eighteenth and early nineteenth centuries. The smallpox epidemic of 1738, brought to South Carolina by slave ships, hit the Cherokees with such force that "nearly half the tribe was swept away within a year."[102] Like the Mississippians two centuries before, the Cherokees had little or no immunity to smallpox, and their remedy for the illness—bathing in cold water—made it worse. The scene at the height of the epidemic must have been ghastly, as "a great many killed themselves . . . some shot themselves, others cut their throats, some stabbed themselves with knives, and others, sharp pointed canes; many threw themselves with sullen madness into the fire, and there slowly expired, as if they had been utterly divested of the native power of feeling pain." In the face of so much unexplainable death, many Cherokees soon lost faith in their medicine men and other traditional curing methods. Because the medicine man's methods also relied upon the use of native herbs and roots and various animal potions, the Cherokees had yet another reason not to continue to value the curative powers of native flora and fauna.[103]

Another factor equally critical to understanding why so many Cherokees adopted the ways of the whites is the heavy loss of life and crops due to warfare. Two major military campaigns against the Cherokees less than two decades apart decimated much of their population, further opening the mountain area for settlement. Soldiers who participated in the campaigns saw firsthand the rich bounty of the mountain region, many later laying claim to the very lands they had once burned and depopulated. The first of these assaults was carried out by the British, who murdered twelve to forty Cherokees in a dispute over stolen British horses. Afterward, the remaining Cherokees soon became "much attached to the French," who encouraged warriors to raid backcountry settlements in neighboring South Carolina.[104] In retaliation for these raids, a number of influential Cherokee chiefs were captured by the British and then held hostage at Fort Prince

George on the Keowee River in the South Carolina upcountry. After a number of attempts at their rescue failed, the Cherokee chiefs were assassinated, initiating a total war.[105] One Cherokee faction retaliated by attacking frontier settlements in western South Carolina, while others laid siege to Fort Loudon, a British garrison located on the Little Tennessee River in eastern Tennessee. In June 1760 a South Carolina militia led by Colonel Montgomery destroyed the Lower Towns, "burning them to the ground, cutting down their cornfields and orchards, killing and taking more than one hundred of their men, and driving the whole population into the mountains before him." In August of that year the British surrendered Fort Loudon to the Cherokees, who killed Capt. Paul Demeré, the British commander of the fort, and took prisoner most of his men.[106]

A year later, in June 1761, a full-scale assault was launched against the Cherokees of the Middle and Overhill settlements. On 10 June Col. James Grant and two thousand Carolina volunteers returned to Fort Prince George, where they defeated the Cherokees in a fierce, bloody battle. Afterward, Grant and his troops quickly pushed their way to the Middle Towns, burning houses and cornfields as they went. The soldiers were no doubt impressed by the mountain landscape and took note of the Cherokees' extensive fields and planting grounds. Upon arrival at a recently deserted Indian town in northern Georgia, one member of the expedition, Capt. Christopher French, observed it to be "one of the finest Spotts I ever saw." The expansive beauty of the verdant Cherokee cornfields and orchards did not deter the plunder. At a Cherokee village in western North Carolina, French and his men were ordered to level the village and croplands, so they "pull'd up all the corn, cut down the fruit trees, & burn'd the Houses, in number about fifty." [107] By the end of July, Grant's regiment had destroyed all fifteen of the Middle Towns and had driven most of the Cherokees into the surrounding mountains.[108]

The decimation of cornfields, granaries, and orchards at the height of harvest was so devastating to the Cherokees that many were reduced to eating their own horses. Many died of starvation, others contracted diseases due to their weakened state. No longer able to adequately defend themselves, the Cherokees sued for peace in 1761. After the official peace treaty between France and England was signed in 1763, the British controlled most of the southern Appalachians. New alliances were forged between the British government and the Cherokees, resulting in the formation of the Proclamation Line, a boundary drawn roughly along the eastern border of the Blue Ridge Mountains. The Proclamation Line established the eastern boundary of Indian territory and was designed to prevent the settling or selling of lands to the west. The line had little effect, as those who had already settled in the region refused to leave. Another treaty was drawn, making the new boundary from the mouth of the Kanawha River in West Virginia to the Holston River in Tennessee. Although this treaty did not ultimately prevent white intruders from entering deeper into the mountain region, it did help to slow frontier expansion and reestablish trade with the British, giving the Cherokees an opportunity to rebuild their conquered villages.[109]

This period of social stability for the Cherokees was short-lived, however. A little more than a decade after the French and Indian War, on the eve of the American Revolution, the British sought Cherokee assistance in subduing the rebellious Americans. The Cherokees complied, in part to protect themselves from those settlers who had been illegally filtering into Cherokee territory. The Watauga and Holston settlements in upper eastern Tennessee, occupied around 1769, were among the first targets of the Cherokees. Carolina and Georgia settlements were also attacked, resulting in the death of women and children and forcing the hand of the Revolutionary forces. In the summer of 1776, six thousand armed men in four military regiments from Virginia, North Carolina, South Carolina, and Georgia were sent into the Cherokee territory. The results were catastrophic.[110]

In August Gen. Griffith Rutherford of North Carolina began the assault, destroying every town—thirty-six in all—located along the Oconaluftee and Tuckasegee Rivers in North Carolina and the upper Little Tennessee and Hiwassee Rivers in southeastern Tennessee. In each village the ripe or ripening corn was destroyed, dwellings were burned, the livestock was killed or driven off, stores of dressed deerskins and other trade goods were stolen, and peach and apple orchards were vandalized or cut down.[111] At one village on the Hiwassee River, soldiers were ordered to burn "upwards of ninety houses and large quantities of corn" and to cut down and burn the remaining vegetables. One soldier remarked that it "was no small undertaking, they being so plentifully supplied." At the smallest Cherokee settlement, no fewer than 200 acres of corn were decimated, not to mention hundreds of bushels of sweet potatoes and beans and numerous peach trees. These assaults on the native landscape—acts of "total war"—were repeated by other revolutionary regiments, including the South Carolina militia, who plundered and burned the Lower Towns along the head of the Savannah River. At Seneca alone, six thousand bushels of corn and other vital foodstuffs were destroyed by the Carolina forces.[112] The Georgia militia, comprised of at least two hundred men, completely leveled two towns near the heads of the Tugaloo and Chattahoochee Rivers, and, entering from the north, the Virginia army destroyed five Overhill Towns and outlying fields. In total, the American forces leveled and burned more than fifty towns, killing hundreds of people, laying waste to thousands of acres of cropland, and destroying numerous fruit orchards. Echota, the capital and sacred "peace town" of the Cherokees, was spared by Colonel Williamson, but only four years later it too, along with nine other Overhill Towns, was destroyed by Cols. John Sevier and Arthur Campbell of Tennessee.[113]

After the widespread destruction of their homes and croplands, it was not long before the Cherokees were forced to sign yet another truce.[114] Peace negotiations soon materialized, and within months, details of a treaty were worked out between the two parties. The Lower Cherokees formally surrendered on 20 May 1777, and the treaty, the first ever in the newly formed United States, relinquished more than 2,000 acres of Cherokee territory, including their most ancient homelands, to South Carolina. A month later, the Middle and Overhill Cherokees finalized the Treaty of Long Island, which ceded an additional 6,000 acres east of the Blue Ridge. These two treaties, along with Henderson's Purchase of 1775, which ceded all lands between the Kentucky and Cumberland Rivers (27,000 square miles), opened up the vast majority of the southern Appalachian region to frontier settlement.

Cut off from their principal hunting lands, the Cherokees were placed in an extremely precarious position. From 1721 to 1775, they had ceded more than 60,000 square miles of territory, which, immediately after the Revolutionary War, began rapidly filling up with settlers. In direct competition with the Cherokees for game, the settlers hunted the remaining deer and trapped the region for furs. After another 12,000 acres were ceded to the whites shortly after the Revolution, the total amount available for hunting and settlement was limited only to the lower Tennessee Valley and portions of the Blue Ridge Mountains. In response to the situation, Chief Dragging Canoe led a band of Cherokees known as the Chickamaugans in a short reprisal, but they too were eventually defeated by American forces.[115] Finally, in 1791, after the Treaty of Holston, the area that today comprises the Great Smoky Mountains was surrendered to North Carolina and Tennessee. In the Oconaluftee and Deep Creek sections of what is now the Great Smoky Mountains National Park, white settlers soon built homes and planted in the very same fields that the Indians once cultivated; several of them had actually accompanied Rutherford on his grisly campaign through the Cherokee settlements.[116] After the death of Dragging Canoe in 1794, the hope of winning back former homelands was fast extinguished.

As the strong presence of the Cherokees receded, the dawning of a new era was at hand in the southern Appalachians. Indian occupation, extensive canebrakes, large expanses of level land, and numerous mineral springs had made the southern Appalachians a prime area for herds of grazing livestock. These ecological factors, as well as the social and political unrest that occurred during the eighteenth century, encouraged the adoption of hog and cattle raising by the Cherokees, further increasing the size and number of open clearings in the mountain forest. Prior to the arrival of European settlers, cattle, hogs, and horses had made notable changes in many areas of the upland environment. Not only did they help to clear forest understories and bottomland canebrakes, they also aided in the proliferation of nonnative grasses and weeds, since wandering livestock, carrying the seeds of these plants in their stomachs, insured their spread throughout the mountain region.

The establishment of permanent settlements by Anglo-Americans initiated a new period of environmental and cultural change in the mountains. Even though a number of important animal and plant species had been seriously depleted, visible changes in the physical environment had not yet occurred over the entire mountain region. Although the forests and river valleys nearest Cherokee settlements—the most susceptible to grazing cattle and hogs—had changed considerably, much of the well-wooded uplands had seen relatively little human impact since the arrival of De Soto. Indeed, a large portion of the southern Appalachians remained a contiguous stand of mature old-growth timber until at least the middle decades of the nineteenth century. Prior to 1780, most environmental change in the mountains was restricted to major river valleys below 2,500 feet in elevation. And even there, change was not universally the same. In areas not formerly inhabited by Mississippians or Cherokees or cleared by the ongoing work of beavers, large stands of mature hardwoods still dominated large expanses of southern Appalachian river bottoms. With the arrival of pioneer settlers, environmental change accelerated, however, extending across major river valleys and into upland coves and along high mountain ridgetops. Soon, a much larger portion of the mountain region would be transformed into a "second nature" or "middle landscape" of log cabins, outbuildings, water mills, stone fences, and open grazing areas.[117] To accomplish the task, the pioneers brought axes, cross-cut saws, plows, and oxen as well as numerous ornamental plants from the Old World. The fur trader and the Revolutionary War soldier had done much to clear the way, but the pioneer settler would do even more to change the mountain environment.

The woodlands, carpeted with grass, and the wild peavine, growing as high as a horse's back, and the wild flowers of every hue, were the constant admiration of the traveler and adventurous pioneer. . . . The trees were generally larger, and stood so wide apart that a deer or buffalo could be easily seen from a long distance . . . peavines and grasses occupied the place of the bushes and young forest growth that render the woods of the present time so gloomy and intricate.—JOHN LOGAN, *A History of the Upper Country of South Carolina*, 1859.

5 Southwestern Mountains

FRONTIER APPALACHIA

HE SOUTHERN MOUNTAINS were not settled in a fortnight. It was an incremental process that was infused with Indian massacres, conflicts over land claims, failed crops, inclement weather, and the trials and tribulations of what was perceived by many as a harsh, unforgiving environment. By the early eighteenth century, the territory comprising the original colonies was already in a state of agricultural decline, forcing many residents to look over the Appalachian divide for new homelands. Land prices were rising in the older, more established communities, and this, along with greater population density, made them far less desirable for farming. Indeed, as early as 1698, the Frenchman Pierre Le Moyne saw the coastal settlement's potential for overcrowding. "The spaces between these mountains and the sea are occupied," he wrote, "by settlers whose children will be obliged to cross these mountains to find room for themselves."[1]

Across the mountain divide lay an abundance of good, relatively inexpensive land made even more attractive by the propaganda of government land companies and private speculators. To individuals who had completed military service in the French and Indian War, Colonial governments offered an additional incentive to move to the region—in essence, a veteran pension in the form of large tracts of arable mountain land. Amounts of the land grants varied from 5,000 acres for field officers to 50 acres for privates. After 1760, the British Crown's London Company allocated property by "head rights," awarding 50 acres to the head of each household and 50 additional acres to each family member, providing the total did not exceed 640 acres.[2]

Settlement in the region began as early as 1745, when Col. James Patton made one of the first purchases in the upper Tennessee Valley, securing 120,000 acres from the governor of Virginia. Using his James River settlement in central Virginia as a base of operation, Patton and his associates traveled deeper into Indian territory, arriving below the headwaters of the Tennessee River in less than a year. As early as 14 March 1746, John Buchanan, Patton's brother-in-law, was surveying tracts along the "Indian" or Holston River in southwestern Virginia.[3]

Land plats were surveyed and recorded by the Pattons and then sold to prospective settlers. One of the first to arrive in the region was Stephen Holston, for whom the Holston River in upper eastern Tennessee is named. Holston, of Swedish or perhaps German ancestry, built his home along the Middle Fork of the Holston sometime before 1748.[4] Like many other settlers of the region at that time, Holston held his land under what was then called "corn rights," which meant that he acquired landownership by growing corn on a portion of the land, allowing him to retain legal title "to a hundred acres of land for every acre planted by him in corn." This must have been a difficult task for Holston, who quickly sold his claim to James Davis, a Welshman, who occupied the land shortly thereafter.[5] Following closely on the heels of Patton was Dr. Thomas Walker, an English representative of the Loyal Land Company who acquired no fewer than 800,000 acres of backcountry land from the Burgesses of Virginia. Although the southern boundary of Walker's enormous grant did not technically extend into what was then North Carolina, Walker ventured as far south as the Long Island on the Holston River, where in 1750 he surveyed what he considered several attractive parcels. In 1753 John Buchanan was granted land at an area known as Sapling Grove, which would later become Bristol, Tennessee. Despite the fact that the land titles of Patton, Buchanan, and Walker were legally in question and their proper jurisdiction still under debate by Colonial governments, lands in the Great Valley south of Roanoke continued to be surveyed, sold, and settled.[6]

The French and Indian War, which unofficially began in 1754, helped to stall, at least for a short time, the settlement process in the mountains. At the height of the war, the French and their Indian allies staged major assaults on frontier settlements, forcing pioneers to seek safety in stockaded forts or abandon the region entirely. Dozens of white settlers perished in the attacks and even more fled to the Piedmont settlements of North and South Carolina. Several of the Holston and New River settlements in upper eastern Tennessee and western North Carolina were completely destroyed or abandoned. John Stuart's "A Map of the Cherokee Country," drafted in 1761, is ample proof of settlement destruction on the early frontier. On Stuart's map is the phrase "Destroyed by the Shawanese [Shaw-nee] Indians," words imprinted directly over the Holston homestead of Samuel Stalnaker. Directly upstream, above the Stalnaker settlement, is the boldly printed caption "Abandoned Plantations."[7]

Prior to the end of the war, largely in order to control the western boundaries of the colonies, the British passed the Proclamation of 1763, prohibiting settlement west of the southern Appalachian divide. By 1767, however, negotiations were under way with the Cherokees for opening more land in the Great Valley of the Appalachians. The Treaty of Hard Labor, signed only a year later in 1768, established a new settlement boundary that ran between Tryon Mountain, North Carolina, to the mouth of the Kanawha River. In accordance with the treaty, settlement by whites was legally permitted only east of the line. However, the new boundary hardly applied to speculators and settlers, who continued to venture far into Cherokee lands and deeper into the mountains. Another round of ne-gotiations with the Cherokees followed, resulting in the 1770 Treaty of Lochaber, which allowed permanent white settlement along the Clinch, Powell, and Lower Holston Rivers.[8]

The Great Valley of Virginia and Tennessee was not the only area in southern Appalachia feeling the pressure of European settlement before the Revolutionary War. In 1763 a Shawnee war party led by Cornstalk ascended the Kanawha River in West Virginia, killing settlers occupying lands near Greenbriar and Muddy Creek. Indian boundaries along the South and North Carolina borders were also being contested by whites, who perceived the mountain region as a vast wilderness waiting to be con-quered and tamed. By 1766 numerous settlers were already living along the headwaters of the Savannah River in the South Carolina upcountry, some well beyond the boundary line established by Indian treaties. "About the Saludy [River]," complained Deputy Indian Superintendent Alexander Cameron, "there are several houses within four miles of the line, and one house, within one mile of it. On the North Carolina side of Reedy River, there are four or five families settled."[9] In western North Carolina the situation was little better. In 1766 the Cherokees felt such grave concern over the encroachment of their Blue Ridge hunting grounds that one was compelled to state that "the number of families that have come from North Carolina and Virginia and settled upon a great deal of our best lands and within an easy day's march of some of our towns, are circumstances very alarming to us . . . we were promised quiet possession of our lands and redress for our grievances."[10] Even though new treaties with the Cherokees were signed and boundary lines drawn, they were repeatedly violated by restless pioneers in search of new land. By 1770 there was no going back: the permanent settlement of southern Appalachia by white Europeans was well under way.

One of the first permanent settlements in the mountain region was Castle's Woods.[11] Founded in Russell County, Virginia, in 1769, Castle's Woods was named after the first settler of the area, Jacob Castle. As was typical of many first settlers, Castle himself did not permanently reside at the "station," as these first settlements were called. Castle, a long hunter who wore the buckskin leggings, moccasins, and leather hunting shirt so common during the frontier period, was most interested in obtaining skins for the fur trade. Long hunters like Castle preferred to travel in groups, however, taking several pack horses with them to carry out deerskins and other valuable forest commodities. They traded their goods at the shops of local store keepers in the developing towns and settlements or took them to the Moravian missionaries in Salem, North Carolina, where they were transported to Charleston.[12]

Long hunters cleared the first overland routes leading into the southern mountains, and fur traders soon extended their hunting expeditions into areas not routinely frequented by Indians. Around 1740 a group of these men crossed the Blue Ridge along the Roanoke River, reaching the Warriors Path, the major Indian trail connecting the Shenandoah and Tennessee Valleys. The discovery and development of this new route—the Great Valley Road—helped to ensure the rapid settlement of the mountain region, since it also connected the port of Philadelphia to the Yadkin River in western North Carolina. Prior to that time, wagon travel into the area from the north was highly restricted, if not altogether impossible. The only major road into the mountains had been the Carolina Road, a route requiring passage from the east through the mountains of western North Carolina. The Wilderness Trail cleared by Daniel Boone in 1775 opened up the rest of the southern Appalachians to white settlement, creating for the first time a major route between Virginia and Kentucky. By cutting an approachable path through the Cumberland Gap, Boone made the lands of the Cumberland Plateau and beyond much more accessible to settlement. The creation of the Great Valley and Wilderness Roads gave new direction to migration by establishing the flow of settlement toward the south and southwest. "It was easier," as Tennessee historian Samuel Cole Williams put it, "to follow the great longitudinal valley to the southwest than to cross the mountain ranges."[13]

Seeking a new life in a new land, the men, women, and children of southern Appalachia quickly followed the newly blazed roads and trails into the heart of the mountain region. Humbling as it must have been to peer across the great mountain divides for the first time, the settlers must have also been disturbed by the lack of "civilized" improvements in the surrounding mountain forest. To the first pioneers, the southern mountains were a wilderness to be tamed, a landscape to be transformed into an earthly paradise, a New Jerusalem. Even Daniel Boone, the quintessential backwoodsman, admitted later in life that he was nothing more than a creature of Providence, "ordained by Heaven as a pioneer in the wilderness, to advance the civilization [and] extension of his country."[14] To ensure that civilization and Providence would endure on the Appalachian frontier, settlers gravitated to openings in the forest, to old fields created by Indians, or to beaver meadows along creeks or rivers. If no openings could be found, they immediately created them. Civilization, as the Europeans understood it, demanded large expanses of open, unobstructed land. For the early pioneer, dark primeval forests and dense imposing canebrakes were uninhabitable landscapes hardly compatible with pastoral ways of life.

Anglo Arrivals

By 1788 more than twenty-five thousand individuals, all intent on making new improvements in the mountain wilderness, had settled the upper reaches of the Tennessee Valley. Thousands more had settled the Cumberland Plateau and the eastern foothills of the Blue Ridge Mountains, bringing the total population of the mountain region to nearly forty thousand. By 1790 there were eighty thousand residents scattered across the mountain region in settlements along the Holston, Yadkin, Cumberland, and upper Kanawha Rivers.[15] Historical records of the period reveal that the majority of these individuals were of English or Scots-Irish ancestry, but Germans, Irish, and even Scandinavians contributed to the ethnic mix. African-Americans were also represented on the southern Appalachian frontier, as the rich soils of the Tennessee Valley made slave labor economically possible. Samuel Cole Williams estimates that in 1790 their numbers totaled more than fifteen hundred in the State of Franklin alone.[16]

Despite frequent claims to the contrary, the Scots-Irish were arguably not the largest European ethnic group to settle the southern Appalachians. In 1790, according to one reputable source, they quite possibly could have constituted less than 20 percent of the entire population. John C. Campbell, who did an extensive surname study of Revolutionary War pension lists, also found the percentages slightly in favor of English, rather than Scots-Irish, dominance. "Of the 497 names on our list from North Carolina," wrote Campbell, "the English and Scotch-Irish appeared to have formed each about one-third; of the 228 from Tennessee the same proportion held; of the 360 from Kentucky, the English constituted four-tenths, and the Scotch-Irish three-tenths." John Knox, who did one of the earliest demographic studies of frontier Tennessee, placed the ethnic distribution for the young state as "English, 80 percent; Scotch, 13 percent; German, 5 percent; Irish, 3 percent; other, 2 percent."[17] Similarly, David Hackett Fischer writes that the Scots-Irish of southern Appalachia were one of several border peoples originating from northern Ireland, lowland Scotland, and northern England. In his analysis of the 1790 census, which collapses both English and Scots-Irish surnames into one category in order to arrive at the total number of backcountry settlers from what he calls the "British borderlands," "90 percent of the backsettlers were either English, Irish, or Scottish," with the vast majority coming from "Ulster, the Scottish lowlands, and the north of England."[18]

Although they may have proportionally represented the largest ethnic group in the southern Appalachians, the English perhaps made the fewest contributions to the land-use culture in the mountains. Although a number of eighteenth-century advancements in animal and plant husbandry—for example, apple growing and sheep herding—can certainly be attributed to the English, the shape and form of domestic houses was perhaps their biggest contribution to frontier culture. The English were well known for their brick-making and brick-laying skills, having perfected the art in the early eighteenth century. In fact, elements of English architecture survive even in the crudest log cabins of the region. Exterior chimneys located at opposite gable ends, for example, originated along the Tidewater region of Virginia and North Carolina, areas of highly concentrated English settlement.[19]

The English also heavily influenced political organization, as the system of English law was transplanted, basically intact, to the region. Historically, English law has always been administered by a county system of government, and so the county became the primary social and geographic unit of the region, if not the entire southeastern United States. The Old World political order also helped to establish the two major settlement types in the region: the county seat, a township historically controlled by merchants and business elites; and the unincorporated hamlet, a settlement area traditionally comprised of farmers and rural farmland. From the beginning county government exercised a great deal of control over economic affairs, licensing gristmills and sawmills, overseeing the maintenance of roads, and even fixing the prices at local taverns.[20]

The Scots-Irish, despite their smaller numbers, had an important influence on the social and cultural development of the southern Appalachians. Like the English, the Scots-Irish left much of their culture behind in the Old World, abandoning by the middle of the eighteenth century customs such as Twelfth of July celebrations, sod and thatch home construction, and the use of the Gaelic language. However, many of their cultural practices and land-use skills proved extremely useful in the mountains, including their advanced knowledge of cattle herding and whiskey making, not to mention the Presbyterian religion, folk ballads, and the art of weaving cloth.[21]

In the southern mountains, as well as in the rest of North America, many Scots-Irish immigrants settled in clusters of farmsteads patterned closely after *clachans,* the name of their Ulster settlements in northern Ireland. In Ulster, clachans were comprised of a number of small homesteads situated around a commons or communally worked area of farmland. Nearest the dwellings was an infield, cropland generally cultivated in staple crops such as oats, wheat, barley, rye, potatoes, and turnips. Beyond the infield lay the outfield, slightly poorer land reserved for oats or wheat that was, after yields gradually declined, allowed to lay fallow and revert back to pasture. Beyond the outfield lay the unclaimed wasteland, a grazing commons reserved exclusively for herds of cattle and sheep.[22]

The southern Appalachian landscape allowed for the direct transference, with notable modifications, of the field, fallow, and forest agricultural cycle. To the southern mountaineer, bottomlands below the house or along the floodplain of a creek and river were regarded as infields, with corn and wheat replacing wheat and oats as the main infield crops. Many Scottish farmers were familiar with the cultivation of this type of soil, having tilled the silt-rich bottom or *haugh* lands of Scotland.[23] Interplanted among the corn were crop varieties borrowed from the Native Americans: beans, tobacco, pumpkins, and squash. The Scots-Irish also continued planting small vegetable gardens adjoining the house just as they had in the Old World. The New World equivalent of outfields were located farther from the house; these were cleared of timber and then annually planted with corn or wheat. In two or three years, after they had exhausted the soil's productivity, Scots-Irish settlers usually returned these fields to fallow pasture. The vast woodlands surrounding the settlement were viewed as a communal grazing area in which livestock were free to range. In the main, the practice of open-ranging cattle in the common woods resembled the practice of transhumance, a grazing system extremely common in eighteenth-century Ireland and Scotland.[24]

Transhumance, as practiced in the British Isles, involved the annual burning of the moorlands during the winter months so that livestock could graze on the regenerated forage that resulted in the spring, summer, and fall. According to agricultural historian John S. Otto, animals were grazed under the care of herdsmen "who mollified stock by feeding them salt . . . When fall frosts killed moorlands grasses, owners collected herds, retained breeding animals, and sold surplus stock to professional drovers who operated in Scotland and Ireland."[25] Similarly, in the Blue Ridge Mountains, cattle and sheep were grazed during the summer months on ridges and mountaintops, far away from settlement croplands. Before ascending the mountains every year, southern Appalachian herdsmen burned mountaintop pastures in late fall or early spring to encourage new growth. One herdsman of Scots-Irish ancestry who left a detailed description of his herding activities reported that "he set out for the top of the mountain" in April and then, after gathering his herd in August, returned home.[26]

Most mountain cattlemen accompanied their livestock during the summer, often living in crude dwellings constructed solely for the purpose. As they had in Britain, southern mountain herdsmen often used salt to keep cattle and sheep from straying too far or, when necessary, to move them from pasture to pasture. One eighteenth-century traveler made the observation that the use of salt rendered cattle "gentle and tame"; otherwise, he noted, the cattle would "roam far beyond the reach of their proprietors." In the fall the cattle were taken down the mountains and sold to overland drovers or, in later years, herded to regional markets in Asheville, Knoxville, Lexington, or Charleston. As a result of its importance in mountain herding traditions, the practice of salting ridgetops has left its mark on the region in the form of numerous place-names. Lickstone Bald in North Carolina, for example, derives its name from the huge flat rock near the summit "whereon the cattle-herders used formerly to place the salt brought by them to the stock which ranged the mountain meadows."[27]

The introduction of the Scots-Irish herding system to the region is also striking evidence that many of southern Appalachia's "balds" were created by human disturbance. Once an ecological mystery, the presence of mountaintop balds is now largely attributed to this once common cultural practice. One of the first recorded instances of mountain grazing occurred in 1781, when an individual known only by the surname "Main" is believed to have cleared several hundred acres on what is today Oldfield Bald near Grandfather Mountain, North Carolina.[28] A 1795 land grant for a parcel of land along Scott's Creek near Wesner's Bald, also in western North Carolina, mentions the location of "Scott's old lick blocks," clearly designating a former cattle range. According to Dr. Abraham Job, whose family moved to Cades Cove in 1821, his father "cleared a considerable amount of his 640 acres of land" to raise "a good deal of stock."[29] John W. Oliver, also of the Cove area, remarked that during the 1830s James Spence burned trees and brush in order to create the mountain meadow known as Spence Field, a grassy bald near Thunderhead Mountain in what is today the Great Smoky Mountains National Park. Clearly, mountaintop cattle herding was a land-use activity that settlers had keen knowledge of prior to their arrival. Roderick Peattie remarked that the Scots-Irish who came to the southern Appalachians "cleared mountain farms by choice."[30]

In southern Appalachia, the herding tradition that involved the grazing of sheep and cattle atop high altitude mountains owes much to the Scots-Irish. Indeed, cattle and sheep raising in Ulster and Scotland offered a prototype for the practice. With the arrival of the first pioneers, the southern mountain landscape became, in effect, an enormous grazing commons in which livestock could grow fat browsing among mountaintop pastures, woodland glades, and river-bottom canebrakes. The herding practice was not without certain dangers to the animals, however, as backcountry settlers had to pen livestock at night in order to protect them from wolves and mountain lions.[31] In order to properly keep track of ownership, frontiersmen also utilized the Ulster custom of marking animals by cutting a small but distinctive portion of the animal's ear. Collecting the animals in the fall was yet another problem, however, since they generally became semiwild in the spacious mountain forest. The animals had to be captured and then temporarily corralled in circular cow pens, a roundup practice more characteristic of the Spanish herding tradition adopted by the Cherokees during the early part of the nineteenth century.[32]

Flax, a crop requiring fields relatively free of stumps and roots, is another important Scots-Irish introduction to the southern mountains. Scots-Irish settlers grew flax primarily to make linen cloth and linseed oil as did their ancestors in northern Ireland and the Scottish highlands. In fact, Ulster had become a major exporter of linen during the late seventeenth century when King William III provided numerous inducements for growing the crop. There, the manufacturing of linen was organized almost exclusively on a domestic basis, "with piecework distributed widely through the homes of the region."[33]

In the southern Appalachians, Scots-Irish settlers grew flax in small fields of several acres or less. After harvest, the plants were set aside to dry before threshing out the small seeds, the major ingredient for the making of linseed oil, a glossy varnish and natural wood preservative. Next the stalks were soaked in water to free the outer bark from the inner fiber. After another drying period, frontier women crushed the flax stems in a "break" and then "hackled" them to separate the fibers into desired weights. The women then spun selected fibers into spools of long thread and wove the thread into linen cloth, the strong and coarse fabric that dominated the dress of the frontier period. In southwestern Virginia, when flax was unavailable, the native wild nettle often served as an important substitute as "the fibrous bark, with the exception of the shortness of the fibres, seemed to be adapted to the same uses."[34] With the introduction of cotton and hemp cultivation into the mountains during the early nineteenth century, flax growing became increasingly less common. By the end of the century comparatively little of the plant fiber could be found anywhere in the southern Appalachians.[35]

The Scots-Irish were certainly not the only ethnic group to influence land-use patterns in the southern Appalachians. Though fewer in number, many German or "Dutch," as they were sometimes called, settlers also changed the mountain landscape in particular ways. Most German immigrants came to frontier America from a region known as the Palatinate, a centuries-old principality on the southwestern border of Germany. Still others came from Alsace, today part of France but historically an area claimed by both the French and Germans. The first wave of overseas migration began in 1689 after a retreating French army had destroyed much of the territory. By the early 1700s, crop failures, religious persecution, and high taxes substantially increased the number of German immigrants destined for North America. Later, between 1727 and 1755, 239 ships carrying mostly Germans anchored in the port of Philadelphia.[36] Although many Germans came to this country as indentured servants, the redemptioner system provided them with free passage to the New World and ultimately, after seven years of contracted labor, their freedom. At the end of indenture, many sought out farms in Pennsylvania, Maryland, North Carolina, and Virginia. The Moravian missionaries of Wachovia, North Carolina, who settled near the foot of the Blue Ridge Mountains were also partly responsible for the influx of Germans to the region, thus making a significant contribution to the development of the southern frontier.[37] When Moravian brothers Abraham Steiner and Frederick de Schweinitz visited Abingdon, Virginia, in 1799, they saw "several German churches," one of which, they noted, was "very large and looks fine." They also visited several German families in the surrounding mountains, remarking favorably on their well-tilled soil and "beautiful plantations."[38]

A smaller number of Germans arriving in southern Appalachia during the late eighteenth century were no doubt Hessian mercenaries, hired by the British to fight in the Revolutionary War. However, muster rolls for the border counties of Virginia for the French and Indian War establish the presence of Germans in the region well before 1770. Germans predominated in parts of the upper Shenandoah Valley during the latter half of the eighteenth century but represented only 5 percent of the total Tennessee population in 1790. Numbers in some mountain communities appear to have been much higher, especially for counties nearest the Moravian tract in North Carolina, where, according to one source, Germans represented more than 20 percent of the population.[39] Although they had no influence on frontier development, it should also be noted that approximately one hundred German-speaking families settled atop the Cumberland Plateau during the mid–nineteenth century, helping to form the Gruetli-Laager community, as it is known today.[40]

Despite their relatively smaller numbers, the Germans' contribution to environmental and cultural change in many parts of the region was significant. Germans preferred level land over rolling hillsides and, unlike the Scots-Irish, frequently spread manure over worn fields to increase fertility.

In preparing the mountain homesite, most German settlers practiced clear-cutting—the felling of all trees within the area—and then grubbed out all of the remaining tree stumps. They also preferred systematic cultivation over land rotation, which meant that all debris had to be thoroughly removed. Excess stones were gathered from plowed fields and used to build fences or the foundations of barns and outbuildings. Felled trees were cut into firewood or burned on the site, providing large amounts of fertile potash that also helped to neutralize soil acidity. In fact, from the full-scale German method of frontier land clearance came the expression "free and clear," a phrase used to describe a parcel of land ready for planting.[41]

Of course, one of the more important contributions that the Germans made to the southern Appalachian subsistence economy was log building and barn construction. In fact, many of the log cabins and barns in the region could not have been constructed without the use of German carpentry methods and designs. According to scholars of frontier material culture, the techniques of horizontal log building construction were first introduced by Germans into southern Pennsylvania as early as 1710. Notching techniques varied according to where the immigrant may have originated in Germany, but the basic principle of corner timbering made the construction of all log houses possible. The very first German log houses in the mid-Atlantic region were rectangular and had two or three major rooms and a central chimney.[42] The Germans built more elaborate barns than any other ethnic group, the most well known and most copied of these being the cantilevered barn. Wooden shingles, the central chimney, board gables, vertical planking, and the rafter-style roof are all among the German contributions to log home building in the southern mountains.[43]

Although Appalachian frontiersmen borrowed many German construction techniques, the log cabin was not entirely German in origin. Most Scots-Irish and English settlers built log structures whose interiors reflected the floor plans of their former homes. In most instances, builders of English ancestry generally chose to modify the three-room German house by squaring the structure into one- or two-room "pens," creating larger and more familiar living quarters. The English, as noted earlier, also placed an external chimney at each end of the cabin, again altering the central chimney form of the German log dwelling. The spaces between the cabin logs required substantial caulking with mud, a building practice familiar to most British settlers. When the Ulster settlers first came to American in the seventeenth century, they initially built houses of stone, thatch, and mud. Lacking many of these construction materials and having a ready supply of wood, they quickly abandoned this practice.[44]

Although the southern Appalachian log cabin is more likely the product of a collaborative cultural effort, that is, the result of a blending of Tidewater English, Pennsylvania German, and Scots-Irish traits,[45] a few notable scholars have argued that frontier building techniques and land-use practices, including log cabin construction, are Scandinavian in origin.[46] Cultural geographers Terry Jordan and Matti Kaups believe that Swedish and Finnish settlers were the only culture group preadapted to the environment of the American frontier, having arrived from a forested land possessing a "satisfactory axe and the ancestral skills to clear woodlands." After providing a successful example for later arrivals to the region, Jordan and Kaups believe that Scandinavian land-use practices spread southward with the flow of frontier migration. The origin of the Virginia rail fence, they argue, can be traced to the Savo-Karelians (Finns), who settled in New Sweden (Delaware) in the seventeenth century. The prototype of the zig-zag rail fence, says Jordan and Kaups, "is an ancient archaic Finnic type called *perkka-aita*, vestiges of which still remain among the Lapps and Savo-Karelians."[47]

Scandinavian methods of land clearance undoubtedly made their appearance during the settling of the frontier, as Swedish and Finnish immigrants brought with them a vast knowledge of forest silviculture. The practice of *svedjebruket*, or svedging, as it was more commonly called, involved the felling of deciduous trees in summer or fall and then, the following year, the removal of the largest limbs for building lumber or firewood. A year later, the remaining trees, stumps, limbs, and underbrush were spread over the ground to be cultivated and then were burned into ashes. Immediately the field was planted in rye or oats and, after the fall harvest, burned again. After several successive years of planting and burning, additional branches and brush were added to the field, and again these were reduced to ashes. Log rolling, a celebrated frontier practice requiring work groups to communally collect, pile, and burn felled timber, also likely evolved out of the intensive Scandinavian tradition of forest clearance.[48]

Svedging, as the attentive reader may have already noted, closely resembles other slash-and-burn agricultural practices common in the southern

mountains. Since the eighteenth century, farmers in the southern Appalachians have girdled, cut, and then burned the natural vegetation before
planting new ground. Harriette Arnow mentions how, on the Cumberland
Plateau, felled trees were generally "dragged into a pile and burned." Indeed, the custom of chopping and firing the natural vegetation to improve
cropland was practiced in the southern mountains from frontier settlement
until the early twentieth century.[49] Stanley Pope remembered that in the
mountains of northern Georgia where he grew up, the process was commonly known as "cleaning up new ground." According to Pope, "we
grubbed up the bushes and trees with a maddock [and] piled up the brush
and the trees and burnt it off. That got rid of it and also improved the
ground." Intentional fires not only cleared lands for agriculture but also
eliminated unwanted pests and improved conditions for grazing livestock.
"Fire do a heap of good," responded another mountaineer when asked his
reasons for burning the woods. It "kill the boll weevil, snakes, ticks, an'
bean beetle [and] greens up the grass."[50]

As persuasive as the evidence for Scandinavian influence on frontier
land clearance might appear, it rests partly on the assumption that the majority of mountain settlers or their ancestors had direct or indirect contact
with individuals who had once lived in or near the Delaware and Monongahela River valleys where Scandinavian influence was greatest. While a
great number of mountain settlers came from this region of North America
and a few even had direct Scandinavian ancestry, not all could have
been directly exposed to these cultural influences.[51] Immigrants originating from the ports of Charleston and Savannah, Hessian soldiers, German
Moravians, British and French fur traders, Creeks and Cherokees, African
slaves, and English transplants from the Tidewater are among those least
likely to have had little if any initial exposure to Scandinavian land-use
techniques. Although cultural borrowing can certainly take place without
direct or even indirect contact, it is highly unlikely that any one subsistence
activity in the southern mountains remained culturally "pure" for any
length of time. Subsistence practices on the southern Appalachian frontier
most likely evolved in syncretic fashion, synthesizing Scots-Irish, English,
German, Spanish, Cherokee, and, yes, Scandinavian traditions.

There is also the very real possibility that more than one ethnic group
was responsible for introducing the same cultural practice to separate
areas of the southern mountains. Both the Cherokees and Scandinavians,

for example, could have introduced woods burning to areas where those communities and cultural traditions predominated. The burning of woodlands in many parts of the Blue Ridge may have Scots-Irish origins (as transhumance suggests), but it could have also been learned from neighboring Cherokees. In pockets of eastern Kentucky and West Virginia where more individuals of Scandinavian ancestry appear to have settled, the custom of slash-and-burn agriculture may well have had Swedish or Finnish roots. The English could have also influenced woods-burning activities in the mountains, however, as paring and burning was also practiced in England as early as the seventeenth century.[52] Because nearly all the culture groups who settled the region held a common penchant for agriculture, it seems only logical that all would share a number of strategies and techniques for altering the mountain landscape. In the southern Appalachians, the mountain environment favored some European subsistence practices over others, and cultural adaptation to the new landscape was necessary for survival.

Nature/Culture

Undoubtedly mountain farmers would have also allowed the local landscape or even the availability of tools to dictate what land-use techniques might be appropriate in a given area. For many it was simply more practical to first make "deadenings" in a maturing forest by pulling up or cutting several acres of the undergrowth, burning the brush, and then girdling the largest trees.[53] To girdle a tree, the settler would only have to remove a wide strip of bark around the base so as not to allow the sap to rise to the upper branches. This practice, first used by Native Americans throughout much of North America, quickly killed even the largest trees.[54] Certainly for the Scots-Irish, with little knowledge of large-scale timbering, the making of forest deadenings had many advantages over other land clearance techniques. Unlike clear-cuts, deadenings were far less labor intensive and did not immediately require the felling of trees, since crops could be planted in shadeless areas among the standing trees the following year. Within a few more years the deadened trees either fell down during high winds or would be cut into usable lengths with steel broad axes. Settlers could then use the trees for log cabins, firewood, and fences or simply heap the logs into piles and burn them.

The intentional burning of trees provided a convenient way to remove large trees from potential croplands as well to produce large amounts of potash, which greatly increased soil fertility. Despite the apparent wastefulness of this clearing process, the felling of trees, as Harriette Arnow has noted, was never done "solely to be rid of the tree." If the trees were hardwoods, they might later become firewood, axe handles, wooden utensils, roof shingles, or pegwood. Poplar and ash were more often used in cabin or barn construction, although where mature stands of the eastern red cedar predominated, such as on the Cumberland Plateau, homes and barns were often built of hewed cedar.[55]

Because the soil and climate of the region greatly favored the growing of Indian corn, all settlers in the southern mountains quickly took up the practice of growing this New World crop. On most southern Appalachian homesteads, corn was immediately interplanted among the remaining tree stumps after the felled trees were removed. As early as 1755, when touring the Rocky River valley in western North Carolina, Arthur Dobbs found settlers planting Indian corn, wheat, barley, rye, and oats in fields cleared among the hardwood forest.[56] Corn was the most frequently planted crop in the deadenings, as it could be planted without the use of plows in soil "too filled with roots and stumps." The smaller Old World grains required a more even seed bed of loose soil, which meant that the first plantings of these crops could only be done in bottomlands or in the deadenings after several years of hoeing and plowing had sufficiently broken the soil. This certainly seems to have been the case on the Cumberland Plateau, where Scots-Irish farmers were growing wheat and rye two or three years after the first corn crop.[57]

Whatever crop was sown in the stump-ridden clearings of the frontier settlements, twenty-four-hour protection was needed from the cattle, hogs, deer, rabbits, squirrels, and other animals of the forest seeking food. In response to the onslaught, all settlers enclosed their gardens with rail, stone, or paling fences to avoid run-ins with unwanted animals. In the environment of southern Appalachia, some fences had a certain advantage over others, however. Split-rail or Virginia "worm" fences, constructed by stacking split rails in a repetitious, zigzag manner, could be easily moved from one location to another and were especially easy to construct on rough and rocky ground.[58] Rail fences—even those nine rails high— hardly kept out rabbits, raccoons, squirrels, and deer, however.

American chestnut trees, 1890.
Photograph courtesy of the Great
Smoky Mountains National Park,
Gatlinburg, Tennessee.

River cane along Cumberland River. Whitley County, Kentucky.

Photograph by the author.

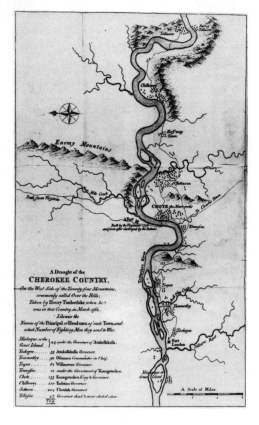

Henry Timberlake map, "A Draught of the Cherokee Country."

Photograph courtesy of Hogkins Library, Special Collections, University of Tennessee.

Etowah Mounds, Dallas, Georgia, 1963.
Photograph courtesy of the Waring Archaeological
Laboratory, State University of West Georgia,
Carrollton, Georgia.

Vann's Tavern, New Echota State Historic Site, Georgia Department of Natural
Resources, Calhoun, Georgia.
Photograph by the author.

Fitchburg or Red River Furnace, Estill County, Kentucky.
Photograph courtesy of the Filson Club Historical Society, Louisville, Kentucky.

Log cabin, Barbourville, Kentucky.
Photograph courtesy of the Forest History
Society, Durham, North Carolina.

Grassy Bald on Big Yellow Mountain, Mitchell County, North Carolina, 1899.
Source: Message from the President, Senate Document No. 84, Plate VIII.
Photograph courtesy of the Forest History Society, Durham, North Carolina.

Forest deadenings, 1900, Grandfather Mountain, North Carolina.
Photograph courtesy of the National Archives, Still Pictures Branch, College Park,
Maryland. NA: 95G: 050971.

Mossy Creek farmstead, 1842, Jefferson County, Tennessee.

Source: Frontispiece, John Gray Smith, *A Brief Historical, Statistical, and Descriptive Review of East Tennessee, United States of America.* London: J. Leath, 1842. Photograph courtesy of Hogkins Library, Special Collections, University of Tennessee, Knoxville, Tennessee.

Cantilever barn, Sevier County, Tennessee.

Photograph courtesy of Museum of Appalachia, Norris, Tennessee.

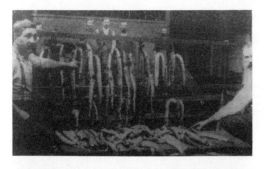

American freshwater eels,
Trion, Georgia, 1896.
Source: *History of Chattooga County.*

Salting sheep, 1900,
Lumpkin County, Georgia.
Photograph courtesy of Georgia
Department of Archives and History,
Atlanta, Georgia.

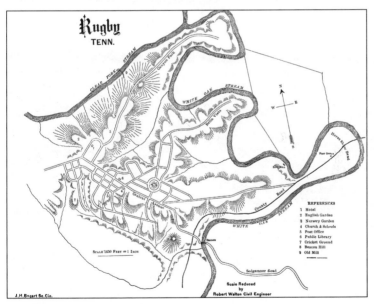

Map of Rugby, Tennessee, 1884.
Source: *The Rugby Handbook of the English American Colony
on the Plateau of the Cumberland Mountains in East, Tennessee.*
Facsimile edition, Historic Rugby Press, 1996.

Findley gold mine, West Cut, Lumpkin County, Georgia.
Photograph courtesy of the Georgia Department of Archives
and History, Atlanta, Georgia.

Placer gold mining, White County, Georgia.
Photograph courtesy of the Georgia Department of Archives
and History, Atlanta, Georgia.

Old growth tulip-tree, Reems Creek, Buncombe County, North Carolina.
Photograph courtesy of the Great Smoky Mountains National Park, Gatlinburg, Tennessee.

Logging operations, southwestern Virginia.

Photograph courtesy of Museum of Appalachia, Norris, Tennessee.

Loading poplar logs, West Virginia.
Photograph courtesy of the Forest History Society,
Durham, North Carolina.

Logging operations, Rabun County, Georgia.
Photograph courtesy of the Georgia Department of
Archives and History, Atlanta, Georgia.

Debris from floods on Nolichucky River, Erwin, Tennessee, 1901.
Source: Message from the President, Senate Document No. 84. Photograph
courtesy of the Forest History Society, Durham, North Carolina.

Devastation caused by logging and fires, Mt. Mitchell, North Carolina, 1923.
Photograph courtesy of the National Archives, Still Records Branch, College Park, Maryland.
NA: 95G-176379.

Yellow poplar and horseback rider, Little Santeethla Creek,
Unicoi Mountains, North Carolina, 1916.

Photograph courtesy of the National Archives, Still Records Branch,
College Park, Maryland. NA: 95G-27294A.

Shelton family with American chestnut, 1920.
Photograph courtesy of the Great Smoky Mountains
National Park, Gatlinburg, Tennessee.

Rail fences created other problems besides their inability to keep out many unwanted pests. In order for the rails to balance exactly upon their diagonally crossed stake supports, each section of fence had to join the next at a 120-degree angle, so the actual path of the fence "stretched almost ten feet wide, and the swath of ground occupied by the rails proved almost impossible to cultivate, even with a hoe." A mile of worm fence literally took dozens of acres of cultivated land out of production, as well as creating an environmental haven for weeds, groundhogs, birds, and other undesirables. It also took a considerable number of large trees to build these fences: circumventing a 10-acre field required more than 4,500 rails, or the cutting of thirty to fifty very large trees. Only where mature timber grew plentifully did the split-rail fence predominate.[59]

More difficult to build but better at keeping out pesky intruders was the paling or stake fence. Mountain settlers used it primarily for smaller garden plots and the yard area immediately around the homesite. The paling fence was constructed by laying narrow boards or stake palings side by side along a panel of horizontal boards that were held upright on sturdy posts. The result was a very tall but solid picket fence, and with the ends of the boards sharpened to discourage deer from jumping over them, the structures were nearly impenetrable.[60]

Settlers in the Blue Ridge Mountains used the stone wall in the same fashion the paling fence was used elsewhere. Stone walls are certainly much rarer in the southern Appalachians than in the Blue Grass region of Kentucky, an area much better known for its picturesque stone fences. There are, nevertheless, excellent examples of stone construction throughout the southern mountain region. On the Old Settlers Trail, for example, in the Great Smoky Mountains National Park, most of the former homesites that one sees along the trail are surrounded by formidable stone fences built to keep wandering animals out of garden areas and cornfields. Many stretch for more than 200 yards without a single opening, and some are more than 7 feet high. Since large stones were extremely plentiful in the Smokies and needed to be removed for successful cultivation, it is not surprising that such construction techniques were adopted by the early settlers there. The Germans and Quakers of Pennsylvania are perhaps best known for stone masonry on the American frontier, but in the mountains the practice of laying stone may have evolved independently of their influence. Interestingly, in National Park Service literature, the still visible stone piles that were used to build the fences are referred to as *carnes,* a Celtic term meaning mounds of stones. According to R. Gerald Avery, many of the early stone walls constructed in parts of north-central Kentucky were clearly built "by people with knowledge of the craft as practiced in Ulster and Britain."[61]

The mountain environment also played an incredibly important role in livestock selection and use on the southwestern frontier. Hogs found very little to dislike about the native mountain ecosystem, devouring great quantities of chestnuts, hickory nuts, acorns, cane stalks, and even the buried roots of trees and shrubs. In fact, pork, rather than beef or mutton, became the principal meat of all classes during the Colonial period. For example, between 1771 and 1796, hogs dominated the inventories of farm estates in Washington County, Tennessee, representing the greatest percentage of all livestock breeds. Archaeological evidence confirms the importance of hogs in the Tennessee Valley; an examination of faunal remains at the Tipton-Hayes Farm in upper eastern Tennessee provides further evidence that pork was probably the most frequently eaten meat of the frontier period.[62]

The proliferation of hogs in the southern Appalachians directly influenced mountain culture, changing eating habits, land-use practices, and, eventually, the landscape itself. After butchering, portions of the hog were either hung in a smokehouse to cure or stored in large wooden casks filled with salt, saltpeter, and brown sugar. For many, the proper time for killing hogs depended a great deal on the weather or "proper sign," since the best days for slaughtering the animal were those with "a moon on the wane." Hogs were raised not only for food, as the animals supplied lard for cooking, hides for leather, and even grease for metal gears and guns.[63]

In the Old World, pork was not as popular among common folk, particularly among the Scots-Irish and English, who generally avoided the flesh of pigs. In fact, Scottish Highlanders held such an overt disdain for pork that they were sometimes called "the Jewish Scots."[64] England's mast-rich oak forests had disappeared by A.D. 1400, so it was never really practical to keep hogs there after that time. While black cattle and sheep remained the principal livestock of the Scottish Highlands, hogs were the most practical animal for the southern mountains, meaning that pork, hominy, and corn pone—not mutton, beef, and rye bread—were the most commonly eaten foods.[65] This isn't to say that cattle were not numerous in the region during the early Colonial period. Cattle ranching was certainly being done on a large scale, although usually by professional drovers. Cattle herding was also more common on the Cumberland Plateau, where the practice flourished until well after the Civil War. For home consumption, however, hogs were still the animal of choice.

Besides hog husbandry, another subsistence practice that nearly all culture groups shared after their arrival to the mountain region was hunting. Here the environment played perhaps its biggest role in directing the daily activities of the pioneer. Because clearing the land and successfully harvesting crops sometimes took several years, hunting of both large and small game became necessary for survival. The first mountain settlers hunted deer, elk, buffaloes, and bears, but many also relied upon smaller animals like turkeys, rabbits, squirrels, ducks, geese, and even the migratory whistling swans. On 27 March 1780 John Donelson, an early Tennessee resident, reported killing a large swan on the Cumberland River that he claimed was "very delicious."[66] According to Arnow, these magnificent birds were "a favorite summer food" on the Cumberland Plateau as well as many other parts of southern Appalachia where they were regular seasonal residents.

The earliest settlers of the region, however, sought primarily the largest game: buffaloes, elk, and deer, and of these, buffaloes were preferred. As noted in chapter 3, buffaloes provided meat, hides, and large quantities of tallow, an important eighteenth-century commodity traded in developing local townships and distant cities where butter and lard were scarce. In 1767, in a single two-month period, one group of English hunters killed "upwards of 700 buffaloes" and then rendered their tallow for market.[67] Not all buffaloes were taken by professional hunters involved in the business of trading skins or rendering tallow, however. In the winter of 1776, after clearing homesites for cropland, the first settlers of Carter's Valley, Virginia, are said to have "hunted and killed buffalo twelve or thirteen miles north-west of their settlement."[68] After a decade of intense hunting from both long hunters and settlers alike, most of the biggest buffalo herds were driven north and west off the Cumberland Plateau. However, in 1779, according to one eyewitness, a few buffalo herds could be found near the Big South Fork of the Cumberland and Obed Rivers. Within just a few years, however, even these had been eliminated from the southern mountains.[69]

The American elk, much like the buffaloes, also vanished from the region as a direct result of frontier settlement. Naturalist John Lawson, who referred to elk as the "Monster of the Venison sort," recorded their presence in western North Carolina around 1700, noting that "the Stags of Carolina are lodged in the mountains."[70] In 1753 James Burke, one of the original settlers of the Draper's Meadows in southwestern Virginia, wounded an elk and followed it through Henshaw Gap into the fertile mountain valley now known as Burkes Gardens. Early eyewitness accounts also mention elk following well-worn paths to mineral licks along the banks of the New River in North Carolina. Not surprisingly, they also note the many place-names derived from the large numbers of elk that once resided in southwestern Virginia and southern West Virginia: Elk Creek, Elk View, Elk Garden, Elko, Elk Hill, Elkton, and Elkwood.[71]

Fleeing the approach of settlement, a few elk herds found their way to the Virginia and West Virginia mountains, where they remained until the eve of the Civil War. According to William Bartram, a few elk were even found in the mountains of northeastern Georgia and eastern Tennessee prior to the Revolutionary War. In recounting his travels for the year 1773, Bartram wrote: "there are but few elks and those only in the Appalachian mountains."[72] In 1806 Thomas Ashe wrote that elk still roamed the mountainous areas of Tennessee but that they were much more rare. When an elk was killed in Dickson County, Tennessee, that same year, "the hunter had a great barbecue and invited all his neighbors." By that time, says Harriette Arnow, elk meat was already a curiosity or distant memory. As late as 1847, naturalists John Audubon and James Bachman heard rumors of an elk herd in West Virginia that was known to "range along the high and sterile mountains west of Red Sulfur Springs."[73]

By 1780 big game was scarce in most of eastern Kentucky, southwestern Virginia, and eastern Tennessee. Prior to the 1780s, most frontiersmen had hunted deer, elk, and buffaloes in any season, sometimes leaving the edible flesh of the animal to rot in the woods. Deer harvests could be particularly staggering: when long hunter Jesse Bledsoe had his entire stash of peltries stolen by unknown Native Americans, he carved on a tree, "2300 deerskins lost, ruination by God."[74] Deer populations suffered so greatly that territorial assemblies were forced to pass game laws restricting the killing of deer solely for their skins. Night hunting also was thought to be excessive and dangerous, and South Carolina forbade it in the upcountry as early as

1769. The same South Carolina law not only restricted night hunting but placed restrictions on killing does and fawns: "No doe or fawn should be killed between the first day of January and the last of July, in any year after; nor any buck between the first day of September and the last Friday of October." The legislation did not seem to stop or even slow the slaughter, at least in South Carolina, where additional laws and even stiffer penalties were needed to protect the deer. In 1785 it was ordained "that any person who should thereafter hunt with fire, or kill any deer, or horse, or cattle or stock of any kind, in the night-time, should pay the sum of twenty pounds sterling."[75] Similar legislation was passed in North Carolina, where deer populations had been declining since the 1740s. After 1784 it was unlawful to kill deer "by firelight and at unreasonable times."[76]

The small farmer, less ambitious than the long hunter and fur trader, also took his share of wild game. On any given day or night, the mountain settler might hunt bear, elk, deer, wild turkey, rabbit, squirrel, raccoon, grouse, or even opossum. Some animals were occasionally taken using snares or deadfalls, others were shot with flintlock rifles. All supplied meat during the winter months when home fruit and vegetable supplies became low or absent entirely. The furs and skins were also valuable commodities and were exchanged at frontier stores for such things as sugar, coffee, chocolate, tobacco, rifle bullets, and garden seeds.[77]

At the same time the legal system cracked down on some hunting practices in the southern mountains, it sanctioned the wholesale slaughter of other animals. Settlers frequently complained that timber wolves were killing their livestock and soon demanded bounties on their heads. North Carolina was the first to enact such legislation, placing monetary bounties as early as 1748 on the scalps of panther, wolf, and wildcat. The state of Tennessee passed a similar act in 1812, and by the 1830s three dollars a scalp was the going rate. Between 1830 and 1840 a few scalps continued to be cashed in around the area of the Great Smoky Mountains, where wolves were known to exist until the Civil War.[78] In western North Carolina, bounty hunters received $2.50 per scalp, regardless of the animal's size. To take advantage of the situation, hunters sometimes followed a mother wolf into her den and killed her pups, allowing the mother to escape and insuring another year's litter and new supply of scalps.[79]

As a result of the loss of big game animals, the competition for mast—acorns, chestnuts, beechnuts, and hickory nuts—became less intense among the remaining forest animals. In some areas of the region, small animal populations actually rose during the last quarter of the eighteenth century. Gray and fox squirrels were so common and were taken so regularly that they soon became a major source of frontier subsistence. According to one eye witness, the woods were so "infested with squirrels" that the children were "sent around to the fields to frighten them away." [80]

Squirrels apparently did so much damage to the corn crop in the mountains that the state of Tennessee made squirrel scalps legal tender. In the fall months they appeared in such great numbers "that the inhabitants are obliged to meet together in order to destroy them . . . they generally go two by two, and sometimes kill thirty or forty in a morning." [81] An experienced pioneer rifleman would often "bark the squirrel," meaning that he would take careful aim at the piece of bark on which the animal was resting. With the report of the gun, the wood under the squirrel would splinter to pieces, and the stunned squirrel would fall to the ground. This style of hunting attests not only to the sharpshooting skills of the frontiersmen but also to their desire not to waste meat. Designed for larger game, the .45-caliber Kentucky rifle could do great damage to the flesh of small mammals. Barking the squirrel minimized waste. [82]

Turkeys, like squirrels, also benefited greatly from local increases in oak and chestnut mast. Their size, numbers, and relative tameness made them easy targets for many mountain settlers. Frontier people ate or used nearly all parts of the wild turkey, even fashioning the large wing and tail feathers of the bird into useful feather dusters. A common method of capture was to build a "turkey pen," a partially underground trap that was baited with handfuls of corn. After capture, the 20-pound birds were roasted in a large Dutch oven or "cooked in a pit beneath a mound of hot coals." [83]

Turkeys were especially abundant atop the Cumberland Plateau, where their numbers often astonished newcomers. In 1785 General Butler, traveling up the Kanawha River in West Virginia, "had nothing to do but spring from the boats among flocks of turkeys and kill as many as desired." Around 1800, at the time of his first arrival in eastern Kentucky, John James Audubon claimed that "turkeys were so abundant, that the price of one in the market was not equal to that of a common barnyard fowl." According to Kentucky resident Sylvester Judd, the birds sold "for six cents apiece, though the largest ones, sometimes weighing from twenty-five to thirty pounds, sometimes brought a quarter of a dollar." Gilbert Imlay believed that the abundance of turkeys in the area was best explained by the "rapidity of settlement," which, he believed, had driven the turkey out of the "middle countries" of the Tennessee Valley.[84]

Raccoons, another mammal frequently taken in the frontier hunt, were valued more for their fur than as a food source, since their flesh isn't as palatable as that of most small game. In fact, the hides of all small mammals—raccoon, mink, otter, beaver, and even opossum—were extremely important to the frontier economy. Because raccoons are nocturnal, capturing them generally required the use of hunting dogs, who would help isolate the elusive prey. Dogs were trained to "tree" the raccoon, holding it at bay in a tall tree until the hunter arrived with gun and axe. If the treed animal could not be seen with the aid of moonlight or a fire-lit pine knob, the hunters would sometimes cut down the tree.[85] Dogs were invaluable companions and could be found traveling with pioneer families from the very earliest period of settlement. In fact, pioneers could not kill black bears in large numbers without the use of dogs, who forced the bears up trees or held them at bay under rock ledges or in caves. The Plott hound, developed in North Carolina sometime during the late eighteenth century, is probably the best-known bear dog of southern Appalachia.[86]

For the pioneers, hunting the animals of the forest was paramount to survival. For this reason, the natural world exerted a considerable amount of control over the lives of the newly transplanted Europeans. Whether the hunt was for bears or raccoons, the animals of the mountains helped shape the lives of all immigrant groups. At the same time, frontier settlers created recognizable, even dramatic changes in the surrounding mountain landscape. As more and more land succumbed to the axe and plow, many parts of the Appalachian countryside began to take on a different look, at times even resembling Old World environs. To use the terminology of the eighteenth-century Anglican minister Charles Woodsmason, larger and larger areas of the mountain landscape begin to take on "a new face."[87] Indeed, some portions of the southern mountain region soon resembled the Old World more than the New World out of which they had been created.

Environmental changes were hardly universal in scope, occurring first along major river valleys, particularly in the Ridge and Valley section of the mountains. In the Blue Ridge Mountains and Cumberland Plateau, large-scale environmental change was much slower in coming. In fact, isolated areas of the southwestern mountains saw little or no human disturbance until the last decade of the nineteenth century. However, almost no part of the region escaped the environmental changes that resulted from the introduction of European trees, vines, shrubs, flowers, grasses, and animals. These "natural aliens," including many plants erroneously thought to be native to the region, spread quickly across the southern Appalachians. Most species adapted well to the mountains; others, such as privet and multiflora rose, grew so prodigiously that they eventually choked out all other native vegetation.

Natural Aliens

Grasses were among the first exotic plants introduced to the mountains by Europeans. After their first arrival on the Atlantic Coast, many settlers had been greatly deceived by the luxurious summer growth of the native vegetation and soon discovered that North American grasses, more often than not, withered away in the fall, leaving cattle to forage on lifeless brown foliage. As a result, settlers coming to America were often instructed to bring grass seed along with them as part of their required provisions. A London pamphlet published as early as 1635 instructed the prospective settler to take "a good store of calver-grasse seed to make good meadow."[88] Of course some grasses were introduced unintentionally to North America, arriving among the livestock fodder stored on transAtlantic ships.

The general consensus among agricultural historians is that grasses from the Welsh and English countryside were among the first plants brought to this country by the pioneer settlers. In fact, prior to 1800, the adjective "English" was often used to distinguish all introduced grass species from indigenous North American vegetation. Timothy grass was a favorite of European settlers and was brought from the British Isles sometime during the seventeenth century. In England timothy was known locally as "cat's tail grass" and grew naturally in isolated wastelands. The grass is actually named for Timothy Hanson, the settler who first took the seed into the southeastern United States, where he distributed it in Virginia and North Carolina sometime before the Revolutionary War. By 1799 Moravian missionaries Abraham Steiner and Frederick de Schweinitz could report seeing meadows of timothy grass and red clover growing among the verdant fields of southwestern Virginia.[89] In fact, prior to the Civil War, cattle herders in the mountain region preferred timothy grass over all others, commenting it was "the best grass we have for making hay."[90]

Settlers also frequently sowed red and white clover—two other important nonnative plants—in the mountains prior to the beginning of the nineteenth century. Red clover was generally planted with timothy grass as a mixed hay crop, a practice that continued well into the twentieth century. White clover, cultivated in the southern United States as early as 1739, was used both as a honey crop and as forage for cattle in the mountains. A highly prolific ground cover, white clover was also a marker of ethnic advancement across the southern Appalachians. English clover, observed the Cherokees, "follows the white man."[91]

Another important grass species brought by European settlers to the mountain region was orchard grass. The cultivation of orchard grass appears to have started in Virginia prior to 1760, although it did not achieve popularity in that state until sometime after 1780. The grass grew extremely prolifically in limestone soils and, as the name implies, did exceptionally well when sown among apple and peach trees.[92] Bermuda grass, a native grass of the tropics, first arrived in the Southeast as bedding for slaves and then spread into the interior as a result of Spanish trade. Exactly when it reached the southern mountains is hard to discern with certainty, but it was probably being grown in the upper Tennessee Valley by the early 1800s. Today it is commonly planted in lawns, golf courses, and pastures, and its microscopic pollen is considered a major cause of hay fever. Its ability to spread rapidly has made it an unwanted pest in the modern era, a trait that originally brought it many accolades. In 1807 James Meese, in his "Geologic Account of the United States," stated that Bermuda, which "grows with great luxuriance and propagates with astonishing rapidity by means of its numerous jointing," was as important "a grass as any in the southern states."[93]

Red and white clover, timothy, orchard, and Bermuda grass are just a few of the hundreds of herbaceous plants that were brought to the region as a result of frontier settlement. Many spread so rapidly across the landscape that many people thought them native to the region. In 1785 Thomas Jefferson wrote, for example, that our native grasses "are Lucerne, St. Foin, Burnet, Timothy, rye, and orchard grass; red, white, and yellow clover, greensward, blue grass, and crab grass." In truth, none of these varieties are native to the United States, an observation that Jefferson, himself an accomplished horticulturalist, failed to make.[94] Collectively, all these European grasses helped change the complexion of the mountain landscape, choking out native plants and weeds as they helped to turn canebrakes and adjoining woodlands into pasture.

Along with exotic grasses came a variety of weeds and herbaceous plants, many of which became extremely important to mountain culture and folklore. Like grasses, some of the exotics found their way to the mountains randomly; others were brought here specifically as food sources. Chicory, introduced into the United States in 1785, quickly made its way into the southern Appalachians, where it served as both a salad green and coffee substitute. When nineteenth-century mountaineers reported eating varieties of field cresses ("narrow dock" and "greasy greens," for example), they were discussing the consumption of nonnative European plants.[95] Winter cress, yellow rocket, prickly lettuce, English plantain, bitter cress, Queen Anne's lace, common yarrow, field pennycress, common chickweed, shepherd's purse, bitter nightshade, henbit, and wild and field garlic are all from the European continent.

While many plants were simply eaten for their obvious nutritional value, others served as tonics and herbal remedies. Common mullein, for example, a European plant sometimes employed in the making of candle wicks in Colonial America, was used in the southern mountains as the major ingredient in cough syrup. To make the syrup, pioneers boiled a handful of mullein roots and leaves in a pint of water. Sweetener was then added to this light tea, and the patient was instructed to take a spoonful at a time.[96]

Many herbs and so-called weeds of the frontier environs were first cultivated in the kitchen gardens of mountain homesteads. In Europe women had developed the use of herbal remedies for common illnesses, and they continued to advance folk medicine traditions in the southern mountains.[97] Eighteenth-century women gardeners also planted a variety of ornamental flowers among their herb patches, and, like exotic grasses, these quickly spread into the surrounding countryside. Many are now assumed to be native wildflowers, but their presence in the region is primarily due to frontier settlement. Star-of-Bethlehem, multiflora rose, dandelion, oxeye daisy, wisteria, bouncing Bet, several species of violets, butter-and-eggs, daylily, and viper's bugloss are all naturalized flowers of southern Appalachia.[98] The Cherokee rose, once common around nineteenth-century Cherokee homesites and the state flower of Georgia, is a nonnative species introduced from China in 1757.[99] Ornamental roses, shrubs, and trees were favorites in the yards of the first settlers, and finding them today is a good indicator of former homesites. The royal paulownia, or "princess tree," another native of China, was planted widely in the region during the nineteenth century. Privet, the common shrub of hedge and fencerow, is another introduced species that has flourished throughout the southern mountains.[100]

To help pollinate Old World flowers and shrubs, the pioneer settlers also brought "English flies," or honeybees. Some bees had already escaped from parent hives on the coastal settlements, where they were first introduced in the late seventeenth century. According to agricultural historian Lyman Carrier, these initially introduced honeybees helped to stock the woodland forest with numerous bee trees in advance of settlement. "Wild" honeybees were not unknown on the southern Appalachian frontier, but most settlers preferred to manage their own beehives in order to have ready access to sweetener or to assist in the pollination of crops. Beeswax, an important by-product of keeping bees, was a chief ingredient in making tapered candles. In the Washington County, Tennessee, tax inventories for 1778, no fewer than sixty bee gums were listed among the possessions of the first settlers, along with thirty-one candle sticks, thirteen snuffers, and five candle molds.[101]

Plants and insects were not the only exotics introduced to southern Appalachia during the eighteenth century. Numerous small mammals were also brought to the region from the European continent. Red foxes were brought to Colonial America sometime prior to 1750, when, according to German naturalist Peter Kalm, an English fox hunter "brought over a great number of foxes [and] let them loose in his territories." These introductions were later corroborated by the "unanimous testimony" of many Native Americans, who claimed that "this kind of fox never was in the country before the Europeans settled it."[102] In 1802 André Michaux observed Norway and other European rats in the southern mountains, particularly in "settlements belonging to whites," but noted their absence atop the Cumberland Plateau. Apparently the common black crow, a native species, also followed the path of human migration across the mountain region. According to the observant François Michaux, crows were "a true plague in the Atlantic states" but had "not yet made their appearance in Tennessee."[103]

Like the exotic plants and animals that flourished in the mountain environment, European settlers both took and gave something to southern

Appalachia. They came to the region in order to carve civilization out of a wilderness and, with the aid of Old World land-use techniques and considerable knowledge gained from the Cherokees, were largely successful. They also introduced European plants and mammals into the mountains, changing the southern Appalachian ecosystem in ways we may never fully understand.[104] Living closer to the cycles of nature than those who would follow, the men and women of the southwestern frontier felt the intense heat of summer and the bitter cold of winter. They relied on the moon and sun to direct their planting and harvesting, gathered medicinal herbs from the forest floor, hunted the lush woodlands, and fished the mountain streams. And like those who came before and after them, they were seduced by the enormous beauty of the region and its seemingly unlimited supply of natural resources. Yes, a few were certainly a "people of waste," such as the entrepreneurial long hunters and fur trappers, yet many were also enormously inventive and resourceful in making do when the abundance they imagined failed to materialize.[105]

For those settlers who fully attempted to live entirely off the bounty of land, life was not easy. Hard currency was extremely scarce on the frontier, so furs, ginseng, corn, and tobacco were used to purchase rifles, nails, tools, salt, and seeds. By 1785, after most land grants had been issued to surviving veterans of the Revolutionary War, the head right system expired, making the purchase of good quality farmland increasingly difficult for the average mountain yeoman. Afterward, more and more land fell into the hands of private speculators, further decreasing opportunities for small farmers wanting to purchase large, fertile, bottomland tracts.

When new land was available, it was often on hillsides or on much poorer soils, since most of the best farmland had been acquired by that time. This forced later arrivals to locate their homesteads at the mouths of creeks, cut the timber on the creek bottoms, and then plant their crops on the adjacent hillsides. After several years of growing corn under these severe conditions, hillside soils often washed away, forcing the settlers to move on or clear lands higher up and repeat the process. Many settlers chose instead to leave the region entirely, seduced by tales of better, cheaper lands to the south and west.

As difficult as it was for the pioneers to acquire and hold good arable land, settlement in the region never slowed. By 1800 more than 150,000 residents lived in the southern Appalachians, individuals who shaped, and were shaped by, the mountain environment. Of course, not every parcel of land was settled in the region at that time, nor was every settler equally successful in taming the wilderness. As late as 1810, large areas of the Blue Ridge Mountains and Cumberland Plateau remained unoccupied, and large stands of old-growth timber were still left uncut. Huge stores of iron ore and coal also lay just beneath the land's surface, ready for the bellows of industry and market commerce. Frontier settlement made significant changes to the mountain environment, but there were more changes yet to come.

And behold what a change has passed over the face of the land!
—J. W. M. BREAZEALE, *Life As It Is,* 1842

6 Alleghenia

ANTEBELLUM APPALACHIA

$\mathcal{B}$Y 1830 FRONTIER SETTLEMENT had finished in much of the southern mountains. At that time, only the most remote areas of the mountain region could claim little or no human occupancy. After 1800 land settlement and clearance greatly intensified as an increasing number of second- and third-generation settlers began moving deeper into the mountain interior. By 1810 most of the region had a population density of more than six persons per square mile, which, even by Frederick Jackson Turner's standards, hardly qualified the region as frontier. By the 1820s the Tennessee Valley could claim as many as thirty persons per square mile, making it the most populated area in the southern Appalachians.[1]

Land scarcity in the East and relatively cheap land prices made even the most secluded mountain valleys and coves attractive to settlement. The Oconaluftee River valley, high in the Blue Ridge Mountains of western North Carolina, was occupied as early as the 1790s. John Jacob Mingus and his family led the way, migrating to the mountain valley in 1792. Mingus, of German ancestry, settled on the Raven Fork of the Oconaluftee River, where his youngest son, John Mingus, lived until the end of the nineteenth century. Settlement in Oconaluftee progressed slowly until the War of 1812, after which the flow of immigrants steadily increased.[2] Nearby Cades Cove shared a similar settlement history, the first settler, John Oliver, arriving in the cove in early 1818. Even though Oliver and his young family immediately began farming the land, he did not legally claim title to the property until 1826, when he finally purchased his 100-acre farm.[3]

John Oliver, like the majority of the original occupants of the Blue Ridge Mountains, initially owned between 100 and 300 acres of land. Much of the property was not under cultivation, with two thirds or more left completely forested. Major crops included corn, oats, rye, and wheat, although agricultural census records reveal that most residents of the Blue Ridge grew a variety of staples, including sweet and Irish potatoes, peas, beans, flax, tobacco, and sorghum.[4] Genuinely committed to animal husbandry, mountain farmers also raised hogs, sheep, horses, mules, oxen, and numerous beef cattle. The climate and soil of the Blue Ridge Mountains made growing southern cash crops like tobacco and cotton difficult, relegating them to a position of relative insignificance in the agricultural economy.[5] Of perhaps less economic importance but still acutely vital to the household economy were kitchen gardens, milk cows, and poultry yards, each traditionally the responsibility of women and all influential in shaping nineteenth-century mountain life and culture. Farm wives had managed dairy herds in the British Isles and on the Continent, a practice continued in some areas of the southern mountains until well into the twentieth century. The raising of poultry was also a woman's domain in both the Old and New Worlds. In her last will and testament, Mattie Boggs Davis remarked that the largest debt owed her was a loan made to a son-in-law of her entire life savings—$235—that she earned "when eggs were a good price for that purpose."[6]

The settlement of the Cumberland Plateau, unlike the Blue Ridge, progressed slowly but still relatively unabated during the first two decades of the nineteenth century. Families were first drawn to the Cumberland River and its major tributaries, but even remoter areas such as Cranks Creek in Harlan County, Kentucky, had permanent settlements by that time. As early as 1820 approximately two thousand people lived in Harlan County, largely around the area where the Martin's Fork, Clover Fork, and Poor Fork Rivers join to form the Cumberland River.[7] In southeastern Kentucky, land acquisition intensified as a result of state land disposal laws that, according to scholar Mary Beth Pudup, permitted individuals "to claim survey, and purchase two-hundred-acre parcels of uninhabited land for a minimum price of twenty cents an acre."[8] The so-called knob country along the Kentucky and Tennessee border also afforded many opportunities for settlement, even though the best river bottomlands had been taken by the first settlers before 1810. One commentator wrote that for the second-wave immigrant of the Cumberland Plateau, the best option for finding farmland was to go inland from the river and establish a homesite on one of the series of ridges that rose steeply above the river bottoms.[9]

Even though ridgetop farms were less profitable than those along rich bottomland, rivers were no less important to their successful operation. For the first half of the nineteenth century, steam- and keelboats were the only modes of transportation other than foot or horseback over much of the area. Despite their isolation from conventional overland routes, Cumberland Plateau settlements in both Kentucky and Tennessee developed a considerable transportation network. The Big Sandy River watershed, for example, located in eastern Kentucky and southern West Virginia, was navigable for several hundred miles, including considerable stretches along the Tug and Levisa Fork Rivers. Even before 1800 plateau farmers were shipping cotton, oats, wheat, corn, tobacco, hemp, and ginseng to major ports downstream. New Orleans was the preferred destination until the second decade of the nineteenth century, when Nashville, less than 100 miles away, became an important commercial center.[10]

Early-nineteenth-century transportation improvements like the steamboat were a great boon to mountain settlement and development. The establishment of regular water transportation helped to provide settlers with essential goods and markets for their crops. Likewise, the building of roads and turnpikes made the region more accessible to wagon and foot travel, connecting mountain communities to more densely populated settlements outside the region. As early as 1808, post roads bisected even the smallest village settlements, allowing the U.S. Postal Service to advertise weekly mail delivery throughout much of the mountain area. The first roads through the mountains were little more than improved foot trails or well-traveled horse paths, forcing local and state officials to quickly solicit the building of larger turnpikes and toll roads. After a narrow wagon road was opened up across the Blue Ridge Mountains in 1800, the South Carolina legislature, wanting to improve trade with Tennessee, granted Gabriel Benson the power "to lay out and build at his own expense a turnpike road from the Saluda River to the North Carolina boundary." Even though such roads were generally considered "distasteful to the people," Benson's road—the Saluda Turnpike—became one of the first toll roads in all of southern Appalachia. Widespread public dislike for toll roads is understandable when considering the high cost of traveling over them. Upon completion, operators were allowed to collect as much as 75 cents for four-horse wagons and 1 cent per head for hogs, sheep and goats.[11]

Lack of sufficient roads was a perennial concern of merchants and the landed gentry who wanted access to distant markets on the Atlantic and

Gulf Coasts. Recognizing the necessity of roads in the lower Tennessee Valley for stimulating commerce, James Vann, a prominent Cherokee planter and merchant, initiated the building of the Federal Road, the first major route to bisect the entire Cherokee Nation. Completed in 1807, the road connected Nashville to Augusta, Georgia, one of the most important trading centers in the Southeast. Although the federal government provided most of the funds for building the road, Tennessee and Georgia were only required to maintain it outside the official boundaries of the Cherokee Nation. Within the Nation itself, the Cherokees were instructed to establish a schedule of tolls and ferry charges in order to keep the road in good repair. At the two major Cherokee toll gates, the rates were fairly typical of the period: a wagon and team cost $1; a two-wheel carriage, 50 cents; a man and his horse, 12.5 cents; and hogs, sheep, and goats, 1 cent per head.[12]

The Saluda Turnpike and Federal Road were just two of dozens of roads constructed in the region during the first quarter of the nineteenth century. With the completion of the Kanawha Turnpike in southern West Virginia, the Owningsville Turnpike in eastern Kentucky, and the Buncumbe Turnpike in western North Carolina, nearly every corner of the southern mountains had become accessible to settlement and commerce. These thoroughfares did more than simply bring settlers and market goods to the southern mountains, as enterprising settlers opened businesses along these turnpikes in order to take advantage of the increasing number of merchants and travelers using them.[13] Taverns, inns, stores, and stock stands sprang up along the roads, creating social and economic relations never before seen on the frontier. As one eyewitness fondly remembered in his autobiography: "Enterprising men soon established stands on the road and built frame houses and clusters of log houses, also stables and stake-and-rider fence lots [and] made provision for the traveling public . . . Sometimes half a dozen or more people met at one of these stands. They found plenty of good things to eat, and around a wide fireplace good cheer prevailed."[14] Jeremiah Evarts, who visited the region in 1818, similarly noted that it had been "quite an object" for settlers to furnish food and shelter to travelers, particularly along the Federal Road in northwestern Georgia and southeastern Tennessee.[15]

Arriving with these improvements in roads and transportation was the central village township, the precursor to the southern Appalachian city.

Asheville, Knoxville, Charleston, and Chattanooga (Ross's Landing) were founded at this time, and their subsequent commercial development was due largely to their proximity to major transportation routes. In 1800 Knoxville was already a village of more than two hundred frame, brick, and log homes. François Michaux, traveling through the eastern Tennessee village of Jonesborough, observed "a hundred and fifty houses, built of wood, and disposed on both sides of the road." Over the next two decades, the population of mountain townships steadily rose, with Knoxville, one of the largest townships in the region, numbering fifteen hundred by 1830. All were important centers of regional trade, and Greeneville, Tennessee, became the site of one of the first chartered colleges in the southern Appalachians. Chattanooga, one of the region's most important river towns, also advanced considerably during the period, becoming a central location for shipping large quantities of commercial goods to major ports downstream.[16]

Increased population, improved transportation routes, and the introduction of new manufacturing technologies were clear indications that the southern Appalachians were feeling the direct impact of the Market Revolution. Manufacturing had been introduced into the mountains well before 1800, and its impact did not go unnoticed. The level of industrial development is reflected in an early historical sketch of Kingsport, Tennessee, that in 1806 claimed the city "had as many as four [gun]powder mills in operation for powder was as necessary in the family as salt. A charcoal iron furnace and iron works were built and the tilt-hammer pounded away along the river. The oil mills turned out at least pure linseed oil. Tanneries made leather to replace rawhide moccasins. The grist mill and saw mill worked together."[17]

Communities like Kingsport were hardly commercial satellites for an advancing industrial market. Industrial production was certainly commonplace, but it did not represent the dominant mode of economic production in the southern Appalachians. The widely held Physiocratic notion that agriculture was morally superior to other vocational pursuits arguably prevented the factory system from rising to economic ascendancy in the mountains until after the Civil War. As late as 1848, Asa Faulkner, an eastern Tennessee cotton manufacturer, found most native whites indifferent or even hostile to the idea of working in factory mills.[18] Moreover, early manufacturing, more often than not, complemented agricultural pursuits.

As historian Kathleen Bruce has noted, industrial revolutions have historically promoted agricultural revolutions, "for the two provide each other with markets and thus serve as a mutual stimulus."[19] The fledgling iron industry, for example, supplied mountain farmers with nails, iron plows, wagon rims, horseshoes, and other metal implements needed for agricultural improvements. Likewise, the manufacturing of salt, one of the earliest commercial pursuits in the mountain region, created new markets for the sale of local cattle. Packed in salt, a preservative, mountain beef could be sold locally in nearby towns or driven to regional meat-processing establishments such as Atlanta, Nashville, Knoxville, or Lexington.

Drivers, Drovers, Herders

Central to the agricultural economy of southern Appalachia during the antebellum era was the raising of livestock. By the third decade of the 1800s, hundreds of thousands of cattle and hogs were being driven across the mountains to eastern trade centers. Many were herded northward along what was then called the Carolina Road, on which early-nineteenth-century travelers often met "a thousand cattle and hogs heading north to Philadelphia markets." Frederick Jackson Turner estimated that in 1824 alone more than a million dollars' worth of horses, cattle, and hogs came through the Saluda Gap, many on their way to cotton and tobacco plantations in South Carolina.[20] With the completion of the Buncombe Turnpike in 1828, which provided convenient and affordable passage over the Blue Ridge Mountains, Asheville, North Carolina, became the irrefutable center of the antebellum hog and cattle trade. In less than a decade, more than 140,000 animals were annually passing along the "fine new road" into Asheville, where drovers stopped before making their way east to Charleston, Charlotte, Augusta, Norfolk, Columbus, or Savannah.[21] The Tennessee Valley and Cumberland Plateau regions were the principal source of mountain livestock, with the majority coming from eastern Tennessee. In fact, as early as 1840, Ridge and Valley counties—from northeastern Alabama to southwestern Virginia—were annually raising two thousand head of cattle and more than five thousand hogs each. By 1848 Reverend Charles Lanman could report that most farmers in eastern Tennessee derived their principal revenue from what he referred to as "the business of raising cattle." Livestock herding was unquestionably the central occupation along the French Broad River between Newport and Dandridge, where drovers annually fattened somewhere between twenty and thirty thousand hogs for market.[22]

The Blue Ridge Mountains also had their share of livestock herdsmen, even though the area generally fell short of the Ridge and Valley and Cumberland Plateau in antebellum livestock production. In 1859 farmers in Cherokee County, North Carolina, in the extreme southwestern portion of the state, produced 21,075 hogs, 5,702 cattle, and 9,270 sheep, placing it second only to Asheville's Buncombe County in livestock production.[23] The ready availability of hardwood mast was a major boon to Blue Ridge drovers, who turned stock out in the fall to feast on the abundant chestnuts. Frederick Law Olmsted, in his travels through the Blue Ridge in 1856, reported that even though hog raising in the mountains had decreased under the competition it had recently met from Tennessee and Kentucky, the matter was of "inferior concern" in areas where chestnut mast was "remarkably fine." Olmsted also added that swine in the Blue Ridge Mountains were "of superior taste" and looked better than he had seen "anywhere else in the South."[24]

By most accounts, antebellum livestock herding in the southern Appalachians was associated with at least three kinds of individuals or social types. First were drivers, men who specialized in simply driving livestock on foot or horseback from one destination to the next. Second were drovers, livestock herdsmen who raised hogs and cattle for the sole purpose of taking them to distant markets. Third were the traditional yeoman farmers, who raised beef primarily for their own consumption but who also sold surplus hogs and steers to passing drivers or drovers.[25]

Hog and cattle drives in the mountains were extremely hard on the livestock, which often arrived at their destinations gaunt and sick. To help remedy the problem, large quantities of grain were fed to the animals at designated stock stands, providing local farmers with additional markets for surplus corn. Some enterprising farmers even timed their fall grain harvest to correspond with the annual hog and cattle drives, which took place in late summer or early fall. The roadside inn and stock stand were no doubt essential to the successful completion of the drives, providing drovers with food, drink, and dry beds, and hungry livestock with essential grains. At the peak of the herding season, one western North Carolina innkeeper, David Vance, is reported to have fed as many as ninety thousand hogs in a single month. During peak periods, his Madison County establishment lodged fifty men a night.[26]

The rise in the importance of livestock herding in the mountains was due not only to the existence of a favorable ecological niche that included the availability of a vast grazing commons but also to internal improvements such as passable roads and the building of stock stands for travel-weary drovers. Regional population growth and expanding cotton and tobacco markets on the Atlantic Coast also contributed to the rise of livestock production in the southern Appalachians during the antebellum period. As more land was converted into cotton fields in the Deep South, planters had to rely more on upland farms for meat and produce. Sea Island plantations in Georgia and South Carolina consumed a great deal of these agricultural products: in 1843 alone, South Carolina imported from Kentucky and Tennessee 52,000 barrels of flour, 300,000 bushels of corn, 100,000 bushels of oats, 40,000 bushels of peas, 24,826 bundles of hay, 5,000 hogsheads of bacon, butter valued at $225,000, cheese worth $30,000, and livestock valued at $1,775,000.[27] It should be noted, however, that a considerable portion of these products was produced by Nashville and Lexington area farmers—not all of these agricultural products came exclusively from the southern Appalachians. There is also considerable evidence that some of the region's livestock and agricultural goods were destined for urban areas like Atlanta, where the terminus of the Western and Atlantic Railroad was built in 1842. Annual reports of the W&A Railroad do reveal large quantities of upland freight being shipped to the station. While a large portion of these goods was shipped down the rails to be sold to plantations or exported to foreign ports, a significant share of mountain agricultural products remained in larger southern cities, consumed there by an ever-growing population.[28]

The dominance of livestock raising in the mountains also reflects the drovers' importance to subsistence culture in the region during the antebellum period. Drovers made up a measurable portion of the mountain population, and their activities certainly influenced the building and maintenance of roads, hotels, and stock stands. Indeed, entire communities were affected by their presence: local farmers often sowed and harvested crops to correspond with their annual visits, and innkeepers worked diligently to provide them with food and lodging along major routes. It is important to note, however, that drovers were neither traditional yeoman farmers nor commercial planters. Leaving their cattle and hogs to run on the open range for much of the year, mountain herdsmen were not actively engaged in traditional agricultural pursuits. For this reason, drovers were often viewed as indolent or shiftless by outside observers, who erroneously interpreted their apparent lack of interest in soil cultivation as a severe character flaw. Frederick Law Olmsted's disapproving comments about mountain residents and their techniques of animal husbandry are indicative of the general lack of knowledge about southern herding traditions. "In the severest weather they [cattle] are only fed occasionally, hay or corn being served out upon the ground," writes Olmsted, "but this is not done daily, or as a regular thing, even by the better class of farmers." Obviously, Olmsted was not aware that the upland forest understory served as a reasonable substitute for bottomland pasture, so the additional feeding of the cattle herds was only necessary under extraordinary conditions.[29]

The proliferation of hogs and cattle throughout the southern Appalachians was not without important environmental consequences. Across the mountain uplands, particularly in areas undergoing natural succession or recovering from timber cutting initiated by iron and coal industries, grazing livestock suppressed the growth of young saplings and herbaceous plants. Over time, particularly in areas experiencing heavy livestock use, the result was an open, parklike forest, with greater distances between standing trees. In many of the disturbed areas, nonnative plants such as privet, multiflora rose, and mullein, to name only a few, rapidly replaced native varieties. In drier locales, particularly along higher ridgetops, it became necessary to burn the woodlands every year in order to "green up" the forest floor, providing additional soft browse for hungry livestock. In isolated areas receiving the heaviest use, cattle herding even had an important impact on soil productivity. While the effects certainly varied according to the season of use and the type and original condition of the soil, the repeated trampling of the woodlands by cattle no doubt contributed to greater soil compaction, higher surface runoff, and increased soil erosion.[30]

Hogs were by far the most destructive of the animals, rooting up and devouring vegetation and killing significant numbers of snakes and salamanders in the mountain forest. Heavy consumers of hardwood masts, large swine herds would have locally prohibited the natural regeneration of oak and chestnut stands in the mountains. Hogs would have certainly consumed less understory vegetation than cattle, but they would have made a significant mark on the native landscape in terms of sheer natural disturbance. River cane was certainly a victim of all roaming livestock, which had eliminated the plant from most mountain river bottoms by the 1850s. J. W. M. Breazeale recognized the disappearance of the reed in the Ridge and Valley as early as 1842, writing that "the rich and fertile valleys where we now behold widespread farms, flowery gardens, verdant meadows and splendid mansions, were then [one hundred years ago] covered with tall and rank cane."[31]

Although their importance to mountain agriculture has been grossly underestimated in the literature, sheep were second only to hogs in the mountains, outranking all other livestock, including cattle, in actual numbers. The gradual decline in gray wolf and mountain lion populations, along with the clearing of additional woodlands for pasture and grasslands, made the southern mountains an ideal grazing environment.[32] A largely English cultural tradition, sheep herding was practiced on a fairly important scale throughout the mountains by 1830. Impressed by large herds of sheep grazing among the peaks of the Blue Ridge Mountains, Olmsted went so far as to say that "sheep raising and wool growing should be, I think, the chief business of the mountains." Of course, the primary purpose of raising sheep was for wool, the raw material used for woolen fabrics and coverlets. Although lamb and mutton were occasionally eaten by a few mountain residents, many avoided mutton, a centuries-old food prejudice originating with the Scots-Irish.[33]

By 1850 most sheep in the southern Appalachians were of Merino or Saxony stock, common but improved breeds producing 1–3 pounds of wool per animal. Before then, sheep raising was less than scientific, with most herders showing a modicum of interest in owning purebred varieties. Improved breeds existed among more serious herdsmen, nonetheless: Leicester, Southdown, Cotswold, and Bakewell breeds had all been imported to the southern Appalachians before the Civil War.[34] No geographic province conspicuously dominated sheep production during the first three decades of the nineteenth century, although by 1840 eastern Tennessee clearly had the greatest number of sheep. In fact, in that year alone the entire state of Tennessee produced more wool than any other state except for New York at an estimated value of nearly $3 million. By 1850 upper eastern Tennessee and southwestern Virginia were the major sheep-raising areas in the southern mountain region, with most counties in that vicinity supporting populations of five thousand sheep or more. In 1859 Hawkins County, Tennessee, farmers raised more than sixteen thousand sheep, an extraordinary figure when one takes into account the small number of farms in that geographically small county. With one of the largest average herd sizes in the southern Appalachians, Hawkins County families kept at least twenty head for home and market use.[35]

On the Cumberland Plateau, sheep raising became especially prominent in the knob country of Kentucky and Tennessee, due partly to the area's proximity to Lexington and Nashville, the two most important sheep-raising areas in the entire Southeast. Pulaski County, Kentucky, was by far the largest producer, with U.S. Census records reporting 22,007 sheep for the crop year 1859.[36] A few areas in the Blue Ridge also had herds of considerable size, as mountaintop pastures were well suited to these grass-loving creatures. Alleghany County, in the highlands of western North Carolina, could boast a total of 6,755 sheep on just 347 homesteads. The high altitude mountains of northeastern Georgia also afforded good sheep range during the antebellum era. On just 267 farmsteads, Rabun County herdsmen kept a total of 7,824 sheep, for an astounding average of 29 animals per farm family. More typical of the Blue Ridge Mountains was Buchanan County, Virginia, however, where the average mountaineer raised no more than eight or nine sheep.[37]

Most wool in the mountains remained on the farmstead, where it was carded, spun, and dyed before being made into homespun blankets and clothing. As more and more looms made their way into mountain communities, the art of dyeing and weaving flourished among women, becoming in some areas a small cottage industry. Carding mills also sprang up in many areas, giving those who could afford it the option of exchanging freshly sheared wool for finished and dyed yarn. In fact, wool was considered gold and silver to many merchants, who often used it as currency when purchasing their own wares for the crossroads or village store.[38]

For most women in the southern mountains, an intimate knowledge of local flora and their various chemical properties was as essential as the art of weaving. Native plants, routinely gathered from surrounding fields and woodlands, were the principal mordants and coloring agents used to dye homespun yarns and fabrics. Pokeweed berries created rose dyes, staghorn sumac or bloodroot produced red ones, wild indigo or blue ash gave blue dyes, walnut hulls produced shades of brown, and yellowwood or birch leaves yielded yellow. The palette of the experienced dyer was virtually unlimited, and with the help of various tree barks and flowers she could produce shades of almost any hue.

Central to the household economy, sheep raising, including wool production and weaving and dyeing, was almost entirely a woman's domain. Sheep were invaluable to the homestead, especially to women, who generally oversaw the feeding and shearing of the animals. This fact may partially explain the lack of serious treatment this subsistence practice has received in the scholarly literature. Unlike beef or pork, wool and mutton were not value-added products; few external cash markets existed for these items, and so raising the animals brought little additional cash to the homestead. The great value of sheep to the individual farm family is indicated, however, by the amount of prime pastureland set aside for their exclusive use.[39] Sheep also required shelter, fencing, and hay for extended periods and, like cattle, needed frequent salting to survive. By overlooking the significance of wool and sheep raising in the mountain economy, scholars not only fail to recognize the importance of women's labor to subsistence culture but also their unique contribution to managing the local mountain environs.[40] Carolyn Merchant makes a similar point in her significant environmental history of eighteenth- and nineteenth-century New England, where traditional production activities such as the care of herb and vegetable gardens, dairying and cheese making, and poultry and sheep raising demanded that women have a uniquely intimate relationship with their local environment. Women were indeed important agents of economic production, and they too left their mark on the mountain landscape.[41]

Growing with the Grain

As meaningful as livestock were to the average household, it was crop production that interested mountain families most or at least occupied much of their labor around the homestead. Livestock herding and the raising of crops were not entirely unrelated, however, as the successful agriculturalist needed large grain supplies to feed his many horses, hogs, cattle, and poultry. Because of its serviceability as a food to both livestock and humans, Indian corn, as it was then called, remained the principal mountain crop. The extent to which corn and other grain production dominated the lives of mountaineers is important not only because it tells us a great deal about land-use activities in the mountains but also because it allows us to reconstruct the typical nineteenth-century farmstead.

Almost all farmers in the southern mountains grew large quantities of corn, particularly those living in eastern Tennessee. By 1840 Tennessee had become, as one antebellum writer put it, "the greatest Indian corn growing state in the union." The entire crop was estimated at 46,285,259 bushels, a good portion coming from the fertile bottomlands in the eastern section of the state.[42] By 1860 the Tennessee corn crop had risen to 52,089,926 bushels, with nearly 9 million bushels coming from the eastern counties. Cumberland Plateau corn production did not lag far behind, with most farmsteads producing 43 bushels of grain per household in 1840, at that time the highest per capita ranking in the mountain region. By 1860 per capita corn production had declined considerably on the plateau, with nineteen Kentucky counties producing 6,883,913 bushels. In the Blue Ridge counties of western North Carolina, where crop selection was much more diversified, only 3,595,338 bushels of corn were grown in 1860.[43] Corn growing took a substantial amount of land, although very few farmers tilled more than 20 acres for that purpose. Corn production took up about one tenth of the average farmer's improved land, but that figure varied across the region, with Ridge and Valley farmers having by far the most acreage in corn production.

Corn was not only important as a primary foodstuff, it was central to mountain subsistence culture. Corn was ground into meal and made into whiskey; its husks and leaves were woven into hats, dolls, mops, and chair bottoms. Corncobs served as primitive toilet paper, fire starters, bowls for tobacco pipes, and hog and cattle fodder. The harvesting of corn also greatly influenced social relations, bringing neighbors and communities together for annual fall cornshuckings. Cornshuckings, or "frolics," were ritual celebrations, yearly events in which community members assisted friends and neighbors in the gathering and preparation of the annual corn harvest. Cornshuckings were certainly not unique to the southern Appalachians, being observed throughout most of the eastern United States during the nineteenth and early twentieth centuries. On the day of the event, the ears of corn were gathered in the fields, loaded onto a wagon, and brought to the site of the cornshucking—usually a barn or a cleared field. There the corn was unloaded and then stacked and arranged in equal piles on the ground. Each team of participants, which included men, women, and children from the local community, worked enthusiastically to shuck its pile of corn before the other teams could finish. Sometimes a red ear was hidden in one of the piles, and the lucky finder was given a prize. Singing, dancing, drinking, and speech making often accompanied the corn frolics, which generally ended with the eating of a large meal prepared and served by women.[44]

Cornshuckings, as practiced in the southern mountains, combined a number of Old and New World traditions. The harvest home celebrations of Britain and the African-American practice known as "singing the master" were important influences on both the execution and spirit of mountain frolics. Folklorist Roger Abrahams, in his lengthy study on the subject, reminds us that the cornshucking was adapted largely from "seasonal practices of the English countryside," which included the use of a grain crop as a central symbol of celebration as well as "the procession and feast . . . speech making, singing, and joking." Abrahams also reminds us that corn was originally a Native American crop "cultivated in different climates and soils, and carrying a very different technology of sowing, cultivation, reaping, and preparation as food and fodder." In other words, mountain residents had to alter Old World cultural practices to the growing season of a totally unfamiliar New World crop. The cornshucking is therefore best understood as a syncretism of cultural vocabularies and ecological practices, the result of several ethnic traditions coming together in order to mark, concludes Abrahams, "the passage of life."[45]

The widespread growing and harvesting of corn in the southern mountains are interesting for yet another reason. In recent years, scholars have used corn production as a way to measure self-sufficiency on mountain farmsteads. Many now believe that because mountain farmers produced large amounts of surplus corn, their operations cannot be viewed as self-sufficient, that is, operating independently of external cash markets. As already noted, the plantation economy of the Deep South was an important force in mountain agriculture during the antebellum period, but there is equal evidence to suggest that the level of "market incorporation," to use the language of world-system theorist Immanuel Wallerstein, was not so important in the mountains that external markets were the modus operandi of all agricultural pursuits. As Paul Salstrom, Durwood Dunn, Robert McFarland, David Hsiung, Robert Lynn Nelson, and other scholars of the southern mountains have noted, entrepreneurial agricultural capitalism was often tempered in the mountains by social forces such as familism, conviviality, and the presence of local community allegiances—not to mention limited physical access to larger commercial markets.[46] To date, lack of sufficient knowledge about the many cultural uses of corn and other grains on the mountain farmstead has certainly made it easier for those arguing on the side of external market dominance. However, what is often perceived as corn "surpluses" by writers promoting such views is grain merely destined for other uses on the farmstead.

For example, when considering grain surpluses, it is much more instructive to first focus on the operations of specific farmers or groups of farmers before building arguments about the role of all southern Appalachian farmsteads in supplying agricultural goods to markets outside the region. Ralph Mann's study of farming communities in Tazewell County, Virginia, is a good example of this approach. Mann convincingly demonstrates that Tazewell had not one farming community but three, and of those, only one township—the Cove—was socially and economically driven by large-scale agricultural pursuits. This helps to explain why there is considerable diversity in corn production across the southern Appalachians. Mountain farms in the central Blue Ridge Mountains, for example, yielded, on average, 400 bushels of corn, and yet those to the south in Fannin County, Georgia, routinely fell below 300 bushels. Moreover, yields of 200 bushels and less for individual farmers were not uncommon. In 1850 Stephen Caudill's Letcher County farm in eastern Kentucky produced 150 bushels of corn, 7 bushels of wheat, and 15 bushels of sweet potatoes on 30 improved acres. Likewise, James Chadwick, on his 40-acre farm in Dade County, Georgia, raised no more than 200 bushels of corn, including fewer than 10 bushels of wheat and rye.[47]

Some farms even showed incredible deficits. In 1840 James G. Smith, who is certainly not known for understating the agricultural potential of the southern mountain region, observed a considerable number of farmers in eastern Tennessee falling short of grain. He noted that in late spring, many of these farmers were obliged to purchase additional corn for the farmstead, being advanced 50 to 100 percent of their next corn crop.[48] In 1856, after spending the entire afternoon cribbing corn, western North Carolina yeoman Basil Thomasson wrote: "Dont think I've got more than ten bushels to my shear [share]. It was so dry last summer our corn crop failed."[49]

On most southern mountain farmsteads, a considerable portion of the harvested grain was used as livestock feed, as corn was routinely fed to horses, mules, cattle, hogs, milk cows, and goats as well as numerous chickens, geese, and turkeys. Home consumption accounted for a great deal of use; a family of seven generally consumed about 100 bushels in a single year. If the corn was taken to the local miller, as much of it was, one eighth or more of the total amount—the "miller's cut"—was removed as payment from the total supply. Corn whiskey, used extensively by mountain folk as both beverage and medicinal tonic, required at least 2 bushels of grain for each 5-gallon batch. This meant that a considerable portion of the mountaineers' grain harvest was used in whiskey making, a not at all uncommon trade in the mountains. As early as 1796, David Hsiung found that Washington County, Tennessee, residents were taxed for distilling 15,000 gallons of alcohol in stills ranging in capacity from 40 to 130 gallons, for an incredible per capita production of 291 gallons.[50] In Blount County, Tennessee, alone, tax records show that fifty-two individuals made $26,000 worth of whiskey at forty-seven legal stills in 1820. Even if the average farmer/whiskey-maker distilled only 50 gallons per year, which is probably closer to the actual per capita figure, then one fourth to one half of the total corn harvest might have been allocated to the production of corn liquor.

In addition, 1 or 2 bushels of grain would also be retained on each farmstead as seed—or about .125 bushel per acre of corn grown. Wedding gifts also consisted of large quantities of corn: in many areas it was expected that the groom's father would give his son "a horse, a hog for meat, and a wagonload of corn." Because of persistent problems with rats, spoilage, and other catastrophes such as droughts and floods, farmers always stored a considerable amount of surplus corn in their cribs to guard against such unforeseeable events.[51] As late as February 1856, Basil Thomasson remarked that he and his wife had "nineteen bushels of corn stored away," enough, he believed, "to bread Mollie and me till next corn harvest."[52]

Shedding additional light on corn production and subsistence levels in nineteenth-century southern Appalachia is Paul Weingartner, Dwight Billings, and Kathleen Blee's community study of Beech Creek, Kentucky. Using a methodology developed largely by economic historians interested in calculating grain surpluses for the antebellum South, the authors were able to determine that the average amount of grain consumed by both humans and animals in the Beech Creek community was 162 "corn-equivalent" bushels. After comparing the total grain consumed with the total amount of grain produced on each farm, it was discovered that "twenty-nine farms were producing below subsistence levels and fifty-five were producing above subsistence levels." In sum, they found that subsistence farms—that is, those without any surplus grain supplies—accounted for at least one third of the farms in the community.[53] A more recent and more refined study of the Beech Creek community yielded similar findings, demonstrating clearly that corn surpluses are closely linked to farm size, population gains, and soil fertility.[54]

It is my contention that the number of Beech Creek subsistence farms would be even larger if additional cultural uses for surplus grain had been entered faithfully into the equation. "Corn-equivalency ratios" do not consider, among others things, the local variability of miller's cuts, feed for raising poultry, or seed for whiskey making. One of the deficiencies of calculating corn consumption levels based solely on strict quantitative measures is that grain surpluses, even when they do occur, do not always reflect a market orientation on the part of producers. Farmers might barter surplus corn or meal for tools, seeds, or tobacco at the crossroads store or give corn to their neighbors or relatives in exchange for a day's work. Even if farmers did actively participate in external markets, it should not mean that their subsistence mentality was driven solely by them. While corn productivity was extremely important to the success of mountain agriculture, the growing of other crops, as well as commitments to family, home, and church, greatly tempered the influence of the market on the typical mountain homestead. Steven Hahn goes so far as to argue that because the very center of economic life in the antebellum upcountry was the household, agricultural activities were mediated foremost by "ties of kinship rather than by the marketplace."[55]

Moreover, scholars relying solely on federal census data to tabulate corn surpluses have failed to recognize that census takers only enumerated those farms with annual crop production values of $100 or more. Such omissions in their sample base greatly skew the evidence toward market orientation, since thousands of marginal and submarginal farms were eliminated from enumeration on federal census rolls.[56] Nineteenth-century mountain agriculture is therefore best understood when placed in a continuum of market participation, recognizing the importance that geographic location, topography, and farm size had on everything from production levels to crop selection. Farms along the most fertile river bottoms of the Ridge and Valley, for example, particularly those of 200 acres or more, consistently outproduced farms farther removed from major transportation networks. Obviously, the region's largest farms produced the greatest surpluses, while those of 200 acres or less—which constituted the vast majority of all mountain farms by 1850—had relatively little left over for regional or national markets. To classify farmers as either subsistence-oriented yeoman, on the one hand, or market-driven capitalist planters, on the other, based solely on grain surpluses creates a false dichotomy of social types in the southern mountains.

It is conceivable that as late as 1860 a small but significant majority of mountain farmers had not accepted the concept of agriculture as a market-driven, profit-making business, refusing to accumulate the wealth and with it many of the problems of the minority planter class.[57] As one upcountry farmer in northern Alabama stated in the 1850s, "The richer a man is . . . the poorer he seems to live. If you want to fare well in this country you stop to poor folks' houses: they try to enjoy what they got, while they can, but these big planters they don't care for nothing but to save."[58] The tendency of late to equate all agricultural economic exchange transactions in the mountains with capitalist social relations is premature if not unfounded.[59] First, it ignores the important role of the home division of labor in mountain life and culture, a division of labor shared with women. It also overlooks the many obstacles to large-scale capitalist agriculture in general, which in many parts of the southern mountains has historically been constrained by natural physical boundaries, poor soil productivity, and the market viability of local crops.[60]

In order to feed themselves and their children, mountain families grew a variety of grains and vegetables, including wheat, rye, oats, beans, barley, peas, beans, squash, and pumpkins. Other grains, like sorghum and buckwheat, were also planted extensively by antebellum mountain farmers, especially those living in the Blue Ridge Mountains of Georgia, North Carolina, and southwestern Virginia. Wheat was second only to corn in its agricultural importance to the region, although it was certainly not grown as ubiquitously. Ridge and Valley counties dominated wheat production in the region, producing 8 bushels per person by midcentury. Upper eastern Tennessee, with its wider bottomlands and close proximity to river traffic and major roads, was the heart of the region's wheat-growing belt. In 1859 neighboring Greene and Jefferson Counties together grew 423,602 bushels of wheat on just 2,900 farms, a staggering figure if one considers that the total wheat production for all farms in eastern Kentucky—numbering 12,550—was fewer than 380,000 bushels. Blue Ridge farms also fell behind Ridge and Valley farms in wheat production, with most growing 4–6 bushels per person. Farmers in Buncombe County, North Carolina, had the largest amount of tillable land in wheat, raising 76,180 bushels on 924 farms. Farmers in Rabun County, Georgia, on the other hand, saw fit to grow no more than 656 bushels of wheat, demonstrating its relative unimportance to some mountain communities.[61]

Where wheat was grown, it was used as feed for livestock and ground into flour for home consumption. Rye was also grown for this purpose, and the two were often mixed for the making of rye bread. The Connecticut-born Olmsted once remarked that the only difference he saw between the table fare of the mountains and that of the "lower country" was "the occasional presence of unleavened rye bread." Adding that it was made with much "saleratus and fat," he said that mountain bread was unlike any he had eaten elsewhere and was "more palatable" than the usual cornbread.[62] Rye was an equally important hay crop, used to feed hungry livestock during cold winter months. Because draft horses required large amounts of nutrient-rich hay, rye was grown specifically for that purpose. Rye was most common in the Blue Ridge Mountains of southwestern Virginia and North Carolina, where 200,000 bushels were harvested annually. Ashe, Buncombe, and Cherokee Counties in western North Carolina cultivated the most rye—about 24 bushels per farm in 1859.[63]

Buckwheat was another important crop, though it has received scarce attention in the literature. Buckwheat served two purposes: the grain could be made into a nutritious pancake flour, and the entire plant could be fed to livestock as fodder. In fact, western North Carolina counties led the entire state in the production of both rye and buckwheat for the two decades prior to the Civil War. As a whole, the southern Appalachians cultivated more of these two grains than did the farmers below its southern borders, who had abandoned such crops for the exclusive production of cotton and corn. In many respects, mountain agriculture resembled northern agriculture in that it placed more emphasis on crop diversity as well as the production of home-manufactured goods like wool, butter, beeswax, and honey.[64] Corn may have been king of the southern mountain homestead, but it certainly did not rule the entire farm.

Indeed, the relative lack of interest in large-scale commercial farming in the region allowed for considerable horticultural experimentation on the part of local growers, resulting in a much greater diversity of crop varieties. Bean, pea, and corn varieties were hand selected or cross-fertilized in order to produce strains better suited for mountain microclimates. Some particular strains were bred for exceptional flavor, others for a unique color or a particular shape or size. Many antebellum fruits and vegetables would not even be recognizable to modern growers, including gourdseed corn, a variety whose ears could be easily shelled by flocks of foraging turkeys. Green nutmeg muskmelons known as Rocky Fords were raised in favor of commercial cantaloupe varieties. In eastern Kentucky, a pole bean variety known as Ruth Bible became popular for its resistance to drought, whereas Turkey Craw was grown in northeastern Tennessee, North Carolina, and southwestern Virginia. Of course, all families saved their own vegetable seed every year, giving rise to a cultural tradition that in some mountain areas continues to this day.

The mountaineer's ties to the landscape extended to the surrounding woodlands, providing additional staples not supplied by the home farm. The making of maple syrup and sugar became an important enterprise for many mountain settlers, particularly those living near stands of large sugar maple trees, from which those sweeteners were annually made. James Gray Smith noted an abundance of "sugar trees" in eastern Tennessee, stating that in certain localities farms have from one to five hundred trees, forming "as it were an Orchard." Making the syrup was relatively simple. In early spring the trees were first bored with a half-inch auger in two or three adjoining places and then tapped with crude spigots that drained the watery sap into wooden vessels. The sap was then boiled repeatedly until it reached the consistency of a thick dark syrup. To make maple sugar, an egg was put in the liquid at the appropriate time to "grain it," creating a product not unlike that found commercially.[65] Not surprisingly, sugar making was most prominent in the mountains, where groves of maple trees dominated. The Cumberland Plateau, an area of mixed mesophytic hardwood forests, had the most individuals engaged in sugar making, with all counties producing at least some quantities of sugar or syrup. Both sweeteners were equally popular on the plateau, with more than 200,000 pounds of sugar and 40,000 gallons of syrup being processed in 1859. Maples were much less prevalent in the Ridge and Valley, with the largest concentrations of trees found at the northern end of the range. Even there, maple sugaring was scattered along only a few ridges where larger trees continued to grow in small pockets and hardwood coves. The Blue Ridge also had considerable stands of maple trees, despite the fact that many had been cut for the iron industry or for use in furniture making prior to 1850. Farmers in Sevier County, Tennessee, for example, excelled in sugar making, refining 38,455 gallons of syrup in 1859. Those farmers who did not have access to large maple trees quickly turned to sorghum molasses, arguably the most popular sweetener in the Blue Ridge Mountains prior to the Civil War. Those with the luxury of owning a sizable stand of large maples, however, continued making sugar for at least another half-century.[66]

As might be expected, beekeeping and honey production rose to greatest prominence in areas where maple trees and sorghum cane were in shortest supply, although most families generally consumed all three sweeteners over the course of a single year. In 1859 farm families in Giles County, Virginia, for example, produced on average 34 pounds of maple sugar, 31 gallons of molasses, and 10 pounds of honey.[67] In areas too steep to grow sorghum, some farmers focused almost exclusively on raising bees for honey. Perry County Kentuckians, for example, produced more than 100,000 pounds of honey in a single year, a yield of more than 185 pounds per homestead.[68]

Household manufactures such as maple syrup were an important part of mountain life and culture, though only slightly more so than in other parts of the United States during the antebellum period. Pointing to the low economic values given to them by federal census enumerators, many scholars have even questioned their overall economic importance to the region. The problem with assessing their true social and economic value is that home manufactures are not value-added products like hogs or cattle, whose ultimate cash worth was determined by the distant urban dweller or wealthy plantation owner. The value of household goods, whether homemade lye soap or homespun cloth, was dictated almost exclusively by community needs, desires, and wants, which, in turn, were influenced by local cultural and family traditions. The fact that census enumerators applied little monetary value to these products tells us only about their lack of importance to externally driven cash markets, rather than their ultimate use value to the mountain household or to individual members of that household. The value of pure sourwood honey to women who used it in medicinal tonics is not measurable in strictly monetary terms.

Without question, the spread of settlement across the southern Appalachians had a significant impact on the mountain environment. More farms meant more improved land, more free-ranging cattle and hogs in the surrounding countryside, and fewer virgin forests. By 1850 the largest farmsteads of the Ridge and Valley were even beginning to exhibit the effects of soil loss and erosion, particularly in northwestern Georgia and northeastern Alabama, where cotton was fast becoming the dominant cash crop. By the eve of the Civil War, crop yields had decreased dramatically enough in some areas that growers were forced to abandon their farms entirely. Soon, sedge grasses and exotic weeds were flourishing in bottomlands that had for many years yielded 50 bushels of corn to the acre. Commenting on the status of mountain agriculture in 1853, one northwestern Georgia farmer near Rome wrote: "Our farmers trust too much to their rich, fresh lands . . . corn one year and wheat the next, with a little oats occasionally . . . is the most universal practice of our farmers. Manure is never thought of . . . In short, they are farmers of the old school. The idea never entering their heads that theirs is an exhausting . . . system. Already the broom sedge begins to wave over some of these beautiful lands."[69]

Despite these important environmental changes, there was still a significant amount of land in the region left untouched by human settlement, particularly areas now owned by iron merchants and capitalist land speculators. Many farmers were still leaving a majority of their land unimproved, although the amount varied considerably across the mountain region. In eastern Kentucky and southern West Virginia, for example, improved acreage seldom accounted for more than one fifth of the total farmland, with some farmers leaving as much as 90 percent of their farms in woodlands. In the Blue Ridge, land clearance patterns resembled those on the Cumberland Plateau, with farmers cultivating about one fourth of their entire estate. Farmers of the Ridge and Valley saw the greatest loss in forested land, in many areas clearing more than half of their total acreage.[70] The frontispiece to James Gray Smith's 1842 historical review of eastern Tennessee is indicative of the many improvements made not only to Jefferson County farmsteads but to many farms in the Ridge and Valley portion of the southern mountains. These improvements, along with the timber cutting practiced by the antebellum iron industry, left large portions of the major river valleys completely deforested, helping to create a pastoral landscape of verdant meadows, large corn and wheat fields, peach and apple orchards, and occasional woodlots.

Mineral Wealth

While agriculture certainly had an important effect on the southern Appalachian landscape prior to the Civil War, the industry that had the biggest environmental impact on the region was iron manufacturing. From West Virginia to northern Alabama, iron manufacturing rose to such great prominence that it made, in some areas, a lasting and "indelible impression upon the prevailing agricultural economy."[71] Iron forges and furnaces were among the earliest industries to locate in the mountains; indeed, by the third decade of the nineteenth century, the pounding of the great iron hammers could be heard echoing across the southern Appalachians.

Nineteenth-century iron manufacturing required vast quantities of natural resources, all of which could be readily found in the mountains, including ore deposits such as hematite, limonite, magnetite, and field limestone and an unlimited supply of hardwood trees. The trees were needed for the production of charcoal, the only fuel hot enough to melt the various ores used in the iron-making process. Because southern Appalachia possessed great stands of mature oak, hickory, beech, and maple, not to mention an abundant water supply, it rapidly became a prime location for the nineteenth-century ironmaster.

During the antebellum era, iron manufacturing involved two distinct operations: blast furnaces and bloomery forges. The much more numerous and smaller bloomery forges used smaller quantities of charcoal for fuel but still required considerable amounts of timber. The typical bloomery forge, sometimes referred to as a catalan forge, was comprised of a large hammer and anvil, both usually made of iron and each weighing as much as 750 pounds. The fires of the forge were fueled by charcoal and continuously controlled by a stream of water that created blasts of air in the same manner as a bellows. Most bloomery forges in the mountains produced what was then known as hollowware, that is, kettles, pots, and pans, as well as stove plates, wrought-iron bars for nails, tools, wagon rims, mill gears, and plow points. The Amerine Forge in Miller Cove, the largest and most productive in Blount County, Tennessee, produced 12 tons of bar iron in a single year.[72]

Nineteenth-century iron production was central to the economy of many southern mountain communities, a fact attested to today by the numerous place-names referring to these former ironworks. Pigeon Forge, Furnace Creek, Furnace, and Laurel Bloomery are just four of dozens of southern Appalachian place-names inspired by the iron industry. Forge Creek, located at the foot of Gregory Ridge in the Great Smoky Mountains, got its name from the Cades Cove Bloomery Forge that was built there in 1827. Several hundred yards upstream was Coalen Ground Branch, the location where men then known as colliers produced huge piles of charcoal used for stoking the bloomery fires.[73] In fact, because of the large deposits of iron ore discovered in the Blue Ridge, the Great Smoky Mountains were initially called the Great Iron Mountains. It wasn't until the late 1700s, after North Carolina ceded its western lands to the federal government, that the name "Smoky Mountains" actually appeared on official maps and documents of the mountain region. The two names were used almost interchangeably for at least another forty years, until the major iron deposits in the mountains were completely exhausted.[74]

Despite its significant economic impact on the region, the history of the southern Appalachian iron industry is, to paraphrase Samuel Cole Williams, an obscure one.[75] No systematic study of iron production across the entire mountain region has ever been undertaken, because the majority of scholars focus on individual furnaces, forges, or their owners. The recent history of the Chattanooga Bluff furnace, *Industry and Technology in Antebellum Tennessee,* is a notable exception, as the authors go to great pains to place eastern Tennessee iron production in a broader regional context.[76] What almost all studies to date have failed to sufficiently demonstrate, however, are the profound ecological effects of the industry on the mountain environment.

For the first half of the nineteenth century, charcoal was virtually the only fuel used in commercial iron smelters in the United States. Hardwoods such as white and red oak, maple, hickory, and beech were the preferred wood types for charcoal production, since these trees yielded the most pounds of fuel per cord.[77] Under normal operating conditions, at least 22 cords of wood were needed daily to make a typical charcoal mound.

This figure becomes even more compelling considering that an acre of mature forest generally contains no more than 30 cords of wood (a cord of wood is a stack 4 feet high, 4 feet wide, and 8 feet long).[78]

The average nineteenth-century blast furnace, producing 2 tons of iron a day, consumed about 300 acres of mature timberland a year. The demand for land and trees was so great that the North Carolina legislature passed the "Act to Encourage the Building of Iron Works in This State," awarding 3,000 acres of vacant land to anyone establishing a furnace operation.[79] The state of Tennessee passed a similar law in 1807, granting 3,000 acres of land, "unappropriated and unfit for cultivation," to anyone wanting to build an ironworks facility. The land was also tax exempt, provided that the owner build and operate a forge within the first two years. In upper eastern Tennessee, where the largest percentage of the region's iron was produced prior to 1850, the environmental effects are telling. In 1820 alone, twelve small ironworks in Johnson and Carter Counties consumed 12,000 cords of wood, collectively eliminating more than 500 acres of hardwoods from nearby mountain forests (1 square mile equals 640 acres).

One of the oldest and most productive of these iron establishments was Union Forge, located in Greasy Cove near present-day Unicoi, Tennessee. In 1820 owners Elihu and Elijah Embree reported using 375 tons of iron ore and 1,825 cords of wood that same year. Before subsequent owners abandoned the site in 1852, timber cutters employed at the factory cleared more than 2,000 acres of mountain hardwoods.[80] By 1840 one prominent Tennessee iron maker was asserting that to keep a large furnace "in continuous and sustained operation," 7–10,000 acres of mountain timberlands were needed "to supply fuel for that purpose."[81]

In the Blue Ridge Mountains of western North Carolina iron production was never as large or widespread, but its effect on the environment was, in many areas, no less destructive. The U.S. Census of 1810 reported eleven forges or foundries operating in the Blue Ridge area alone—five in Surry County and six in Buncombe County. Two decades later, Elisha Mitchell's geological survey of the state listed dozens of additional active forges in the western North Carolina mountains, including the North Fork Bloomery in Ashe County. Producing 200 pounds of charcoal iron per day, the North Fork Bloomery consumed more than 200 cords of oak, beech, and maple wood in a single year.[82]

On the Cumberland Plateau, iron production also rose to prominence in the early 1800s as part of the general westward expansion of the iron industry. By the 1830s Kentucky was the third largest producer of iron products in the country. One of the state's most important furnaces was the Estill Furnace of Furnace, Kentucky, which was built in 1829. The Estill Furnace possessed a stack 34 feet high and was one of the very first to use steam, rather than water power, to operate its enormous blasts. The nearby Red River Iron Region, where the largest iron ore and timber reserves were found, supplied Lexington and Frankfort with iron products throughout the antebellum era. When operating at full capacity, the Red River or Fitchburg Furnace, as it is sometimes called, was one of the most productive blast furnaces in the entire mountain region, annually consuming more than 400 acres of timber.[83] Smaller operations in the mountains supplied raw iron to blacksmiths, who in turn produced finished farm implements such as plow points or axe heads. In 1849 Robert Morris, who owned a large blacksmithing establishment in Cumberland County, Kentucky, produced twelve hundred horseshoes, four hundred wagon wheels, and twenty-five plows. The Morris smithing establishment, like hundreds of others throughout the mountain region, required charcoal for fuel, creating an even greater demand for local timber supplies.[84]

The iron industry peaked at various times and places throughout the mountains, reaching its greatest economic importance during the 1840s and 1850s. As already noted, one of the most productive iron-making areas in the southern Appalachians was upper eastern Tennessee, where iron production had, by 1840, risen to 3,124 tons. At that time, Tennessee could claim thirty-four blast furnaces and ninety-nine bloomeries, forges, and rolling mills, with the largest portion of these located in the eastern part of the state.[85] One ironmaster operating a furnace in the vicinity of Bumpass Cove in Washington County owned 70,000 acres of timber.[86] James Smith's advertisement to prospective industrialists in an 1842 publication for the East Tennessee Land Company is telling: "To the Iron Manufacturer, the same remarks will apply; inexhaustible beds of Ore, water power and fuel in abundance, with water carriage, and a market from thence to New Orleans."[87]

The antebellum iron boom was hardly restricted to eastern Tennessee since rich iron deposits could be found in every state in the region. In Cherokee County, North Carolina, seven 3,000-acre claims were filed by individuals wanting to erect forges between 1843 and 1851. At the Red

River Furnace in Kentucky, census returns for the year 1850 show that 150 workers turned out more than 1,500 tons of pig and bar iron and 75 tons of nails.[88] Of the four furnaces erected along the Etowah River in northern Georgia during the 1840s, the largest, the Etowah Furnace, employed more than five hundred hands at peak production. In fact, the production of iron became so central to the economy in these communities that iron was regularly used as specie or currency. When Henry D. Johnson of Carter County, Tennessee, bought land from Joseph Cooper in 1823, he paid for it in iron.[89]

By the early 1840s the iron industry was having a noticeable effect on large portions of the mountain landscape. Clear-cutting of timber left entire hillsides devoid of vegetation, making them less desirable for agricultural pursuits. The continued use of specific sites for charcoal production drastically decreased soil fertility, resulting in the creation of sterile patches of ground that, for decades, supported little or no plant life.[90] Observing the environs around a blast furnace in the South Carolina upcountry, a nineteenth-century traveler commented that the woodlands surrounding the establishment were cut over for miles, leaving "a most desolate and gloomy landscape."[91]

There were, of course, less obvious environmental effects resulting from iron production. Most furnaces were nearly always located near creeks and rivers since a great deal of water was needed to operate the hammer, stamper, and blasts. In order to direct the greatest volume of water into the furnace operations, small dams had to be constructed next to the forge, resulting in the flooding of the surrounding countryside. Recognizing the iron industry's propensity for flooding valuable farmland, the state of Tennessee passed a law in 1807 providing the proprietors of ironworks clear title to any inundated lands. According to stipulations in the act, the ironmaster was allowed three years to annually make "ten tons of iron [or] forfeit the land acquired for his dam."[92]

The environmental impact of the iron industry was not limited to charcoal production, the building of dams, or the general forge operations, however. There was also the clearance of land for hauling roads and employee housing. By the 1850s the largest iron establishments employed upwards of five hundred individuals, most of whom resided close to the furnaces in crude or makeshift dwellings. Surrounding these were several hundred additional acres of cultivated fields and pasture, agricultural land needed to feed hungry iron workers and their families. When not all food supplies could be produced by the owner's estate, neighboring farmers supplied operators and their employees with corn, wheat flour, bacon, and feed for livestock. In his well-documented study of industrial development in eastern Kentucky, Tyrel G. Moore found that a single furnace community might annually purchase fifteen thousand dollars' worth of such provisions.[93] In the case of a single furnace community in northwestern Georgia, it is estimated that as many as two thousand individuals, including employees, laborers, farmers, and their families, were directly or indirectly dependent upon the iron facility.[94]

As could be expected, prominent ironmasters were also members of the landed gentry and so were also the first to bring slaves to the mountain region. William B. Carter, who founded the Carter Ironworks in Elizabethton, Tennessee, was one of the leading slaveholders in all of eastern Tennessee, owning twenty-one slaves in 1840.[95] Most slave owners used slaves to construct the ironworks, build roads, mine the heavy ore, and cut wood for making charcoal. Without question, slaves made a significant contribution to the iron industry in the southern United States, their numbers possibly totaling more than ten thousand individuals for the antebellum period. Unfortunately, no exhaustive studies have been done concerning slave labor in southern Appalachian iron production, although we do know that slaves were certainly among the skilled workforce. In 1825 James I. Tipton of Carter County, Tennessee, purchased a single slave, a hammerman by trade, for the then remarkable sum of $900.[96] An early authority on iron production in the Southeast believes there is enough evidence to assert that Anglos and African-Americans were evenly divided among the labor force but adds that ironworks "in more remote districts" recruited "poor whites," who, he noted, "fared badly in comparison with the average negro slave."[97]

An industrial factory owned by ambitious, slave-owning entrepreneurs, the iron furnace challenges many commonly held notions about economic development in the southern mountains. While still largely an area of yeoman farmers, by the 1840s an important part of the local economy was directly linked to heavy manufacturing and extralocal commerce. The mountains, historically viewed as a geographic barrier to trade and commerce, had, in the case of the iron industry, made industrialization possible. However, by midcentury, the industry that had brought early economic development to the region was also beginning to wane. Water navigation was becoming a hindrance to the transport of large quantities of iron, greatly weakening its economic value outside the region. As historian Robert Nave points out, ironmongers who depended solely on river transportation were "hampered by having to wait for the spring floods to move their boats. Since the rises occurred on most of the streams simultaneously it caused the merchants to ship their iron down the rivers at the same time." Operators in the Northeast, on the other hand, had ready railroad access and were by that time firing furnaces with plentiful and cheaper coal, giving them a far more competitive edge in the national, indeed international, iron marketplace.[98]

After midcentury the supply of iron in the region so exceeded demand that prices dropped considerably, making it unprofitable for shippers to transport large quantities of iron over very long routes. David Nelson, an Elizabethton, Tennessee, merchant who bought $1,847 worth of iron goods in 1850, sold the merchandise for only $1,400 after it reached its final destination in Whitesburg, Alabama.[99] Despite lower prices, overall regional tonnage production rose during the 1860s, even though the total number of operating forges and furnaces dramatically declined. In many areas, iron production ceased altogether. Distances to national markets, the continued depletion of large-scale iron and timber reserves, and the economic depression caused by the Civil War forced most ironmasters to abandon the business entirely or, in a few instances, to consolidate their efforts in order to build larger and more efficient facilities.[100]

The shift from charcoal to coal in the production of iron did not signal an end to the widespread cutting of mountain timber. Despite the increase in the use of coal in the industry during the 1850s, charcoal remained an important fuel for the smaller bloomery forges until the last decade of the nineteenth century.[101] In northwestern Georgia, southeastern Tennessee, and northeastern Alabama charcoal production even increased for short periods after the Civil War. Most ironmasters thought mountain timber was an inexhaustible resource, and the few who saw a possible end to the region's timber reserves believed that bituminous coal deposits would help assuage potential shortages. Whatever the ultimate ability of the mountains to reforest themselves, by the end of the 1860s the iron industry had rendered tens of thousands of acres treeless, a fact that has escaped the most ardent students of southern Appalachian history.[102]

Large timber reserves and rich iron ore deposits were vitally important to the early economic development of the region. A third natural resource—coal—played an equally important role in the industrial development of the region during the antebellum era. The logical source for this coal was the Cumberland Plateau, an area long known for its expansive coal reserves. Coal had been mined by blacksmiths and farmers on the plateau since frontier settlement and commercially since at least 1800. After underground mining methods were first employed in 1829, shipments of eastern Kentucky coal made their way to hundreds of foundries across the South and Midwest. According to an 1838 geological report by William Williams Mather, annual shipments of eastern Kentucky coal to Tennessee alone averaged between 1,000 and 2,000 tons.[103]

In urban centers, coal quickly replaced wood as the principal heating source, ultimately altering cookstove, fireplace, and building construction techniques. Tyrel G. Moore notes that demand for coal in Lexington and Frankfort alone had risen to 700 tons as early as 1805, increasing to 3,000 tons by 1835. In 1833 a Nashville newspaper editor remarked upon the superiority of coal as home fuel, adding that it could be bought locally for 10 cents a bushel.[104] The use of coal in salt manufacturing and blacksmithing created further demands for the black ore, increasing regional production at least fourfold by the 1840s. The numerous saltworks situated along the northern edge of the Cumberland Plateau had perhaps the greatest impact on the level of early coal production. A study published in 1836 by University of Virginia geologist William Barton Rogers found 200,000 tons of coal were mined annually for use by the Kanawha River saltworks.[105]

Salt production, another largely ignored industry of antebellum Appalachia, also gained importance in the mountain region during the first decade of the 1800s. The southern mountains were extremely rich in naturally occurring saline waters, which, when boiled in large kettles over open fires, yielded large quantities of palatable salt. Salt, an essential ingredient in home cooking and food preservation, was extremely important to the local mountain economy prior to the Civil War. Used liberally in the making of salt pork and pickled meats, two commodities shipped downstream to markets outside the region, the mineral was, needless to say, in great demand during the first half of the nineteenth century.[106] Not limited to the Kanawha River valley, salt manufacturing also rose to great importance in eastern Kentucky and southwestern Virginia. Saltville, in present-day Smyth County, Virginia, owes its existence to the tens of thousands of bushels of salt that were produced in the town during its formative years. Frederick Jackson Turner argued that salt deposits were an important, if not the primary, attraction promoting frontier migration and settlement in the mountains.

One of the most productive saltworks was found in Clay County, Kentucky, near the headwaters of the south fork of the Kentucky River. Operators of the Clay County saltworks shipped large quantities downriver before 1820, mostly to salt buyers in Lexington and Louisville. From 1835 to 1845 fifteen saline wells annually produced between 100,000 and 250,000 bushels of the mineral.[107] Eastern Tennessee was an important destination for eastern Kentucky salt, since Knoxville, a burgeoning cattle town by the 1830s, needed large quantities for its meat-processing industry.[108] A resource extractive process, salt manufacturing required the use of incredible amounts of saline waters, brine-yielding springs, and, in one method of salt extraction, the salt-laden soil of riparian saltlicks. One early salt producer in the region, James Robertson, claimed that at least 80 gallons of water were required to make 1 bushel of salt.[109] Large-scale salt manufacturing no doubt depleted naturally occurring salt reserves, which had been vitally important to deer, elk, and buffalo herds. Of greatest consequence to the local environment were the large amounts of coal and timber needed to fuel the saltworks' continuously burning fires. The mining of coal seams precipitated acid runoff in mountain streams, and the cutting of cordwood aided in the further clearing of mountain woodlands, intensifying soil erosion and the siltation of creeks and rivers.

Salt was only one of a dozen or so minerals taken from the southern mountains during the antebellum period. Gold, nitre, copper, lead, quartz, limestone, talc, Epsom salts, magnesium, and alum were also mined in considerable quantities, making the region a vast reserve of mineral wealth. One North Carolina resident exclaimed that the mountains were a "Mineral Kingdom," and another believed there may have been enough silver in the region "to depopulate California."[110] Indeed, the discovery of gold in the Blue Ridge Mountains of northern Georgia in the 1820s led to America's first major gold rush, swelling the population of the area and eventually leading to the establishment of a federal mint.[111] As thousands of gold seekers flooded the area, the conflict between whites and Chero-kees intensified, making it more and more unlikely that the Cherokees could continue to peacefully occupy the southern mountains.

Auraria, one of the region's first gold boomtowns, was soon rivaled by Dahlonega in nearby Lumpkin County, Georgia, the undisputed epicenter of gold-mining activity in the mountains. The mining of gold forever changed the mountain landscape, due largely to a hydraulic mining tech-nique so new to the mining industry that it immediately became known as the "Dahlonega method." In effect, the Dahlonega method required the removal of all standing timber and topsoil, which then allowed engineers to blast the exposed subsoil with water cannons, washing away the earth containing the precious gold. The dirt ran down a series of flumes, which trapped the finer pieces of gold and sent larger pieces down to a mill to be crushed. In Lumpkin County, a 33-mile aqueduct system was used to carry water to the mining operations.[112]

By the early 1840s, after a decade of mining more than $20 million in gold, the Lumpkin mines began to close. Many of the miners known in Georgia as the "twenty-niners" would soon become the "forty-niners" of the California gold rush. In 1849 Georgia state geologist Matthew Ste-phenson publicly pleaded with the men to stay in Georgia, saying "there's millions in it"—a phrase that was reportedly corrupted into "there's gold in them thar hills."[113] By 1840 much of the Blue Ridge had been occupied by whites who had settled the mountain region as a result of the gold rush and the Georgia land lotteries, which had awarded white settlers 40- and 160-acre tracts of mountains lands.

Potassium nitrate, or nitre as it is more commonly called, was another important mineral extensively excavated in the southern Appalachians. As early as 1806 Kingsport, Tennessee, had four powder mills, each requiring large amounts of nitre, the essential ingredient in the making of gunpow-der. During the War of 1812 and later during the Civil War, tons of potas-sium nitrate were mined for use in munitions production.[114] Great quanti-ties of the mineral were leached out of the earth with water, then allowed to slowly percolate through large vats of wood ash. Workers then boiled the nitrate solution to create a saltpeter residue, which was dried and then carefully mixed with sulfur and powdered charcoal to produce the final product. One of the most important nitre mine sites was Alum Cave in Sevier County, Tennessee, where mining began in 1841 after a locally owned Epsom salts manufacturing company purchased the property. For more than three decades, alum (used as a mordant for dyes), Epsom salts (used for medicinal purposes and in agriculture), and nitre were taken from the Alum Cave. The cave became legendary during the Civil War, providing a large percentage of the Confederacy's gunpowder.[115]

One of the most environmentally destructive industries in the southern Appalachians during the antebellum period was copper mining. Centered in the great Copper Basin of northern Georgia and southeastern Tennessee, copper mining began in 1850 after the first mine opened near Ducktown, Tennessee. Initially, the extreme remoteness of the mines severely restricted copper production and transport, the nearest railroad being some 40 miles away in Dalton, Georgia. The narrow wagon road to Dalton was passable only during summer months, forcing mining companies to build a new roadbed along the Oconee River Gorge to Cleveland, Tennessee. Although local residents vehemently opposed the building of the road, it was finished in 1853 for the incredible sum of $22,000, a price paid exclusively by the mining companies. The new road allowed the copper mines to operate year-round, drawing hundreds of new mine operators to the Copper Basin area. By 1854 twenty-three companies had filed for incorporation at the state capital.[116]

Copper production, like the making of iron, was truly devastating to the mountain environment, although not for the same reasons. Copper ore contains only a small percentage of copper and has to be heavily processed before it can be rendered into a usable product. First, the ore was placed on enormous piles of cordwood, which were set on fire. After several weeks of continuous burning, the roasting piles released large amounts of sulfur, iron, zinc, and other undesirable contaminants known as "sulfurettes" into the air. The sulfur gases killed all surrounding vegetation, beginning a desertification process in the area that lasted well into the twentieth century.[117] After roasting, the copper ores were placed into large iron smelters, furnaces fueled solely by charcoal. Three hundred bushels of charcoal a day were required to operate the furnaces, placing a huge demand on mountain timber supplies. "Wood choppers" advertised their services in local papers; other residents made charcoal from private woodlots, selling the fuel directly to the mines. Records reveal that one company consumed more than 500,000 bushels of charcoal, roughly the equivalent of 12,500 cords of wood, in a single year. In order to secure adequate supplies, the mines were eventually forced to purchase timber well outside the Copper Basin proper. Stripping some 1,500 acres of mature timberlands each year, by 1876 the Union Consolidated Mining Company was recovering wood from as far away as Morganton, Georgia.[118]

The mining district also greatly influenced the local agricultural economy, providing cash markets for local produce and livestock. In a letter written from Athens, Tennessee, L. W. Gilbert gives a vivid picture of the enormous quantity of provisions required by the copper industry:

> There are some 500 [oxen and horse] teams engaged in the [mine] service, besides many others employed at the mines in hauling logs, boards, feed, etc. It requires no small amount of feed to support 500 or 600 teams . . . The mines furnish a good cash market for every kind of produce from the farm, besides employment for hundreds of men, and many hundreds of teams. One farmer told me today, as I was coming from the mines, that not withstanding he had a good crop this year, yet he could not feed all the teams employed by the mines for a single night.[119]

Farmers in surrounding Cherokee, Bradley, and Fannin Counties also sold surplus hogs, cattle, goats, and sheep to the mines. Copper haulers returning from Cleveland daily loaded their wagons with several thousand pounds of dry goods. All this went to feed a growing and prosperous mining town whose movers and shakers had consented, in effect, to ridding the entire basin of its standing trees.

In fact, nearly 40 square miles of timber had been eliminated from the surrounding forests by the end of the 1860s. Union Consolidated stripped some 15,000 acres, while the Burra Burra Copper Company and the Polk County Copper Company consumed 5,000 acres each. Not only were most of the trees gone across the entire basin, but sulfuric gas emissions from the roasters prevented any new growth of vegetation. The area's heavy annual rainfall made matters worse, washing away tons of topsoil and causing severe sheet and gully erosion. Because of local wood shortages, timber cutters employed by the company began floating logs greater and greater distances down the Toccoa and Ocoee Rivers, destroying fish traps and severely impairing stream flows. Despite local opposition to the use of the river for floating timber, the Georgia legislature sided with the monied monopoly, passing a bill making it unlawful to obstruct "by the erection of fish traps or otherwise the main current of the Toccoa River in Fannin County to a width of thirty feet, so as to interfere with rafting or floating timber."[120]

The economic and political clout of the copper mines demonstrates the important role that industrial forces played in many parts of the southern Appalachians during the antebellum period. Entire communities could be created or destroyed by the hubris of capitalists seeking to amass wealth and fortune from the timber and mineral reserves of the region. Early industrialization came with a steep price, however, posing a tremendous threat to the mountain culture that had evolved over several centuries. To be sure, the southern Appalachians still contained some of the largest stands of virgin timber in the eastern United States, but it is equally true that hundreds of thousands of acres of timber had already been cut for the manufacture of iron, coal, salt, and copper.

Despite the important rise of manufacturing during the antebellum era, agricultural was still the most common economic pursuit for the majority of mountain residents. By 1860 more than 80 percent of all households listed their occupation as "farmer" or "farm laborer" when asked by federal census takers. The Market Revolution left its mark on agriculture, too, as improved transportation routes created new markets for crops and live-stock. The growth in the iron industry was also, in part, the result of an increased demand for agricultural improvements like iron plows and plow points, which, in turn, increased the number of acres under cultivation, improving yields and allowing for greater crop diversity. The introduction and spread of certain agricultural pursuits brought new environmental and cultural changes to the southern Appalachians, each with its own unique effect on the mountain landscape.

Slaves and slaveholders also made their presence felt during the ante-bellum era, particularly in areas where their numbers were greatest. In several Ridge and Valley counties in southeastern Tennessee, northwest-ern Georgia, and northeastern Alabama, 15 to 20 percent of the total population was comprised of slaves. Individual farmers across the entire mountain region owned not only slaves but individual tracts of land often totaling tens of thousands of acres. In Harlan County, Kentucky, where only 8 percent of the total population owned farms of 1,000 acres or more, a single landowner, William Turner, owned 38,550 acres—and forty-two slaves.[121] On these vast properties, slaveholders like Turner employed their captive hire to dig roadbeds and millraces, construct large homes and out-buildings, cut and haul timber, and grow and harvest crops. The African contribution to environmental and cultural change in the southern mountains is, therefore, hardly insignificant. Not only were Africans instrumental in the introduction of important foods like okra, field peas, and sweet potatoes to the mountains, their cultural contribution is found in many aspects of southern Appalachian music, dance, and folklore.[122]

To those areas in the southern mountains that may have missed the effects of the axe and plow, the Civil War brought additional environmental changes, accomplishing in half a decade what had taken half a century elsewhere. Along the routes of major campaigns, thousands of trees were cut for firewood, barracks, railroad beds, breastworks, and entrenchments. The actual battlefield sites suffered tremendously, as exploding munitions razed thousands of small trees and saplings across their entire course. Major encampments, often comprised of tens of thousands of hungry soldiers and their mules and horses, were equally destructive to the surrounding countryside. In some areas, entire towns were burned, factories destroyed, fields plundered, and livestock killed.[123] If southern Appalachia was beginning to fall behind the rest of the United States because of its lack of major railroad and other transportation improvements, the social and environmental destruction caused by the Civil War further hindered the economic growth of the region.

After the war, recovery in the mountains was slow. Proportionally the uplands had sent more soldiers to battle than any other southern region, and many did not return home. Farming suffered greatly, with notable reductions in improved acreage and crop production in major agricultural areas. Survivors mined dirt floors of smokehouses for grains of precious salt. Yellow pines, sweetgum, and sassafras invaded untended fields, where corn and wheat had once grown thick and tall in the summer sunlight. Cash was scarce, and political revenge frequent. Into this social and economic vacuum entered a new wave of entrepreneurs, land speculators, and timber barons, northern and foreign industrialists with an eye on transforming the southern Appalachians into a private domain of capital and wealth.

In [the Appalachian] region occur that marvelous variety and richness of plant growth which have led our ablest businessmen and scientists to ask for its preservation by the Government for the advancement of science and for the instruction and pleasure of the people of our own and future generations. And it is the concentration here of so many valuable species and such favorable conditions of growth which has led forest experts and lumbermen alike to assert that of all the continent this region is best suited to the purpose and plans of a national forest reserve in the hardwood region.—THEODORE ROOSEVELT, *Message from the President, 1901*

7 Appalachia

MAKING THE MODERN LANDSCAPE

*I*NITIATED BY THE iron merchants and other capitalists during the early part of the nineteenth century, land speculation escalated to new heights in the southern Appalachians after the Civil War. Politicians, businessmen, and prominent journalists promoted the region as a New South mecca, encouraging northern capitalists to exploit the mountains' remaining mineral and timber reserves. Land was bought sight unseen by many of these wealthy industrialists, often without knowledge of its actual worth or with a specific use in mind. For example, the Southern States Coal, Iron and Land Company, a British firm, purchased all of eastern Tennessee's Bald Mountain and then sold the 25,000-acre tract to the Tennessee Coal, Iron and Railroad Company without ever mining or timbering the area. Acquisitions included lands held previously in speculation but also tax-delinquent properties as well as mountain lands that local landowners believed were too hilly to cultivate. These latter properties were generally acquired by skilled land agents who convinced owners to sell "unused farmlands" for as little as a dollar per acre or, in a few cases, a single hog rifle or shotgun.[1]

One of the most prominent foreign investors in the mountains was Scottish-Canadian capitalist Alexander A. Arthur, the so-called Duke of the Cumberlands, who acquired more than 80,000 acres in the Yellow Creek Valley of southeastern Kentucky. The coal town of Middlesboro, Kentucky, was the direct result of Arthur's entrepreneurial efforts, as more than $20 million of British capital flowed into the valley within just five years.[2] In 1874 James Bowron, another British industrialist, purchased some 150,000 acres of iron, coal, and timberlands in the rural Sequatchie Valley of southeastern Tennessee with hopes of making the area the "Iron Capital of the South." After building a state-of-the-art iron furnace, Bowron quickly realized his dream. By 1880, "South Pittsburgh" was a prosperous boomtown, complete with numerous hotels, offices, supply houses, machine shops, and foundries.[3]

The land acquisitions of English author and entrepreneur Thomas Hughes were no less remarkable. After a trip to the southern mountain region in 1870, Hughes began persuading British investors to establish a settlement colony for England's downtrodden "second sons." By 1880 Hughes's colony had officially opened, named Rugby in honor of the British school where he had studied as a young boy. At that time, Hughes and his international holding company, the Board of Aid to Land Ownership, Limited, held title to 75,000 acres atop the Cumberland Plateau and several options to an additional 300,000 acres. By the summer of 1881, the town housed more than three hundred residents, operated a monthly newspaper, and boasted a large commissary that was owned and operated by community shareholders.[4]

When land speculators found little or no iron or coal on acquired lands, they could always sell to interested timber barons who were increasingly scouting the mountains for virgin timber. Despite more than a century of timber harvesting and industrial charcoal production in the southern Appalachians, the mountain region still contained enormous tracts of old-growth hardwood forests, including vast stands located along isolated stretches of the Cumberland Plateau and in the remoter sections of the Blue Ridge Mountains. According to historian Ronald L. Lewis, as much as two thirds of West Virginia was still covered in old-growth forests as late as 1880, with some southern counties, such as Wyoming, Raleigh, and McDowell, having as much as 80 percent of their woodlands in relatively undisturbed forest growth. This was certainly the case in Swain County, North Carolina, where at least 94 percent of the land was still in forest, and one third of that, reported state forester J. S. Holmes, was "virgin."[5] The Great Smoky Mountains also contained a considerable amount of old-growth timber, with individual stands yielding between 25,000 and 50,000 board feet to the acre. Across the region, the largest uncut timber could be found near the heads of streams or in higher elevation mountain coves and hollows where permanent human settlement had yet to fully penetrate. The most common old-growth species were chestnut, yellow poplar, hemlock, red oak, and basswood, but maple, beech, and spruce also grew to enormous sizes in the yet undisturbed forest.[6]

Prior to the beginning of the twentieth century, individual trees exceeding 10 feet in diameter were still not uncommon sights in the southern mountains. Carl Clendening of the Appalachian Hardwood Club knew of yellow poplars 12 feet in diameter, including specimens in southern West Virginia that reportedly yielded 28 cords, or approximately 1,400 cubic feet, of shingles. Timber cruisers hired by the largest timber companies routinely observed white and red oaks growing to more than 6 feet in diameter, with single trees yielding 15,000 board feet of lumber.[7] Oaks and poplars were not the only trees to grow to astonishing proportions in the southern mountains. American chestnut trees often grew to more than 8 feet in diameter, especially where rich soils and heavy rainfall predominated. Garfield Jenkins, who grew up on Chestnut Branch near Crestmont, North Carolina, in the 1890s recalled seeing a chestnut tree so large that it had to be split into four sections before it could be loaded on a narrow-gauge railroad car and carried to the lumberyard.[8] Today, in the Great Smoky Mountains National Park, a log cabin constructed from a single chestnut tree provides visual testimony to the original greatness of the mountain forest.[9]

It was remoteness, however, and not merely the enormous size of mountain timber that had kept the industrial lumbermen out of the southern Appalachians until the last two decades of the nineteenth century. Prior to the 1870s, the nation's lumber barons had shown little interest in purchasing large tracts of land in the region, having adequate supplies in much more accessible areas in the North and Midwest. That quickly changed, however, as more and more railroad lines began to penetrate the mountain interior, and timber shortages elsewhere in America became more imminent. Many of the large timber and railroad companies were even owned by the same stockholders, who strongly believed that the two industries should be mutually supportive. Railroads, as they saw it, "required a high volume of business to justify their investment," and sawmills "required efficient transportation to urban markets." Recognizing the close relationship between the two enterprises, scholars rightly refer to this period (1880–1920) in southern Appalachian history as the era of industrial railroad logging.[10]

The Forest for the Trees

During the four-hundred-year history of land use that this book chronicles, the single greatest human activity to affect environmental and cultural change in the southern Appalachians is industrial logging. Commercial timbering first began in the region along the largest rivers, down which
large rafts of logs were floated to sawmills at major river ports like Nashville, Tennessee; Cincinnati, Ohio; Huntsville, Alabama; and Huntington,
West Virginia. Nashville was handling more than 22 million board feet of
timber by the 1870s, the majority taken from logs floated down the Cumberland River from eastern Kentucky. As early as 1868, the Clinch River
was used by lumber dealers and manufacturers Richardson, Burr and
Terry, a firm that floated large rafts of logs from southwestern Virginia to
its steam sawmill above Clinton, Tennessee. The Cumberland Plateau was,
in fact, one of the largest suppliers of timber for the nineteenth-century
hardwood industry, since its major rivers—the Big Sandy, Guyandot, Kanawha, and Cumberland—were large enough to permit the easy removal
of vast quantities of logs.[11] Transporting logs on tributaries was more impractical, since logs would pile up against obstructions, become jammed
along narrow river bends, or become stranded along stream banks. In fact,
during summer and fall months, when water levels were at their lowest, it
was nearly impossible to float logs downstream on even the largest rivers.
Splash dams were often constructed to help remedy the problem by arti-
ficially increasing water levels, but these structures were temporary at best
and provided no long-term solution to the log transport problem.[12]

It wasn't until the mid-1880s, after railroad lines had penetrated the interior, that the era of full-scale industrial logging began in the southern
mountains. The timber boom that resulted lasted more than thirty-five
years, leaving a legacy of environmental destruction that remains with us
today. Industrial logging in the region is generally traced to Alexander A.
Arthur, who by 1885 was focusing much of his investment energies on
creating the Scottish Carolina Land and Lumber Company.[13] With monies
supplied by investors from Glasgow, Scotland, and Capetown, South
Africa, Arthur was able to purchase no fewer than 10 square miles—
60,000 acres—of hardwood forests in eastern Tennessee alone. Although
he was certainly among the first timber barons to locate in the southern
Appalachians, Arthur was just one of hundreds of commercial lumbermen

who, over the next few decades, would invest in the region's vast timber reserves.

Following Arthur's lead was Englishman H. N. Saxton, who organized the Sevierville Lumber Company and soon afterward the Saxton Company, a firm involved in exporting high quality hardwoods to Europe. In 1888 stockholders of the Thomas Lumber Company helped purchase substantial tracts in Floyd County, Kentucky, where they immediately began cutting logs for the Ohio Valley timber market. The Burt-Brabb and Swann-Day Lumber Companies were also early developers in eastern Kentucky, as was the Kentucky Hardwood Lumber Company, a large firm owning 30,000 acres of forest land. By 1890 William M. Ritter, who would later become one of the region's most prominent timber barons, was already constructing his first sawmills in southern West Virginia. That same year, owners of the Unaka Timber Company began buying up large timber tracts in the Blue Ridge Mountains of western North Carolina in order to supply their growing mill and log boom operations. Arthur responded by expanding his own already enormous timber holdings, purchasing an additional 120,000 acres of land in the Blue Ridge Mountains of western North Carolina.[14]

The move south by the major timber companies was no surprise to most industry investors, who were well aware that timber production in the Northeast was waning. In fact, the dwindling timber supply in New England led Maine lumberman C. F. Buffum to set up one of the region's first major bandmill operations along the Tuckaseegee River in western North Carolina.[15] Impressed by the twenty new sawmills located in Johnson City, Tennessee, a noted *Garden and Forest* correspondent commented in 1892 on the "push and go of the 'new south.'" By 1895 the southern Appalachian timber boom—financed almost exclusively by northern and foreign investors—was in full swing. Backed by teams of sawyers, locomotives, railroad lines, and steam-powered sawmills, the industrial loggers soon began removing the biggest and oldest trees from the mountain forests with unparalleled speed and efficiency. Virtually no stand of timber was off-limits, including trees old enough to have witnessed the passing of Hernando de Soto in 1540.[16]

The environmental effects of timbering on such a large scale were immediately felt. Within a few short years the high grading of mountain timber—from eastern Kentucky to Alabama, from West Virginia to northeastern Georgia—was beginning to have a noticeable impact on the forest environs. Erosion, fires, and flooding increased significantly in many parts of the region, damaging prime cropland along streams and destroying wildlife habitat. As early as 1892, Gifford Pinchot, who had been given the important task of introducing sustainable forestry practices to the Blue Ridge Mountains of western North Carolina, wrote that "if forest management is successful in producing profit off this burned, slashed, and overgrazed forest, it will do so on almost any land in this part of the country." [17]

The increasing environmental destruction was due not only to the mere cutting of trees but also to the use of new and more technologically efficient logging methods. With the coming of railroads to the remoter sections of the southern Appalachians, it was no longer necessary for logging operations to be confined to the vicinity of larger streams. Narrow-gauge railroad beds, then called "dummy lines," could now be laid along the contours of steep hillsides in places once thought inaccessible by lumbermen. From there, logs of all sizes were "skidded" by cables across steep slopes to awaiting railroad cars for loading and transport. The end result was, in effect, a clear-cut since the skidded logs destroyed everything in their path. As former logger Raymer Brackin remembered, "You hardly ever left a tree of any size standing and all the little [ones] was tore down." [18] The skid trails that remained as a result of these activities created such severe erosion that the cutover landscape often took decades to heal. A U.S. Geological Survey employee asked to investigate the effects of these new logging practices in the Watauga Valley of North Carolina found conditions so severe that he described the watershed as "torn to pieces." [19]

Accompanying the severe erosion were widespread forest fires that further denuded mountain slopes and hillsides. No doubt some of the fires were the creation of local herdsmen, who continued to periodically burn the woods to promote the growth of new browse for cattle and sheep. Many of the fires, however, were the direct result of careless lumbermen, who routinely left behind large piles of brush and downed tree tops at logging sites.[20] During the hottest summer months, these materials became a virtual tinder box, ignitable by campfires, lightning, or carelessly tossed matches. William W. Ashe, the first secretary of the National Forest Reservation Commission (the federal agency that would later become the National Forest Service), estimated that in 1891 alone between 800,000 and 1.2 million acres of woodlands burned in North Carolina due to unchecked forest fires.[21] Seldom admitted by industry spokesmen, many of the fires were caused by sparks from the coal- or wood-fired locomotives used to haul out harvested timber. John H. Finney, secretary and treasurer of the Appalachian Forest Association during the early 1900s, estimated the annual amount of timber destroyed by forest fires started by railroad locomotives at $50 million. At a convention speech reported in the industry's trade magazine, the *Southern Lumberman,* Finney openly advised timber-holding companies to "clear up almost immediately all the downed timber on their land" so that the destructive fires "may be at least to some extent prevented."[22]

By far the most controversial and widely debated topics surrounding early industrial logging and its effect on the mountain environment were soil erosion and flooding. By the early 1890s there was already a consensus among observers that standing timber played an important role in preventing excessive water runoff and the loss of fertile topsoil, especially after heavy rains. In fact, supporters of the Organic Administration Act, formally passed by Congress in 1897, argued that a large amount of forest lands should be set aside not only to secure a continuous supply of timber but also to create more favorable conditions for water and stream flow.[23]

By 1900 there could be little doubt that injudicious lumbering and forest fires resulted in widespread loss of forest topsoil, which had served as a natural sponge for water runoff during heavy rains.[24] According to botanist William W. Ashe and his colleagues, large stands of native trees had served as a natural barrier to heavy rainfall as well as provided thick mats of leaves to hold large amounts of water in the soil. The loss of topsoil due to timber cutting thus prohibited appreciable amounts of rain from soaking into the ground and water table, causing stream courses to run dry during summer months and flood excessively during winter and spring months. "The destruction of the earth cover," explained Horace Ayres and William Ashe in their widely publicized U.S. Geological Survey report, "prevented water from fully penetrating the earth. The roots of trees penetrate deeply into the subsoil, and as they decay leave a network of underground water channels . . . the mosses and humus of a well-conditioned forest form wet blankets, often a foot thick, the function of which is apparent."[25]

The detrimental effects of timbering on soil and water quality were not immediately apparent to the timber industry or its political supporters, who challenged such notions as "a subterfuge and a pretext, not to say a sham."[26] Growing evidence supported the fact that lumbering practices were one of the principal causes of increased flooding in the southern mountains, placing additional pressure on the federal government to do something to permanently correct the situation. By 1899 the federal government had already, in fact, heard enough evidence to order a four-agency investigation of the mountains in order to fully determine the cause and extent of soil erosion and flooding in the region. The final results of the study challenged the wastefulness of industrial logging practices and advocated the use of conservation measures, among them creation of a southern Appalachian forest reserve. James Wilson, one of the authors of the report and the secretary of agriculture under Theodore Roosevelt, placed the destruction squarely on the shoulders of the logging industry, stating that the preservation of the mountain forests should not be left "to the caprice of private capital." In the final draft of the report sent to the president in 1901, Wilson wrote: "The soil, once denuded of its forests and swept by torrential rains rapidly loses its humus, is washed away in enormous volume into the streams, to bury such of the fertile lowlands as are not eroded by the floods, to obstruct the rivers, and to fill up the harbors on the coast." [27]

President Roosevelt, attaching his own response to the document, thought that the evidence was clearly on the side of those who believed that uncontrolled lumbering practices were the primary cause of increased flooding in the region. "[T]he regulation of the flow of these rivers," concluded Roosevelt, "can be accomplished only by the conservation of the forests." [28] Despite overwhelming evidence that conservation measures should be legally mandated in the mountains, the debate concerning the role of standing timber in protecting southern Appalachian watersheds would continue for more than a decade. In the interim, annual timber production in the region steadily increased, peaking in 1909 at 4 *billion* board feet of sawtimber.[29] J. S. Holmes estimated that in western North Carolina alone, some 59 million cubic feet of lumber, pulpwood, tanbark, cross-ties, firewood, rails, and fence posts were consumed by the forest industry that same year.[30]

As could be expected, increased outputs also increased environmental damage to the mountain ecosystem, leaving many to question the extent to which the hardwood forest would, if ever, recover. Industrial logging cleared entire mountainsides of trees and undergrowth, favoring the regeneration of fast-growing, shade-intolerant species such as white and short-leaf pine. Writing in 1907, Forest Service employee R. S. Kellogg pointed out that there had already been a 15 percent decline in hardwood lumber production over the past seven years, adding that "when the utmost has been done that it is possible to do to insure a future supply of hard-woods, there still must remain a considerable gap between the time when the present supply of large timber is exhausted and that when new timber is available for use, since it takes many years to grow a tree to merchant-able size, and unfortunately some of our most valuable hardwoods grow slowly."[31] Kellogg believed that at present consumption rates even the most optimistic calculation would place the future hardwood supply in the southern Appalachians at not more than sixteen years. He recommended that the federal government begin purchasing "the backbone of the vari-ous Appalachian ranges" so that they could be managed "for the good of all interests concerned," which, he believed, included not only those inter-ested in the preservation of hardwoods but anyone who saw the uncut for-est as a means of checking erosion and providing flood control.[32]

Tragic floods in West Virginia and eastern Kentucky in 1907 insured that Kellogg's wish for government involvement in the southern Appalachians would become a reality. With mounting evidence that healthy forests served as the principal protector of our nation's watersheds, more and more pressure was placed on the federal government to stop the forests' destruction by setting aside large tracts of mountain timberlands in forest reserves. After hearing considerable and heated testimony from engineers, industry spokesmen, and conservationists, Congress passed the Weeks Act on 1 March 1911, officially authorizing the purchase of "forested, cut-over, or denuded lands within the watersheds of navigable streams . . . necessary to the regulation of the flow of navigable streams."[33]

The first attempted land acquisitions in the southern Appalachians in-cluded timberlands in the Blue Ridge Mountains of North Carolina, north-ern Georgia, and eastern Tennessee, areas that had received considerable attention and study from Pinchot and others interested in the forest re-serve movement. Under the jurisdiction of the federal government, these scientifically managed forests would serve a dual purpose: to protect ailing watersheds from erosion and to conserve timber for future use. In fact, few of the early managers of the first national forest reserves doubted the relationship between excessive timber harvesting, soil erosion, and long-term forest health. William L. Hall, the first regional forester over the southern Appalachians and certainly the first to write about the role of the federal agency in the mountains, stated in 1914 that "clear cutting as a rule will not be desirable in the Appalachians. A system of selection will be employed by which individual trees or groups of trees will be removed with a large proportion of the stand always remaining." For Hall, the goals of his young federal agency were self-evident: "stream protection, forest conservation, human recreation, and social welfare."[34]

Although the passage of the Weeks Act greatly intensified the land acquisition process for the creation of what would become the first national forests in the United States, the destruction of the southern mountains did not stop. Timber production actually intensified in the Great Smoky Mountains region after 1911 before finally peaking shortly after 1920.[35] World War I brought additional demands on mountain timberlands, forcing logging companies to seek trees even among the highest slopes, areas once thought inaccessible to conventional logging operations. "When Europe burst into the horror of warfare in 1913, demands on the forest mounted," wrote a prominent government forester, "and postwar reconstruction saw no letup. So the large sawmills . . . marched across the face of the remaining Appalachian wilderness."[36] The remaining Appalachian "wilderness," was, in effect, the Great Smokies, where between 1900 and 1938 more than 2 billion board feet of timber were removed before the area was finally taken out of the industrial timber base and managed by the federal government as southern Appalachia's first national park.[37]

It was national forests, not national parks, that conservationists and other supporters of the Weeks Act were most interested in creating after its passage. After the act became law in 1911, nearly 1.5 million acres in four mountain states were immediately designated as "purchase units," giving the newly created Forest Service Reservation Commission the ability to acquire lands within designated watersheds. According to government records, one of the very first acquisitions was an 8,100-acre tract acquired from the Burke McDowell Lumber Company in western North Carolina. It was bought for $7 per acre, as were the 31,000 acres sold to the government by the Gennett brothers of the Gennett Land and Lumber Company of Atlanta, Georgia. The Gennett purchase, the first tract in the entire United States to receive formal approval for purchase by the National Forest Service, was located in Fannin, Union, Lumpkin, and Gilmer Counties, Georgia, and was officially acquired 29 August 1912.[38] Like the Gennett tract, most lands acquired by the Forest Service were purchased from timber companies, which offered lands already cut over or those that remained inaccessible by road or rail. One well-documented Forest Service history of the southern mountains found that the largest tracts were "purchased almost without exception from lumber companies and investment concerns." Of the earlier acquisitions, the report found that "nearly 30 percent of the lands bought in the first five years in North Carolina, Tennessee and Georgia were virgin timber," and by law, most tracts were located almost exclusively near the headwaters of navigable streams. However, the report concluded that by far the majority of the acquired lands, especially in later years, "had been cleared, misused, or at least selectively culled." [39] Of the 8,600 acres sold to the Forest Service in 1927 by a northeastern lumber company operating in upper eastern Tennessee, 12 acres were virgin, 500 acres were thinned, and the remaining 8,088 were entirely cut over. [40]

There was much less uniformity in how national forest lands were acquired from individual private landowners in the mountain region. Because the Forest Service focused on purchasing the largest timber company tracts first, individual landowners often found themselves landlocked by larger acquisitions, making long-term tenure on the site an improbable proposition. Even then, many small landowners were unwilling to sell and chose to negotiate only when approached directly by Forest Service agents. Those who could afford attorneys and threatened lawsuits often received more money for their lands at prices at or slightly above fair market value. [41] Those who could not were at the mercy of the Forest Service land buyer, who had the luxury of waiting out prospective sellers. One eastern Tennessee man thought his 74-acre farm was worth at least $7 an acre—the going price for average farmland in that area—but was told by Forest Service land buyers that they could offer him only $4. Because the individual was decidedly reluctant to sell at that price, the local agent wrote his supervisor, who in turn responded by saying, "I suggest you wait awhile and if possible let them ask you about it and then tell them (reluctantly) that you may be able to get them $5." Four years later, in 1931, the parcel sold for that price. [42]

By the end of 1930, more than 4 million acres of land had been acquired by the Forest Service Reservation Commission in the southern Appalachians. As the final purchase units took shape, boundaries became more formal, and individual national forests were officially declared. In 1916 the Pisgah National Forest, the first national forest in the southern mountain region, was proclaimed. In 1920 four more national forest boundaries were drawn: the Boone in North Carolina; the Nantahala in North Carolina, northern Georgia, and South Carolina; the Cherokee in Tennessee; and the Unaka in eastern Tennessee, North Carolina, and southwestern Virginia. The Monongahela National Forest, also officially proclaimed in 1920, is located in central West Virginia and is therefore outside this volume's study area.

The Chattahoochee and the Sumter National Forests were officially proclaimed in 1936 and the Cumberland in 1937. Of these, only seven remain today, as boundaries were eventually redrawn and names changed after 1940, reportedly to better coordinate their use and management by the federal government: the Jefferson National Forest in southwestern Virginia and southeastern Kentucky; the Cherokee National Forest in eastern Tennessee; the Daniel Boone National Forest in eastern Kentucky; the Pisgah and Nantahala National Forests in North Carolina; the Chattahoochee National Forest in Georgia; and the Sumter National Forest in South Carolina. These national forests comprise more than 5 million acres, making the U.S. Forest Service the largest single landowner in the southern Appalachian region.[43]

In the short term, the acquisition of public lands for conservation did little to benefit local residents, which helps to explain their relative indifference to the creation of the national forest system. Most of the land being acquired had long ago passed into the control of the timber and mining companies, which, taking much of the timber, topsoil, and minerals from the mountains, had left them of little practical value to local residents. With the establishment of game and fish regulations, fence laws, and woods-burning restrictions, the residents' ability to use the lands as a grazing, hunting, and trapping commons was severely limited. At the same time, the mountaineers' lack of a positive response to national forest acquisitions should not be equated with a lack of concern for the mountain environment or for conservation in general. Most mountain residents, reported scholar Henry Canby in *Harper's*, "have an affectionate regard for their forests . . . They regard with a certain melancholy the invasion of the lumberman" and generally deplored "the slaughter of the forests." A cattle herder he met during his travels is quoted as stating that "it seems as if they just naturally tear up everything. Soon there'll be no more big woods."[44] Mountain residents simply saw the federal purchases as another way for timber barons to rid themselves of cutover and useless lands and to profit even more from their speculative endeavors. In 1914, for example, the Vanderbilts sold 87,000 acres to the government for $5 per acre after selling all the marketable timber on the tract for $12 per acre from lands they had purchased only two decades earlier for little more than $2 per acre, for an astonishing $800,000 profit.[45]

Although the short-term benefits of a national forest reserve system were minimal to local residents, setting aside mountain lands for the long-term protection of watersheds and wildlife was certainly, in theory, a good idea. Clear-cut, burned, and scarred, the mountain lands of the southern Appalachians would require considerable time to recover. As conservation reserves, however, national forests were set aside specifically for future use and, above all, for commercial timber production. As early as 1905, Pinchot, the original founder of the U.S. Forest Service, wrote that the primary purpose of forest reserves was for insuring "a perpetual supply of timber for home industries."[46] Pinchot believed that the timber industry, as the supporter of "economic forestry" over "scenic preservation," should and would eventually return to the harvested areas. In fact, timbering was allowed almost immediately in noncutover areas and, shortly thereafter, in areas that had been discernibly thinned or culled. By 1939 millions of board feet of timber were once again leaving the southern Appalachian region, an output that rose even more dramatically after the start of the Second World War. Ironically, the ability of the mountains to fully heal themselves remains jeopardized today by Forest Service policies that continue to ignore the cumulative effects of timber harvesting on mountain watersheds. Some contemporary observers in the mountains believe that the agency continues to violate the original intent of the 1911 Weeks Act and are taking great measures to stop the current destruction of public forests by the timber industry.[47]

While corporate logging operations did much to alter the mountain landscape, reducing forest cover and contributing to flooding and soil erosion, industrial logging had an important impact on the subsistence economy of the region, removing much needed farmland from the community land base as well as eliminating from the forest the native plants and animals that mountain families had long depended upon for survival. Numerous testimonies from mountain residents provide evidence that white-tailed deer, turkeys, black bears, and other important game animals showed significant declines after peak periods of timber harvests. Ginseng, goldenseal, mayapple, galax, and other plants seasonally traded at the mountain store for supplies or cash also experienced marked decreases in abundance.[48] The extent of land acquisition by timber companies and their subsidiaries was staggering, so even if the land was not immediately logged, its continued use by local residents was certainly restricted. By 1930 only 38 percent of all privately owned timberlands in the southern Appalachians was held by individual farmers, which left the ownership of the remaining 62 percent to "industrial organizations."[49]

The largest purchaser of private timberlands in the southern Appalachians was the William M. Ritter Lumber Company, which by 1930 had purchased 200,000 acres, or 300 square miles, of forests in western North Carolina alone. A close rival was Peter G. Thompson, who founded the Champion Fiber Company in 1905. Thompson secured more than 300,000 acres of land in western North Carolina and Tennessee before acquiring an additional 100,000 acres a few years later in order to further expand his company's pulp and softwood operations.[50] Of course, hundreds of smaller tracts were also acquired throughout the region during the first decades of the twentieth century, such as the 78,000- and 34,000-acre tracts acquired in Swain County, North Carolina, by the Foreign Hardwood Log Company of New York and the Dickson-Mason Lumber Company of Illinois. In northern Georgia, 65,000 acres were purchased by the Conasauga Lumber Company of Cincinnati, including the tract that would later become the Cohutta Wilderness Area, currently the largest wilderness area in the eastern United States. The situation was similar on the Cumberland Plateau, where the Tennessee Timber, Coal and Iron Company, owned primarily by New York interests, developed 80,000 acres of timberland. In the southwestern Virginia coalfields, a Wisconsin syndicate purchased 26,000 acres of timberlands, as did the Clinchfield Timber Corporation, an affiliate of the Clinchfield Railroad. To the south, the Grand View Coal and Timber Company of Cincinnati purchased 32,000 acres in order to develop the extensive timber and coal reserves found atop the Cumberland Plateau near Chattanooga, Tennessee.[51]

Needless to say, with the influx of timber and mineral companies, speculation on mountain lands increased dramatically, driving up prices and forcing many residents to pay off property taxes that in some areas had gone uncollected since the Civil War. In several states, when timber companies could show proof that a landowner had failed to pay taxes on a parcel of land, tax sales were conducted that obviously favored the timber barons, who could easily outbid local landowners. In 1906, for example, the state legislature of Kentucky passed an official act permitting speculators who held such claims and who had then paid property taxes for five years to "take such property from previous claimants who had not paid taxes."[52] Farmers failing to show proof of ownership were driven off their land, sometimes at gunpoint by the local sheriff. Removed from their ancestral homes, the mountaineers and their families often found refuge in the lumber and coal camps that increasingly dominated the mountain economy after 1900. Lumber camps did provide shelter for mountaineers but seldom paid more than a subsistence wage, which, in some instances, was dispersed in scrip and redeemable only at the company store. At Ritter lumber camps in southern West Virginia, "men were forced to work in taxing and unsafe conditions" at wages averaging less than $1 a day.[53] In fact, in 1906 a Ritter-owned lumber camp in Wyoming County was formally charged with debt peonage by the federal government, a charge eventually upheld by the courts. Living conditions in southern Appalachian logging camps were indeed difficult: the average lumberman in the North Carolina mountains could expect to work 62.7 hours per week at a pay rate of only 12 cents per hour.[54] This was well below the national average for logging wages, a figure that was closer to 20 cents per hour elsewhere in the United States. Dorie Cope, who lived with her husband in a logging camp near present-day Elkmont in the Great Smoky Mountains, endured everything from poor sanitary conditions and ill health to periodic invasions of rats and mice: "Baby chicks were killed and partially eaten," she recalled after one such rodent invasion. "Holes gnawed in the feed sacks left grain pouring onto the ground. Before morning was over, they found every hole and weak spot in our homes."[55]

The economic and social costs associated with the increasing concentration of land in the hands of corporate timber companies become even more apparent after examining population and outmigration figures for areas where timbering dominated after the turn of the century. The population of Union County, Georgia, for example, declined as much as 18 percent between 1900 and 1910. Nearby Rabun County, Georgia, dropped from a population of 6,285 to 5,562 residents, a 12 percent decrease attributable, says one historian, to "the sale of farms along with their timber by numerous families in the outer districts of the county."[56] Portions of western North Carolina also witnessed population losses even though the state population as a whole grew considerably during the first decade of the twentieth century. Clay County, North Carolina, had the most noticeable decline in population at nearly 14 percent. Ashe and Madison Counties, two other areas of heavy timberland speculation, also showed declines during this same period.[57] The population of other Blue Ridge counties remained relatively stable until the following decade, when additional population decreases are reported after large tracts of timberlands were later purchased by the federal government for the creation of the Pisgah and Unaka National Forests.[58] In contrast, Cumberland Plateau counties with large coal reserves saw enormous population increases during the same period, with Wise and Dickerson Counties in southwestern Virginia increasing by nearly 100 percent and Bell, Harlan, Knott, and Leslie Counties in eastern Kentucky increasing as much as 70 percent.[59]

Population increases could also be attributable to the logging industry. Logging camps usually employed hundreds of men, many of whom traveled across state lines to find work. In 1910 the Tellico River Lumber Company, which then owned about 100,000 acres in Monroe County, Tennessee, employed as many as five hundred men, or about 5 percent of the total county population.[60] By 1915 Champion employed nearly a thousand workers at its Canton plant and was gaining the distinction of being one of the largest wood pulp and paper plants in the world. At the mouth of Forney Creek in the Great Smoky Mountains, one-time resident Tobe Clark remembered that almost fifteen hundred people were living in that immediate area during the early 1920s. According to Clark, the loggers lived in temporary camps near the watershed they were logging, and a railroad spur connected them to the village where the mill stood. In the village, a man and his wife generally took care of each crew—she cooking the meals, and he in charge of feeding animals, mending harnesses, repairing tools, filing saws, and working as general handyman.[61]

The consolidation of land into large private and federal timber holdings had a profound impact on the subsistence economy of the mountain region. Farm sizes decreased considerably as fathers found it more and more difficult to acquire new lands for their sons and daughters or maintain even a modicum of productivity on their own lands. As a result, farmers often sold portions of their property to pay local taxes or leased it to younger tenants who sharecropped the land. As noted in chapter 6, the average farm size in the mountains in 1880 was 187 acres, of which one fourth was cultivated, about 20 percent was in pasture, and the remainder was in forested woodlands. By 1910 the average farm across the region had dropped to fewer than 90 acres, which left very little forested land to be used for grazing hogs and cattle, collecting firewood, or pursuing any other land-use activities that involved forest cover. This trend continued for several decades, particularly in areas where there were considerable national forest purchases. In Rabun County, Georgia, for example, farm sizes decreased by 39 percent between 1910 and 1920. Buncombe County, North Carolina, saw a 37 percent decrease, and Fannin County, Georgia, witnessed a 22 percent reduction in individual farm acreage. By 1930 the average farm size in the southern Appalachians was only 76 acres.[62] The small, marginally self-sufficient mountain homestead of the 1930s was largely a by-product of these shifting economic and landownership patterns, created in no small part by the wanton destruction of our native mountain forests. Now owned exclusively by private and federal timber interests, the surrounding forest was no longer the woodland commons that had for centuries been used and shared by a variety of people for a number of different land-use activities. Timber speculation, along with new fence laws introduced in state legislatures by railroad and timber interests, had greatly narrowed the range of subsistence possibilities for mountaineers and their families. As Gifford Pinchot said of the former residents of the 100,000-acre tract bought in 1886 by millionaire George Vanderbilt for a private hunting preserve: "They regarded this country as their country, their common. And it was not surprising, for they needed everything usable in it—pasture, fish, game—to supplement the very meager living they were able to scratch from the soil."[63] On those lands mountain farmers had not only herded cattle but had also gathered chestnuts, picked berries, hunted, fished, and dug ginseng. To the mountaineers the surrounding forest was much more than board feet on the stump: the mountain woodlands were a living matrix of plants, animals, and shared memories.

This is not to say that mountaineers did not themselves cut trees or substantially alter forest ecology. Before the advent of full-scale industrial logging timber was, in fact, purchased from local farmers who seasonally cut select trees from their landholdings for their own use or for extra cash. Initially this harvest method encouraged a more selective cutting of the largest oaks, walnuts, cherries, and yellow poplars. The logs were then snaked out by teams of oxen, mules, or draft horses, loaded upon horse-drawn wagons, and hauled to river ports, where they could be rafted downstream to large regional sawmills. At that time, timber was seldom purchased for more than 50 cents per foot, and because the tree was measured across the stump, an entire tree seldom brought the seller more than a single dollar.[64] Logging around the mountain homestead was also extremely labor intensive, a slow and arduous process requiring the use of cross-cut saws, wedges, and hand axes.

Although a considerable amount of timber harvesting was done for local use, trees might also be taken to the numerous local water-driven sash sawmills that still existed in the region until the late 1880s.[65] At the local sawmill, trees were cut into lumber for the construction of homes, barns, and outbuildings. The majority of these mills were able to cut only 1–2,000 board feet per day, greatly limiting large-scale timber production. With the introduction of portable steam sawmills into the region during the 1850s, timber could be logged at the homesite and at a much faster rate. Jesse Kerr, after acquiring one of the first portable sawmills in eastern Tennessee, wrote in 1858 that he was "able to cut 3,000 feet of beautiful lumber in 12 hours, with something less than one cord of wood." Kerr added that the portability of the sawmill allowed him to move his sawmill "from five to ten miles per day," which, he noted, "saves the great burden of hauling logs a long distance to the mill."[66]

Comparatively speaking, steam-powered sawmills had relatively little environmental or economic impact on the region until at least the early 1880s. Because steam-powered sawmills were portable, their mobility insured that most farmers could make good advantage of them. By 1889 there were at least twenty-three portable mills in existence in Blount County, Tennessee, alone, where they were even declared "fashionable" by the editor of the *Maryville Times*.[67] However, most of the sawmill owners were fairly small-scale operators who usually custom sawed only enough timber for the local landowner to use around the homestead. The sawmill operator generally charged by the amount of board feet he actually cut or sometimes worked "on the halves," that is, keeping half the lumber in lieu of cash payment. The relatively more affluent residents of the region took the greatest advantage of these portable sawmills for hire and were thus among the first residents in the region to build and live in wooden frame houses.

The steam-powered sawmill not only forced the shift from log to frame home construction during the last decade of the nineteenth century, it also indirectly advanced the cause of commercial lumbering. The proliferation of the portable sawmills helped to increase the pace and scale of logging operations in the mountains, forcing many residents to consider, perhaps for the first time, the timber on their wooded farmlands as an important cash crop. Indeed, local demand for lumber had increased considerably during the 1880s, particularly in areas surrounding county seats across the region where wood was needed by building contractors, coffin makers, cabinet and furniture shops, and window and sash factories. In the coal-field areas of the region, large numbers of trees were cut to aid in the construction of narrow gauge railroads, mine shaft supports, coal tipples, and company housing. In terms of scale, however, local timber-cutting methods usually involved the harvesting of individual trees or groups of trees, thus giving the forest, says historian Robert Lambert, "a chance for reproduction." [68]

Of course, the greatest check on timber harvesting was the mountain-eers' dependence on trees for things other than saw timber. Appalachian hardwoods provided important benefits to mountain farmers, including fuel for heating homes, shade and food for livestock, habitat for wild game, and a means of checking soil erosion. For this reason, as late as 1900, it was still common for mountaineers to leave as much as 60 percent or more of their homestead in uncleared, forested woodlands. [69] In fact, most farmers living on the Cumberland Plateau and in the Blue Ridge Mountains main-tained as much as 90 percent of their farms in forests. Only a small portion of the remaining improved acreage was actually cultivated, and these lands were periodically abandoned by the mountain farmer in order to allow them to revert to woodland pasture. One study found that of the total land owned by farm families in the southern mountains, only 14 percent was actually planted in harvestable crops. The nineteenth-century agricultural system of crop rotation and forest fallowing no doubt helped to minimize the destruction of the surrounding forest, despite the claims of government reformers, who called the centuries-old practice culturally regressive and environmentally unsound.[70]

The Shallow and the Deep

The increased flooding caused by the indiscriminate cutting of southern Appalachian forests resulted in renewed and heightened interest in dam construction and other permanent flood control measures in the southern mountain region. Fast-flowing waterways in the mountains were fully navigable only during certain periods of the year or after successive heavy rains. For this reason, engineers and local boosters had long dreamed of damming the largest mountain rivers in order to provide permanent boat and barge transportation for Appalachian communities. Electrification was another concern of many of these individuals, who by the turn of the century saw mountain rivers as an important source of electric power for a fast-growing urban population. The major obstacle to full-scale water transportation on the largest of these rivers—the Tennessee—had historically been below Chattanooga at the Narrows and at Muscle Shoals in northern Alabama, where the river spread into numerous wide shoals of depths averaging less than 6 inches. The overall average depth of southern Appalachian rivers was a mere 1.5 feet, making large boat or barge traffic impractical, if not impossible, for most of the year.[71]

Increased flooding, the desire for improved navigation, and the fact that the region's largest municipalities were becoming keenly interested in the opportunity to generate hydroelectric power brought dam construction to the political and economic fore during the first decade of the 1900s. One of the first dams in the mountain region was the Hales Bar Lock and Dam below Chattanooga, a project started in 1905 and finished some eight years later in the fall of 1913. Financed from monies obtained from a New York financier and several wealthy Chattanooga businessmen seeking a source of cheap electricity for the growing city, the project was designed and supervised by the Army Corps of Engineers, which, upon completion, retained ownership of the dam, lock, and reservoir. Although it was not the first concrete dam constructed in the mountains, the Hales Bar Dam was the first to successfully combine both navigation and electric power improvements, providing additional incentives for dam construction elsewhere. The end result was a slack-water impoundment stretching 33 miles from the dam site upstream to the city of Chattanooga. The new dam created navigation depths of no less than 6 feet, permanently flooding the Narrows and several other navigation obstacles that had existed along one of the most historically significant sections of the Tennessee River.[72]

Dam and channel construction quickly escalated throughout the entire region as wealthy businessmen, using largely outside capital, saw great opportunities to develop a natural resource that, they believed, had for generations been going to waste. A hydroelectric dam on the Oconee River, which also supplied power to Chattanooga, was completed as early as 1912. The Tallulah River in northeastern Georgia was dammed by the Georgia Railway and Power Company, founded by H. M. Atkinson, a Harvard graduate and native of Boston. Promoters of the dam and the accompanying power plant saw the project as a way to supply needed power to a series of streetcar lines being developed by the company in Atlanta. In 1912 half of the output of all central station electric plants was consumed in the operation of electric streetcars—by 1920, the automobile had, in essence, made streetcars obsolete. Completed in 1914, the five generators of the Tallulah Falls Plant had an aggregate horsepower output of 85,000 units, making it the third largest power plant in the United States. Realizing the need for reserve supplies of water to ensure an uninterrupted supply of power regardless of stream flow or weather conditions, the Georgia Railway and Power Company launched the construction of a series of dams along a 28-mile stretch of the Tallulah, Tugalo, and Chattooga Rivers. Incredibly, by the completion the sixth and final dam in 1927, northeastern Georgia could claim to have the "most completely developed continuous stretch of river in the United States."[73]

Of course, dam construction in the region would not reach its final peak until the creation of the Tennessee Valley Authority (TVA) during the early 1930s. World War I slowed many of the dam-building efforts in the southern Appalachians, but the 1920s saw a return to large-scale dam construction, including the completion of the Wilson Dam in northern Alabama, a structure built to finally solve the problem of Muscle Shoals and river navigation in the Tennessee Valley. Because of political controversies surrounding the construction, use, and ultimate ownership of the Wilson Dam, as well as the perceived inability of individually situated dams to control flooding in the region, the federal government became more and more interested in managing the entire Tennessee Valley river system. A 1930 report drafted by the Army Corps of Engineers that would later become the basis for congressional policy on most matters related to the Tennessee Valley watershed recommended the construction of seven major dams in the region, including possible sites for at least another 149 related hydroelectric projects. On 18 May 1933 the federal act creating the TVA was passed by Congress, making the implementation of those recommendations a very real, if not imminent, possibility.[74]

The first and perhaps most well known project to be implemented by the TVA was the construction of the Cove Creek storage dam on the Clinch River, a structure later named Norris Dam in honor of Senator George W. Norris, a Nebraska politician and an ardent TVA supporter. The dam, completed in 1936, rose 265 feet from the valley floor and stretched more than 1,860 feet across the river gorge. Sixty square miles, or 37,000 acres, along the Clinch and Powell Rivers were permanently flooded to create the Norris Dam. An additional 100,000 acres of land surrounding the reservoir were also purchased for the project, including what historians Michael McDonald and John Muldowny rightly referred to as perhaps "the best agricultural land in the state." Promoted by agency chairman Arthur Morgan as an experiment in "organic" regional planning, the Norris Dam project also involved the creation of a suburban village of more than three hundred homes, a school, and a multipurpose community center.[75]

In 1935 an amendment to the original TVA act decreased Morgan's influence on the agency and made navigation and flood control the primary objectives of the federal agency, including a specific mandate to provide a 9-foot channel from at least Knoxville to the mouth of the river in Paducah, Kentucky. This allowed the TVA to move ahead relentlessly with its dam-building and hydroelectric programs. By the end of the Second World War there were more than a dozen TVA dams in the Appalachian region alone, including the Cherokee and Watauga Dams in upper eastern Tennessee, the Apalachia, Hiwassee, and Cheoah Dams in southeastern Tennessee, and the Blue Ridge Dam in northern Georgia. One of the TVA's most ambitious undertakings was the construction of Fontana Dam along the Little Tennessee River near the Great Smoky Mountains, a project it justified as part of the war effort, since the power the dam would produce would be used for the manufacture of aluminum and other war materials. Upon its completion in 1943, the Fontana Dam inundated more than 10,000 acres of mountain lands, submerging or partly submerging the mountain communities of Fontana, Bushnell, Japan, Forney, Judson, Almond, and Proctor. The lake that resulted also destroyed a diverse population of native plants and animals, including some of the largest specimens of the extremely rare yellowwood tree ever observed in the southern mountains. In just a dozen years, the TVA had, in effect, transformed what once had been a unique network of shallow, swiftly flowing rivers and streams into a uniform series of slack-water lakes.[76]

In Kentucky dam construction fell largely to the Army Corps of Engineers but began well after the 1950s, when nearly all major impoundment projects in the eastern third of state were started. One exception is the Dale Hollow Lake Dam on the Tennessee-Kentucky border, completed in 1943 as one of the initial projects of the original Flood Control Act of 1938. Historically, electricity in eastern Kentucky and West Virginia came largely from coal-fired utility plants, so little if any hydroelectric power was produced on the Cumberland Plateau during the first half of the twentieth century.[77] There are numerous dam impoundments on the plateau today, however, including Paintsville Lake, Fishtrap Lake, Yatesville Lake, Martins Fork Lake, and Dewey Lake, the latter located within the Jenny Wiley State Park in Floyd County, Kentucky. Dams built solely for recreation and flood control in the southern mountain region have had much the same effect as hydroelectric dams, submerging homesites as well as destroying critical habitat for indigenous fish and wildlife.

One of the most scenic and historically significant sites destroyed by a hydroelectric dam in the southern Appalachians was Tallulah Falls in northeastern Georgia. Formerly one of the highest waterfalls in the entire eastern United States, Tallulah Falls had been visited by numerous important individuals over the centuries who unanimously praised the scenic beauty of the falls and the surrounding mountain landscape. In 1914 the picturesque falls were virtually extinguished after the completion of the Tallulah Falls hydroelectric project, a 116-foot-high dam located immediately above the crest of the waterfall. An attempt to stop the destruction of the falls was spearheaded by the Tallulah Falls Conservation Association, an organization founded in 1912 by Helen Dortch Longstreet, widow of Confederate general James Longstreet. Having no other recourse to stop what she considered the "ruthless destruction" of the falls, Mrs. Longstreet claimed that the state of Georgia still held title to the property, a claim that ultimately resulted in a lawsuit against Georgia Railway and Power, the builder of the project. After what one local historian has called the "best prepared civil case ever tried in Georgia," the local superior court ruled in favor of the power company, a decision upheld by the state supreme court on 13 December 1913.[78]

The most obvious social cost of dam construction was the direct removal or dislocation of mountain residents. Over a period of three decades, more than eighty thousand people lost their homes and farms to these development projects. As a result of the construction of Norris Dam, at least three thousand families were displaced and over five thousand graves—many unmarked and dating back to the late eighteenth century—had to be removed and buried elsewhere. Chickamauga Dam was responsible for the removal of 903 households, including 263 property owners and 640 tenants. Cherokee Dam displaced 875 households, and Watauga Dam, almost a thousand families.[79] Regardless of whether these mountain families sold their farms willingly or unwillingly, the loss of their place of residence and the transition to a new one had to be extremely difficult, especially during the Great Depression. Glen Elliot, whose family was removed for the creation of the Watauga Dam in upper eastern Tennessee, was born on the same parcel of land his ancestors had homesteaded in the 1770s. In recalling what removal meant to him and his family, Elliot stated, "The land was in our family for seven generations prior to TVA moving us out. We lost our homeplace. It erased us off the map, so to speak. I tell people that I'm from a little town in Tennessee called Carden's Bluff, it is all under water now." A similar story is told by southern agrarian Andrew Lytle, who recalled a family removed by the TVA from their ancestral homeplace in northern Alabama. According to Lytle, since the fire in the home "had not gone out in one hundred years," the TVA had to move "the chimney intact, its coals covered and hot, to its new location."[80]

One of the most important functions of native mountain rivers and streams was to provide mountain families with an abundant source of edible freshwater fish, including species that are seldom eaten or even commonly observed today. These fish were caught in a number of ways, ranging from the river cane fishing pole and barbed hook to the large weir-dam fish trap. Alex Stewart, the famous craftsman of Hancock County on the Cumberland Plateau, made large fish traps with wooden hoops that he then covered with carefully knitted nets. "You take little blocks of wood and do your knitting around that," recalled Stewart. "You then cover the hoops with your net and make two V-shaped traps inside. One time I went to check my net and I had catched fifty-three catfish in one net and every one weighed at least two pounds."[81]

Prior to the Great Depression, most fish traps in the mountains took the form of smaller wooden baskets made of narrow white-oak splits. According to one source, women would often bake cornbread specifically for the occasion, finely crumble it, and then place it in the center of the fish baskets. Once or twice a week, usually late in the afternoon, the menfolk of the community would lower the basket and its contents into a favored fishing hole along the river's or creek's edge. Early the next morning the basket would be checked and the fish—usually a mix of catfish, drum, bass, and bream—removed. The fish were often cooked immediately for breakfast along with biscuits and hominy grits, but sometimes the catch would be large enough that a fish fry would have to be arranged for the entire community.[82]

Weir-dam fish traps like the ones used by the Mississippians during the sixteenth century were so successful at catching fish that numerous traps were later used commercially. One common location for weir-dam fish traps was the Holston River above Knoxville, Tennessee, where their use has been documented as a "well-established tradition for over 180 years."[83] One of these traps was the Monday Island fish trap located near Mascot, Tennessee, a trap kept in continuous operation for more than forty years. Knoxville resident William McCoy remembers visiting Monday Island, where he lived for a month while on a family vacation, around 1915. "During our stay on the island we were allowed to use any of the fish we wanted," recalled McCoy.

> The rivermen took the remainder to market in Mascot. After I had learned
> to pole the boat along the dam to the trap it became my job to bring in the
> catch. There were usually 35–40 fish in the trap each morning . . . the fish
> were cleaned, rolled in cornmeal and fried in bacon fat in an iron skillet on top
> of a wood burning stove. It seemed to me that we ate fish for almost every
> meal and choking on the tiny bones was a common mealtime hazard.[84]

According to McCoy, caretakers living on the western bank of the Holston monitored the Monday Island fish trap every day, selling the catch to both residents and local diners. J. W. Kirby, who ran the trap during the

1920s, kept detailed records of the exact size and species of each fish caught. For an eleven-month period beginning in November 1921, Kirby caught more than 1,000 pounds of fish for a total income of $311.17 at 30 cents per pound. A ledger covering a three-month period from January to March 1923 reveals that the most common species caught during the coldest months were redhorse suckers and carp. Of those three months, March provided the most diverse catch, including a trout, drum, and three "blackhorse suckers." William McCoy, who saw the trap in operation during the month of May, recalled removing bass, blue catfish, mud catfish, bream, and carp from the trap and even remembered catching, on one occasion, "a shovel-bill catfish."[85] The number and kinds of species caught in the traps fluctuated considerably, due in part to increasing or decreasing water levels, the migratory habits of the fish, and seasonally changing water temperatures.

The use of weir-dam fish traps declined steadily during the first three decades of the twentieth century, coming to an end throughout the region around the beginning of the Second War World. Earlier in the century, many fish traps were dynamited by various state fish and game departments who claimed the traps were threatening native fish populations. Others were destroyed by logging operations, especially where splash dams were used to float logs downstream. There was considerable local debate about the traps' alleged detrimental effect on fish numbers, however, forcing the state of Tennessee to repeal an earlier state law banning their use. Historically, most of the sentiment against fish traps had actually been initiated by the timber or riverboat companies, who considered fish traps a great hazard to logging operations and river navigation. By the mid-1930s, the widespread flooding of mountain streams and rivers by hydroelectric dams made the debate surrounding the use of fish traps irrelevant, although a few fish traps, like the Monday Island fish trap, remained in operation until at least 1940.[86]

Another river-dependent natural resource that played an important role in the southern Appalachians were freshwater mussels and pearls. Although not generally eaten by mountain residents, freshwater mussels were quite often used as fish bait or occasionally even fed to hogs. The shallow, clear-flowing streams of the region provided ideal habitat for a great diversity of mussel species, several of which routinely bore freshwater pearls of considerable value. Although pearls were gathered on nearly every major stream in the mountain region, the economic heart of the pearl industry was along the Clinch and Emory Rivers in southwestern Virginia and eastern Tennessee. In a paper read to the Tennessee Academy of Sciences in 1914, W. E. Myer considered the Caney Fork River as the birthplace of the pearl industry in the region since one of the first and largest pearls was found there in 1876. The Coosa and Etowah Rivers in northwestern Georgia were also important pearl fishery areas, as were the wide shoals of the Tennessee River in northern Alabama.[87]

By 1908 the U.S. freshwater pearl industry had grown to a half-a-million-dollar enterprise, and Tennessee was considered one of the nation's six leading states in the marketing of quality pearls. In eastern Tennessee Anderson County, and specifically the town of Clinton, was by far the region's largest center for pearling activity. As George Kunz and Charles Stevenson noted in *The Book of the Pearl*, pearling excitement developed there in the 1890s, resulting in vivid and picturesque accounts of hundreds of individuals camping along the banks of the Clinch River. Newspaper reports describe the pearl fishermen as "easy-going, pleasure loving people, the men and women working hard all day, subsisting largely on fish caught in the same stream, and dancing at night to the music of a banjo around the camp-fires."[88] In Clinton Saturday was the preferred day for trading pearls, causing a flurry of weekend activity in the small river town. New York jewelers who regularly made trips to Clinton stayed at the Strader Hotel, the preferred destination for most out-of-state pearl buyers. The pearl industry was driven largely by markets in New York, London, and Paris, where enormous sums were routinely paid for exceptionally fine freshwater pearls. While the majority of pearls usually sold locally for ten to seventy-five dollars each, it was not uncommon for an exceptionally large Clinch River pearl to bring a thousand dollars or more. Elsewhere in the region, the quality of the pearls was apparently comparable to those from the Clinch River area. After dredging John's Creek near Rome, a northern Georgia farmer reportedly received $180 from a Baltimore jeweler for several of his most marketable pearls.[89]

Most often practiced when rivers were at their lowest levels, mussel gathering could also be associated with local special events such as town festivals or celebrations, causing hundreds of individuals to join in the search for prized pearls. Of course, the ecological impact of these mass harvests on native mussel populations could be enormous: for every exceptional pearl specimen found by the gathering parties, thousands of mollusks had to be destroyed. Unlike the Mississippians of the sixteenth century, white mountain families did not regularly eat freshwater mussels, although there are a few reports that Civil War soldiers occasionally ate them "as a change," pronouncing them "no bad article of diet."[90] Later, as fashionable buttons began to be made from the mother-of-pearl mantles of the largest and most unusual species, the wastefulness of mussel harvesting was greatly reduced, although the additional incentive to harvest the colorful shells continued to deplete mussel populations.

Not surprisingly, the overcollecting of mussels was already a public concern by the end of the first decade of the twentieth century. In 1908 Kunz and Stevenson wrote that in many localities "the fishery has been prosecuted so vigorously that it appears probable the resources will be materially impoverished if not ruined in a few years, unless prompt and decisive protective measures are adopted." The authors added, however, that solving the problem would entail not only restricting "methods of fishery" but curtailing the disposal of sewage by "the cities and the large factories, through which great quantities of mussels have been destroyed."[91] Water pollution had already become a major problem in the southern mountains by the first decade of the twentieth century, especially downstream from major riverport towns like Charleston, West Virginia, and Chattanooga, Tennessee. Mussel enthusiast A. E. Ortmann voiced his concerns about the situation, observing in 1909 that the worst damage to mussels was done not by overharvesting but by "sewage . . . coal mines . . . chemical factories . . . woodpulp mills, saw mills, tanneries, etc." Increased flooding and the damming of southern Appalachian rivers also contributed greatly to the destruction of native mussels, since most species require clear, shallow, and swift waters to successfully reproduce.[92]

Indeed, with the building of each new hydroelectric dam, more and more mussel habitat became submerged under deep water and tons of murky silt. Below the spillways immediately downstream, several mussel species were "chilled into reproductive stupor," thus becoming functionally extinct. Before the damming of the Tennessee River, for example, Muscle Shoals had quite possibly the greatest diversity of mussel species in North America. In 1924, after viewing firsthand the destruction caused by the building of the Wilson Dam, Ortmann described the area that once formed the original shoals: "The beautiful islands, and the general feature of the river itself are gone, as well as a large portion of the fauna, chiefly that of mussels." In 1963, when the area was again surveyed by mussel experts, only thirty of the original sixty-three mussel species were found inhabiting the former mussel paradise.[93]

In the end, the TVA system of reservoirs collectively destroyed hundreds of miles of important mussel waters, including, according to Anderson County residents, some of the best pearl fishery areas in the entire Tennessee Valley. Young's Island, among the narrow shoals of the Clinch River in waters now flooded by the Norris Dam, was a particularly favored location for pearling. Some localities even derived their place-names from the type of mussels commonly found there: "blue-point," "pancake," "buckhorn," and "butterfly" were once commonly recognized locations along the Clinch River. Today only a handful of prime mussel sites remain in the southern Appalachians, the most notable being the narrow channels surrounding Pendleton Island along the upper stretches of the Clinch River in southwestern Virginia. There, at least forty-five species still exist among the river's shallow and truly pristine headwaters.[94]

The environmental, social, and cultural effects of public and private dam construction on the southern Appalachians cannot be underestimated. Collectively, these hydroelectric and navigation projects inundated more than a million acres of mountain lands, submerged over a thousand miles of natural flowing streams and rivers, and permanently flooded hundreds of important cultural and historical sites significant to the region's history. The overall water quality of the region's rivers greatly diminished, as did the number of species dependent upon the native river ecosystem. Freshwater eels, paddlefish, sturgeons, quillbacks, not to mention the recently rediscovered robust redhorse and other migratory fish species declined dramatically in numbers or, as in the case of several freshwater mussels, became extinct altogether. By far the best agricultural land in the region was taken out of the agriculture land base, resulting not only in a decline in farming as a primary occupation but also in the loss of millions of dollars' worth of valuable property that was permanently removed from the local tax base.[95]

The damming of southern Appalachian rivers had a profound impact on mountain life and culture. Most residents had lived close enough to a large stream that fishing had remained an integral part of daily subsistence, particularly from March through September. Sherman Hartley, who lived along the Watauga River before the construction of the Watauga Dam, remarked that even though his family were "just country people," they raised all their food, adding that "we had all the fish we wanted, had all the wild ducks, and everything that goes with the river."[96] Winter and early spring floods improved bottomland soils and summer harvests. The lack of attention given to rivers in discussions about southern Appalachia is an error committed too often by scholars who have associated mountain life only with the mountains and not with the many rivers, creeks, and streams that crisscross the region.

A Whole World Dying

Rivaling the loss of mussels in ecological importance was the death of the American chestnut, formerly the most dominant tree species in the southern Appalachian forest. In fact, as important as commercial logging and dam construction were to environmental and cultural change in the region, few events in North American environmental history compare with the loss of this unique tree species. "The devastation of the American chestnut by the chestnut blight," writes William MacDonald, a professor of plant pathology at West Virginia University and a leading expert on the tree, "represents one of the greatest recorded changes in natural plant population caused by an introduced organism." Chestnut trees once comprised roughly 20 percent of the entire forest in the mountains, although in specific areas they accounted for as much as one third of all standing trees. William Ashe reported seeing locales where the trees "occur pure or nearly pure over areas as large as 100 acres."[97] In 1901 he and Horace Ayres estimated that their southern Appalachian study area contained more than 884,000 acres of chestnut timber. The trees were largely confined to the Blue Ridge Mountains and Cumberland Plateau, where they commonly grew at altitudes between 1,000 and 4,000 feet.[98] The Ridge and Valley province had a few important stands of chestnuts as well, but these were found only on the slopes of the highest ridges where richer soils and heavier rainfall predominated. A well-documented reconstruction of nineteenth-century forests in northwestern Georgia found chestnut trees comprising no more than 6 percent of the area, with hickories, the most dominant tree species, making up 10 percent of the total forest. According to estimates made by William MacDonald, chestnut-dominated forests once covered more than 200 million acres of land from Maine to Georgia.[99]

The death of the American chestnut was due to an exotic blight introduced in the United States from Japanese chestnut nursery stock just after the turn of the century. A forester at the New York Zoological Park first reported the disease in 1904 after observing an immense number of dead and dying chestnut trees on park lands under his supervision. Five years later, the first scientific bulletin appeared about the disease, a fungus later named *Endothia parasitica*.[100] Only a year after the bulletin's publication, an editorial in the *Southern Lumberman* referred to a "mysterious blight" that had recently been observed in Pennsylvania and New York. "Large timbered sections of [Pennsylvania] are already in an alarming manner affected by the disease," stated the report. By 1912 all the chestnut trees in New York City were dead, and the chestnut blight had reached ten states. Scientists in Pennsylvania launched a vigorous control program that included burning dead trees, monitoring the advance of the fungus, and spraying infected trees. This effort, a scientist later commented, was a little like using toy swords to battle an enemy equipped with atomic bombs. Yet foresters told the public that "the control and ultimate extermination of [the chestnut blight] . . . will sooner or later become a real accomplishment."[101]

The disease spread relentlessly southward at an astounding rate of some 50 miles per year. Aided by woodsmen who carried it on their shoes and axes, the blight first entered North Carolina near Stokes and Surry Counties about 1913. Shady Valley in upper eastern Tennessee had been hit by 1915. By 1920 the American chestnut in the Great Smokies was ultimately doomed, though there were few visible signs of the blight there before 1925.[102] North Carolina lumbermen even used the encroaching disease as their excuse to attempt a last-ditch effort to defeat the proposed Great Smoky Mountains National Park. "Certainly nothing could be more unsightly than the gaunt and naked trunks of these dead trees, standing like skeletons in every vista which the eye turns," they wrote.[103]

According to Harry Caudill, the chestnut blight had reached the Cumberland Plateau of Kentucky as early as 1929, killing 17 percent of all standing trees in just two years. By the mid-1930s, the blight had reached much of northern Georgia, and by 1940 there was scarcely a tree in the entire Appalachian region that was not dead or showing some sign of being infected with the disease.[104] Although few people alive today remember what the southern Appalachian forests looked like before the blight devastated the region, those who did provide indisputable testimony to the trees' significance to the mountain environment. "This is an unbelievable thing: how many chestnuts there were," remembered Paul Woody, who grew up near Cataloochee, North Carolina. Gifford Pinchot himself recalled seeing chestnut stands with individual trees 13 feet across and with crowns spreading more than 120 feet above the forest floor. Charles Grossman, one of the first rangers at the new Great Smoky Mountains National Park, recorded a chestnut tree 9 feet, 8 inches in diameter at a point 6 feet off the ground. "The hollow portion is so large that [an adult] could stand up in it," wrote Grossman after discovering it. "This hollow runs more than 50 feet up the trunk and at its narrowest point is not less than three feet. This must be the tree of which I heard. A man lost some stock during a snowstorm and later found them safe in a hollow chestnut tree."[105]

Due to its abundance and enormous size, the American chestnut ranked as the most important wildlife plant of the eastern United States. The largest trees could produce 10 bushels or more of nuts. Reports of chestnuts 4 inches deep on the forest floor were not uncommon in the southern mountains. Many of the wildlife species that mountain people thought of as game—squirrel, wild turkey, white-tailed deer, bear, raccoon, and grouse—depended on these chestnuts as a major food source. "The worst thing that ever happened in this country was when the chestnut trees died," said Walter Cole of eastern Tennessee. "Turkeys disappeared, and the squirrels were not one-tenth as many as there were before." Will Effler, who grew up on the West Fork of the Little River in what is today the Great Smoky Mountains National Park, recalled shooting a wild turkey that had ninety-two chestnuts, "still in the hulls and undigested," in its swollen craw.[106] Other nongame animals were equally dependent on the chestnut, including several unique insect species that relied upon chestnut trees as their principal food source. Paul Opler of the U.S. Fish and Wildlife Service has estimated that at least seven native moths became extinct in the southern Appalachians as a result of the chestnut blight. The loss of the chestnut also slowed the recovery of wildlife populations already suffering from loss of habitat by logging operations. Randoph-Macon College biologist James M. Hill ascribes the slow recovery of deer, wild turkey, goshawk, Cooper's hawk, cougar, and bobcat in the mountains to habitat destruction directly caused by the chestnut blight.[107]

Of course, humans ate chestnuts too, making them an important dietary supplement when the trees dropped their nuts after the first major frost.

Each October, mountain children scooped up chestnuts by the sackful, then hung the cloth bags on nails outside the door and ate the nuts until December, when they began to get wormy. The Cherokees made more use of the nuts, which they frequently added to cornmeal dough that was then boiled or baked. Some families gathered many bushels of chestnuts, taking them by wagon to urban markets.[108] John McCaulley, whose family foraged for chestnuts in the Great Smoky Mountains around 1910, remembered seeing in one mountain cabin a "hundred bushels of chestnuts, piled up there, and about four men packing off, every day." McCaulley himself recalls gathering as many as 7 bushels of chestnuts in a single day's outing. These, he said, were taken to Knoxville on mules, where they were sold for "four dollars a bushel."[109] Chestnuts were also routinely shipped by rail to major cities on the eastern seaboard. In 1911 West Virginia reported that one railroad station alone shipped 155,000 pounds of chestnuts to destinations along the train's northerly route.[110]

Another important use of chestnuts in the mountain region was as food for hogs. For a month or two each fall, hogs ran loose in the woods to feast on chestnuts and other mast littering the forest floor. Maggie Wachacha, recalling the scene around her home in Cherokee, North Carolina, said, "There were about a hundred pigs when I first moved here. Pigs and hogs were so fat. There was plenty of chestnuts back then."[111] In late November, or as soon as the weather got cold enough, mountain residents rounded up the fattened hogs for slaughter. Chestnut-flavored pork hung in the smokehouse all winter, where it continued to be the primary source of protein for most families. A southwestern Virginia farmer commenting on the role of chestnuts in mountain agriculture noted that it "didn't cost a cent to raise chestnuts or hogs in those days. It was a very inexpensive way to farm. The people had money and had meat on the table too."[112]

As a building material, the chestnut was unsurpassed. Chestnut wood was highly rot-resistant, making it ideal for fences, shingles, and furniture. Valuable sources of tannic acid used in the leather industry, chestnut bark and rough chestnut cordwood were important sources of income for mountain residents. In Tennessee alone, fifty thousand cords of wood were cut every year to supply those tanneries in operation before 1912. This "tanbark" or "acid wood," as it was called locally, was taken largely from trees already cut for other purposes or small defective trees that were not of nut-bearing age. Commercial operations were also heavily engaged in the harvesting of chestnut trees for tanbark and cordwood. One observer remarked in 1931 that even though chestnut timber was once cut by lumbermen for the bark alone, "very little waste of this kind is now noted."[113]

As might be expected during the era of industrial logging, the blight did not slow the harvest of chestnut trees; in fact, the cutting actually increased after the initial introduction of the disease. In fact, most lumber barons were harvesting the largest chestnut trees even before the blight was officially observed in the mountain region. Early on, lumbermen even doubted the potential devastation of the disease, believing that the fast-growing trees would eventually regenerate across the mountain landscape. Moreover, they knew that a chestnut tree was worth money dead or alive, since foresters soon determined that it was possible to manufacture lumber from standing chestnuts for up to ten years after the death of the tree. For acid wood, the salvage period was even longer: Reuben Robertson, president of the Champion Fibre Company, estimated that the company cut chestnut trees for pulp and tannin twenty years after the blight first arrived in North Carolina.[114]

The chestnut was therefore responsible for bringing another major industry to the upper South: leather tanning. By 1930 there were twenty-one chestnut-fueled plants in the southern Appalachians, producing over half of the U.S. supply of vegetable-based tannins. Within a decade, almost all the chestnut trees had vanished from the mountains, as the growing tanning industry, the largest consumer of chestnuts, had found ways to use every part of the tree. After 1940, with the development of synthetic replacements in the production of tannin, the demand for chestnut trees greatly diminished, leaving only a few ghost-white skeletons to stand lone sentry over the once great southern Appalachian forest.[115] The dead and dying chestnut snags were painful reminders to southern mountaineers that the mountain landscape, including an entire way of life, was all but gone. "Man, I had the awfulest feeling about that as a child, to look back yonder and see those trees dying," recalled Joe Tribble, a native of eastern Kentucky. "I thought the whole world was going to die."[116]

Mountain residents were right to mourn the lost of the chestnut. The chestnut tree was possibly the single most important natural resource of the southern Appalachians, providing inhabitants with food, shelter, and, in the early twentieth century, a much-needed cash income. Born in 1914, Knott County, Kentucky, native Verna Mae Sloan recalled that life without the chestnut tree was almost unthinkable. "At first we thought they would come back, we didn't know they were blighted out forever," she remembered. "But the chestnut tree was the most important tree we had. We needed those chestnuts." [117] In fall and winter chestnuts could be boiled or roasted over an open fire or traded at local stores for needed supplies. Chestnut timber, with the greatest durability of available native woods, was made into long-lasting boards, posts, shingles, and split-rail fences. The tender and abundant sprouts could even be pulled from the ground and fed to cattle as fodder. As a wildlife food, the chestnut was unsurpassed and helped to keep local game populations at high levels. In a memoir written shortly before his death, Shady Valley, Tennessee, native William Cole aptly summed up the extraordinary value of the tree to southern mountain residents. "A favorite outing for me and my friends was to go to the ball ground on Sunday to collect chestnuts," wrote Cole. "The chestnut tree was a great tree, chestnut wood was a great wood, and chestnuts a good food." [118]

Now depending less and less on the mountain farmstead environs, the food and folkways of the region's inhabitants began to conspicuously change. By the early 1930s mountain families were consuming less buttermilk and more whole milk, less rye and wheat breads and more light breads, and more processed sugar and less maple syrup and honey. While there were some dietary constants throughout the region, such as the consumption of cornbread and biscuits, the use of canned and other storebought foods increased significantly during the first three decades of the twentieth century.[119] For those who remained exclusively farmers, crop monoculture became a much more common way to farm. Family size dropped by more than 2 individuals, from 10 family members per household in 1910 to 7.62 per household in 1934. Home-building techniques changed as well. "Boxed" houses—that is, frameless structures made exclusively with sawn planks and boards—gradually replaced log cabins as residents working seasonally for lumber companies had less time and help to build traditional log homes. The number of working outbuildings on the homestead also diminished, including the smokehouse, springhouse, and separate kitchen facility. Furniture was no longer homemade, and looms and spinning wheels largely became things of the past.[120] Needless to say, everything from architecture to social relations was altered by the separation of the mountain environment from the mountaineers.

In many ways, the death of the chestnut symbolized the end of a waning, albeit arguably vital, subsistence culture in the mountains. The loss of the tree no doubt gave additional advantage to the forces of industrialization that were gaining a stronger and stronger foothold in the regional and local economy. No longer able to range hogs and cattle in the woodland commons, trap fish in free-flowing streams, or gather chestnuts on the hillsides, the rural mountaineers turned increasingly to milltowns and urban centers for economic salvation. The environmental abuse of the mountains, along with the residents' permanent removal from their traditional land base, made it extremely difficult for mountaineers to continue a semi-agrarian and intimately forest-dependent way of life. With the death of the chestnut, an entire world did die, eliminating cultural practices that had been viable in the southern Appalachians for more than four centuries.

To see nature as active is to recognize its formative role over geologic and historical time. Only by according ecology a place in the narrative of history can nature and culture be seen as truly interactive. — CAROLYN MERCHANT, *Ecological Revolutions*

8 Conclusion

NATURE, CULTURE, HISTORY

*I*N WRITING HUMAN HISTORY, scholars have largely over-looked the role that nature has played in shaping American life and culture. Their arrogance in exaggerating differences between humans and other organisms, between human history and the natural environment, has created an enormous intellectual gap in our present understanding of the human condition. As William Barrett has forcefully stated, many of those who study and write about our species have done so as if they "were sealed in the privacy of their study, and did not live on a planet surrounded by the vast organic world of animals, plants, insects, and protozoa, with whom their own life is linked in a single history."[1] Because social life and the natural world are inextricably intertwined, an entire history remains to be written of humanity's association with the natural world. Human history is natural history.

In the field of Appalachian studies, the relationship between environment and culture has long been an enigmatic one. Most attempts at finding environmental influences on southern Appalachian culture have resulted in a crude geographic determinism in which the isolation or severity of the mountains is said to be the fundamental cause of the "primitive" or "frontierlike" behavior of the mountain people. Ellen Churchill Semple, for example, writing at the beginning of the twentieth century, argued that cultural persistence in eastern Kentucky was a direct result of the social isolation created by the rugged mountain environment. Semple, however, an American disciple of the German antropogeographer Frederick Ratzel, was more interested in how territorial *space* influenced culture and politics and less concerned about the role that dynamic ecological forces such as indigenous flora and fauna played in the lives of mountain residents. Like other commentators writing about southern Appalachia before and since, Semple saw the region as territorially and culturally homogeneous and attached little importance to variations found in mountain topography, ecology, and culture.[2]

In more recent years, scholars studying the mountain region have equally failed to recognize the important contributions that the Mississippians and the Cherokees have made to the environmental and cultural history of the southern Appalachians. Europeans did not settle an empty wilderness; rather, they reoccupied lands made vacant by two centuries of disease, famine, and warfare. Even though European groups did bring specific skills to the southern Appalachian frontier, their way of life did not go unchanged.

Today there is considerable disagreement among scholars studying the mountain region as to which ethnic group holds the key to the origins of southern Appalachian subsistence culture, with most advancing the general notion that most land-use practices in the mountains have their origins somewhere in the Old World. In their book *The American Backwoods Frontier,* for example, folk historians Terry Jordan and Matti Kaups maintain that mountain culture has "significant northern European roots" but more specifically argue that the Savo-Karelians, an eastern Finnish group, are "the most significant shapers of the American backwoods way of life."[3] Other scholars maintain that southern Appalachian culture owes much to the Scots-Irish, as does historian David Hackett Fischer, who has documented the persistence of numerous Ulster folkways in the southern mountains.[4]

In all these discussions, the role of ecological forces in the development of mountain culture is largely deemphasized in order to prove the adaptive superiority of one ethnic group over another. Advanced in this volume is the argument that if a single ethnic group does deserve special mention in this context, it would be the Cherokees, who for several centuries prior to pioneer mountain settlement existed in relative ecological harmony with the southern mountain landscape. These "first peoples" did alter the local terrain to suit their own needs, but they also adapted their land-use techniques and technology to the peculiarities of the mountain environment.

Using the landscape of the sixteenth century as a starting point, there are six discernible periods of environmental and cultural change in the southern Appalachians. The Spanish began the process during the sixteenth century, introducing important new crops such as peaches and sweet potatoes into the region and initiating trade in furs and other material goods. The Spanish also brought deadly microbes into the mountains, decimating a large percentage of the Mississippian population and forcing surviving native peoples to migrate to and from the area. Within a single century, pre-Columbian Mississippian life had all but vanished from the southern mountains.

Seventeenth-century environmental change was, globally speaking, minimal, with some bottomland hardwood forests recovering from the lack of corn and bean cultivation. Yellow and white pines, sassafras, sweetgum, and other shade-intolerant tree species would have certainly increased in numbers, especially in areas of concentrated Mississippian occupation along meander-belt floodplains and river bottoms. The migration of bison herds to the area in the late sixteenth century would have also made visible alterations to the upland forest, especially around mineral springs and other grazing areas. Locally, elk, deer, and beaver populations would have risen slightly in numbers, increasing, at least in the short term, the number of early succession clearings in the surrounding upland forest.

The third period of environmental and cultural change occurred after the English and French initiated trade with the Cherokees during the early part of the eighteenth century. Initially, the Cherokees saw the fur trade as beneficial to their people, and thus participation in it was not necessarily discouraged by all members of the community. As deer and other important game became increasingly scarce in the mountains, the Cherokees became more and more dependent on English goods for sustenance. Debts were often paid in large tracts of land, further limiting the Cherokees' access to vital hunting grounds. Scots-Irish and French fur traders were among the first Europeans to actively live among the Cherokees, and so their presence in the region also had an important influence on many of their cultural activities and agricultural practices. Fur traders also introduced cattle and hogs into the upland forest, which helped to enlarge existing woodland clearings as well as reduce native vegetation in the surrounding woodland understory. After the French encouraged Cherokee warriors to fight against the British, English armies retaliated by destroying Cherokee dwellings, croplands, and grain supplies. As a result of these losses, the natives found it more and more difficult to maintain many of their cultural traditions, including hunting game with bow and arrow, flint knapping, and traditional pottery making.

The permanent settlement of the mountain region by white settlers represents the fourth major period of ecological and cultural change to occur in the southern mountains. As early as 1760, after land became harder to find east and north of the mountains, Europeans cleared and settled land in what is today southwestern Virginia and soon thereafter occupied the mountains of the Blue Ridge and Cumberland Plateau. However, Indian occupation made it difficult for settlers to push deeper into the area until after the Revolutionary War, when the Cherokees relinquished control over much of their original territory. These first settlers to the region were largely of English, Scots-Irish, and German ethnic origin, and all brought a variety of European crops, grasses, plants, and livestock with them into the mountains. The newly introduced plants flourished in the rich soils of the mountain river valleys, gradually overtaking indigenous species in areas where land disturbance was greatest. As settlers cut timber for fences and dwellings and cleared land for gardens and pasture, more and more openings appeared in the surrounding forest, starting a land clearance process that continued throughout the nineteenth and early twentieth centuries.

Because the Cherokees occupied the region throughout much of the frontier period, their influence on mountain culture, as noted earlier, was significant. Many Europeans were forced to abandon Old World crops for varieties commonly grown by the Cherokees and other southeastern Indians. Corn, squashes, beans, and melons became immediately popular among white settlers, as did many Cherokee preservation methods such as the drying of shuckbeans and pumpkins. Fishing techniques, such as grappling fish by hand and the use of weir-dam fish traps, were also borrowed from the mountain Cherokees. Pioneer women learned medicinal uses of mountain herbs from Cherokee women and soon were making their own home remedies in much the same manner. Likewise, Cherokee women learned how to milk dairy cows, tend poultry flocks, and spin and weave European cloth. Plants brought by Europeans to the region were also adopted by the Cherokees, many taking a central place in their home and kitchen gardens.

The industrialization of the mountains ushered in the fifth period of cultural and environmental change in the southern Appalachians. Iron ore mining, which rose to ascendancy during the 1830s in parts of upper eastern Tennessee, eastern Kentucky, and western North Carolina, was responsible for the largest land clearances in the mountain region prior to the Civil War. Copper mining, which did not reach its peak in the mountains until after the war, also did noticeable damage to the mountain landscape, although almost exclusively within the Copper Basin of north-eastern Georgia and southeastern Tennessee. Both industries served as catalysts for mountain agriculture, which also rose to ascendancy during the antebellum era, especially in the Ridge and Valley province, where farmers took the greatest advantage of the growing market economy. Iron ore and copper mining, the clearing of land for new farms, and large-scale commercial agriculture left a significant portion of the mountain landscape treeless by the end of the 1870s, although by no means did all of southern Appalachia become a pastoral landscape of verdant fields, scattered wood-lots, and bucolic farmsteads.

The final period of environmental and cultural change in the region re-sulted from industrial logging, which began in the mountain region on a grand scale shortly after 1880. Associated with industrial logging was rail-road construction, which allowed the harvesting of forests once thought inaccessible by conventional logging methods. Industrial railroad logging also allowed the highest ridgetops and mountains to be cleared, areas that had largely escaped both the axe and the plow of the original white settlers. The widespread cutting of timber caused extensive flooding in the region, initiating public discussions not only about the construction of dams for flood control but also the creation of forest preserves to be managed by the federal government. Both the TVA and the National Forest Service had considerable influence upon settlement patterns, the latter becoming, by the mid-1930s, the largest single landowner in the entire mountain region. By the end of the Great Depression, farmers had, in many ways, become less rather than more self-sufficient, causing many residents to leave their marginal farms for logging or coal camps or migrate into neighboring towns and cities where textile mills and tanneries had begun to dominate the local economy.

Of course, many environmental and cultural practices in the mountains persisted across several centuries and can be associated with different time periods, mountain subregions, and ethnic groups. The girdling of trees in order to clear local woodlands for cultivation, for example, was a practice possibly initiated by the Mississippians throughout southern Appalachia, but it certainly continued until the early twentieth century, when it was still practiced by many white mountaineers. Peaches and sweet potatoes—both Spanish-introduced crops—became central to the diets of the Chero-kees and later became important to the first European settlers of the mountain region. The building of weir-dam fish traps, originally a practice of the Mississippians, was also taken up by the Cherokees and later the first pioneer settlers, who used the traps for many generations. In fact, the early Cherokees inherited a considerable amount of material culture from the Mississippians, including wattle-and-daub building construction and the making of cane mats and baskets. Iron ore mining had begun in the region as early as the eighteenth century but continued in some parts of the mountains, such as northwestern Georgia, after 1900. Commercial logging, which initially involved the floating of logs down major waterways, was first practiced in southern Appalachia during the antebellum era but peaked in the region in both the 1890s and 1920s, as railroad lines and logging crews penetrated into different parts of the southern Appalachians.

Without question, from the sixteenth century forward, warfare, population pressures, and numerous other social and economic forces originating outside the region have had a profound impact on the settlement and cultural development of the southern mountains. The desire for gold and silver brought the Spanish to the area, the trade in animal skins brought the fur traders, and the European settlers came seeking refuge from servile living conditions in the Old World. Prior to the sixteenth century, the region remained largely outside the world economic system, a luxury that ended with the arrival of Hernando de Soto in 1540. By the early seventeenth century mountain Indians were trading in furs, Old World crops from Europe and Africa had already been introduced into the mountains, and thousands of natives had perished from introduced diseases. As the Mississippian case demonstrates, world commerce and trade had an enormous impact on both the ecology and culture of the southern mountain region.

The Cherokees were also drawn directly into world economic relations, trading in skins, ginseng, and other commodities from the well-wooded mountain forests. Initially, Cherokee participation in the fur trade changed their lives and culture relatively little. Hunting deer had long been part of traditional hunting practices, and the killing of surplus animals did not immediately bring significant changes to their lives. Early on, the Cherokees were able to barter judiciously for weapons, tools, and other European goods. As competition for furs increased, however, traders made permanent settlements in the area, enticing the Cherokees into acquiring more skins by offering them such items as durable fabrics, colorful glass beads, and alcohol. Because of their close proximity to Charleston, South Carolina, the Cherokees living in the southern Blue Ridge Mountains were the first to engage in these trade networks and thus also the first to experience the resulting environmental and cultural changes.

The extraction of natural resources for the global economy did not, by any means, stop with European settlement. Fur trappers and long hunters, in direct competition with the Cherokees, traded elk, buffalo, deer, and beaver skins to exporters from Charleston, Augusta, and Savannah. Frontier settlers also collected and sold ginseng, which was shipped in large quantities to France and then China. Because overland travel across the mountain region was often difficult, river settlements became important outposts for commercial trade. On the Cumberland Plateau, products for export were regularly sent down the Cumberland River to shipping ports as far away as New Orleans. From there, goods from the southern Appalachians might find their way to the Caribbean, Spain, England, France, and the Asian continent.

While external economic forces were certainly powerful in shaping the subsistence culture of the region, they do not tell us everything about the process of environmental and cultural change in the southern mountains. Economic models of social and cultural evolution portray individuals as being caught in a system of market relations over which they have little or no control. As early as 1820, Johann von Thünen believed that subsistence activities of a geographic region were determined solely by their market accessibility. In explicating his theory, von Thünen created the image of an isolated state whose economic center was a thriving urban metropolis. Outside his city was a homogeneous "wilderness," accessible by animal-drawn wagons on straight and level roads. According to von Thünen, only those areas immediately surrounding the city would possess enough capital for intensive commercial agriculture, particularly given the difficulties of long distance wagon travel. Because of spatial, temporal, and other obvious constraints caused by transportation problems, the most intensive kinds of agriculture were found closest to urban markets.[5] On the periphery of these intensive farming zones are plantations and other farms that produce both meat from fenced cattle and hogs and feed grains for fattening the livestock. Beyond that zone are the grazers, who, according to von Thünen, graze livestock on the open range and drive them relatively long distances to market. Lastly is the peripheral zone of hunters and trappers, who in the isolated wilderness procure skins and peltries, easily transported over long distances.

Central to von Thünen's model are the concepts *core* and *periphery*, ideas borrowed in this century by a number of social theorists who have used the market accessibility model to represent the Western world as a whole.[6] In the sixteenth century one could say that western Europe, especially Britain and Spain, represented the world metropolis or core, and the North American continent, including the Appalachian frontier, represented the peripheral economic zone. As the "world city" grew, demand for raw materials and natural resources increased, enlarging markets in the North American periphery. By the eighteenth century, considerable portions of the United States were, in fact, producing cash crops, livestock, and peltries for European markets. Proponents of the core/periphery model, including Appalachianist Wilma Dunaway, argue that the settlement of the southern Appalachian frontier—and the social organization that accompanied it—is best explained within the context of this ever-expanding world economic system.[7]

Implicit in this theory of social and economic transformation and central to our discussion here is the idea that an unequal exchange of goods must always occur between the core and periphery. The core, controlled by elite capitalists forever seeking surplus wealth, grows richer at the expense of a progressively impoverished peripheral population. As conventionally formulated, those in the periphery participate in this economic system, however unfair it may be, because the absolute power of the core precludes all other options. In the southern Appalachians, the Cherokees did become progressively involved in the fur trade, despite the fact that participation in it was destroying their local environment and culture.

Illustrative and provocative as the core/periphery theories are, they alone do not tell how or why cultures or, for that matter, environments change over time. Market incorporation of the periphery is seldom a universal process affecting all social groups or locales equally. Human agency very often leaves room for individuals or even entire communities to maneuver within or around the world economic system. Ideology, ethnicity, as well as the physical environment can, over time, restrict the ability of the core to extract resources from peripheral areas.[8]

Mississippians, for example, chose peaches over other Spanish cultigens, partly because of the trees' prolific fruit-bearing qualities and partly because of their resemblance to native plum trees. At the same time, because of a cultural prejudice against European livestock, the Cherokees did not raise hogs for more than a century after initial contact with the animals. European settlers, themselves from vastly different regions of the core metropolis, brought a range of subsistence practices to the region, none of which fully replaced indigenous agriculture practices. Some core subsistence activities, such as flax growing, did persist well into the nineteenth century, but other Old World practices, such as mud and thatch building construction, were quickly abandoned. During the antebellum era, many mountain farmers resisted slaveholding and single-crop production, participating in the market economy that controlled the deeper South only as they thought necessary.[9]

As important as core/periphery models are for illuminating the role that economic forces play in shaping social life, another conceptual framework is needed to more fully explain the process of environmental and cultural change in southern Appalachia. One theory gaining popularity among contemporary scholars of culture change is syncretism. Proponents of cultural syncretism argue that when peoples, cultures, and economic systems interact, a by-product of their interaction is completely new cultural forms.[10] These theorists suggest that over time, no single culture group, including imperial powers, gains absolute hegemony or avoids absorbing aspects of the other. The armies of Hernando de Soto and Juan Pardo survived excursions into the southern Appalachian backcountry by eating Indian corn, a New World crop that became the agricultural mainstay of the Iberian peninsula. The Cherokees eventually adopted the practice of cattle raising, and the white Europeans borrowed a great number of subsistence techniques from the Cherokees. Corn, squashes, beans, and melons became popular among white settlers, as did many Cherokee food preservation methods. Cherokee women, on the other hand, were soon milking dairy cows, utilizing European herbs, and spinning and weaving European cloth. Unlike simple acculturation, cultural syncretism suggests that all culture groups, not just subordinate ones, share in the process of cultural change.

This is certainly not to suggest that political and economic forces did not influence the cultural development of the region. Obviously, those in power helped determine which cultural traits would persist on the frontier. In some instances, the success of a group did have less to do with adaptive superiority than with the group's sheer economic and military might. In the eighteenth century, both British and American forces drove the Cherokees into submission by violent acts of warfare and destruction. Unable to adequately defend themselves against these powerful militias, the Cherokees had little choice but to adapt their culture to the changing political and economic environment.

Despite devastating military defeats, the Cherokees did, however, retain some agency in governing their own affairs. For the Cherokees, cultural change involved both pro- and reactive responses to outside forces. In the early 1760s, for example, the Cherokees became political allies of the French and by doing so partially directed the course of world trade. Certain Cherokee factions always resented the European presence in the region, including Chief Dragging Canoe, who fought to the death to save his native homelands from white encroachment. Cherokee women, who were devoted agriculturalists, basket makers, and weavers of native fabrics, maintained many of their cultural traditions until well into the twentieth century. At the same time, the southern Appalachians were hardly a region of "cultural refuge," to use the language of social theorist Gonzalo Aguirre-Beltran.[11] They were, more accurately, a cultural "middle ground," a place between the "historical foreground of European invasion and occupation and the background of Indian defeat and retreat."[12]

Clearly, syncretism offers many conceptual advantages over conventional theories of cultural acculturation. It should be noted, however, that proponents of cultural syncretism do not necessarily see the natural environment as a major component of cultural change. Advocates of cultural syncretism generally focus attention almost entirely on social relationships: the cultural dynamics between two or more groups. Yet, as this study demonstrates, the natural environment often remains the fulcrum upon which cultural identity rests. As powerful as they may be, members of imperial or colonizing groups almost always find themselves strangers in a strange land. Having little knowledge of their new surroundings, they rely heavily on the ecological knowledge of indigenous peoples, in turn changing the nature of the relationship between the two groups. Ecological forces are therefore critical to the culture change equation. In the southern mountains, culture did not arise in a social vacuum, it was the product of both human and natural history.

If we assume that a reciprocal relationship exists between social groups and their surrounding environments, then culture must always have an ecological component. In the long view, southern Appalachian subsistence culture can thus be seen as the heterogeneous blending of many ethnic practices, a cultural matrix that was influenced to an important degree by the ecological specificity of the mountain environment.

By studying the environmental and cultural history of the southern Appalachians, it is possible to see, perhaps for the first time, the full impact of human settlement on the mountain landscape. It also becomes clear that ecological forces in the region retained considerable control over the course of human action. Regardless of the historical epoch in question, human beings who have called the southern Appalachians home have been greatly aware of both the possibilities and limitations imposed on them by this lofty and foreboding landscape. In the 1930s, when the chestnut blight decimated the chestnut tree, the residents of the region lost not only a major wood source for housing and fencing but an important food source for themselves and their livestock. Even today, the southern mountains continue to supply the region with timber for homes, wells for drinking water, trails and rivers for recreation, and game and fish for sportsmen.

Did the southern Appalachians, over the four centuries covered in this volume, suffer more from the hands of a single group? Clearly, yes. Before European settlement, the mountain landscape was perceived less as a resource to be consumed than as a living matrix for sustaining individual and community life. Traditionally, the Mississippians and the Cherokees did not consider land a commodity that could be bought, sold, or permanently altered. As Douglas Hurt has described it, Native American groups such as the Cherokees believed that uncultivated land was owned by the community, while the individual "created a control or use claim by cultivating a specific field or plot of land." The practice of communal property rights in the southern Appalachians not only helped maintain a relatively egalitarian social order, it also helped preserve the overall ecological integrity of the mountain environment.[13]

European expansion in the southern mountains, on the other hand, was enormously shortsighted. After 1750, the use of the local environment became increasingly directed by profit, rather than purely subsistence, motives. Absentee ownership became widespread in the mountains, and many farmers were landless for much of their lives. Nonetheless, most mountains settlers, well into the nineteenth century, acted upon their belief that the surrounding upland forest was a commons to be shared. Those elite mountain residents who adopted the fundamental principles of agrarian capitalism did more damage to the mountain landscape, indiscriminately draining swamps, harvesting timber, and growing successive crops on worn-out soils.

In the twentieth century, the building of dams by the federal government and private industry altered miles of southern Appalachian rivers and streams, permanently destroying biotic and human communities. The iron ore and timber industries, both capitalist-driven enterprises, also did irreparable damage to the mountain ecosystem, leveling thousands of acres of first- and second-growth forests. Industrial logging not only caused widespread erosion and flooding in the region, it also created major changes in the species composition of mountain ecosystems. Large areas of the southern Appalachians changed as much in the first half of the twentieth century as they had in the previous three centuries. The rate and scale of environmental degradation, as this study demonstrates, increased almost exponentially with the advent of commercial logging during the late nineteenth and early twentieth centuries.

While the southern mountains have shown great resiliency and have recovered to a certain degree from past abuses, the forest of the late twentieth century hardly resembles the forest of the sixteenth century. Presently there are only 1.5 million acres of old-growth and potential old-growth forests across the entire southern Appalachians, less than 3 percent of the entire forest. And of these trees only an extremely small portion would be considered virgin, that is, forests demonstrating no visible effects of past human presence. The Lilley Cornett Woods in eastern Kentucky is one of the best examples of an old-growth or climax mesophytic forest in the southern mountains—individual trees there are more than five hundred years old. Another remaining ancient stand of timber is the Joyce Kilmer Memorial Forest in western North Carolina, where some yellow poplars stretch 150 feet into the air and exceed diameters of 8 feet or more. In the forests of sixteenth-century southern Appalachia, stands of timber such as those found in the Lilley Cornett Woods and Joyce Kilmer Memorial Forest would be the rule rather than the very rare exception, another important indication of the vast changes that have occurred in the forests of the mountain region.

Apologists for the timber industry, among them environmental historians, wrongly assume that simply because there are numerous trees in the mountains today, the southern Appalachian forest is relatively normal and healthy. Tragically, such writers are less inclined to denounce the large-scale disturbance of commercial logging as ecologically destructive, arguing instead that mountain ecosystems have been damaged as much by precapitalist economic systems as capitalist ones. Many also argue that because some forests have recovered from centuries of logging, timber cutting can continue at present rates without irreversible damage to mountain ecosystems. As early as 1950, ecologist Lucy Braun saw the fallacy of such arguments, stating that the extensive clear-cutting of mountain forests contributes not only to the increased dryness of local soils but also to more rapid water runoff and soil erosion. In other words, when large areas are removed of all standing trees, the remaining soil is either washed away or becomes xeric, losing its ability to soak up life-sustaining moisture. When this happens, the remaining soil base is no longer able to grow trees in mature climax associations, and so the forest never fully returns to its original biological state.[14]

In the southern Appalachians, the current widespread clear-cutting of timber for paper and pulp production could, in a few short years, irreversibly destroy one of the most ecologically diverse forests on the planet. The proliferation of chip mills in the southern mountains—there are presently more than 140 across the entire Southeast—is causing unprecedented forest destruction in the southern Appalachians, in some communities devouring more than a hundred truckloads of trees per day. Air pollution, acid rain, and ozone damage are also killing thousands of acres of trees in the region, particularly at elevations higher than 4,000 feet, where acid deposition and ozone levels are at their greatest. On the Cumberland Plateau, mountaintop removal, a method of strip-mining for coal that flattens the tops of entire mountains, threatens to destroy hundreds of thousands of acres of native southern Appalachian forests. One report found that in many places in southern West Virginia, one fourth of all surrounding mountaintops have already been leveled by these massive strip-mining operations.[15]

The death of southern Appalachia's remaining native forests, if and when it does occur, will also spell the end of traditional mountain culture. In the past, when humans and the environment came together in the southern mountains, they influenced each other. Nature was never entirely opposed to social life, and mountain culture has always exhibited ecological aspects. For this reason, environmental and cultural preservation in the southern Appalachians are closely intertwined. Mountain native Zell Miller, in a statement written during his tenure as governor of Georgia, underscored the connection between the preservation of mountain culture and the mountain forests upon which it has, for centuries, been so dependent. "Growing up, I experienced a way of life created by the forests of Appalachia," wrote Miller. "I believe that the future of Appalachia is inexorably tied to forests. How the story of the region ends depends simply and surely upon whether the trees of Appalachia are saved." [16]

NOTES

Preface and Acknowledgments

1. A preliminary attempt at an environmental history of southern Appalachia appeared in the traveling museum exhibit "The Great Forest: An Appalachian Story" and the accompanying thirty-page booklet by that same name. The authors of the four essays in *The Great Forest* volume (edited by Buxton and Crutchfield) present a chronological outline of environmental change in the southern Appalachians, from prehistory to the present, but their treatment for each period is very brief and exploratory. Cowdrey's earlier and much more general survey, *This Land, This South,* documents environmental changes in the larger southern landscape but lacks a specific treatment of Appalachia. By contrast, *Where There Are Mountains* provides a more detailed account of environmental and cultural change, with particular emphasis on the evolution of land-use techniques and subsistence strategies.

2. Jordan and Kaups, *Backwoods Frontier,* 89, fig. 4.3. Data are drawn from the U.S. Census.

3. See, for example, Pudup, Billings, and Waller, eds., *Appalachia in the Making;* and Dunaway, *The First American Frontier.*

4. In 1920 approximately 98 percent of coal produced in America came from deep mines. In 1950 deep mining still accounted for 76 percent of all production in the United States. The incredible degree of ecological change brought on by the strip-mining of the mountains warrants an entire volume and is therefore beyond the scope of the present study. See President's Commission on Coal, *Coal Data Book,* 1–10.

5. Silver's analysis of the South Atlantic forests stops at 1800. His book focuses primarily on the ecological and cultural history of the forests of the southern Piedmont and Atlantic Coast regions of Georgia, South Carolina, North Carolina, and Virginia.

1. Apalatchi: Naming the Mountains

1. Walls, "On the Naming of Appalachia," 58. See also Drake, "Appalachian America," 6; Raitz and Ulack, *Appalachia, a Regional Geography,* 11; Hann, *Apalachee,* 160–80, 227–36.

2. Le Moyne quoted in Cumming, Skelton, and Quinn, *The Discovery of North America,* 187.

3. Cumming, *The Southeast in Early Maps,* 2.

4. Quote from ibid., 10. See also Walls, "On the Naming of Appalachia," 56–58; Hann, *Apalachee,* 5.

5. Quoted in Kephart, "Report," 1, 3.

6. Adair, "A Map of the American Indians Adjoining to the Mississippi, West and East Florida, Georgia, South and North Carolina, Virginia, etc.," in Williams, ed., *Adair's History,* frontispiece.

7. Ibid., 239–40; Kephart, "Report," 1; Van Doren, ed., *The Travels of William Bartram,* 60. The Michaux brothers are quoted in Thwaites, ed., *Travels West,* 48, 147, 187, passim.

8. Quoted in Kephart, "Report," 2.

9. Featherstonhaugh, *Excursion through the Slave States,* 1: 131. However one may feel about the descriptive validity of travel accounts, they were the first to give visual shape and form to the mountain landscape. Prior to that time, the southern Appalachians were terra incognita to most Americans and Europeans.

10. Zeigler, *The Heart of the Alleghenies.*

11. Walls, "On the Naming of Appalachia," 66; Guyot, "On the Appalachian Mountain System," 157–87.

12. Muir, *A Thousand Mile Walk,* 17–46; Kephart, *Our Southern Highlanders,* 26.

13. Powell, *Physiographic Regions.*

14. One of the first of these maps was drafted by William G. Frost, the former president of Berea College. In 1894 Frost identified 194 counties in Maryland, West Virginia, Virginia, Kentucky, Tennessee, North Carolina, South Carolina, Georgia, and Alabama as what he called "the Mountain Region of the South." See also Frost, "Our Contemporary Ancestors," 311.

15. Harney quoted in Shapiro, *Appalachia on Our Mind,* 3; Shapiro, "America and the Idea of America," 43.

16. Campbell, *The Southern Highlander,* 11–12.

17. Ford, ed., *The Southern Appalachian Region,* 3–4.

18. Ergood, "Toward a Definition of Appalachia," 34. See also Salstrom, *Appalachia's Path to Dependency.*

19. Ulack and Raitz, "Perceptions of Appalachia," 742, 743, 744; Ulack and Raitz, "Appalachia," 45.

20. Southern Appalachian Man and the Biosphere Cooperative, *The Southern Appalachian Assessment,* report 1, 1. Another recent attempt at defining Appalachia is found in Salstrom, *Appalachia's Path to Dependency,* an exploration of economic and social underdevelopment in the region. Salstrom divides Appalachia into three chronological subdivisions, "Old," "Intermediate," and "New," stating that "the pace and geographic pattern of settlement are . . . crucial in understanding the history of Appalachia." While this statement is certainly true and supported by his own research, Salstrom's definition could have been improved by a closer adherence to geographic landforms rather than state lines. See the frontispiece.

21. Raitz and Ulack, *Appalachia, a Regional Geography,* 18, 50; Works Project Administration, *Tennessee,* 507; Jillson, "Geology," 12.

2. Mississippia: Native Appalachia

1. La Florida is the term used by the Spanish to refer to the entire southeastern United States, which includes the area De Soto and his men explored in the mountains of North Carolina, Tennessee, and Georgia.
2. Robertson, ed., *True Relation,* 2: 311.
3. Elliot, *Imperial Spain,* 10–13, passim.
4. Robertson, ed., *True Relation,* 2: 100; Hudson, "The Hernando de Soto Expedition," 84; Duncan, *Hernando de Soto,* 345; Hudson, *Knights of Spain,* 190.
5. Quotation in Nabokov, *Native American Architecture,* 93–94.
6. Reynolds counted as many as sixty "reedy" or "caney" place-names in Georgia, West Virginia, Tennessee, and North Carolina. About half of those "caney places," he reported, were in the state of North Carolina (*The Southern Appalachian Region,* 2: 67–68).
7. Brown, "Bogs of East Tennessee," E1; Delcourt and Delcourt, "Late-Quaternary Paleoecology," 25–30; Cole, *Tales from a Country Ledger,* 101–2.
8. Robertson, ed., *True Relation,* 2: 103; Clayton, Knight, and Moore, eds., *The De Soto Chronicles,* 1: 78; Duncan, *Hernando de Soto,* 345–51.
9. Van Doren, ed., *The Travels of William Bartram,* 57; Hatley, "Cherokee Women Farmers," 290 n. 16.
10. Robertson, ed., *True Relation,* 2: 106; Hudson, "The Hernando de Soto Expedition," 84; Hudson, *Knights of Spain,* 199–205.
11. Robertson, ed., *True Relation,* 2: 104–5.
12. Ibid., 104, 116.
13. Odum, *Fundamentals of Ecology,* 18; Smith, "Variation in Mississippian Settlement Patterns," 480–88; Hudson, *The Juan Pardo Expeditions,* 53–59; Lewis and Kneberg, *Tribes that Slumber,* 80–89; Stuart, "Etowah," 56–66.
14. Robertson, ed., *True Relation,* 2: 108.
15. Arnow, *Flowering of the Cumberland,* 297; Imlay, *A Topographical Description,* 41 n.
16. "In the meadows," wrote Imlay, "grew wild-rye, buffalo grass, and pea vine" (*A Topographical Description,* 41 n.).
17. Firestone, *Bubbling Waters,* 79–80.
18. Drooker, *The View from Madisonville,* 47–48; Henderson, ed., *Fort Ancient Cultural Dynamics,* 2.
19. Robertson, ed., *True Relation,* 2: 116–17. A detailed map of De Soto's journey through northern Georgia is found in McCain et al., "Vision of Conquest," 83; see also Hudson, *Knights of Spain,* 214–15.
20. Fowler, *Cahokia,* 25; Hudson, *The Southeastern Indians,* 77; Korp, *The Sacred Geography,* 4, 27–28; Milner, "The Late Prehistoric Cahokia Cultural System," 1–43.
21. Smith, "Research on the Origins," 1–7; R. P. S Davis Jr., "Explaining Mississippian Origins," 175–95; Hudson, *The Juan Pardo Expeditions,* 52–60.

22. Helkamp, "Biosocial Organization," 158; Hudson, *Knights of Spain,* 11–15; Smith and Hally, "Chiefly Behavior," 99–109.

23. Kroeber, *Cultural and Natural Areas,* 95.

24. Henderson, ed., *Fort Ancient Cultural Dynamics,* 1–3.

25. See also Hudson, *The Juan Pardo Expeditions,* 52–73; Hally, "The Chiefdom of Coosa," 227–29; Hally and Langford, *Mississippi Period Archaeology,* passim; Donald E. Davis, "Before Albion's Seed," 59, 63 n. 2. Only the Fort Ancient people appear to have evolved relatively independently of larger Mississippian influences. See Henderson and Turnbow, "Previous Fort Ancient Chronologies," 9–23.

26. Quote from Korp, *The Sacred Geography,* 26. See also Hudson, *The Juan Pardo Expeditions,* 55; DePratter, *Late Prehistoric and Early Historic Chiefdoms,* 57–64; Widmer, "The Structure of Southeastern Chiefdoms," 147.

27. Hudson, *Knights of Spain,* 211.

28. Robertson, ed., *True Relation,* 2: 52. See also Hudson, *The Juan Pardo Expeditions,* 110; Nabokov, *Native American Architecture,* 94.

29. Quotation in Lefler, ed., *A New Voyage,* 23–24; Hudson, *The Juan Pardo Expeditions,* 110.

30. Quote in Robertson, ed., *True Relation,* 2: 52; see also Hudson, *The Juan Pardo Expeditions,* 54, 110; Nabokov, *Native American Architecture,* 94; DePratter, *Late Prehistoric and Early Historic Chiefdoms,* 105–19.

31. Hudson, *The Juan Pardo Expeditions,* 60.

32. Earle, "Chiefdoms," 289; Service, *Origins of the State,* 15–16; DePratter, *Late Prehistoric and Early Historic Chiefdoms,* 122–32; Widmer, "The Structure of Southeastern Chiefdoms," 146.

33. Swanton, *Social Organization,* 443. See also Williams, ed., *Adair's History,* 436.

34. John Smith, in sixteenth-century Virginia, also saw women and children hilling soil around the roots of corn "when the corne is growne midle high." Quotation in Arber, ed., *Travels and Works,* 2: 952; see also Smith, "Variation in Mississippian Settlement Patterns," 492; Williams, ed., *Adair's History,* 438. This could well be the first North American reference to scarecrows.

35. Williams, ed., *Adair's History,* 438; Hatley, "Cherokee Women Farmers," 40–41.

36. Cridlebaugh, "American Indian and Euro-American Impact," 46–47. Interestingly, maygrass is absent from Fort Ancient archaeological excavation sites. By the time the Spanish reached the Southeast, it appears that domesticated varieties of sumpweed were already extinct and that it existed only in its wild state. For the history of goosefoot cultivation in the Southeast, see Smith, "The Role of *Chenopodium,*" 51–72.

37. According to Charles Hudson, it took 100 pounds of hickory nuts to produce 1 gallon of oil (*The Southeastern Indians,* 301).

38. Davis and Stotik, "Feist or Fiction," 193–202.

39. Quote from Robertson, ed., *True Relation,* 2: 100. See also Father Membré, *Narrative of La Salle's Voyage down the Mississippi,* in French, ed., *Historical Collections of Louisiana,* 4: 169.

40. Nabhan, *Enduring Seeds,* 164; Schorger, *The Wild Turkey,* 60.

41. Broida, "Maize in Kentucky Fort Ancient Diets," 76–78.

42. Carrier, *The Beginnings of Agriculture,* 45–46; Baden, "A Dynamic Model," 76.

43. Baden, "A Dynamic Model," 94; Hally, "The Chiefdom of Coosa," 231; Ethridge interview.

44. Russell, "Indian-Set Fires," 80–86; quote in Cridlebaugh, "American Indian and Euro-American Impact," 124.

45. Morton quotation in Force, ed., *Tracts and Other Papers,* 37. See also Russell, "Indian-Set Fires," 82; Cridlebaugh, "American Indian and Euro-American Impact," 123; van der Donck, "A Description," 20–21.

46. Steiner and de Schweinitz quoted in Williams, ed., *Early Travels,* 478. The date for the observation was 13 November 1799. See also Williams, ed., *Adair's History,* 435. For Cherokee burning practices, see Mooney, "Myths," 317, 322, 470; Lanman, *Letters,* 195; Gersmehl, "A Geographic Approach," 77–79, 82.

47. Sondley, *Asheville and Buncombe County,* 23; DeVivo, "Indian Use of Fire," 308.

48. Cridlebaugh, "American Indian and Euro-American Impact," 122–25; Silver, *A New Face on the Countryside,* 59–64. See also Southern Appalachian Man and the Biosphere Cooperative, *The Southern Appalachian Assessment,* 95.

49. This number excludes the hundreds of excavated post holes that have no known function. The post dimensions apply specifically to structures excavated at Hiawassee Island but should apply to most dwellings found throughout the southern Appalachian region. Lewis and Kneberg, *Tribes that Slumber,* 83; Cridlebaugh, "American Indian and Euro-American Impact," 105.

50. In almost all cases, the mention of pine groves or forests occurs when the group is approaching or very near a Mississippian village.

51. Lederer quotation in Murie, *Elk of North America,* 39–40. To my knowledge no one has critically discussed the possible role that elk herds played in the formation of upland balds. Although deer are not generally reported at higher elevations, elk are very fond of high altitude habitats and actually seek them out.

52. "Fish of Tennessee," 14; McClane, *McClane's Field Guide,* 189–90; Henderson, "Physical Setting," in Henderson, ed., *Fort Ancient Cultural Dynamics,* 26. Another interesting species affected by dam construction is the quillback, a native carpsucker that browses for plant and animal organisms along rocky river bottoms.

53. Coxe, *A Description,* 82–83.

54. When the chieftainess of Cofitachequi escaped from De Soto in the mountains of western North Carolina, she carried with her a box of canes filled with these precious pearls. Twenty-five years later, Juan Pardo was also given gifts of pearls by the Mississippians of eastern Tennessee, largely to show their deference to the Spanish governor. Shipp, *The History,* 372; Kunz and Stevenson, *The Book of the Pearl,* 254–55; Hudson, *The Juan Pardo Expeditions,* 156–57, 190; Robertson, ed., *True Relation,* 2: 101.

3. Apalachee: Spanish Appalachia

1. Smith, "Indian Response"; Hudson et al., "The Tristan de Luna Expedition," 40–42; Hudson, *The Juan Pardo Expeditions,* 135–39; Smith, *Archaeology,* 23–53; Waselkov, "Seventeenth-Century Trade," 120–27; Hudson, *Knights of Spain,* 31–61, 72–85, 185–219.

2. Worth, "Late Spanish Military Expeditions," in Hudson and Tesser, eds., *The Forgotten Centuries*, 104–5, 108, 110–11.

3. Bennett, *Laudonniere and Fort Caroline*, 70, 120, 135; Bushnell, *The King's Coffer*, 9.

4. Hann, "Demographic Patterns," 382; Hudson, *The Juan Pardo Expeditions*, 144–56; Waselkov, "Seventeenth-Century Trade," 117; Hann, *Apalachee*, 24–69.

5. Hann, *Apalachee*, 243; Waselkov, "Seventeenth-Century Trade," 118.

6. Waselkov, "Seventeenth-Century Trade," 117–20; Hudson, *The Juan Pardo Expeditions*, 153–56; Hann, *Apalachee*, 147–48.

7. Arthur quoted in Alvord and Bidgood, *The First Explorations*, 213, 219–20. See also Briceland, *Westward from Virginia*, 163.

8. Weber, *The Taos Trappers*, 12–31; Gray, *History of Agriculture*, 1: 109; Waselkov, "Seventeenth-Century Trade," 11; letters from Governor Juan Marquez Cabrera, in Secretaría de Estado; Wilson, "Multicultural Mayhem," 21.

9. Waselkov, "Seventeenth-Century Trade," 129.

10. Crane, *The Southern Frontier*, 17.

11. Swanton, "The Kaskinamo Indians," 406–7; Cumming, *The Southeast in Early Maps*, plates 45, 48, 59.

12. Hann, *Apalachee*, 9.

13. Hudson, *The Juan Pardo Expeditions*, 153. See also Worth, "Late Military Expeditions," 111–16.

14. Hann, *Apalachee*, 16, 182–83.

15. Kennedy, *The Melungeons*, 27; Schroeder, "First Union," 36–41.

16. See, for example, Smith, *Archaeology*, 55. See also Hudson, "An Unknown South," passim.

17. Smith, *Archaeology*, 55–60; Hudson, *Southeastern Indians*, 103–10. For an excellent discussion of the general effects of Old World diseases in the Americas, see Crosby, *The Columbian Exchange*, 35–63.

18. Robertson, ed., *True Relation*, 2: 99–100.

19. Quoted in Crosby, *The Columbian Exchange*, 37.

20. Robertson, ed., *True Relation*, 2: 101, 112; Smith, "Aboriginal Depopulation," in Hudson and Tesser, eds., *The Forgotten Centuries*, 259.

21. Dobyns, *Their Number Become Thinned*, 8–32; Smith, *Archaeology*, 55–58; Milner, "Epidemic Disease," 46; J. Leitch Wright Jr., *The Only Land They Knew*, 23–25; Smith, "Aboriginal Depopulation," 257–75; Cowdrey, *This Land, This South*, 41–42. Lawson quoted in Lefler, ed., *A New Voyage*, 232.

22. Smith, *Archaeology*, 101–2, 108–12; Smith, "Indian Response," 144–45.

23. Hudson et al., "The Tristan de Luna Expedition," 41–42.

24. Dickens, "Mississippian Settlement Patterns," 134–35.

25. Purrington, "The Status and Future," 48.

26. Smith, "Indian Response," 143–44; DePratter, *Late Prehistoric and Early Historic Chiefdoms*, 116–19. For the origin and evolution of temple mounds, see Rudolph, "Earthlodges and Platform Mounds," 33–37.

27. Quoted in Van Doren, ed., *The Travels of William Bartram*, 297. Ethnologist James Mooney, around 1900, also recorded what appears to be a fairly accurate description of

the ancient mound-building practice. This would suggest that at least some of the Cherokee shamans knew of the former tradition. See Mooney, "Myths," 395–96.

28. Hudson, *Knights of Spain*, 193–96.

29. Roy S. Dickens, a major authority on Cherokee prehistory, places the Qualla transformation at around 1500. If he is correct, this would mean that cultural evolution was occurring prior to Spanish contact. Charles Hudson says that the cultural transformation may have begun "a half century or so later." Even if Dickens's estimation is accurate, the Spanish were responsible for accelerating culture change. Dickens, "Mississippian Settlement Patterns," 119; Hudson, *The Juan Pardo Expeditions*, 86; see also Dickens, *Cherokee Prehistory*, 13–14, 206, 210.

30. For Cherokee migrations, see Hudson, *The Juan Pardo Expeditions*, 186, fig. 43. For historical accounts of the Overhill Cherokee, see Williams, ed., *Early Travels*, 115–43, 177–200; Mooney, "Myths," 29–65. For Overhill ethnohistory and archaeology, see Schroedl and Russ, "An Introduction," 1–42.

31. Smith, *Archaeology*, 78, 83–84. For more on Dallas culture, based largely on archaeological evidence, see Lewis and Kneberg, *Tribes that Slumber*, 91–123; Sabel, "Trade and Development," 14–29.

32. The Creeks, well into the eighteenth century, continued to lay out their towns according to a pattern reminiscent of the Mississippian plan. At the center of the Creek village was a plaza upon which was situated a public townhouse. Surrounding this central commons were the houses of the townspeople. For the Creek town plan, see Bartram, "Observations," 55; Hudson, *Southeastern Indians*, 213–14. On the formation of the Creek Confederacy, see especially Smith, *Archaeology*, 129–42.

33. Waselkov, "Seventeenth-Century Trade," 120–21; Smith, *Archaeology*, 41–43; Arthur quoted in Alvord and Bidgood, *First Explorations*, 214. For a much more complete summary of Fort Ancient culture change during the sixteenth and seventeenth centuries, see Drooker, *The View from Madisonville*, 39–62.

34. Steward and Faron, *Native Peoples of South America*, 176; Smith, *Archaeology*, 128.

35. Theodorson and Theodorson, *A Modern Dictionary of Sociology*, 3. The classic formulation of acculturation is "those phenomena which result when groups of individuals having different cultures come into continuous first hand contact" (Redfield, Linton, and Herskovits, "Memorandum," 149). Alfred Kroeber saw acculturation as "those changes produced in a culture by the influence of another which result in an increased similarity of the two" (quoted in Foster, *Culture and Conquest*, 7). Acculturation as defined by Redfield, Kroeber, and others certainly occurred in the region during the sixteenth century, but the influence of the Spanish on the Mississippians was much more subtractive than additive. For an excellent discussion of the deculturation process in the interior Southeast, see Smith, *Archaeology*, 5–10, 113–28.

36. Hann, *Apalachee*, 239. For the importance of the slave trade in New World crop introductions, see Wagner, "The Introduction," 112–23.

37. Wing, "Evidences," 72–79; Crosby, *The Columbian Exchange*, 64–74; Carrier, *The Beginnings of Agriculture*, 41; Sauer, *Sixteenth Century North America*, 286–88; Hobhouse, *Seeds of Change*, 192–232; Gray, *History of Agriculture*, 1: 9–13.

38. Williams, "The Joe-Bell Site," 79; Hann, *Apalachee,* 133; Smith, *Archaeology,* 125; Sauer, *Seventeenth Century North America,* 242.

39. Hann, *Apalachee,* 133; Hudson, *Southeastern Indians,* 295; Merrell, *The Indians' New World,* 16; Gray, *History of Agriculture,* 1: 5.

40. Sheldon, "Introduction of the Peach"; Smith, *Archaeology,* 125; Williams, "The Joe-Bell Site," 425–27.

41. Williams, "The Joe-Bell Site," 425–27, 434; Hann, *Apalachee,* 133.

42. Smith, "Indian Response," 148–49.

43. Hatley, "Cherokee Women Farmers," 39; Robertson, ed., *True Relation,* 2: 103, 311. Bartram quoted in Van Doren, ed., *The Travels of William Bartram,* 291. See also Hudson, ed., *Black Drink,* passim. The Yaupon tree (*Ilex vomitoria*) was used extensively by nearly all southeastern tribes from the early historic period on.

44. Hamel and Chiltoskey, *Cherokee Plants,* 47–48; Moerman, *Medicinal Plants,* 373.

45. Quoted in Williams, ed., *Early Travels,* 464.

46. Georgia Department of Natural Resources, "The Vann House," n.d. For peach growing in late-eighteenth-century Kentucky, see, for example, Thwaites, ed., *Travels West,* 242; Bonner, *History of Georgia Agriculture,* 150–51.

47. Hufford, "Weathering the Storm," 148, 150.

48. In 1492 Christopher Columbus found Indians growing sweet potatoes in Cuba, where he saw "a great deal of tilled land some sowed with these roots." Cultural geographer Carl O. Sauer claimed that the sweet potato was the second most important crop of the Caribbean. In speaking of its importance to the natives, Columbus went so far as to say that the root was "their life" (Sauer, *The Early Spanish Main,* 54). See also Carrier, *Beginnings of Agriculture in America,* 60–63; Herndon, "Indian Agriculture," 295–96.

49. Hamilton, "What the New World Gave the Old," 2: 856; Wagner, "The Introduction," 113–14; Taylor, *Eating, Drinking, and Visiting,* 38.

50. Gray, *History of Agriculture,* 1: 4. See also Herndon, "Indian Agriculture," 287–88.

51. Brett Riggs, personal communication. On the general influence of British traders on Cherokee subsistence patterns, see Williams, ed., *Adair's History,* 442–47; Mooney, "Myths," 213–14; Bogan, LaValley, and Schroedl, "Faunal Remains," 489–92. For sweet potato cultivation during the Colonial era, see Bonner, *A History of Georgia Agriculture,* 21.

52. Brett Riggs, personal conversation, 10 March 1993. See also Mooney, "Myths," 50–51.

53. Mooney, "Myths," 214.

54. Hatley, "Cherokee Women Farmers," 41.

55. Fearing Burr Jr., *The Field and Garden Vegetables,* 91–94; Hilliard, *Hog Meat and Hoe Cake,* 50, 175; Dick, *Dixie Frontier,* 290–91; Romans, *A Concise Natural History,* 86; Taylor, *Eating, Drinking, and Visiting,* 37–38.

56. Carrier, *Beginnings of Agriculture,* 247; Wagner, "The Introduction," 114; Waselkov, "Seventeenth-Century Trade," 127.

57. Du Pratz, *The History of Louisiana,* 204; Surrey, *The Commerce of Louisiana,* 271, 379; Carrier, *Beginnings of Agriculture,* 231.

58. Quoted in Carrier, *The Beginnings of Agriculture,* 250.

59. Waselkov, "Seventeenth-Century Trade," 127; Russ and Chapman, *Archaeological Investigations*, 98.
60. Of course, new bean varieties could have entered the region as the result of direct trade with other Indians outside the area. For the introduction and dispersal of beans in North America, see Carrier, *Beginnings of Agriculture*, 49, 247; Crosby, *The Columbian Exchange*, 172; Heiser, *Seed to Civilization*, 125–26; Nabhan, *Enduring Seeds*, xviii–xxiii.
61. Gray, *History of Agriculture*, 1: 12; Sauer, *Seventeenth Century North America*, 241.
62. In 1748 Peter Kalm noted that "the Indians plant great quantities of watermelon at present, but whether they have done it of old is not easily determined, for an old Oneida Indian (of one of the six Iroquois nations) assured me that the Red Man did not know watermelons before the Europeans came into the country and showed them to the Indians." Ribault quoted in Carrier, *Beginnings of Agriculture*, 69, 70–78; White quoted in Gilmore, *Uses of Plants*, 75–77. See also Wagner, "The Introduction," 118; Benson, ed., *The America of 1750*, 2: 515.
63. Cridlebaugh, "American Indian and Euro-American Impact," 104–6.
64. Silver, *A New Face on the Countryside*, 51. John Hann notes that the first reports of buffaloes in northwestern Florida occur in the 1680s, "a decade or so after the destruction of the Apalachee and Timucuan missions" (*Apalachee*, 186).
65. Rostlund, "The Geographic Range," 395–407; Roe, *The North American Buffalo*, 228–56.
66. Quote from Robertson, ed., *True Relation*, 2: 113; Haines, *The Buffalo*, 73–79. Roe also does a good job of debunking the myth that the buffalo of the mountains was a subspecies of bison—the so-called woodland or woods buffalo.
67. Quoted in Van Doren, ed., *The Travels of William Bartram*, 276, 280–83, 288. A few scholars have argued that these open fields were caused by Indians who are said to have burned these areas for agriculture purposes or in order to create game lures. Woodland meadows such as those observed by Bartram and others could not have been created solely by such fires, however. As noted in the previous chapter, the Cherokees did ignite the woods to clear the forest floor of litter in order to gather chestnuts, but this practice probably did not create large treeless areas in the upland forest. Indian burning, if and when it occurred, was largely concentrated in mountain river valleys around village sites.
68. Donelson and English visitor quoted in Roe, *The North American Buffalo*, 237, 234. See also Allen, *The American Bison*, 114; Garretson, *American Bison*, 22–23.
69. Roe, *The North American Buffalo*, 234.
70. Ibid., 245; Allen, *The American Bison*, 117; Haines, *The Buffalo*, 77–78.

4. Kituah: Cherokee Appalachia

1. McLoughlin, *Cherokee Renascence*, 8; Mooney, "Myths," plates II, III; Goodwin, *Cherokees in Transition*, 6–16, 45, fig. 6.1.
2. Thorton, *The Cherokees*, 17; Goodwin, *Cherokees in Transition*, 16–17, 46, 111, table 16; Mooney, "Myths," 11.

3. Gavin Cochrane letter; Finger, *The Eastern Band of the Cherokee*, 3; French and Hornbuckle, eds., *The Cherokee Perspective*, 16.

4. Goodwin, *Cherokees in Transition*, 42, 45, fig. 6; McLoughlin, *Cherokee Renascence*, 9. Another possible reason for the diffcrence in settlement patterns could be the stronger influence of Mississippian culture on the Lower and Middle Towns. The Overhill Towns were newly settled villages and would have been less inclined to retain the older, more centralized settlement clusters.

5. Map Library, Special Collections, Hogkins Library, University of Tennessee, Knoxville; Fernow, *The Ohio Valley in Colonial Days*, 273–75; Goodwin, *Cherokees in Transition*, 108–9. The mean population of the fifty-three towns enumerated in 1721 was 197, but the population of the average Cherokee village was closer to three hundred residents.

6. Williams, ed., *Adair's History*, 437; McLoughlin, *Cherokee Renascence*, 9.

7. Hill, "Weaving History," 115–36; Hill, *Weaving New Worlds*, 35–109.

8. Bogan, LaValley, and Schroedl, "Faunal Remains," 480.

9. Quotation in Martin, *Sacred Revolt*, 20. The quotation is a paraphrase of Mooney, "Myths," 250–51. For other myths involving animals, see ibid., 231, 252, 279.

10. Williams, ed., *Adair's History*, 239; Van Doren, ed., *The Travels of William Bartram*, 60; Logan, *A History of the Upper Country*, 1: 4.

11. On Indian trails in southern Appalachia, see Myer, *Indian Trails of the Southeast*, 1–81, 99–117; Hemperley, *Historic Indian Trails of Georgia*, 1–6, 8–10, 22–24; Norburn, "The Influence of Physiographic Features," 66–69.

12. Alvord and Bidgood, *First Explorations*, 210–26; Hudson, *The Southeastern Indians*, 163; McLoughlin, *Cherokee Renascence*, 16–17; Newman, "Euro-American Artifacts," 415–17.

13. Quoted in Corkran, *Cherokee Frontier*, 14.

14. For the declining influence of Spanish in the Southeast, see Bolton, "Spanish Resistance," 115–30; Coleman, ed., *A History of Georgia*, 9–15; J. Leitch Wright Jr., *The Only Land They Knew*, 102–98.

15. Wilms, "Cherokee Land Use," 2–3; Hatley, *The Dividing Paths*, 8–10, 163–66, 211–15.

16. Rothrock, "Carolina Traders," 6, 17; Williams, ed., *Early Travels*, 123; Williams, *Dawn of Tennessee Valley*, 70, 89; Schroedl and Russ, "An Introduction," 8.

17. Franklin, "Virginia and the Cherokee Indian Trade," 9; Crane, *Southern Frontier*, 155; quotation from a letter dated 1708 in Rothrock, "Carolina Traders," 10; Mooney, "Myths," 32. Mark Catesby noted that as late as 1724, the Indians of the mountains still bred "no tame animals for food" (*The Natural History*, 19).

18. Williams, ed., *Adair's History*, 443. Within the very first decades of contact with the English, Cherokees were hardly slaves to imported goods and most likely did not, says James Merrell, "pursue European commodities once [they] first donned a matchcoat, raised a musket to [their] shoulder, or drew a metal knife to [their] sheath." Prior to the beginning of the eighteenth century, the Cherokees' tools and clothing served them well: the desire for European commodities would have largely been an acquired one, understood only within the social, economic, and environmental transformation that resulted from the fur trade. See Merrell, *The Indians' New World*, 33.

19. For the social and environmental impact of the fur trade in New England, see Merchant, *Ecological Revolutions,* 29–68; Cronon, *Changes in the Land,* 82–107. For the southern Piedmont, see Merrell, *The Indians' New World,* 34–35, 52–56; Silver, *A New Face on the Countryside,* 88–97.

20. In 1755 a single buckskin was worth $2.50, whereas beaver skins brought "four shillings, three pence half penny." Carroll, *Historical Collections,* 2: 237.

21. The original source for these data is the records of William Brown, comptroller and searcher for His Majesty's Customs in the Port of Savannah. Gray, *History of Agriculture,* 1: 102, table 2.

22. Rothrock, "Carolina Traders," 8, 9–10.

23. Goodwin, *Cherokees in Transition,* 97–98; Logan, *A History of the Upper Country,* 241.

24. Logan, *A History of the Upper Country,* 241, 255.

25. Ibid., 384.

26. Franklin, "Virginia and the Cherokee Indian Trade," 13.

27. Ibid., 14; Crane, *Southern Frontier,* 176–77; Hatley, *The Dividing Paths,* 36.

28. Crane, *Southern Frontier,* 112; Gipson, *The British Empire,* 54. According to Carroll, the value of beaver and deerskin exports from Charleston for the year 1747–48 was $1.25 million (*Historical Collections,* 237).

29. Logan, *A History of the Upper Country,* 383–84; Doherty information from Rothrock, "Carolina Traders," 10; Goodwin, *Cherokees in Transition,* 98.

30. Goodwin, *Cherokees in Transition,* 98; Stuart information in Crane, *The Southern Frontier,* 331, table IV; Gipson, *The British Empire,* 54.

31. Logan, *A History of the Upper Country,* 319; Coleman, ed., *A History of Georgia,* 51.

32. Rothrock, "Carolina Traders," 16–17; Goodwin, *Cherokees in Transition,* 99.

33. Williams, ed., *Adair's History,* 444–45; Meriwether, *The Expansion of South Carolina,* 191. For additional reports about the dishonest atrocities of traders, see also Logan, *A History of the Upper Country,* 281–85; Mancall, *Deadly Medicine,* 48, 73, 80, 122.

34. Logan, *A History of the Upper Country,* 151–66; Goodwin, *Cherokees in Transition,* 133–36; Bays, "The Historical Geography of Cattle Herding," 72–78, passim; Williams, ed., *Adair's History,* 241, 436, 445.

35. Crane, *The Southern Frontier,* 328, table I.

36. Goodwin, *Cherokees in Transition,* 95; Logan, *A History of the Upper Country,* 263.

37. Wells, "Castoreum and Steel Traps," 479–80, 482; Wells, "More on Castoreum and Traps," 603; Silver, *A New Face on the Countryside,* 99.

38. Silver, *A New Face on the Countryside,* 99; Logan, *A History of the Upper Country,* 385. The figure of six hundred assumes that each beaver pelt weighed around 5 ounces, a fairly conservative estimate for skins still in the curing process.

39. Gavin Cochrane letter.

40. Logan, *A History of the Upper Country,* 49, 50; Van Doren, ed., *The Travels of William Bartram,* 232; Matthiessen, *Wildlife in America,* 81. Today, thanks to restocking programs, beavers are steadily making a comeback in many parts of southern Appalachia.

41. Merchant, *Ecological Revolutions,* 36–37.

42. Mooney, "Myths," 425; Hamel and Chiltoskey, *Cherokee Plants,* 36; Moerman, *Medicinal Plants,* 322.

43. Silver, *A New Face on the Countryside*, 83–84. On the use of snakeroot as a Cherokee antidote to snakebite, see Williams, ed., *Adair's History*, 247–48, 389.

44. Fries et al., eds., *The Records of the Moravians*, 2: 571; Williams, ed., *Adair's History*, 389.

45. Pinkerton, *Voyages and Travels*, 13: 639–41; Benson, ed., *The America of 1750*, 2: 436–37.

46. Kains, *Ginseng*, 5.

47. Silver, *A New Face on the Countryside*, 83–84, 101; Williams, ed., *Lieutenant Henry Timberlake's Memoirs*, 70–71; Mooney, "Myths," 425; Hill, *Weaving New Worlds*, 60–62.

48. South Carolina, at that time, included portions of North Carolina, Tennessee, and Georgia. Drayton quoted in Meriwether, ed., *The Carolinian Florist*, 109. Apparently, the Cherokees did not limit their trade to the white man, as they also sold the root to Florida natives dwelling near the sea coast, "where [it] never grows spontaneously" (Van Doren, ed., *The Travels of William Bartram*, 267).

49. Of cane and its uses, Adair also wrote that its foliage was "always green, and hearty food for horses and cattle" (Williams, ed., *Adair's History*, 241).

50. Firestone, *Bubbling Waters*, 81. For additional evidence about the importance of cane to the settlement of the Cumberland Plateau, see Arnow, *Seedtime on the Cumberland*, 101, 127, 237, 247, 401; Arnow, *Flowering of the Cumberland*, 239, 214, 241.

51. Firestone, *Bubbling Waters*, 81; Silver, *A New Face on the Countryside*, 180; Fries et al., eds., *The Records of the Moravians*, 2: 564.

52. The swamp rabbit remains a threatened species in southern Appalachia, a good indication of how few canebrakes exist in the region today. Although large populations are still found along the Mississippi River, there are only a handful of counties in northwestern Georgia and eastern Tennessee where one can still find the swamp rabbit.

53. Drayton, *A View of South Carolina*, 62; Silver, *A New Face on the Countryside*, 180.

54. Schneider quoted in Bays, "The Historical Geography of Cattle Herding," 105; Williams, ed., *Early Travels*, 261.

55. Williams, ed., *Early Travels*, 484.

56. Klink and Talman, eds., *The Journal of Major John Norton*, 72, 33–38; Bays, "The Historical Geography of Cattle Herding," 102.

57. Quote in Williams, ed., *Early Travels*, 139–40. See also Bays, "The Historical Geography of Cattle Herding," 75.

58. Williams, ed., *Adair's History*, 242; Goodwin, *Cherokees in Transition*, 135; Gray, *History of Agriculture*, 1: 201–2. For a more detailed analysis of the problems created by cattle herding in Colonial New England, see Cronon, *Changes in the Land*, 129–31. On problems between colonists, Indians, and cattle on the Atlantic Coast, see Silver, *A New Face on the Countryside*, 172, 173, 175–79.

59. Mooney, "Myths," 49.

60. Bays, "The Historical Geography of Cattle Herding," 55; Arnade, "Cattle Raising," 3–11. For the spread of Spanish ranching traditions in the New World, see Bennett and Hoffman, "Ranching in the New World," 90–111.

61. Hann, *Apalachee,* 133, 137; Hann, "Demographic Patterns and Changes," 383; Arnade, "Cattle Raising," 3–5; Waselkov, "Seventeenth-Century Trade," 117.

62. Arnade, "Cattle Raising," 116–23; Bays, "The Historical Geography of Cattle Herding," 58; Bennett and Hoffman, "Ranching in the New World," 93–98.

63. Quoted in Williams, ed., *Early Travels,* 464.

64. Bays, "The Historical Geography of Cattle Herding," 86.

65. Brown, *Old Frontiers,* 153–54; Mooney, "Myths," 48, 204; Bays, "The Historical Geography of Cattle Herding," 104.

66. Hudson, *Knights of Spain,* 76–78; Bennett and Hoffman, "Ranching in the New World," 101–2.

67. Mayer and Brisbin, *Wild Pigs of the United States,* 9; Bennett and Hoffman, "Ranching in the New World," 101–3; Goodwin, *Cherokees in Transition,* 135.

68. Alvord and Bidgood, *First Explorations,* 223; Briceland, *Westward from Virginia,* 167–68. There is documented evidence that in 1651 Virginia Indians were also stealing hogs and killing cattle from coastal settlements. It should also be noted that the feral pig is not to be confused with the Russian wild boar, a twentieth-century introduction to the southern Appalachians.

69. Williams, ed., *Adair's History,* 436.

70. Goodwin, *Cherokees in Transition,* 136; Bays, "The Historical Geography of Cattle Herding," 78. Because they were fed large quantities of chestnuts, pigs raised by the Cherokees were esteemed more than those raised in white settlements. See also Mooney, "Myths," 82; Hill, *Weaving New Worlds,* 85.

71. Quote from Bays, "The Historical Geography of Cattle Herding," 83. See also Goodwin, *Cherokees in Transition,* 141–44.

72. Logan, *A History of the Upper Country,* 25; Van Doren, ed., *The Travels of William Bartram,* 280.

73. Quotation is from Jefferson, *Notes on the State of Virginia,* 72. The effect of the honeybee on native plant associations remains largely unexplored. For reports of the introduction and migration of honeybees in North America, see Carrier, *The Beginnings of Agriculture in America,* 258; Crosby, *Ecological Imperialism,* 187–90.

74. Van Doren, ed., *The Travels of William Bartram,* 330; Hawkins quoted in Mooney, "Myths," 82.

75. Williams, ed., *Lieutenant Henry Timberlake's Memoirs,* 77.

76. McLoughlin, *Cherokee Renascence,* 5.

77. On fishing techniques using cane spears, see Williams, ed., *Lieutenant Henry Timberlake's Memoirs,* 69; Williams, ed., *Adair's History,* 432–34.

78. Hill, "Weaving History," 121.

79. Quoted in de Vorsey, *The Indian Boundary Line,* 102.

80. Goodwin, *Cherokees in Transition,* 147–51; McLoughlin, *Cherokee Renascence,* 33–91, passim.

81. Quote from Witthoft, "Cherokee Indian Use of Potherbs," 250. See also Neely, *Snowbird Cherokees,* 15–35; Brown, "Smoky Mountain Story," 30–36, 42–46.

82. Dykeman and Stokely, *Highland Homeland,* 52–55; quote from Wiggington, ed., *The Fox-*

fire Book, 235. Durwood Dunn found "no evidence that they [Cades Cove mountaineers] ever used the herb in any home remedy or were even cognizant of its reputed properties" (*Cades Cove*, 32). Considering the secrecy surrounding this plant, his finding is not surprising.

83. Williams, ed., *Adair's History*, 139.

84. Witthoft, "Cherokee Indian Use of Potherbs," 251; Hudson, *The Southeastern Indians,* 308.

85. Hamel and Chiltoskey, *Cherokee Plants*, 50; Witthoft, "Cherokee Indian Use of Potherbs," 251; Mooney, "Myths," 425; Moerman, *Medicinal Plants*, 337.

86. Speck, *Gourds of the Southeastern Indians*, 40–41; Hudson, *The Southeastern Indians*, 294–95, 298–99.

87. Williams, ed., *Adair's History*, 447. Granted, this statement does not refer specifically to the Cherokees or rule out the possibility that the first settlers were already familiar with the practice.

88. Chamberlain, "Maple Sugar and the Indians," 381–83; Barbeau, "Maple Sugar," 75–86; Mancall, *Valley of Opportunity*, 195–98.

89. The suburbs of seventeenth-century London were famous for apple cultivation, and as many as two hundred varieties could be collected from a single orchard. On thermal belts, see Chickering, "Thermal Belts," 1: 147; Norburn, "The Influence of the Physiographic Features," 54–56.

90. Bonner, *A History of Georgia Agriculture*, 155.

91. Arnow, *Seedtime on the Cumberland*, 411.

92. Bonner, *A History of Georgia Agriculture*, 156.

93. Ibid., 156–57.

94. Ibid., 157.

95. Fischer, *Albion's Seed*, 640. By analyzing place-names one is able to trace the influence of various culture groups in the settlement of a region. The presence of numerous Cherokee place-names only reinforces the importance of the Cherokees to the development of southern Appalachia.

96. Hatley, *Dividing Paths*, 233; Finger, "Cherokee Accommodation," 27–29. See also data in McLoughlin and Conser, "The Cherokees in Transition," 678–703.

97. Hill, *Weaving New Worlds*, 115.

98. Mooney, "Myths," 214. See also Wilms, "Cherokee Land Use," 23–24.

99. Quoted in Williams, ed., *Early Travels*, 459.

100. Govan and Livingwood, *The Chattanooga Country*, 68. The Cherokee Census of 1809 is found in the Moravian Archives, Winston-Salem, N.C. For the other census and a discussion of both, see *The Cherokee Phoenix*, 18 June 1828; McLoughlin, *Cherokee Renascence*, 294–301, table 7; Wilms, "Cherokee Land Use," 6–9, table 1.

101. Shadburn, *Cherokee Planters in Georgia*, passim. Not all Cherokees fully adopted the white man's system of agriculture and religion. The most conservative Cherokees fled into the Blue Ridge Mountains and held on to many cultural traditions until the twentieth century. A majority, however, saw Anglo-American agriculture, or some variation of it, as their only means of survival.

102. Quote from Mooney, "Myths," 36. See also Williams, ed., *Adair's History*, 244.

103. Quotation from Williams, ed., *Adair's History*, 245. See also McLoughlin, *Cherokee Renascence*, 17–18; Mooney, "Myths," 86–88; Goodwin, *Cherokees in Transition*, 106–7. For a list and description of plants commonly utilized by the Cherokees and other Native Americans, see Moerman, *Medicinal Plants of Native America;* Witthoft, "Cherokee Indian Use of Potherbs," 250–55.

104. Gavin Cochrane letter.

105. Williams, ed., *Lieutenant Henry Timberlake's Memoirs*, 96; Williams, *Dawn of Tennessee Valley*, 235–36; Mooney, "Myths," 41; Ramsey, *Annals of Tennessee*, 54.

106. Quotation in Mooney, "Myths," 43; Brewer and Brewer, *Valley So Wild*, 37–39; Williams, *Dawn of Tennessee Valley*, 225–56; Schroedl and Russ, "An Introduction," 12; Robinson, *The Southern Colonial Frontier*, 220–21.

107. French, "Journal of an Expedition," 283, 285.

108. Corkran, *The Cherokee Frontier*, 225; King, "Powder Horn," 23–40; Goodwin, *Cherokees in Transition*, 105–6.

109. Williams, ed., *Adair's History*, 242; de Vorsey, *The Indian Boundary Line*, 34–40, passim.

110. Roosevelt, *The Winning of the West*, 1: 294–302, passim; Ramsey, *The Annals of Tennessee*, 164–71; French, "Journal of an Expedition," 275–301.

111. Mooney, "Myths," 49, 205; Myer, *Indian Trails of the Southeast*, 39; French, "Journal of an Expedition," 283–89.

112. Quotation in Mooney, "Myths," 52. See also Roosevelt, *Winning of the West*, 1: 296–303; Ramsey, *Annals of Tennessee*, 163–64; Mooney, "Myths," 50–51; Schroedl and Russ, "An Introduction," 13.

113. King, "Long Island of the Holston," 113–27; Brown, *Old Frontiers*, 157–59; Mooney, "Myths," 51.

114. Williams, "Colonel Joseph William's Battalion," 109; Roosevelt, *Winning of the West*, 1: 303–5; Ramsey, *Annals of Tennessee*, 165–70.

115. Van Every, *Ark of Empire*, 254–58; Mooney, "Myths," 63; Hatley, *The Dividing Paths*, 218–28.

116. Myer, *Indian Trails of the Southeast*, 39; Mooney, "Myths," 49, 205.

117. On the creation of "middle landscapes" on the American frontier, see Marx, *The Machine in the Garden*, 130; Kolodny, *The Land before Her*, 53.

5. Southwestern Mountains: Frontier Appalachia

1. Quoted in Williams, *Dawn of Tennessee Valley*, 24; See also Arnow, *Seedtime on the Cumberland*, 110, 185.

2. Kegley, *Kegley's Virginia Frontiers*, 268; Arnow, *Seedtime on the Cumberland*, 179; Hagy, "Castle's Woods," 3; Otto, *The Southern Frontiers*, 51–52; Raitz and Ulack, *Appalachia, a Regional Geography*, 92.

3. De Vorsey, *The Indian Boundary Line*, 34, 49 n., 57; Booth, "The Watauga Settlements," 32–33, 34; Summers, *History of Southwest Virginia*, 44; Folmsbee, Corlew, and Mitchell, *History of Tennessee*, 1: 96–97. Before settlement, early explorers com-

monly referred to the Holston as the Indian River. The French, on the other hand, called it the Cherokee River, and the Cherokee knew it as the Hogoheegee.

4. Williams, "Stephen Holston and Holston River," 26–27. Burke's Garden was settled by James Burke in 1753, although it is often considered the first settlement in the southern Appalachian region.

5. Summers, *History of Southwest Virginia*, 53; Dick, *The Dixie Frontier*, 8. Davis's 1,300-acre tract was surveyed by John Buchanan in March 1748, which meant that Davis planned to cultivate at least 13 acres in corn. According to Summers, descendants of Davis occupied portions of this original tract well into the twentieth century. Squatters also were common on the frontier, which along with erratic surveying practices made the acquisition of these lands a legal quagmire.

6. Folmsbee et al., *History of Tennessee*, 1: 97; Booth, "The Watauga Settlements," 33; Summers, *History of Southwest Virginia*, 46–54.

7. De Vorsey, *The Indian Boundary Line*, 57, 73; Stuart map in Cumming, *The Southeast in Early Maps*, 231. The "Stalnaker's place," as it was then called, was found on maps as early as 1755. "Plantation" is a general term used for all eighteenth-century farms. See also Franklin, "Virginia and the Cherokee Indian Trade," 19. John Stuart's original map is currently housed in the British Museum, Additional MSS. 14,036, folio 5.

8. Pendleton, *History of Tazewell County*, 227, 228–29; Williams, *Dawn of Tennessee Valley*, 298; Adams, *Atlas of American History*, plate 61.

9. Quoted in de Vorsey, *The Indian Boundary Line*, 132.

10. Quoted in ibid., 95.

11. A distinction shared with Abingdon, Virginia.

12. In 1764 five wagonloads of furs, weighing a total of 9,400 pounds, were taken by the Moravians to the bustling Atlantic port. Arrow, *Seedtime on the Cumberland*, 155; Marks, *Southern Hunting*, 29; Fries et al., eds., *The Records of the Moravians*, 1: 301.

13. Williams, *History of the Lost State*, 268. See also Campbell, *The Southern Highlander*, 22–27; Norburn, "The Influence of the Physiographic Features," 1–38.

14. Boone quotation in Sparks, ed., *Lives of Daniel Boone and Benjamin Lincoln*, 13: 186–89; Smith, *Virgin Land*, 61.

15. These figures are close approximations. The 25,000 figure is for the State of Franklin (Sullivan, Washington, Wayne, Greene, Caswell, Spencer, Sevier, and Blount Counties) given by Brissot de Warville, a French traveler. Major Elholm, at the Greenville convention of 1787, estimated the population of Franklin at 30,000. By 1790, using government census records, it is evident that the population of those counties had risen to 35,691. In Kentucky the population increased from 50,000 in 1787 to 73,677 in 1790. Even considering the fact that a majority of settlers resided in the Blue Grass, a considerable number of Kentucky residents must have occupied the Cumberland Plateau at that time. For population estimates on the southern frontier, see Williams, *History of the Lost State*, 268–69; Green and Harrington, *American Population*, 192–94; Friis, "A Series of Population Maps," map for 1790, facing 464; Rohrbough, *The Trans-Appalachian Frontier*, 25, table 1. In 1792 Gilbert Imlay put the population of the Holston, Clinch, and Powell River settlements at 70,000 (*A Topographical Description*, 49). See also Knox, *The People of Tennessee*, 2–10.

16. Williams, *History of the Lost State*, 269 n. 4. Rossiter estimated the total number of slaves in the Southwest Territory in 1790 at 3,417, but by 1800 the number had increased to 13,584. This number would be lower in the study area, since the Southwest Territory would also include the Shenandoah Valley of Virginia and Blue Grass regions of Kentucky. See Rossiter, *A Century of Population Growth*, 132, 133.

17. Campbell, *The Southern Highlander*, 65; Fischer, *Albion's Seed*, 635; Knox, *The People of Tennessee*, 9, chart 2.

18. Fischer, *Albion's Seed*, 635.

19. Brick architecture was not unknown on the Appalachian frontier, particularly in the first permanently settled townships. While most early brick structures are associated with planter elites, a small number of Federal-style brick homes were inhabited by middle-class farmers. Brickyards were themselves an important economic influence on the region after the early nineteenth century.

20. On county government, see Porter, *County Government in Virginia*, 12–16; Guess, *County Government*, 29–34; Rohrbough, *The Trans-Appalachian Frontier*, 48–49, 52–53; Newton, "Cultural Preadaptation," 150 n. 13; Raitz and Ulack, *Appalachia, a Regional Geography*, 101, 121.

21. Arthur, *Western North Carolina*, 77; Boyd, ed., "Information," 614–15; Campbell, *The Southern Highlander*, 53–71; Jordan and Kaups, *The American Backwoods Frontier*, 118, 120; MacLean, *An Historical Account*, 70; Ross, *The Pagan Celts*, 64–65.

22. McCourt, "Infield and Outfield in Ireland," 369–70, 375–76; Otto, *The Southern Frontiers*, 57; Jordan and Kaups, *The American Backwoods Frontier*, 125–26.

23. Evans, *The Personality of Ireland*, 55–61, 160; Handley, *Scottish Farming*, 37–45; Whittington, "Field Systems of Scotland," 534; Ernle, *English Farming*, 160.

24. Evans, "Culture and Land Use," 72–79; Evans, "The Scotch-Irish," 80–81; Ernle, *English Farming*, 160–61.

25. Otto, *The Southern Frontiers*, 57. See also MacLysaght, *Irish Life*, 167–70; Whyte, *Agriculture and Society*, 80–83; McWhiney and McDonald, "Celtic Origins," 168–69.

26. McCammon, "Diary"; Dunn, *Cades Cove*, 33; Callahan, *Smoky Mountain Country*, 10–11; Gersmehl, "Factors Leading to Mountaintop Grazing," 67–72; Lindsay and Bratton, "The Vegetation of Grassy Balds," 264–75.

27. First quotation in Smyth, *A Tour of the United States*, 1: 143; second quotation in Zeigler and Grosscup, *Heart of the Alleghenies*, 315; Gersmehl, "A Geographic Approach," 244–53; Evans, "Folk Housing," 63.

28. Arthur, *Western North Carolina*, 194; Gersmehl, "A Geographic Approach," 245.

29. Gersmehl, "A Geographic Approach," 245; Arthur, *Western North Carolina*, 194; Job quotation in Burns, "Settlement and Early History," 61.

30. Dunn, *Cades Cove*, 33, 34; Gilbert, "Vegetation of the Grassy Balds," 22; Peattie, *Mountain Geography*, 224. There is additional evidence that Nathan Sparks was grazing more than seven hundred head of cattle around the environs of Spence Field in the 1890s.

31. Anburrey, *Travels*, 1: 326–27; Smyth, *A Tour*, 1: 338, 363; Otto, *The Southern Frontiers*, 56; Jordan, *Trails to Texas*, passim; Macmaster, "The Cattle Trade," 142–45, 147–49.

32. Fletcher, *Pennsylvania Agriculture*, 1: 85; Stilgoe, *Common Landscape*, 192–98; Bays, "The Historical Geography of Cattle Herding," 62, 63, passim. Logan, who called the

frontier cowpen "an important institution," said cowpens were used in the South Carolina upcountry "to collect the cattle at proper seasons; for the purpose of branding and counting them" (*A History of the Upper Country*, 151–52). As Bays points out, in tracing the cultural origins of frontier cattle herding, the best scholars argue for the diffusion and blending of certain cultural practices but maintain that although certain traits are shared, many cultural complexes retain diagnostic attributes that are traceable across geographic regions and through time.

33. Quote from Leyburn, *The Scotch-Irish*, 159; Arnow, *Seedtime on the Cumberland*, 91–92.

34. Summers, *History of Southwest Virginia*, 124. The Scots-Irish were not the first or the sole cultivators of flax. The French Huguenots, Swedes, and Germans also grew the plant and continued doing so on the American frontier.

35. Thwaites, ed., *Travels West*, 241; Arnow, *Flowering of the Cumberland*, 250–52; Arnow, *Seedtime on the Cumberland*, 222, 351; Carrier, *Beginnings of Agriculture*, 162–63; Ernle, *English Farming*, 136, 240, 312; Leyburn, *The Scotch-Irish*, 121.

36. In 1749 alone, twenty-five ships carrying 7,049 German immigrants arrived in that Atlantic port city. Moltmann, ed., *Germans to America*, passim; Schier, *Dietz Family History*, 1–5.

37. See, for example, Thorpe, "Assimilation," 19–42; Thorpe, *The Moravian Community*.

38. Quoted in Williams, ed., *Early Travels*, 448.

39. Kercheval, *A History*, 49; Arnow, *Seedtime on the Cumberland*, 102 n. 122; Merrens, *Colonial North Carolina*, 53–81; Fischer, *Albion's Seed*, 635.

40. Works Projects Administration, *Tennessee*, 510–11; Manning, *The Historic Cumberland Plateau*, 239–40.

41. Fromm, "The Migration and Settlement," 39–40; Raitz and Ulack, *Appalachia, a Regional Geography*, 124; Dyer, "The Farmstead Yards," 14; Stilgoe, *Common Landscape*, 177.

42. Fletcher, *Pennsylvania Agriculture*, 50; Glassie, *Pattern in Material Folk Culture*, 78.

43. Glassie, "The Old Barns of Appalachia," 21–30; Raitz and Ulack, *Appalachia, a Regional Geography*, 123–24; Morgan, *The Log House*, 9.

44. Evans, "The Scotch-Irish in the New World," 78 n. 3; Glassie, "The Appalachian Log Cabin," 5–6. The word "cabin" is of Scots-Irish origin. The Oxford English Dictionary defines it as "a permanent human habitation of rude construction. Applied especially to mud or turf built hovels."

45. Fisher, *Albion's Seed*, 658; quotation in Glassie, *Pattern in Material Folk Culture*, 78. See also Glassie, "The Appalachian Log Cabin," 5–14; Glassie, "The Types of the Southern Mountain Cabin," 391–420; Raitz and Ulack, *Appalachia, a Regional Geography*, 122, 123.

46. See, for example, Fletcher, *Pennsylvania Agriculture*, 1: 64–66, 167–69; Otto, *The Southern Frontiers*, 46–47; Johnson, *The Swedes of the Delaware*, 103–35.

47. Jordan and Kaups, *American Backwoods Frontier*, 96, 107, passim.

48. Stilgoe, *Common Landscape*, 175–77; Johnson, *The Swedish Settlements*, 2: 527–28; Vanberg, *On Norwegian Ways*, 138–40, 217–19; Montelius, "The Burning of Forest Land," 41–54.

49. Arnow, *Seedtime on the Cumberland,* 256; Pyne, *Fire in America,* 143–60; Otto and Anderson, "Slash-and-Burn Cultivation," 131–40.

50. Pope quoted in Thompson, ed., *Touching Home,* 138; Shea, "Our Pappies Burned the Woods," 143–45.

51. Surnames of probable Scandinavian origin include Bankston, Clemson, Holston, Olson, Yokum, and Swanson. In southern Appalachia, at least by 1820, these and other diagnostic surnames were found in pockets of western North Carolina, eastern Kentucky, southwestern Virginia, and northeastern Georgia. See Jordan and Kaups, *The American Backwoods Frontier,* 235–40. For a more in-depth discussion of the concept of cultural core or hearth and its relationship to cultural identity, see Meining, *The Shaping of America,* 1: 52–53, 250–53.

52. Ernle, *English Farming,* 107.

53. Otto and Anderson, "Slash-and-Burn Cultivation," 133–42; Fletcher, *Pennsylvania Agriculture,* 36, 64; Jordan and Kaups, *The American Backwoods Frontier,* 96–100; Stilgoe, *Common Landscape,* 171–73.

54. John Smith remarked in 1625 that "the best way to spoil the woods was to cut a notch in the bark a hand broad round about the tree, which pull off and the tree will sprout no more and all the small boughs in a year or two will decay" (Stilgoe, *Common Landscape,* 172–73); Smith, *Advertisements,* 38. See also Williams, ed., *Adair's History,* 434–35. John Stilgoe tells us that tree girdling was being practiced as early as the second decade of the seventeenth century in Tidewater Virginia.

55. Arnow, *Seedtime on the Cumberland,* 256, 257–58.

56. Saunders, ed., *The Colonial Records,* 5: 356.

57. Arnow, *Seedtime on the Cumberland,* 323.

58. Stilgoe, *Common Landscape,* 188; Jordan and Kaups, *The American Backwoods Frontier,* 105–6; Arnow, *Flowering of the Cumberland,* 236. In the southern Appalachians, chestnut and locust logs were very often used for fence railing since they were easily split and resisted rotting. Fence posts made from chestnut wood can still be seen in the area of the Great Smoky Mountains National Park.

59. Stilgoe, *Common Landscape,* 189, 191–92; Mather and Hart, "Fences and Farms," 201–23; Jordan and Kaups, *The American Backwoods Frontier,* 106–7. In determining the number of trees, I divided the number of rails needed to enclose a 10-acre field (4,500) by the number of rails in a single large tree (150). If smaller trees were used, the figure would be considerably higher.

60. Upon seeing one erected in North Carolina in 1728, William Byrd II remarked that "such a fence doth surprising well" (Bassett, ed., *The Writings of Colonel William Byrd,* 84). See also Arnow, *Flowering of the Cumberland,* 226.

61. Because it is unclear whether the use of the term was borrowed from the former residents who built the fences, it is impossible to determine if the practice in the Great Smoky Mountains has Scots-Irish or Celtic roots. See Dyer, "The Farmstead Yards," 14, 67 n.; Great Smoky Mountains National Park, "Stone Walls, Cairns and Old Roads." On German building construction, see, for example, Fletcher, *Pennsylvania Agriculture,* 65; Avery, *Kentucky Bluegrass,* 38. On stone building construction in Great Britain, see Evans, "Folk Housing," 53–64.

62. Gump, "Possessions and Patterns of Living," 98–100.

63. Arnow, *Seedtime on the Cumberland,* 401–3.

64. MacKensie, *Scottish Folk-Lore and Folk Life,* 42; Berthoff, "Celtic Mist," 539–43.

65. Hagy, "Castle's Woods," 98. As we know from the ledgers of Thomas Amis, a storekeeper on the Tennessee frontier, corn was used for barter more than any other item and gave "local farmers an outlet for their dominant crop" (Gump, "Half Pints to Horse Shoes," 6).

66. Donelson quoted in Williams, ed., *Early Travels,* 240. See also Arnow, *Seedtime on the Cumberland,* 57, 152, 237.

67. Arnow, *Seedtime on the Cumberland,* 126. See also Haines, *The Buffalo,* 76–77.

68. Ramsey, *Annals of Tennessee,* 144.

69. In fact, André Michaux noted in 1802 that a short time after the Europeans settled the area several mammal species "wholly disappeared, particularly the elk and bisons." Their once abundant numbers were due, Michaux believed, to "the non-occupation of the country, the quality of rushes and wild peas, which supplied them abundantly with food the whole year round" (Thwaites, ed., *Travels West,* 234). See also Ramsey, *Annals of Tennessee,* 144; Rice, *The Allegheny Frontier,* 7.

70. Quoted in Harris, *Lawson's History,* 127.

71. Audubon and Bachman, *The Quadrupeds of North America,* 1: 93; Hays, "Notes on the Range," 387–92; Johnson, "Elk," 506–11.

72. Van Doren, ed., *The Travels of William Bartram,* 62.

73. Harris, *Lawson's History,* 127; Rhoads, "Contributions to the Zoology," 180; Ashe, *Travels in America,* 267; Murie, *Elk of North America,* 27. Quotation in Arnow, *Seedtime on the Cumberland,* 170. Elk Valley, a small town near Jellico, Tennessee, was also named for the numerous elk that ranged in the valley and surrounding mountains during the eighteenth century. In nearby Kentucky a small number of elk were thought to be present in 1847, although these too had vanished by the end of the decade.

74. Quoted in Clark, *Kentucky,* 12.

75. Logan, *A History of the Upper Country,* 29, 31; quote in *Statutes of South Carolina,* 4: 719.

76. Clark, ed., *The State Records,* 24: 595–96; Arnow, *Flowering of the Cumberland,* 266. In North Carolina the general assembly placed regulations on killing deer as early as 1745. Night hunting after 1784 was only considered a misdemeanor, but a more stringent law was passed in 1810. "Such laws," as Stuart Marks has observed, "had little effect on maintaining stocks of deer in settled areas" (*Southern Hunting,* 31).

77. Gump, "Half Pints to Horse Shoes," 5–6.

78. Dunn, *Cades Cove,* 30.

79. Marks, *Southern Hunting,* 30, 289 n.; Arthur, *Western North Carolina,* 523; Tober, *Who Owns Wildlife?,* 23–24.

80. Arnow, *Seedtime on the Cumberland,* 239.

81. On squirrel scalps, see Gump, "Possessions and Patterns of Living," 115. Quote from Thwaites, ed., *Travels West,* 235.

82. White, *Tennessee,* 79.

83. Williams, ed., *Adair's History,* 387. Quote from Arnow, *Seedtime on the Cumberland,* 143.

84. Butler, "Journal of General Butler," 447; Bent, *Life Histories*, 328; Mosby and Handley, *The Wild Turkey*, 13. Audubon and Judd quoted in Imlay, *A Topographical Description*, 65.

85. White, *Tennessee*, 59–60.

86. For the use of hounds in the southern Appalachians, see Jordan, "An Ambivalent Relationship," 238–48; Young, "Pets," 1233. On mountain feists as bear dogs, see Davis and Stotik, "Feist or Fiction?" 197.

87. Hooker, ed., *The Carolina Backcountry*, 63; Woodsmason quoted in Silver, *A New Face on the Countryside*, 184.

88. John Smith, as early as 1619, warned that native American grasses, "good and sweet in summer," will "deceive your cattle in winter" (quoted in Stilgoe, *Common Landscape*, 182–84). See also Carrier, *Beginnings of Agriculture*, 239, 240; Gray, *History of Agriculture*, 1: 177–79.

89. Carrier, *Beginnings of Agriculture*; Stilgoe, *Common Landscape*, 183; Williams, ed., *Early Travels*, 448.

90. Killebrew, *Introduction to the Resources of Tennessee*, 116, 117.

91. Haragan, *Weeds of Kentucky*, 38; quote in Mooney, "Myths," 412. When plants and animals are introduced to a new region, they generally explode in numbers, disrupting the ecological balance of the area. In his classic ecological treatise *The Ecology of Invasions by Animals and Plants*, Charles Elton argued that introduced species such as privet and dandelion are able to proliferate rapidly because they fill an empty niche in an ecosystem, "a means of living which is not being used by anything else" (5); see also Donald E. Davis, *Ecophilosophy*, 40.

92. Carrier, *Beginnings of Agriculture*, 242; Killebrew, *Introduction to the Resources of Tennessee*, 115–16.

93. Quotation in Haragan, *Weeds of Kentucky*, 228. Large crabgrass, which closely resembles Bermuda grass, was not officially introduced into the country until 1849, when it was brought from Europe to alleviate a shortage in livestock forage. In the eighteenth century, Bermuda grass was also referred to as crab grass (Haragan, *Weeds of Kentucky*, 253). See also Carrier, *Beginnings of Agriculture*, 243. Bonner maintains that in Georgia there were only "a few individuals who devoted any sustained effort to improved grasses before 1850" but that in the Cotton Belt, which includes portions of northern Georgia, Bermuda grass became well known by 1840 (*A History of Georgia Agriculture*, 129).

94. Jefferson, *Notes*, 37; Gray, *History of Agriculture*, 1: 177; Stilgoe, *Common Landscape*, 183. For grass introductions, see Haragan, *Weeds of Kentucky*, 194, 233, 238, 247, 252; Silver, *A New Face on the Countryside*, 182–83, 188.

95. On the use of mountain cresses, see, for example, Shields, *The Cades Cove Story*, 20. On the introduction and use of chicory, see Peterson, *A Field Guide to Edible Wild Plants*, 58, 144; Haragan, *Weeds of Kentucky*, 173. The curious reader should always consult a reputable field guide before consuming any plants mentioned above or below. Some are highly toxic, particularly when eaten in large quantities.

96. Quoted in Wigginton, ed., *The Foxfire Book*, 236. In 1802 François Michaux found mullein "very abundant in the United States" but saw little of it "beyond the Alleghany

Mountains" (Thwaites, ed., *Travels West,* 187). Its entry into the region probably post-dates Michaux's travels into the region, if only by a few years.

97. For women's images of gardens and domestic space on the frontier, see Kolodny, *The Land before Her,* 48–54, passim.

98. Haragan, *Weeds of Kentucky,* 15, 88, 144, 160, 172; Niering and Olmstead, *The Audubon Society Field Guide,* 370, 371, 420, 425, 600, 798.

99. McCuller, *This Is Your Georgia,* 52. Brought by way of England from China, the Cherokee rose was first described by André Michaux.

100. Brockman, *Trees of North America,* 264, 265.

101. Gump, "Possessions and Patterns of Living," 130; Arnow, *Seedtime on the Cumberland,* 38, 415; Carrier, *Beginnings of Agriculture,* 258.

102. Quoted in Benson, ed., *The America of 1750,* 1: 148–49. The gray fox is an indigenous North American species.

103. Quoted in Thwaites, ed., *Travels West,* 277. André Michaux, who toured the region five years earlier, does not mention seeing crows in Kentucky or Tennessee.

104. Exotics flourish best where there is ecological disturbance. The rapid environmental change caused by human settlement, to which most plant and animal introductions are related, gives the nonnative plant or animal, without any natural predators, an advantage over its native competitors. The fact that "natural aliens" have historically done well in the mountains is confirmation of the changes that have occurred in the region over the past two hundred years.

105. In his book about New England colonists, William Cronon concludes that "ecological abundance and economic prodigality went hand in hand: the people of plenty were a people of waste" (*Changes in the Land,* 107).

6. Alleghenia: Antebellum Appalachia

1. Turner defined the frontier as the edge of settlement having a population density of no more than two persons per square mile. In 1820 only small portions of West Virginia, eastern Kentucky, western North Carolina, and northern Georgia had not achieved population densities of at least six persons per square mile. See Turner, "The Significance of the Frontier," 199–227; Hart, "The Spread of the Frontier," 73–84; Hilliard, *Atlas of Antebellum Agriculture,* 20, 21, 22.

2. Brown, "Smoky Mountain Story," 12–13; Wilburn, "The Indian Gap Trail," n.p.; Myers, *Indian Trails of the Southeast,* 771–75.

3. Dunn, *Cades Cove,* 11; Burns, "Settlement and Early History," 59–68.

4. Lambert, "The Oconaluftee Valley," 421–23.

5. Ibid., 423. See also U.S. Bureau of the Census, *Sixth Census,* Agriculture Schedules, Haywood County.

6. Mattie Boggs Davis, "Last Will and Testament," 1.

7. Salstrom, "The Agricultural Origins of Economic Dependency," 266; Egerton, *Generations,* 51–52.

8. Pudup, "Social Class and Economic Development," 252.

9. Egerton, *Generations*, 23; Montell, *The Saga of Coe Ridge*, 1–20.

10. Thomas, *Big Sandy*, 5–6; Arnow, *Flowering of the Cumberland*, 34 n. 21, 234, 298, 367–68. The two-month return trip from New Orleans was an arduous one, requiring a thirty-day walk on foot.

11. Phillips, *A History of Transportation*, 63.

12. Tracy, *The Life of Jeremiah Evarts*, 176; Hemperley, *Historical Indian Trails*, 22–29; Evans, "Highways to Progress," 395.

13. For an excellent discussion of the importance of early roads in the social and economic development of southern Appalachia, see Hsiung, *Two Worlds in the Tennessee Mountains*, 55–73.

14. Cotter, *My Autobiography*, 55.

15. Tracy, *The Life of Jeremiah Evarts*, 176.

16. Thwaites, ed., *Travels West*, 265–66; Featherstonhaugh, *A Canoe Voyage*, 2: 210–20; Works Project Administration, *Tennessee*, 297. Chattanooga was first known as Ross's Landing.

17. Kingsport Rotary Club, *Kingsport*, 11.

18. Belissary, "The Rise of Industry," 195.

19. Bruce, *Virginia Iron Manufacture*, 85.

20. Turner, *Rise of the New West*, 101–2. For the impact of cattle drives on the economy of antebellum western North Carolina, see also Arthur, *Western North Carolina*, 236–38; Blethen and Wood, "A Trader," 162–64.

21. Burnett, "Hog Raising," 86–103; Inscoe, *Mountain Masters*, 46; Van Noppen and Van Noppen, *Western North Carolina*, 39.

22. Lanman, *Letters*, 153; McDonald and McWhiney, "The Antebellum Southern Herdsman," 161; U.S. Bureau of the Census, *Agriculture of the United States in 1860;* U.S. Bureau of the Census, *Sixth Census,* Agriculture Schedules; U.S. Bureau of the Census, *Seventh Census,* Agriculture Schedules; Hilliard, *Atlas of Antebellum Agriculture,* 46, 47, maps 56, 57.

23. U.S. Bureau of the Census, *Agriculture of the United States in 1860,* 104.

24. Olmsted, *A Journey,* 22.

25. McDonald and McWhiney, "The Antebellum Southern Herdsman," 155; Salstrom, *Appalachia's Path to Dependency,* 5–7; McWhiney, *Cracker Culture,* 51–79.

26. Baker, "East Tennessee Agriculture Production," 6–10; Burnett, "Hog Raising and Hog Driving," 86–103. According to McDonald and McWhiney, there were fifteen "hog hotels" on the 50-mile road from Big Creek to Asheville, North Carolina ("The Antebellum Southern Herdsman," 162).

27. Gray, *History of Agriculture,* 1: 457. The year was 1843.

28. During fiscal year 1852–53, 29,193 hogs, 6,754,552 pounds of bacon, lard, and tallow, 239,302 bushels of wheat, 18,795 barrels of flour, 510,923 bushels of corn and oats, and 65,486 bales of cotton arrived at the terminal from Chattanooga. See Western and Atlantic Railroad, *Annual Reports;* Russell, *Atlanta,* 23, table 1. For an excellent discussion of the flow of livestock and other agricultural goods out of the Upper South, see Lindstrom, "Southern Dependence," 101–13.

29. Olmsted, *A Journey,* 223.

30. Cattle hooves exert on average about 24 pounds of static pressure per square inch and in wet or clay soils severely damage organic material. See also Johnson, "Effects of Farm Woodland Grazing," 109–13.

31. Harper, Frank, and McQuilkin, "Forest Practices and Productivity," 23; Breazeale, *Life As It Is,* 7.

32. Olmsted, *A Journey,* 225; U.S. Bureau of the Census, *Agriculture of the United States in 1860;* U.S. Bureau of the Census, *Sixth Census,* Agriculture Schedules; U.S. Bureau of the Census, *Seventh Census,* Agriculture Schedules. Gray, for example, notes that the mountains' better adaptability for cattle "prevented the extensive development of sheep herding in Appalachia" (*History of Agriculture,* 2: 835).

33. Smith, *A Brief Historical, Statistical, and Descriptive Review,* 41, 63. Mutton was seldom eaten in Scotland or Ireland before the nineteenth century, since the herding of sheep had been forced "upon the Irish and the Scots by their English conquerors" (McWhiney, *Cracker Culture,* 89). See also Leyburn, *The Scotch-Irish,* 262; Olmsted, *A Journey,* 225.

34. Smith, *A Brief Historical, Statistical, and Descriptive Review,* 8, 39–41; *Southern Cultivator* 3 (1845): 73; Randall, *Sheep Husbandry,* 7–8, 64; Bonner, *A History of Georgia Agriculture,* 141–42; Gray, *History of Agriculture,* 2: 847.

35. Smith, *A Brief Historical, Statistical, and Descriptive Review,* 3; Hilliard, *Atlas of Antebellum Agriculture,* 46, 48, maps 55, 48; U.S. Bureau of the Census, *Agriculture of the United States in 1860,* 132, 215; U.S. Bureau of the Census, *Sixth Census,* Agriculture Schedules.

36. U.S. Bureau of the Census, *Agriculture of the United States in 1860,* 62, 210; Hilliard, *Atlas of Antebellum Agriculture,* 46, 48, 49, maps 55, 58, 61; Arnow, *Flowering of the Cumberland,* 223–24; Gray, *History of Agriculture,* 2: 835, 837, 847, 853.

37. U.S. Bureau of the Census, *Agriculture of the United States in 1860,* 23, 104, 154, 196, 210, 218.

38. Arnow, *Flowering of the Cumberland,* 299–300; Smith, *A Brief Historical, Statistical, and Descriptive Review,* 40.

39. I am indebted to John Lewis for information about sheep raising in southern Appalachia.

40. For an excellent introduction to the role of women in mountain agriculture, see, for example, Anglin, "Lives on the Margin," 185–209.

41. Merchant, *Ecological Revolutions,* 150–54, 167–72. The "age of homespun," as the antebellum period in America has sometimes been called, was almost entirely dependent on the successful raising of sheep. Gus Hallum, of Fannin County, Georgia, recalled how sheep were sheared on most nineteenth-century mountain farms: "Yep, I've seen them shear anywhere from 75 to 100 in a day. . . . When you go to shearin', you start at the stomach. You take one hand and roll the wool back as the sheep is being sheared. Take my mother. She'd shear a sheep and it'd all come off in one blanket" (Thompson, ed., *Touching Home,* 175–76).

42. Quote from Smith, *A Brief Historical, Statistical, and Descriptive Review,* 2. See also U.S. Bureau of the Census, *Seventh Census,* Agriculture Schedules.

43. Compiled from U.S. Bureau of the Census, *Agriculture of the United States in 1860,* 3, 23, 27, 59, 63, 105, 109, 133, 137, 155. Per capita corn production followed a similar pattern for the period. In 1850 the valley of eastern Tennessee produced 49.41 bushels per individual; the Kentucky mountains, 39.07; and the Blue Ridge counties of southwestern Virginia, 26.97 bushels per person. U.S. Bureau of the Census, *Seventh Census,* Agriculture Schedules; Gray, *History of Agriculture,* 2: 876, table 33; Salstrom, *Appalachia's Path to Dependency,* 14–15, table 2.

44. Tate, *History of Pickens County,* 63–64; Owsley, *Plain Folk of the Old South,* 111–14; Taylor, *Eating, Drinking, and Visiting,* 50.

45. Abrahams, *Singing the Master,* 56–57, 83.

46. See, for example, Wallerstein, *The Modern World System,* 1: passim; Dunn, *Cades Cove,* 63–89; Salstrom, *Appalachia's Path to Dependency,* 32, 41–59; Hsiung, *Two Worlds in the Tennessee Mountains,* 74–88; Nelson, "Planters and Hill People," passim.

47. U.S. Bureau of the Census, *Agriculture of the United States in 1860,* 210; U.S. Bureau of the Census, *Seventh Census,* Agriculture Schedules; Moore, "Development in Appalachian Kentucky," 226, table 13.1; Mann, "Mountains, Land, and Kin Networks."

48. Smith, *A Brief Historical, Statistical, and Descriptive Review,* 27.

49. Quoted in Escott, ed., *North Carolina Yeoman,* 155.

50. Brewer and Brewer, *Valley So Wild,* 114; Hsiung, *Two Worlds in the Tennessee Mountains,* 76–77.

51. Kennamer, *History of Jackson County, Alabama,* 16; Raulston and Livingood, *Sequatchie,* 98. For additional cultural uses of corn, see Arnow, *Flowering of the Cumberland,* 240, 242; Thompson, ed., *Touching Home,* 135; Dick, *Dixie Frontier,* 289–92. For consumption levels, see *Southern Cultivator* 1 (1843): 17; Gallman, "Self-Sufficiency in the Cotton Economy," 5–23.

52. Escott, ed., *North Carolina Yeoman,* 123.

53. Weingartner, Billings, and Blee, "Agriculture in Preindustrial Appalachia," 75–78; Ransom and Sutch, *One Kind of Freedom.*

54. Billings and Blee, "Agriculture and Poverty," in Pudup, Billings, and Waller, eds., *Appalachia in the Making,* 252–59.

55. Hahn, "The Unmaking of the Southern Yeomanry," 181.

56. Thorndale and Dollarhide, *Map Guide,* vii.

57. There has recently been a tendency in the literature to equate all exchange transactions in the mountains with market or capitalist social relations. See, for example, Dunaway, *The First American Frontier,* 229–32. For conflicting views, although not necessarily about discussions of Appalachia, see Danhof, *Change in Agriculture,* 22; Salstrom, "The Agricultural Origins of Economic Dependency," 278–83; Merchant, *Ecological Revolutions,* 172–97.

58. Olmsted, *A Journey,* 210–11.

59. See, for example, Dunaway, "The Incorporation of Mountain Ecosystems," 355–81; Dunaway, *The First American Frontier,* 257–85, passim.

60. Natural obstacles such as mountains, soil types, and geographic isolation have long impeded the growth of agrarian capitalism in the United States. For a more in-depth anal-

ysis of the role the environment has played in the development of American agriculture, see Mann, *Agrarian Capitalism,* 28–46.

61. U.S. Bureau of the Census, *Agriculture of the United States in 1860,* 3, 23, 27, 59, 63, 105, 109, 133, 137, 155.

62. Olmsted, *A Journey,* 231. On bread eating and preparation in the upper South, see Taylor, *Eating, Drinking, and Visiting,* 21; Hilliard, *Hog Meat and Hoe Cake,* 8; Arnow, *Flowering of the Cumberland,* 261.

63. U.S. Bureau of the Census, *Agriculture of the United States in 1860.* See also Inscoe, *Mountain Masters,* 14–15, table 1.1; Thompson, ed., *Touching Home,* 135.

64. Inscoe, *Mountain Masters,* 17–18; Wagenen, *The Golden Age of Homespun,* 76–82; Brinkman, "Home Manufactures," 50–58.

65. Smith, *A Brief Historical, Statistical, and Descriptive Review,* 13–14.

66. U.S. Bureau of the Census, *Agriculture of the United States in 1860,* 61, 65, 135, 139.

67. Ibid., 57.

68. Ibid., 65.

69. Quote from *Southern Cultivator* 11 (1853): 78. See also Bonner, *History of Georgia Agriculture,* 66. Bonner attributes population losses in northwestern Georgia between 1850 and 1860 to soil erosion.

70. U.S. Bureau of the Census, *Agriculture of the United States in 1860,* 2, 22, 26, 58, 62, 104, 108, 132, 136, 154, 158.

71. Cappon, "History of the Southern Iron Industry," 2.

72. Burns, "Settlement and Early History," 64; Arthur, *Western North Carolina,* 277.

73. Burns, "Settlement and Early History," 60; Dunn, *Cades Cove,* 82.

74. The current name—the Great Smoky Mountains—is a combination of two former place-names. See Kephart, "Origin of Place Names," 1–2; Fink, "Early Explorers," 40–53.

75. Williams, "Early Iron Works," 39.

76. Council, Honerkamp, and Will, *Industry and Technology,* 56–65. Two additional studies that contain considerable treatment of southern Appalachia are Smith, "Historical Geography," and Cappon, "History of the Southern Iron Industry."

77. Gerard Troost, one of the first in the region to evaluate charcoal yields for various wood types, found that white pine produced 455 pounds of charcoal per cord, whereas hickory yielded 1,172 pounds per cord (*Fifth Geological Report,* 41). See also Arnow, *Flowering of the Cumberland,* 296–97 n. 92.

78. Council, Honerkamp, and Will, *Industry and Technology,* 16.

79. Scott, comp., *Laws of the State of Tennessee,* 403; Delfino, "Antebellum East Tennessee Elites and Industrialization," 104; Blethen and Wood, "The Antebellum Iron Industry," 80.

80. Merritt, *Early History of Carter County,* 153; Nave, "A History of the Iron Industry," 71–77, 102; Wallach, "The Slighted Mountains," 363.

81. Quote in Troost, *Fifth Geological Report,* 37. See also Smith, "Historical Geography," 295, table 39.

82. Mitchell, *Diary of a Geological Tour,* 26–27; Clark, ed., *The State Records,* 24: 978–79; Swank, *History of the Manufacture of Iron,* 272–74.

83. Coleman, "Old Kentucky Iron Furnaces," 6–7; Geological Survey of Kentucky, *Reports of Progress*, 212, 213; Moore, "Economic Development," 230.

84. U.S. Bureau of the Census, *Seventh Census*, Manufacturing Schedules.

85. Council, Honerkamp, and Will, *Industry and Technology*, 56; Lewis, *Coal, Iron, and Slaves*, 248, appendix 6.

86. Smith, *A Brief Historical, Statistical, and Descriptive Review*, table 36.

87. Ibid., 39.

88. Blethen and Wood, "The Antebellum Iron Industry," 82; U.S. Bureau of the Census, *Seventh Census*, Manufacturing Schedules.

89. Lesley, *Guide*, 246; Cappon, "History of the Southern Iron Industry," 244; Swank, *History of the Manufacture of Iron*, 299; Council, Honerkamp, and Will, *Industry and Technology*, 46; Nave, "A History of the Iron Industry," 92–93.

90. Kurry, "Iron and Settlement," 20.

91. Quoted in Lander, "The Iron Industry," 337; see also Smith, "Historical Geography," 297. Traveling in the northern Appalachians a century earlier, Johann Schoepf remarked that cutover lands were "of trifling value" to farmers (*Travels*, 1: 36–37).

92. Caruthers and Nicholson, eds., *A Compilation of the Statutes of Tennessee*, 409; Nave, "A History of the Iron Industry," 10.

93. Moore, "Economic Development," 231. See also Smith, "Historical Geography," 237–38.

94. Knight, *Standard History*, 3: 1785; Lesley, *Guide*, 246; Cappon, "History of the Southern Iron Industry," 244.

95. Delfino, "Antebellum East Tennessee Elites and Industrialization," 103–5. See also Council, Honerkamp, and Will, *Industry and Technology*, 176–77.

96. Merritt, *Early History of Carter County*, 153; Nave, "A History of the Iron Industry," 23; Starobin, *Industrial Slavery in the Old South*, 15. For an excellent overview of the role of slaves in the Virginia and Maryland iron industry, see Bruce, *Virginia Iron Manufacture*; Lewis, *Coal, Iron, and Slaves*.

97. Cappon, "History of the Southern Iron Industry," 149. See also, for example, Dunaway, *The First American Frontier*, 269–76.

98. Nave, "A History of the Iron Industry," 98.

99. Ibid.

100. The southern Appalachian iron industry was highly concentrated by the late 1870s, predictably in areas where transportation was most feasible and where large stores of iron ore and coal (which replaced charcoal as the primary furnace fuel) were readily attainable. This helps explain why seemingly remote rural areas like the Sequatchie Valley in southeastern Tennessee, near present-day Chattanooga, and Middlesboro, Kentucky, experienced enormous levels of economic growth during the postwar era. Raulston and Livingood, *Sequatchie*, 189, 193–96; Govan and Livingood, *The Chattanooga Country*, 339–40; Gaventa, *Power and Powerlessness*, 55–58.

101. U.S. Department of Agriculture, *Iron Ore Mining*, passim.

102. Many areas now thought to contain virgin stands of timber more accurately support inferior stands of second or third growth. This fact should be important to forest prac-

titioners interested in reconstructing earlier forest types since large-scale clear-cutting changes forest composition, a topic explored in greater detail in chapter 7.

103. Mather, "Report of the Geological Reconnaissance," 249. Figures are for the years 1829–34.

104. *Nashville Banner-Advertiser,* 12 December 1833.

105. U.S. Bureau of the Census, *Sixth Census,* Manufacturing Schedules; Rogers, *Report of the Geological Reconnaissance,* 1213; Lewis, *Coal, Iron, and Slaves,* 46; Raitz and Ulack, *Appalachia, a Regional Geography,* 98, 100; Moore, "Development in Appalachian Kentucky," 231.

106. See, for example, Clark, "Salt," 42–43; Turner, *Frontier and Section,* 47.

107. Verhoff, *The Kentucky River Navigation,* 155.

108. Jakle, "Salt on the Ohio Valley Frontier," 698; *Knoxville Register,* 4 July 1831; Moore, "Development in Appalachian Kentucky," 230.

109. Arnow, *Flowering of the Cumberland,* 292.

110. First quote in S. G. R. Mount to William H. Thomas, 5 April 1853, second in H. H. Johnson to William H. Thomas, 13 May 1853, both in William Holland Thomas Papers.

111. Williams, *The Georgia Gold Rush;* Coleman, ed., *A History of Georgia,* 170; Inscoe, *Mountain Masters,* 66–67, 71–73.

112. Coulter, *Auraria,* 1–15; Cain, *History of Lumpkin County,* 91–100.

113. Donald E. Davis, "Living on the Land," 44–45; Harshaw, *The Gold of Dahlonega,* 33–36. Stephenson quoted in Coulter, *Auraria,* 110–12.

114. Kingsport Rotary Club, *Kingsport,* 11; Avery and Boardman, "Arnold Guyot's Notes," 251, 253.

115. According to mountain explorer Paul Fink, the log vats used in this long, laborious process could still be seen on the cave floor as late as the 1920s. See Jenkins, "The Mining of Alum Cave," 81–85; Fink, *Backpacking Was the Only Way,* 32. Upon viewing Alum Cave in the 1850s, George T. Ferris wrote that it contained "alum, epsom salts, saltpetre, magnesia, and copperas" (*Our Native Lands,* 3). For early travelers' descriptions of the cave, see also Brown and Davis, "Trail History Notebook," n.p.

116. Barclay, *Ducktown Back in Raht's Time,* 31–33, 51.

117. Walker, Dunn, and Kisselburg, "A Short History of Copper Mining," in Thompson, ed., *Touching Home,* 127; "Madison et al. v. Ducktown Sulphur, Copper, and Iron Co."

118. Barclay, *Ducktown Back in Raht's Time,* 262; Blethen and Wood, "The Antebellum Iron Industry," 86; Callahan, *Smoky Mountain Country,* 101.

119. Gilbert, 6 December 1854, quoted in Barclay, *Ducktown Back in Raht's Time,* 41.

120. The bill, introduced by Representative B. C. Duggar, was passed 26 February 1876. See also Barclay, *Ducktown Back in Raht's Time,* 263.

121. U.S. Bureau of the Census, *Seventh Census,* Population Schedules; U.S. Bureau of the Census, *Eighth Census,* Population Schedules; Pudup, "Social Class and Economic Development," 246, 249.

122. Not only did black Appalachians introduce the "banjar" (banjo) to the mountains, clog-

ging and buck dancing were partially derived from slave dances such as the "Buck." See also Vlach, "African Influences," 139; Turner, "Black Appalachians," 139–41.

123. For the effects of the Civil War on mountain communities and commerce, see Dunn, *Cades Cove*, 69, 123–41; Raulston and Livingood, *Sequatchie*, 141–66; Thompson, ed., *Touching Home*, 92–123; Foner, *Reconstruction*, 11, 13–18; Salstrom, "The Agricultural Origins of Economic Dependency," 272–78; Barclay, *Ducktown Back in Raht's Time*, 87–101.

7. Appalachia: Making the Modern Landscape

1. Ayers, *The Promise of the New South*, 117–31; Eller, *Miners, Millhands, and Mountaineers*, 94–111; U.S. Department of Agriculture, *Mountaineers and Rangers*, xxv, 1–4; Watson, "The Economic and Cultural Development," 131; Clarkson, *Tumult on the Mountains*, 10–40; W. M. Ritter Lumber Company, *The Romance of Appalachian Hardwood Lumber*, 10–15; Wallach, "The Slighted Mountains," 363; Gaventa, "Property, Coal, and Theft," 144.

2. Gaventa, "Property, Coal, and Theft," 143–44; Gaventa, *Power and Powerlessness*, 53–55; Kincaid, *The Wilderness Road*, 322.

3. Raulston and Livingood, *Sequatchie*, 155.

4. Egerton, *Visions of Utopia*, 37–39; *Rugbeian* (Rugby, Tenn.) (April 1881).

5. Holmes, "Forest Conditions," 16, table 1; Lewis, *Transforming the Appalachian Countryside*, 18, 24, 44.

6. Ayers and Ashe, *The Southern Appalachian Forests*, Land Classification Map, plate 37.

7. Clendening, "Early Days in the Southern Appalachians," 101. By one lumberman's estimate, which includes timberlands in West Virginia and Pennsylvania, the southern Appalachians contained 400 billion board feet of hardwood timber and an additional 50 billion board feet of softwoods such as hemlock, spruce, and white pine. When surveyed by Horace Ayres and William W. Ashe in 1900, the Blue Ridge Mountains contained 10 billion board feet of lumber and 69 billion cords of small wood (*The Southern Appalachian Forests*, 52–53).

8. Hannah interviews, 22–24.

9. The cabin is located near the Old Settlers Trail in the Great Smoky Mountains National Park. See also Trout, *Historic Buildings of the Smokies*, 14; Van Noppen and Van Noppen, *Western North Carolina*, 224.

10. Quote from Lewis, "Railroads, Deforestation, and the Transformation of Agriculture," 302. See also Lewis, *Transforming the Appalachian Countryside*, passim; Donald E. Davis, "Logging History Facts," 1–2; DeVivo, "The Deforestation of Western North Carolina," 89, 90–91.

11. Clendening, "Early Days in the Southern Appalachians," 102; Raitz and Ulack, *Appalachia, a Regional Geography*, 191; Clarkson, *Tumult on the Mountain*, 49; Eubank, "Early Lumbering," 100; Seeber, "A History of Anderson County," 77–78.

12. Lambert, "Logging on the Little River," 34; McCracken, "Comparison of Forest Cover," 9–10; Williams, "Early Logging," 6.

13. Eubank, "Early Lumbering in East Tennessee," 100; Wallach, "The Slighted Mountains," 363; Dykeman, *The French Broad*, 167–74; O'Dell, *Over the Misty Blue Hills*, 195; *Manufacturers' Record*, 31 October 1901.

14. Van Noppen and Van Noppen, *Western North Carolina*, 292–98; Lambert, "Logging the Great Smokies," 353–54; Eller, *Miners, Millhands, and Mountaineers*, 81–84; U.S Department of Agriculture, *Mountaineers and Rangers*, 1–3; Webb, "Retrospect of the Lumber Industry," 175–76.

15. In 1839, for example, New York was producing 30 percent of the lumber in the United States; in 1849 New York timber production peaked and thereafter declined. *Manufacturers' Record*, 31 October 1901, 23.

16. *Garden and Forest* 5 (1892): 333; Brender and Merrick, "Early Settlement and Land Use," 322–23; Clendening, "Early Days in the Southern Applachians," 103–5.

17. Quoted in Goodwin, "Eight Decades of Forestry Firsts: A History of Forestry in North Carolina, 1889–1969," 1; Van Noppen and Van Noppen, *Western North Carolina*, 301–3.

18. Brackin interview; Brown, "Smoky Mountain Story," 99; Holmes, "Forest Conditions," 76.

19. Glenn, *Denudation and Erosion*, 9. In many parts of the southern Appalachians, many of these gullies are still visible to the careful observer.

20. *Southern Lumberman*, 18 January 1908, 21; Holmes, "Forest Conditions," 79–81.

21. "Appalachian Logging Congress," 1077.

22. Finney quoted in *Southern Lumberman*, 14 August 1909, 725. See also *Southern Lumberman*, 6 May 1916, 1076.

23. U.S. Department of Agriculture, *Mountaineers and Rangers*, 13, 473–82, 551.

24. Ashe, *Preliminary Report*, 521; Wallach, "The Slighted Mountains," 364 n. 18.

25. Ayres and Ashe, *The Southern Appalachian Forests*, 18.

26. *Congressional Record*, February 15, 1911, 2578. Among those challenging the idea that forest cover had little or no effect on stream flow was the Army Corps of Engineers. See U.S. House of Representatives, *Report 1514 on H.R. 365* (60th Cong., 1st sess., 1908). See also Wallach, "The Slighted Mountains," 364–65.

27. Quote in Roosevelt, *Message from the President*, 34 n. 21.

28. Quote in ibid., 1, 36. See also Graves, "The South's Forestry and Water Resources," 379.

29. Clendening, "Early Days in the Southern Appalachians," 105.

30. Holmes, "Forest Conditions," 16, table 2.

31. Kellogg, "Future of the Appalachian Forest," 55.

32. Ibid.

33. U.S. Department of Agriculture, *Weeks Act of March 1, 1911*, 1021–30; Clark, *The Greening of the South*, 47–48; Salstrom, *Appalachia's Path to Dependency*, 26–27; Shands and Healey, *Lands Nobody Wanted*, 15.

34. U.S. Department of Agriculture, "July Field Program," 4–19; Hall, "To Remake the Appalachians," 338, 323–24.

35. Brown, "Smoky Mountain Story," 74–75, 88, 91, 99–102; Schmidt and Hooks, *Whistle over the Mountain*, xiii, 34–39; Peattie, ed., *The Great Smokies and Blue Ridge*, 154–56.

36. Quoted in Frome, *Strangers in High Places,* 168.

37. Brown, "Smoky Mountain Story," 99; Lambert, "Logging the Great Smokies," 13.

38. U.S. Department of Agriculture, *Mountaineers and Rangers,* 23; U.S. Department of Agriculture, *The National Forests and Purchase Units of Region Eight.*

39. U.S. Department of Agriculture, *Mountaineers and Rangers,* 25. Sixty percent of the Nantahala National Forest was acquired from only twenty-two sellers.

40. Wallach, "The Slighted Mountains," 366. These were Tracts WT 64 and U 62 in the Watauga Ranger District, Elizabethton, Tennessee.

41. Although the Weeks Act did not contain a specific provision for condemnation, the Forest Service assumed it had the authority to do so and did so. See also Wallach, "The Slighted Mountains," 367–69; Eller, *Miners, Millhands, and Mountaineers,* 118–21.

42. Wallach, "The Slighted Mountains," 367, parentheses in original. The tract was located in Erwin, Tennessee, in the Unaka Ranger District. See also U.S. Department of Agriculture, *Mountaineers and Rangers,* 57–60.

43. Kahn, *The Forest Service and Appalachia,* 2, 136; Appalachian Land Ownership Task Force, *Who Owns Appalachia?,* 35; Shands and Healey, *Lands Nobody Wanted,* 15; Pomeroy and Yoho, *North Carolina Lands,* 213, 217; Hall, *Environmental Politics,* 108, 110–11, 112.

44. Canby, "Top O'Smoky," 581.

45. Phenis, "Southern Appalachian Forest Reserve," 41–43; Van Noppen and Van Noppen, *Western North Carolina,* 314.

46. Quoted in Steen, *U.S. Forest Service,* 79.

47. An informed discussion of the effects of excessive timber harvesting on southern Appalachian forests and watersheds can be found in Jackson, *Mountain Treasures at Risk.*

48. Though it seems impossible today, the white-tailed deer was practically an extinct species in the mountains prior to its reintroduction during the 1930s. See, for example, Inscoe, "Appalachian Otherness," 191; Brown, "Smoky Mountain Story," 104–5, 162–64. For the long-term effects of timber removal on forest vegetation, see Duffy and Meir, "Do Appalachian Herbaceous Understories Ever Recover," 199–200.

49. U.S. Department of Agriculture, *Economic and Social Problems and Conditions,* 32. This figure excluded the 2 million acres of timberland that had already been acquired by the federal government.

50. *Manufacturers' Record,* 8 April 1892, 17 August 1894, 42, 7 December 1894, 286; U.S. Department of Agriculture, *Mountaineers and Rangers,* 2; W. M. Ritter Lumber Company, *The Romance of Appalachian Hardwood Lumber,* 12–14; Champion Fibre Company, "An Industrial Forest Policy," n.p.; Van Noppen and Van Noppen, *Western North Carolina,* 308–10.

51. U.S. Department of Agriculture, *Mountaineers and Rangers,* 2–3; *Manufacturers' Record,* 20 January 1910, 57, 13 July 1911, 52, 14 September 1905, 219; Eller, *Miners, Millhands, and Mountaineers,* 98–99, 107–8.

52. Kimbrough, *Taking up Serpents,* 84; Watson, "The Economic and Cultural Development of Eastern Kentucky," 62–71; U.S. Department of Agriculture, *Mountaineers and Rangers,* 4.

53. Quote from Reedy, "The W. M. Ritter Family History Book," 76. See also Alwin Schenck, *Birth of Forestry in America,* 148. At a West Virginia lumber mill, Ritter officials were even indicted for holding laborers in what the federal court called "a condition of peonage." See Reedy, "The W. M. Ritter Family History Book," 77.

54. U.S. Department of Labor, *U.S. Wages and Hours of Labor;* Lewis, *Transforming the Appalachian Countryside,* 179–80.

55. Dorie quoted in Bush, *Dorie,* 173. Several accounts of these invasions give proof that this was not an isolated incident and may have had something to do with decreasing corn supplies in the mountains. For more on community life in the lumber camps, see also Brown, "Smoky Mountain Story," 94–97; Brashler, "When Daddy Was a Shanty Boy," esp. 63–67.

56. Quoted in Ritchie, *Sketches of Rabun County History,* 424, 425; U.S. Bureau of the Census, *Twelfth Census;* U.S. Bureau of the Census, *Thirteenth Census.*

57. U.S. Bureau of the Census, *Twelfth Census;* U.S. Bureau of the Census, *Thirteenth Census;* Williams, "Counting Yesterday's People," 13, table 1; Salstrom, "Newer Appalachia," in Pudup, Billings, and Waller, eds., *Appalachia in the Making,* 84, table 3.1. One scholar estimated that as many as twenty-five families a year left the Bryson City area between 1900 and 1910 to work in the Piedmont textile mills. See Cummings, "Community and the Nature of Change," 64.

58. The Unaka National Forest purchase unit originally included much of upper eastern Tennessee, including Bald Mountain. Today much of this original purchase area is within the boundaries of the Cherokee National Forest.

59. U.S. Bureau of the Census, *Twelfth Census,* Population Schedules; U.S. Bureau of the Census, *Thirteenth Census,* Population Schedules; U.S. Department of Agriculture, *Mountaineers and Rangers,* xix.

60. U.S. Bureau of the Census, *Thirteenth Census.*

61. Brown and Davis, "Trail History Notebook," "Loop Trail, Deep Creek," n.p.

62. Between 1900 and 1910, farm acreage in the counties of northeastern Georgia, southwestern North Carolina, and southeastern Tennessee dropped nearly 20 percent. By 1930 a considerable portion of farms along the Cumberland Plateau were smaller than 50 acres. U.S. Bureau of the Census, *Thirteenth Census,* Population Schedules; U.S. Bureau of the Census, *Fourteenth Census,* Population Schedules. See also Salstrom, "Newer Appalachia," 88, table 3.2; U.S. Department of Agriculture, *Mountaineers and Rangers,* 39. Local counties also lost important tax revenue because of national forest acquisitions, since the land purchased by the government was removed from "the total acreage of the assessable property."

63. Quoted in Van Noppen and Van Noppen, *Western North Carolina,* 305.

64. Horn, *This Fascinating Lumber Business,* 108; Eller, *Miners, Millhands, and Mountaineers,* 89.

65. Van Noppen and Van Noppen, *Western North Carolina,* 292; Donald E. Davis, "Logging History Facts," 1; Lambert, "Logging the Great Smokies," 32–34.

66. Kerr quoted in *East Tennessean,* 19 February 1858. See also Morgan, *The Log House in East Tennessee,* 90; DeVivo, "The Deforestation of Western North Carolina," 90–91.

67. *Maryville Times,* 23 October 1889.

68. Portable sawmills were also limited in that they could only cut smaller trees—generally logs 20 inches or less in diameter. See Lambert, "Logging the Great Smokies," 38.

69. D. H. Davis, "A Study of Succession of Human Activities," 95, 97–99; Schockel, "Changing Conditions in the Kentucky Mountains," 115–18; Otto, "The Decline of Forest Farming," 20; Brown, "Smoky Mountain Story," 30; West Virginia Board of Agriculture, *Second Biennial Report of the West Virginia State Board of Agriculture,* 45; Ayres and Ashe, *The Southern Appalachian Forests,* 22. Farmers in the Ridge and Valley, on the other hand, maintained the least amount of their farms in woodlands, in some counties cultivating as much as 60 percent of the total land area held in farmland. See also Campbell, *The Southern Highlander,* 251; Case, "The Valley of East Tennessee," 3, fig. 3.

70. Gray, "Economic Conditions and Tendencies," 9. Two excellent defenses of nineteenth- and early-twentieth-century southern agricultural practices are Otto and Anderson, "Slash-and-Burn Cultivation," 138–43; Hart, "Land Rotation in Appalachia," 150–54. For a critique of those methods, see, for example, Glenn, *Denudation and Erosion,* 10–12.

71. Droze, *High Dams and Slack Waters,* 14. See the original source from footnote 42 on that page. Today it is hard to imagine that prior to 1933 the Tennessee River had a year-round minimum depth of 4 feet upon 40 percent of its course, 2 feet upon 30 percent of its course, and .5 foot upon the remaining 30 percent of its length. It has been turned into a safe and dependable transportation artery usable year-round by river craft loaded to 9-foot depths.

72. *Chattanooga News,* 13 November 1913; Govan and Livingood, *The Chattanooga Country,* 445–48; Davidson, *The Tennessee,* 1: 177.

73. Wade H. Wright, *History of the Georgia Power Company,* 116–18, 126–27, 132–34, 156, 183.

74. Lowitt, "The TVA," 35; Droze, *High Dams and Slack Waters,* 20–23; Davidson, *The Tennessee,* 2: 191–93, 233–37.

75. McDonald and Muldowny, *TVA and the Dispossessed,* 246; Davidson, *The Tennessee,* 2: 227–31; Creese, *TVA's Public Planning,* 240–68.

76. Moore, "Damming the Valley," 34–35; Brown, "Smoky Mountain Story," 203–40; Parris, "Gopherwood, Both Rare, Beautiful," 5A.

77. Raitz and Ulack, *Appalachia, a Regional Geography,* 216; Lander, *A Guide to Kentucky Outdoors,* 83.

78. Wade H. Wright, *History of the Georgia Power Company,* 130–31; Ritchie, *Sketches of Rabun County History,* 342.

79. Tennessee Valley Authority, Division of Reservoir Properties, Record Group 142; Tennessee Valley Authority, *The Chickamauga Project,* 3–10, passim.

80. Elliot quoted in Whetstone, "When the Valley Became a Lake," 32; Lytle, *From Eden to Babylon,* 227.

81. Irwin, *Alex Stewart,* 111.

82. Donald E. Davis, "Homeplace Geography," 18.

83. Quote from Cobb, "Historic Fish Traps," 33. See also Brown, *History of Tennessee Wildlife Conservation Laws,* 1–10.

84. McCoy, "Recollections of an Early Fish Trap," 182.

85. Ibid. The shovelbill catfish is the colloquial name for the paddlefish (*Polyodon spathula*).

86. Cobb, "Historic Fish Traps," 45. See also Headden and Headden, *Conservation of Wildlife and Forests*, 17, 44–45.

87. Myer, "Pearl Fisheries of Tennessee," 20–21.

88. Kunz and Stevenson, *The Book of the Pearl*, 263, 276; *Knoxville Journal*, 26 April 1936; Hoskins, *Anderson County, Historical Sketches*, 115–16; "Pearl Fishing Has Vanished," 1.

89. Kunz and Stevenson, *The Book of the Pearl*, 267–68.

90. Quote from Rau, *Ancient Trade*, 38. See also Kunz and Stevenson, *The Book of the Pearl*, 494.

91. Kunz and Stevenson, *The Book of the Pearl*, 277.

92. Quoted in Stolzenburg, "The Mussels' Message," 18. The twentieth-century decline of mussel populations is easier to fathom after one learns of their incredibly unique reproductive cycles. Mollusks require specific fish species to be found in the same waters in order for them to act as living hosts for the larval stage mussel. The microscopic mollusks, known as glochidia, must first attach to the gills of the host fish, where they remain for two or three weeks. Because of the size, shape, and elastic nature of the embryonic mussel, only certain kinds of fish have the appropriate kinds of gills to act as a host environment. After developing into juvenile mussels, the stage is complete, allowing the mussel to finally leave the fish and fall safely to the streambed.

93. Stolzenburg, "The Mussels' Message," 19.

94. Ibid.; Hoskins, *Anderson County*, 49, 115–16, 344–45.

95. McDonald and Muldowny, *TVA and the Dispossessed*, 246; Brown, "Smoky Mountain Story," 235–37; Moore, "Damming the Valley," 31; Davidson, *The Tennessee*, 2: 237; Tennessee Valley Authority, *Changed Land, Changed Lives*, 53–60. For the recent rediscovery of the robust redhorse as well as efforts to recover populations in the upper south, see Bryant et al., "The Mystery Fish," 27–35.

96. Quoted in Whetstone, "When the Valley Became a Lake," 33.

97. MacDonald quoted in Davis and Brown, "I Thought the Whole World Was Going to Die," 31; Ashe, "Chestnut in Tennessee," 5–6. Charlotte Pyle determined that the American chestnut once covered 31 percent, or 159,165 acres, of what is today the Great Smoky Mountains National Park ("Vegetation Disturbance History," 11).

98. Ayres and Ashe, *The Southern Appalachian Forests*, 30, 49, 52–53; Buttrick, *Chestnut in North Carolina*, 7.

99. Plummer, "18th Century Forests in Georgia," 7; MacDonald quoted in Davis and Brown, "I Thought the Whole World Was Going to Die," 30–31.

100. Gravatt, *Chestnut Blight*, 1–3; Hepting, "Death of the American Chestnut," 61–62; Anagnostakis and Hillman, "Evolution of the Chestnut Tree and Its Blight," 3–10. The fungus, which germinates in the infected tree, sends fine threads called mycelia into the inner bark that kill each vital cell they invade. The resulting cankers, as they are called by plant pathologists, exude sticky masses onto the feet of birds, insects, animals, and human beings, who in turn carry the fungus deeper into the forest.

101. *Southern Lumberman,* 6 August 1910, 38C; Metcalf, "The Chestnut Tree Blight," 241–42; second quote from Davis and Brown, "I Thought the Whole World Was Going to Die," 30. See also Kuhlman, "The Devastation of American Chestnut by Blight," 1–2.

102. Cole, *Tales from a Country Ledger,* 105; Gravatt, *Chestnut Blight,* 3, fig. 1; Murrill, "The Spread of the Chestnut Disease," 23–30; Brown, "Smoky Mountain Story," 154–55.

103. Western Carolina Lumber and Timber Association, "Report of Committee," 4; U. S. Department of Agriculture, "Deterioration of Chestnut," 1; Exum, "Tree in a Coma," 20–23.

104. Caudill, *Night Comes to the Cumberlands,* 182.

105. Pinchot in Donald E. Davis, "Where There Be Mountains," 82; Woody interview; Grossman quoted in Wheeler, "Where There Be Mountains, There Be Chestnuts," 3.

106. Cole interview; Effler quoted in Weals, *Last Train to Elkmont,* 128.

107. Opler, "Insects of American Chestnut," 83–85; Hill, "Wildlife Value of *Castanea dentata* Past and Present," n.p.

108. Manning interview, 58–59; Newman interview; Nash, "The Blighted Chestnut," 16; Dunn, *Cades Cove,* 226; Williams, *Great Smoky Moutains Folklife,* 96.

109. McCaulley quoted in Brown and Davis, "Trail History Notebook," "Wolf Ridge," n.p. See also Brown, "Smoky Mountain Story," 49–50.

110. Giddings, *Untitled Report on Chestnut Blight,* 173–74; Kuhlman, "The Devastation of American Chestnut by Blight," 1.

111. Wachacha interview, transcript, 50; Brown, "Smoky Mountain Story," 50.

112. Quoted in Nash, "The Blighted Chestnut," 16.

113. Ashe, "Chestnut in Tennessee," 5. Quote from Frothingham, *Timber Growing and Logging Practices,* 12.

114. Baxter, "Deterioration of Chestnut," 19; Nelson and Gravatt, "The Tannin Content of Dead Chestnut Trees," 479–99; Robertson interview.

115. Gravatt, *Chestnut Blight,* 14, fig. 12. According to Robertson of Champion Fibre, when "the pulp yield decreased . . . synthetic tannin materials came in and the price dropped" (Robertson interview).

116. Tribble quoted in Hawkins, "Building Community," 7.

117. Sloan interview.

118. Cole, *Tales from a Country Ledger,* 104.

119. Wheeler, "Changes in the Dietary Habits," 169, 173–74; Black, "A Study of the Diffusion of Culture," 57–83.

120. Wheeler, "A Study of the Remote Mountain People," 34–36; Williams, "Pride and Prejudice," 218, 220, 226–27; Williams, *Homeplace,* 30–32; Morgan, *The Log House,* 98, 102, 105, 107, 109; Williams, *Great Smoky Mountains Folklife,* 73–78; Trout, *Historic Buildings of the Smokies,* 33–35.

8. Conclusion: Nature, Culture, History

1. Barrett, *The Illusion of Technique,* 335.

2. Semple, "The Anglo-Saxons of the Kentucky Mountains," 588–623.

3. Jordon and Kaups, *American Backwoods Frontier*, 19–36.

4. Fischer, *Albion's Seed*, 605–782.

5. Hall, ed., *Von Thünen's Isolated State*, xii–xv, 7–153. For two excellent discussions of the relevance of von Thünen's work to frontier development, see Otto, *The Southern Frontiers*, 3–8; Jordan and Kaups, *American Backwoods Frontier*, 24–28.

6. See, for example, Schlebecker, "The World Metropolis," 187–208; Peet, "The Spatial Expansion of Commercial Agriculture," 283–301; Peet, "Von Thünen Theory," 181–201; Wallerstein, *The Modern World System*, 1: passim; Paynter, *Models of Spatial Inequality*, passim.

7. Dunaway, *The First American Frontier;* Dunaway, "The Incorporation of Mountain Ecosystems," 355–81.

8. See, for example, Hall, "Peripheries, Regions of Refuge, and Nonstate Societies," 282–97; Hall, "The Effects of Incorporation"; Jordan and Kaups, *American Backwoods Frontier*, 26–28, 32–35.

9. See, for example, McFarland, "Head for the Mountains," n.p.

10. Advocates of cultural syncretism, which is not a formal school, belong to a variety of disciplines and credit a number of thinkers in their scholarly work. One of the most frequently cited is James Clifford, an ethnologist who has studied cultural change in both primitive and modern societies. Relevant works promoting syncretic models of cultural evolution include Otto, *The Southern Frontiers;* White, *Middle Ground;* Axtell, *The Invasion Within;* Joyner, *Down by the Riverside;* Clifford, *The Predicament of Culture*.

11. Aguirre-Beltran, *Regions of Refuge*.

12. White, *Middle Ground*, x.

13. Hurt, *Indian Agriculture*, 74.

14. Braun, *Deciduous Forests*, 48.

15. "Special Report: Shear Madness" n.p.

16. Miller, "Southern Appalachia," 80.

BIBLIOGRAPHY

Books and Articles

Abernethy, Thomas Perkins. *From Frontier to Plantation in Tennessee*. Chapel Hill: University of North Carolina Press, 1932.

———. "Social Relations and Political Control in the Old Southwest." *Mississippi Valley Historical Review* 16 (1929–30): 529–37.

———. *Western Lands and the American Revolution*. New York: Russell and Russell, 1959.

Abrahams, Roger D. *Singing the Master: The Emergence of African American Culture in the Plantation South*. New York: Pantheon Books, 1992.

Adair, James. *History of the American Indians*. London, 1775.

Adams, James Truslow. *Atlas of American History*. New York: Macmillan Library Reference, 1985.

Adas, Michael. *Machines as the Measure of Men: Science, Technology, and Ideologies of Western Dominance*. Ithaca, N.Y.: Cornell University Press, 1989.

Agnew, John, and James Duncan. *The Power of Place: Bringing Together Geographical and Sociological Imaginations*. Boston: Unwin Hyman, 1989.

Aguirre-Beltran, Gonzalo. *Regions of Refuge*. Washington, D.C.: Society for Applied Anthropology, 1979.

Alden, John R. *John Stewart and the Southern Colonial Frontier: A Study of Indian Relations, War, Trade, and Land Problems in the Southern Wilderness, 1754–1775*. Ann Arbor: University of Michigan Press, 1944.

———. *The South in the Revolution, 1763–1789*. Baton Rouge: Louisiana State University Press, 1957.

Allen, Barbara, and Thomas J. Schlereth. *Sense of Place: American Regional Cultures*. Lexington: University Press of Kentucky, 1990.

Allen, Joel Asaph. *The American Bison, Living and Extinct*. New York: Arno Press, 1974.

Allen, Turner W. "The Turnpike System in Kentucky: A Review of State Road Policy in the 19th Century." *Filson Club Quarterly* 28 (1954): 239–59.

Altsheler, Brent. "The Long Hunters and James Knox." *Filson Club Quarterly* 5 (1888): 173–74.

Alvord, Clarence, and Lee Bidgood. *The First Explorations of the Trans-Allegheny Region by the Virginians, 1650–1674.* Cleveland: Arthur H. Clark Company, 1912.

Anagnostakis, S. L., and B. Hillman. "Evolution of the Chestnut Tree and Its Blight." *Arnoldia* 52 (1992): 3–10.

Anburrey, Thomas. *Travels through the Interior Parts of America in a Series of Letters by an Officer.* 2 vols. London: William Lane, 1789.

Anderson, William L., ed. *Cherokee Removal: Before and After.* Athens: University of Georgia Press, 1991.

Androsko, Rita J. *Natural Dyes and Home Dyeing.* New York: Dover Publications, 1971.

Anglin, Mary K. "Lives on the Margin: Rediscovering the Women of Antebellum Western North Carolina." In Mary Beth Pudup, Dwight Billings, and Altina Waller, eds., *Appalachia in the Making: The Mountain South in the Nineteenth Century.* Chapel Hill: University of North Carolina Press, 1995.

Appalachian Land Ownership Task Force. *Who Owns Appalachia?: Landownership and Its Impact.* Lexington: University Press of Kentucky, 1983.

"Appalachian Logging Congress Meets in Asheville." *Southern Lumberman,* 6 May 1916: 27–30.

Appleby, Joyce. "Commercial Farming and the 'Agrarian Myth' in the Early Republic." *Journal of American History* 68 (March 1982): 833–49.

Arber, Edward, ed. *Travels and Works of Captain John Smith, President of Virginia and Admiral of New England, 1580–1631.* 2 vols. Edinburgh: John Grant, 1910.

Archdale, John. "A New Description of That Fertile and Pleasant Province of Carolina, by John Archdale, 1707." In Alexander Salley, ed., *Narratives of Early Carolina, 1650–1708.* New York: Charles Scribner's Sons, 1911.

Archer, Margaret. *Culture and Agency: The Place of Culture in Social Theory.* New York: Cambridge University Press, 1988.

Armstrong, Zella. *The History of Hamilton County and Chattanooga.* Vol. 1. Chattanooga: Lookout Publishing Company, 1931.

Arnade, C. W. "Cattle Raising in Spanish Florida, 1513–1763." *Saint Augustine Historical Society Publications* 21 (1965): 3–11.

Arnow, Harriette Simpson. *Flowering of the Cumberland.* Lexington: University of Kentucky Press, 1984.

———. *Seedtime on the Cumberland.* New York: Macmillan, 1960.

Arthur, John P. *Western North Carolina: A History from 1730 to 1913.* Raleigh, N.C.: Edwards and Broughton Printing Company, 1914.

Asbury, Francis. "Journal." In Samuel Cole Williams, ed., *Early Travels in the Tennessee Country.* Johnson City, Tenn.: Watauga Press, 1928.

Ashe, Thomas. "Carolina, or a Description of the Present State of That Country, by Thomas Ashe, 1682." In Alexander Salley, ed., *Narratives of Early Carolina, 1650–1708.* New York: Charles Scribner's Sons, 1911.

———. *Travels in America; Performed in 1806 for the Purpose of Exploring the Rivers Allegheny, Monongahela, Ohio, and Mississippi, and Ascertaining the Produce and Condition of Their Banks and Vicinity.* London, 1808.

Atherton, Lewis E. *The Southern Country Store*. Baton Rouge: Louisiana State University Press, 1949.

Audubon, John James. *Delineations of American Scenery and Character*. New York: Arno, 1970.

Audubon, John James, and Robert Bachman. *The Quadrupeds of North America*. New York, 1846.

Avery, Myron H., and Kenneth S. Boardman. "Arnold Guyot's Notes on the Geography of the Mountain District of Western North Carolina." *North Carolina Historical Review* 15 (1938): 250–56.

Avery, R. Gerald. *Kentucky Bluegrass Country*. Jackson: University of Mississippi Press, 1992.

Axtell, James. *The Invasion Within: The Contest of Cultures in Colonial North America*. New York: Oxford University Press, 1985.

Ayers, Edward L. *The Promise of the New South: Life after Reconstruction*. New York: Oxford University Press, 1992.

Ayers, Harvard, Jenny Hager, and Charles Little, eds. *An Appalachian Tragedy: Air Pollution and Tree Death in the Eastern Forests of North America*. San Francisco: Sierra Club Books, 1998.

Bailes, Kendall, ed. *Environmental History: Critical Issues in Comparative Perspective*. Lanham, Md.: University Press of America, 1985.

Bailey, Fred. "Caste and the Classroom in Antebellum Tennessee." *Maryland Historian* 13 (1982): 39–54.

———. "Class and Tennessee's Confederate Generation." *Journal of Southern History* 51 (February 1985): 31–60.

———. "Tennessee's Antebellum Society from the Bottom Up." *Journal of Southern Studies* 7 (Fall 1983): 260–73.

Bailey, James. "Tennessee's $3,000,000 Fur Industry." *Tennessee Wildlife* (January 1938): 7.

Bailyn, Bernard. *The Peopling of British North America: An Introduction*. New York: Vintage Books, 1988.

Baker, Robert S. *Chattooga County: The Story of a County and Its People*. Roswell, Ga.: W. H. Wolfe Associates, 1988.

Banks, Alan J. "Emergence of a Capitalist Labor Market in Eastern Kentucky." *Appalachian Journal* 7 (Spring 1980): 188–98.

———. "Land and Capital in Eastern Kentucky, 1890–1915." *Appalachian Journal* 8 (Autumn 1980): 8–18.

Barbeau, M. "Maple Sugar: Its Native Origin." *Transactions of the Royal Society of Canada* 40 (1946): 75–86.

Barclay, R. E. *Ducktown Back in Raht's Time*. Chapel Hill: University of North Carolina Press, 1946.

Barnhardt, Wilton. "The Death of Ducktown." *Discover* 8 (October 1987): 35–43.

Barrett, William. *The Illusion of Technique: A Search for the Meaning of Life in a Technological Age*. London: William Kimber, 1979.

Bartram, William. "Observations on the Creek and Cherokee Indians, 1789." *Transactions of the American Ethnological Society* 3 (1853): 20.

————. "William Bartram's Observations on the Creek and Cherokee Indians." In Gregory Waselkov and Kathryn E. Holland Braund, eds., *William Bartram on the Southeastern Indians*. Lincoln: University of Nebraska Press, 1995.

Bassett, John Spencer, ed. *The Writings of Colonel William Byrd, Esquire of Westover in Virginia*. New York, 1901.

Batteau, Allen. *Appalachia and America: Autonomy and Regional Dependence*. Lexington: University of Kentucky Press, 1983.

————. "Appalachia and the Concept of Culture: A Theory of Misunderstandings." *Appalachian Journal* 7 (1979–80): 9–31.

————. *The Invention of Appalachia*. Tucson: University of Arizona Press, 1990.

Beaver, Patricia D., and Burton L. Purrington, eds. *Cultural Adaptation to Mountain Environments*. Athens: University of Georgia Press, 1984.

Beeman, Richard R. "The New Social History and the Search for 'Community' in Colonial America." *American Quarterly* 29 (1977): 422–43.

Belissary, Constantine G. "The Rise of Industry and the Industrial Spirit in Tennessee, 1865–1885." *Journal of Southern History* 19 (1953): 193–215.

Bennett, Charles E. *Laudonniere and Fort Caroline: History and Documents*. Gainesville: University of Florida Press, 1964.

Bennett, Deb, and Robert S. Hoffman. "Ranching in the New World." In Herman J. Viola and Carolyn Margolis, eds., *Seeds of Change: A Quincentennial Commemoration*. Washington, D.C.: Smithsonian Institution Press, 1991.

Benson, Adolph B., ed. *The America of 1750: Peter Kalm's Travels in North America, the English Version of 1770*. Vols. 1 and 2. New York: Dover, 1964.

Bergeron, Paul H. *Paths of the Past: Tennessee, 1770–1970*. Knoxville: University of Tennessee Press, 1979.

Berkeley, Edmund, and Dorothy Smith Berkeley, eds. *The Correspondence of John Bartram, 1734–1777*. Gainesville: University of Florida Press, 1992.

Berthoff, Rowland. "Celtic Mist over the South." *Journal of Southern History* 52 (November 1986): 523–46.

Bible, Jean Patterson. *Melungeons Yesterday and Today*. Rogersville: East Tennessee Printing Company, 1975.

Billings, Dwight. "Culture and Poverty in Appalachia: A Theoretical Discussion and Empirical Analysis." *Social Forces* 53 (1974): 315–23.

Billings, Dwight, and Kathleen Blee. "Appalachian Inequality in the Nineteenth Century: The Case of Beech Creek, Kentucky." *Journal of the Appalachian Studies Association* 4 (1992): 113–23.

Billings, Dwight, Kathleen Blee, and Louis Swanson. "Culture, Family, and Community in Preindustrial Appalachia." *Appalachian Journal* 13 (Summer 1986): 154–70.

Billington, Ray Allen. *America's Frontier Culture: Three Essays*. College Station: Texas A&M University Press, 1977.

————. *Land of Savagery, Land of Promise: The European Image of the American Frontier in the Nineteenth Century*. Norman: University of Oklahoma Press, 1981.

Billington, Rosamund, Sheelagh Strawbridge, Lenore Greensides, and Annette Fitzsimons. *Culture and Society: A Sociology of Culture*. London: Macmillan Education, 1991.

Blackmun, Ora. *Western North Carolina: Its Mountains and Its People to 1880.* Boone, N.C.: Appalachian Consortium Press, 1977.

Blakely, Robert L. *The King Site: Continuity and Contact in Sixteenth Century Georgia.* Athens: University of Georgia Press, 1988.

Blethen, H. Tyler, and Curtis Wood Jr. "The Antebellum Iron Industry in Western North Carolina." *Journal of the Appalachian Studies Association* 4 (1992): 79–87.

———. "The Pioneer Experience to 1851." In Max R. Williams, ed., *The History of Jackson County.* Sylva, N.C.: Jackson County Historical Association, 1987, 5–14.

———. "A Process Begun: The Settlement Period." In Barry Buxton and Malinda Crutchfield, eds., *The Great Forest: An Appalachian Story.* Boone, N.C.: Appalachian Consortium Press, 1985.

———. "A Trader on the Western Carolina Frontier." In Robert D. Mitchell, ed., *Appalachian Frontiers: Settlement, Society, and Development in the Preindustrial Era.* Lexington: University of Kentucky Press, 1992.

Bloom, L. "The Acculturation of the Eastern Cherokee: Historical Aspects." *North Carolina Historical Review* 19 (October 1942): 325–58.

Bode, Frederick A., and Donald E. Ginter. "A Critique of Landholding Variables in the 1860 Census and the Parker-Gallman Sample." *Journal of Interdisciplinary History* 15 (Autumn 1984): 277–95.

———. *Farm Tenancy and the Census in Antebellum Georgia.* Athens: University of Georgia Press, 1986.

Bogan, Arthur E., Lori LaValley, and Gerald F. Schroedl. "Faunal Remains." In Gerald F. Schroedl, ed., *Overhill Cherokee Archaeology at Chota-Tennessee.* University of Tennessee Department of Anthropology Report Investigations 38, Tennessee Valley Authority Publications in Anthropology 42. Knoxville, 1984.

Bolton, Herbert E. "Spanish Resistance to the Carolina Traders in Western Georgia." *Georgia Historical Quarterly* 9 (June 1925): 115–30.

Bonner, James C. *A History of Georgia Agriculture, 1732–1860.* Athens: University of Georgia Press, 1964.

Bonner, James C., and Lucien E. Roberts. *Georgia History and Government.* Athens: University of Georgia Press, 1940.

Bookchin, Murray. *The Ecology of Freedom.* Palo Alto, Calif.: Cheshire Books, 1982.

Botkin, Benjamin Albert, ed. *A Treasury of Southern Folklore: Stories, Ballads, Traditions, and Folkways of the People of the South.* New York: Crown, 1949.

Boyd, Clifford C. "Prehistoric and Historic Human Adaptation in Appalachia: An Archaeological Perspective." *Journal of the Appalachian Studies Association* 1 (1989): 15–27.

Boyd, William K., ed. "Information Concerning the Province of North Carolina." *North Carolina Review* 3 (October 1926): 614–15.

Brashler, Janet G. "When Daddy Was a Shanty Boy: The Role of Gender in the Organization of the Logging Industry in Highland, West Virginia." *Historical Archaeology* 25 (1990): 54–68.

Braun, Lucy E. *Deciduous Forests of Eastern North America.* New York: Hafner Press, 1974.

———. "The Development of Association and Climax Concepts: Their Use in Interpretation of the Deciduous Forest." *American Journal of Botany* 43 (December 1956): 906–11.

Breazeale, J. W. M. *Life As It Is; or Matters and Things in General.* Knoxville, Tenn.: James Williams, 1842.

Breeding, Robert Lee. *From London to Appalachia: A Fascinating Chronicle about the Ancestry of the Southern Highlander.* Knoxville, Tenn.: Breeding, 1979.

Brender, Ernst V., and Elliot Merrick. "Early Settlement and Land Use in the Present Toccoa Experimental Forest." *Scientific Monthly* 71 (November 1950): 318–25.

Brewer, Carson, and Alberta Brewer. *Valley So Wild: A Folk History.* Knoxville: East Tennessee Historical Society, 1975.

Briceland, Alan Vance. *Westward from Virginia: The Explorations of the Virginia-Carolina Frontier, 1650–1710.* Charlottesville: University of Virginia Press, 1987.

Brickell, John. *The Natural History of North Carolina.* Murfreesboro, N.C.: Johnson, 1968.

Briggs, Hilton, and Dinus Briggs. *Modern Breeds of Livestock.* New York: Macmillan, 1980.

Brinkman, Leonard W. "Home Manufactures as an Indication of an Emerging Appalachian Subculture, 1840–1870." *West Georgia College Studies in the Social Sciences* 12 (June 1973): 50–58.

Brockman, C. Frank. *Trees of North America.* New York: Golden Press, 1979.

Brown, Cecil H. *Language and Living Things: Uniformities in Folk Classification and Naming.* New Brunswick, N.J.: Rutgers University Press, 1984.

Brown, Fred. "Bogs of East Tennessee." *Knoxville News-Sentinel,* 22 November 1992: E1.

———. *The Faces of East Tennessee: An Historical Perspective on the Counties of East Tennessee.* Knoxville, Tenn.: Knoxville News-Sentinel, 1990.

Brown, John P. *Old Frontiers: The Story of the Cherokee Indians from Earliest Times to the Date of Their Removal to the West, 1838.* Kingsport, Tenn.: Southern Publishers, 1938.

Brown, Richard D. *Knowledge Is Power: The Diffusion of Information in Early America.* New York: Oxford University Press, 1989.

Bruce, Kathleen. *Virginia Iron Manufacture in the Slave Era.* New York: Augustus M. Kelley, 1968.

Bryant, Richard T., et al. "The Mystery Fish." *Southern Wildlife* (April 1996): 27–35.

Bullard, Helen. *Crafts and Craftsmen of the Tennessee Mountains.* Falls Church, Va.: Summit Press, 1976.

Burchell, R. A. *The End of Anglo-America: Historical Essays in the Study of Cultural Divergence.* Manchester, England: Manchester University Press, 1991.

Burgess, Jacquelin, and John R. Gold, eds. *Geography, the Media, and Popular Culture.* London: Croom Helm, 1985.

Burnett, Edmund C. "Big Creek's Response to the Coming of the Railroad." *Agriculture History* 21 (1947): 129–48.

———. "Hog Raising and Hog Driving in the Region of the French Broad River." *Agriculture History* 20 (1946): 86–103.

Burns, Inez. "Settlement and Early History of the Coves of Blount County, Tennessee." *East Tennessee Historical Society Publications* 24 (1952): 59–68.

Burns, Sarah. *Pastoral Inventions: Rural Life in Nineteenth-Century American Art and Culture*. Philadelphia: Temple University Press, 1989.

Burr, David H. *Map of Kentucky and Tennessee Exhibiting the Post Offices, Post Roads, Canals, Railroads, etc.* London: J. Arrowsmith, 1839.

Burr, Fearing, Jr. *The Field and Garden Vegetables of America: Containing Full Descriptions of Nearly Eleven Hundred Species and Varieties; with Directions for Propagation, Culture, and Use.* Boston, 1865.

Bush, Florence Cope. *Dorie: Woman of the Mountains.* Knoxville: University of Tennessee Press, 1992.

Bushnell, Amy Turner. *The King's Coffer: Proprietors of the Spanish Florida Treasury, 1565–1702.* Gainesville: University of Florida Press, 1981.

Butler, R. "Journal of General Butler." *Olden Time* 2 (1848): 433–64.

Buttel, Frederick, Olaf Larson, and Gilbert Gillespie. *The Sociology of Agriculture.* New York: Greenwood Press, 1990.

Buxton, Barry, and Malinda L. Crutchfield, eds. *The Great Forest: An Appalachian Story.* Boone, N.C.: Appalachian Consortium Press, 1985.

Cain, Andrew W. *History of Lumpkin County for the First Hundred Years, 1832–1932.* Atlanta: Stein Printing Company, 1932.

Calhoun, Creighton Lee. *Old Southern Apples.* Blacksburg, Va.: McDonald and Woodward Publishing Company, 1995.

Callahan, North. *Smoky Mountain Country.* New York: Dell, Sloan and Pearce, 1952.

Camp, W. H. "The Grass Balds of the Great Smoky Mountains of Tennessee and North Carolina." *Ohio Journal of Science* 3 (1931): 157–64.

Campbell, John C. *The Southern Highlander and His Homeland.* Lexington: University of Kentucky Press, 1969.

Canby, Henry Seidel. "Top O'Smoky." *Harpers* (March 1916): 574–83.

Cantwell, Robert. *Ethnomimesis: Folklife and the Representation of Culture.* Chapel Hill: University of North Carolina Press, 1993.

Carrier, Lyman. *The Beginnings of Agriculture in America.* New York: McGraw-Hill, 1923.

Carroll, B. R. *Historical Collections of South Carolina: Embracing Many Rare and Valuable Pamphlets Relating to the History of That State.* New York: Harper and Brothers, 1836.

Carter, Charles H. "The New World as a Factor in International Relations, 1492–1739." In Fredi Chiappelli, ed., *First Images of America: The Impact of the New World on the Old.* 2 vols. Berkeley: University of California Press, 1976, 1: 231–57.

Caruthers, R. L., and A. O. P. Nicholson, eds. *A Compilation of the Statutes of Tennessee.* Nashville, Tenn.: James Smith, 1836.

Catesby, Mark. *The Natural History of Carolina, Florida, and the Bahama Islands.* London, 1731–43. Reprint, Savannah, Ga.: Beehive Press, 1974.

Caudill, Harry M. *Night Comes to the Cumberlands: A Biography of a Depressed Area.* Boston: Little, Brown, 1963.

Chamberlain, A. F. "Maple Sugar and the Indians." *American Anthropologist* 4 (October 1891): 380–84.

Chapman, Jefferson. "Archaeology and the Archaic Period in the Southern Ridge and Valley Province." In Roy S. Dickens Jr. and H. Trawick Ward, eds., *Structure and Process in Southeastern Archaeology.* Birmingham: University of Alabama Press, 1985.

Chapman, Jefferson, Hazel R. Delcourt, and Paul A. Delcourt. "Strawberry Fields: Almost Forever." *Natural History* 9 (1989): 50–58.

Chapman, Jefferson, Paul A. Delcourt, Patricia A. Cridlebaugh, Andrea B. Shea, and Hazel Delcourt. "Man-Land Interaction: 10,000 Years of American Indian Impact on Native Ecosystems in the Lower Little Tennessee River Valley, Eastern Tennessee." *Southeastern Archeology* 1 (Winter 1982): 115–21.

Chapman, Jefferson, and Andrea Brewer Shea. "The Archaeobotanical Record: Early Archaic Period to Contact in the Lower Little Tennessee River Valley." *Tennessee Anthropologist* 6 (Spring 1981): 61–84.

Chard, Thorton. "Did the Spanish Horses Landed in Florida and Carolina Leave Progeny?" *American Anthropologist* 42 (1940): 90–106.

Chiappelli, Fredi, ed. *First Images of America: The Impact of the New World on the Old.* 2 vols. Berkeley: University of California Press, 1976.

Chickering, J. W. "Thermal Belts in North Carolina." *Science* 1 (June 1883): 146–48.

Clark, Joe. *Tennessee Hill Folk.* Nashville, Tenn.: Vanderbilt University Press, 1972.

Clark, Thomas D. *The Greening of the South.* Lexington: University of Kentucky Press, 1984.

———. *Kentucky: Land of Contrast.* New York: Harper and Row, 1968.

———. *Pills, Petticoats and Plows: The Southern Country Store.* New York: Bobbs-Merrill Company, 1944.

———. "Salt: A Factor in the Settlement of Kentucky." *Filson Club Quarterly* 12 (1938): 40–50.

Clark, Victor S. *History of Manufactures in the United States, 1860–1914.* Washington, D.C.: Carnegie Institution of Washington, 1928.

Clark, Walter, ed. *The State Records of North Carolina: Laws 1777–1788.* Vol. 24. Goldsboro, N.C.: Nash Brothers, 1905.

Clarkson, Roy B. *Tumult on the Mountains: Lumbering in West Virginia, 1770–1920.* Parsons, W.Va.: McCalin, 1964.

Clay, James W., et al. *The Land of the South.* Birmingham, Ala.: Oxmoor Press, 1989.

Clayton, LaReine Warden. "East Tennesseans Begin to Advertise." *Tennessee Historical Quarterly* 39 (1980): 149–66.

Clayton, Lawrence A., Vernon James Knight Jr., and Edward C. Moore, eds. *The De Soto Chronicles: The Expedition of Hernando de Soto to North America in 1539–1543.* Vols. 1 and 2. Tuscaloosa: University of Alabama Press, 1993.

Clendening, Carl H. "Early Days in the Southern Appalachians." *Southern Lumberman,* 15 December 1931: 101–5.

Clifford, James. *The Predicament of Culture: Twentieth Century Ethnography, Literature and Art.* Cambridge, Mass.: Harvard University Press, 1992.

Clutton-Brock, Juliet. *The Walking Larder: Patterns of Domestication, Pastoralism, and Predation.* London: Unwin Hyman, 1989.

Cobb, James E. "Historic Fish Traps on the Lower Holston River." *Tennessee Anthropologist* 3 (1978): 31–58.

Cole, William E. *Tales from a Country Ledger.* Acton, Mass.: Tapestry Press, 1990.

———. "Urban Development in the Tennessee Valley." *Social Forces* 26 (October 1947): 67–75.

Coleman, J. Winston. "Old Kentucky Iron Furnaces." *Filson Club Quarterly* 31 (1957): 227–42.

Coleman, Kenneth, ed. *A History of Georgia.* Athens: University of Georgia Press, 1991.

Coles, Robert. *Migrants, Sharecroppers, Mountaineers.* Boston: Little, Brown, 1972.

Collard, Andree, with Joyce Contrucci. *Rape of the Wild: Man's Violence against Animals and the Earth.* Bloomington: Indiana University Press, 1989.

Conzen, Michael P., ed. *The Making of the American Landscape.* Winchester, Mass.: Unwin Hyman, 1990.

Cook, Frederick A., Larry Brown, and Jack E. Oliver. "The Southern Appalachians and the Growth of Continents." *Scientific American* 243 (1980): 160–61.

Coontz, Stephanie. *The Social Origins of Private Life: A History of American Families, 1600–1900.* London: Verso Books, 1988.

Corkran, David H. *The Cherokee Frontier: Conflict and Survival, 1740–62.* Norman: University of Oklahoma Press, 1962.

———. *The Creek Frontier, 1540–1783.* Norman: University of Oklahoma Press/Council of Commerce of Louisiana, 1967.

Cotter, William Jasper. *My Autobiography.* Nashville, Tenn.: Publishing House, Methodist Episcopal Church, 1917.

Coulter, E. Merton. *Auraria: The Story of a Georgia Gold-Mining Town.* Athens: University of Georgia Press, 1956.

———. "The Georgia-Tennessee Boundary Line." *Georgia Historical Quarterly* 35 (December 1951): 269–86.

———. *The South during Reconstruction, 1865–1877.* Baton Rouge: Louisiana State University Press, 1947.

Council, R. Bruce, Nicholas Honerkamp, and M. Elizabeth Will. *Industry and Technology in Antebellum Tennessee: The Archaeology of Bluff Furnace.* Knoxville: University of Tennessee Press, 1992.

Cowdrey, Albert. *This Land, This South: An Environmental History.* Lexington: University Press of Kentucky, 1983.

Coxe, Daniel. *A Description of the English Province of Carolina by the Spaniards Call'd Florida, and by the French La Louisiane, as Also of the Great and Famous River Meschacebe or Mississippi.* London, 1722.

Craig, Alan K., and Christopher Peebles. "Ethnoecologic Change among the Seminoles, 1740–1840." *Geoscience and Man* 5 (June 1974): 83–96.

Crane, Verner. *The Southern Frontier, 1670–1732.* Durham, N.C.: Duke University Press, 1928.

Creekmore, Polly Anna. "Early East Tennessee." *East Tennessee Historical Society Publications* 28 (1958): 146–64.

———. "Early East Tennessee Taxpayers, I, Anderson County, 1802." *East Tennessee Historical Society Publications* 23 (1953): 115–35.

Creese, Walter L. *TVA's Public Planning: The Vision, the Reality.* Knoxville: University of Tennessee Press, 1990.

Crisp, Mitchell. "A Rare Archaeological Occurrence: De Soto Era Beads with a Serpent Gorget." *Artifact News* 1 (May–June 1990): 29.

Cronon, William. *Changes in the Land: Indians, Colonists, and the Ecology of New England.* New York: Farrar, Straus and Giroux, 1983.

———. "Modes of Prophecy and Production: Placing Nature in History." *Journal of American History* 76 (March 1990): 1122–29.

———. "A Place for Stories: Nature, History, and Narrative." *Journal of American History* 78 (March 1992): 1347–76.

———, ed. *Uncommon Ground: Reinventing Nature.* New York: W. W. Norton, 1995.

Crosby, Alfred W. *The Columbian Exchange: Biological and Cultural Consequences of 1492.* Westport, Conn.: Greenwood Publishing Company, 1972.

———. *Ecological Imperialism: The Biological Expansions of Europe, 900–1900.* New York: Cambridge University Press, 1987.

Cumming, William P. "Geographical Misconceptions of the Southeast in the Cartography of the Seventeenth and Eighteenth Centuries." *Journal of Southern History* 4 (1938): 476–92.

———. *The Southeast in Early Maps with an Annotated Check List of Printed and Manuscript Regional and Local Maps of Southeastern North America.* Princeton, N.J.: Princeton University Press, 1958.

Cumming, William P., R. A. Skelton, and D. B. Quinn. *The Discovery of North America.* New York: American Heritage Press, 1972.

Cummings, Joe. "Community and the Nature of Change: Sevier County, Tennessee in the 1890s." *East Tennessee Historical Society Publications* 58–59 (1985–86): 63–88.

Cunningham, Rodger. *Apples on the Flood: The Southern Mountain Experience.* Knoxville: University of Tennessee Press, 1987.

———. "Scotch-Irish and Others." *Appalachian Journal* 18 (Fall 1990): 84–90.

Danhof, Clarence H. *Change in Agriculture: The Northern United States.* Cambridge, Mass.: Harvard University Press, 1969.

Dary, David. *The Buffalo Book: The Full Saga of the American Animal.* Chicago: Sage Books, 1974.

Davenport, Guy. "The Anthropology of Table Manners from Geophagy Onward." In Guy Davenport, *The Geography of the Imagination.* San Francisco: North Point Press, 1981, 345–52.

Davidson, Donald. *The Tennessee.* Vol. 1, *The Old River: Frontier to Secession.* New York: Rinehart and Company, 1946.

———. *The Tennessee.* Vol. 2, *The New River: Civil War to TVA.* New York: Rinehart and Company, 1948.

Davis, D. H. "A Study of Succession of Human Activities in the Kentucky Mountains: A Dissected Highland Area." *Journal of Geography* 29 (March 1930): 94–100.

Davis, Donald E. "Appalachia Revisited." *Utne Reader* (May–June 1989): 26.

———. "Before Albion's Seed: Environmental and Cultural Change in the Appalachian South." *Journal of the Appalachian Studies Association* (Spring 1994): 1–10.

———. "Damming Diversity: The Shallow and the Deep." *Chattooga Quarterly* (Summer 1997): 15–18.

———. *Ecophilosophy: A Field Guide to the Literature.* San Pedro, Calif.: R. & E. Miles, 1989.

———. "Homeplace Geography." *Now and Then* 7 (Spring 1990): 18–19.

———. "Living on the Land: Blue Ridge Life and Culture." *Georgia Wildlife: The Blue Ridge* 6 (1997): 38–53.

———. "On Building Ecological Fences." *Trumpeter* 2 (1988): 70–72.

Davis, Donald E., and Margaret Brown. "I Thought the Whole World Was Going to Die: The Story of the American Chestnut." *Now and Then* (Spring 1995): 30–31.

Davis, Donald E., and Jeffrey Stotik. "Feist or Fiction?: The Squirrel Dog of the Southern Mountains." *Journal of Popular Culture* 26 (Winter 1992): 193–201.

Davis, R. P. Stephen, Jr. "Explaining Mississippian Origins in East Tennessee." In Bruce Smith, ed., *The Mississippian Emergence.* Washington, D.C.: Smithsonian Institution Press, 1990.

Day, Gordon M. "The Indian as an Ecological Factor in the North-Eastern Forest." *Ecology* 34 (April 1953): 329–46.

Delfino, Susanna. "Antebellum East Tennessee Elites and Industrialization: The Examples of the Iron Industry and Internal Improvements." *East Tennessee Historical Society Publications* 56–57 (1984–85): 102–19.

DePratter, Chester. *Late Prehistoric and Early Historic Chiefdoms in the Southeastern United States.* New York: Garland Publishing Company, 1991.

DePratter, Chester, Charles Hudson, and Marvin Smith. "The Hernando de Soto Expedition: From Chiaha to Mabila." In Reid R. Badger and Lawrence A. Clayton, eds., *Alabama and the Borderlands, from Prehistory to Statehood.* Tuscaloosa: University of Alabama Press, 1985.

Devall, Bill, and George Sessions. *Deep Ecology: Living as if Nature Matters.* Layton, Utah: Gibbs Smith, 1985.

DeVivo, Michael S. "The Deforestation of Western North Carolina: 1900–1920." *Pioneer American Society Transactions* 9 (1986): 89–94.

De Vorsey, Louis. *The Indian Boundary Line in the Southern Colonies, 1763–1775.* Chapel Hill: University of North Carolina Press, 1966.

Deyton, Jason B. "The Toe River Valley to 1865." *North Carolina Historical Review* 24 (October 1947): 423–66.

Dick, Everett. *The Dixie Frontier: A Social History of the Southern Frontier from the First Transmontane Beginnings to the Civil War.* New York: Capricorn Books, 1964.

Dickens, Roy S. *Cherokee Prehistory: The Pisgah Phase in the Appalachian Summit Region.* Knoxville: University of Tennessee Press, 1976.

———. "Mississippian Settlement Patterns in the Appalachian Summit Area: The Pisgah and Qualla Phases." In Bruce D. Smith, ed., *Mississippian Settlement Patterns.* New York: Academic Press, 1978, 115–39.

Dirlik, Arif. "Culturalism as Hegemonic Ideology and Liberating Practice." *Cultural Critique* 6 (Spring 1987): 13–50.

Dobyns, Henry F. *Their Number Become Thinned: Native American Population Dynamics in Eastern North America.* Knoxville: University of Tennessee Press, 1983.

Dohrenwend, Bruce P., and Robert J. Smith. "A Suggested Framework for the Study of Acculturation." In Verne F. Ray, ed., *Cultural Stability and Cultural Change: Proceedings of the 1957 Annual Spring Meeting of the American Ethnological Society.* Seattle, Wash.: American Ethnological Society, 1957.

Doran, Michael F. "Antebellum Cattle Herding in the Indian Territory." *Geographical Review* 66 (1976): 48–58.

Dosse, François. *New History in France: The Triumph of the Annales.* Urbana: University of Illinois Press, 1994.

Drake, Daniel. *Pioneer Life in Kentucky, 1785–1800.* New York: H. Schuman, 1948.

Drake, Richard. "Appalachian America: The Emergence of a Concept, 1895–1964." *Mountain Life and Work* 40 (Spring 1965): 6–9.

Drayton, John. *A View of South Carolina: As Respects to Her Natural and Civil Concerns.* Charleston, S.C.: W. P. Young, 1802. Reprint, Spartanburg, S.C.: Reprint Company, 1972.

Drooker, Penelope Ballard. *The View from Madisonville: Protohistoric Fort Ancient Interaction Patterns.* Ann Arbor: Memoirs of the Museum of Anthropology, University of Michigan, No. 31, 1997.

Droze, Wilmon Henry. *High Dams and Slack Waters: TVA Rebuilds a River.* Baton Rouge: Louisiana State University Press, 1965.

Duffy, David Cameron, and Albert J. Meir. "Do Appalachian Herbaceous Understories Ever Recover from Clearcutting?" *Conservation Biology* 6 (June 1992): 196–201.

Dunaway, Wilma A. *The First American Frontier: Transition to Capitalism in Southern Appalachia, 1700–1860.* Chapel Hill: University of North Carolina Press, 1996.

———. "The Incorporation of Mountain Ecosystems into the World-System." *Review* 19 (Fall 1996): 355–81.

Duncan, David Ewing. *Hernando de Soto: A Savage Quest in the Americas.* New York: Crown Publishers, 1995.

Dunn, Durwood. *Cades Cove: The Life and Death of a Southern Appalachian Community, 1818–1937.* Knoxville: University of Tennessee Press, 1988.

Du Pratz, Antoine Le Page. *The History of Louisiana.* London: T. Becket, 1774.

Dykeman, Wilma. *The French Broad.* New York: Rinehart and Company, 1955.

Earle, Timothy K. "Chiefdoms in Archaeological and Ethnohistorical Perspective." *Annual Review of Anthropology* 12 (1987): 276–95.

Eaton, Allen. *Handicrafts of the Southern Highlands.* New York: Dover, 1937.

Edmunds, R. David. *The Shawnee Prophet.* Lincoln: University of Nebraska Press, 1983.

———. *Tecumseh and the Quest for Indian Leadership.* Boston: Little, Brown and Company, 1984.

Egerton, John. *Generations: An American Family.* New York: Simon and Schuster, 1983.

———. *Visions of Utopia: Nashoba, Rugby, Ruskin, and the "New Communities" in Tennes-*

see's Past. Knoxville: Tennessee Historical Commission/University of Tennessee Press, 1977.

Elledge, Barry. "The Influence of the Smoot Tannery on the Economic Development of Wilkes County, N.C., 1897–1940." *Journal of the Appalachian Studies Association* 1 (1989): 105–13.

Eller, Ronald. "Land and Family: An Historical View of Preindustrial Appalachia." *Appalachian Journal* 6 (Winter 1979): 83–109.

———. "Land as Commodity: The Industrialization of the Appalachian Forests, 1880–1940." In Barry Buxton and Malinda Crutchfield, eds., *The Great Forest: An Appalachian Story*. Boone, N.C.: Appalachian Consortium Press, 1985, 15–22.

———. *Miners, Millhands, and Mountaineers: Industrialization of the Appalachian South, 1800–1930*. Knoxville: University of Tennessee Press, 1982.

Elliot, J. H. *Imperial Spain, 1469–1716*. New York: St. Martin's Press, 1963.

Elton, Charles. *The Ecology of Invasions by Animals and Plants*. London: Methuen, 1958.

Ely, William. *Big Sandy Valley: A History of the People and County from Earliest Settlement to the Present Time*. Catlettsburg, Ky.: Central Methodist Publishing Company, 1887.

Enebak, Scott. "The Holiday Nut." *The World and I* (December 1990): 330–35.

Ergood, B. "Toward a Definition of Appalachia." In B. Ergood and B. E. Kuhre, eds., *Appalachia: Social Context Past and Present*. 3rd ed. Dubuque, Iowa: Kendall Hunt, 1991, 31–41.

Ergood, B., and B. E. Kuhre, eds. *Appalachia: Social Context Past and Present*. 3rd ed. Dubuque, Iowa: Kendall Hunt, 1991.

Ernle, Lord. *English Farming Past and Present*. London: Longmans, Green and Company, 1936.

Escott, Paul D., ed. *North Carolina Yeoman: The Diary of Basil Armstrong Thomasson, 1853–1862*. Athens: University of Georgia Press, 1996.

Eubank, F. D. "Early Lumbering in East Tennessee." *Southern Lumberman,* 15 December 1935: 100.

Evans, E. Estyn. "Culture and Land Use in the Old West of North America." *Heidelberger Geographische Arbeiten* 15 (1966): 72–79.

———. "Folk Housing in the British Isles in Materials Other than Timber." *Geoscience and Man* 5 (June 1974): 53–64.

———. *The Personality of Ireland: Habitat, Heritage, and History*. London: Cambridge University Press, 1973.

———. "The Scotch-Irish: Their Cultural Adaptation and Heritage in the American Old West." In Edward Rodney Richey, ed., *Essays in Scotch-Irish History*. London: Routledge and Kegan Paul, 1969.

———. "The Scotch-Irish in the New World: An Atlantic Heritage." *Journal of the Royal Society of Antiquaries of Ireland* 95 (1965): 76–92.

Evans, E. Raymond. "The Graysville Melungeons: A Tri-Racial People in Lower East Tennessee." *Tennessee Anthropologist* 4 (Spring 1979): 1–31.

———. "Highways to Progress: Nineteenth Century Roads in the Cherokee Nation." *Journal of Cherokee Studies* 2 (1977): 394–98.

Ewan, Joseph. "The Columbian Discoveries and the Growth of Botanical Ideas with Special Reference to the Sixteenth Century." In Fredi Chiappelli, ed., *First Images of America: The Impact of the New World on the Old.* 2 vols. Berkeley: University of California Press, 1976, 2: 807–12.

Exum, Ellen Mason. "Tree in a Coma." *American Forests* (November–December 1992): 20–59.

Featherstonhaugh, George W. *A Canoe Voyage up the Minnay Sotor with an Account of the Lead and Copper Deposits in Wisconsin; of the Gold Region in the Cherokee Country; and Sketches of Popular Manners.* London: Richard Bentley, 1847.

———. *Excursion through the Slave States.* Vols. 1 and 2. London: Albemarle Street, 1844.

Ferguson, Robert. "Arnold Village Site Excavations of 1965–1966." In Robert Ferguson, ed., *The Middle Cumberland Culture.* Nashville, Tenn.: Vanderbilt Publications in Anthropology, 1972, 3–49.

Fernow, Berthold. *The Ohio Valley in Colonial Days.* New York: J. Munsell's Sons, 1890. Reprint, New York: Burt Franklin, 1971.

Ferris, George T. *Our Native Lands.* New York: D. Appleton and Company, 1856.

Finger, John R. "Cherokee Accommodation and Persistence in the Southern Appalachians." In Mary Beth Pudup, Dwight Billings, and Altina Waller, eds., *Appalachia in the Making: The Mountain South in the Nineteenth Century.* Chapel Hill: University of North Carolina Press, 1995, 25–49.

———. *The Eastern Band of Cherokees, 1819–1900.* Knoxville: University of Tennessee Press, 1984.

Fink, Paul. *Backpacking Was the Only Way.* Johnson City: Research Advisory Council, East Tennessee State University, 1975.

———. "Early Explorers in the Great Smokies." *East Tennessee Historical Society Publications* 51 (1979): 40–53.

Firestone, Clark B. *Bubbling Waters.* New York: Robert McBride, 1938.

Fischer, David Hackett. *Albion's Seed: Four British Folkways in America.* New York: Oxford University Press, 1990.

"Fish of Tennessee." *Tennessee Wildlife* 1 (August 1937): 14.

Fisher, Stephen, and Mary Harnish. "Losing a Bit of Ourselves: The Decline of Small Farmers." In *Proceedings of the Appalachian Studies Conference, 1980.* Boone, N.C.: East Tennessee State University/Appalachian Consortium Press, 1981, 68–88.

Flamming, Douglas. *Creating the Modern South: Millhands and Managers in Dalton, Georgia, 1884–1984.* Chapel Hill: University of North Carolina Press, 1992.

Fletcher, Stevenson W. *Pennsylvania Agriculture and Country Life, 1640–1840.* Harrisburg: Pennsylvania Historical and Museum Commission, 1950.

Folmsbee, Stanley J., Robert E. Corlew, and Enoch L. Mitchell. *History of Tennessee.* 4 vols. New York: Lewis Historical Publishing Company, 1960.

Foner, Eric. *Reconstruction: America's Unfinished Revolution, 1863–1877.* New York: Harper and Row, 1988.

Force, Peter, ed. *Tracts and Other Papers . . . to the Year 1776.* Washington, D.C.: Peter Force, 1838.

Ford, Lacy K. *Origins of Southern Radicalism: The South Carolina Upcountry, 1800–1860.* New York: Oxford University Press, 1988.

Ford, Thomas, ed. *The Southern Appalachian Region: A Survey.* Lexington: University of Kentucky Press, 1962.

Foreman, Grant. *Indians and Pioneers: The Story of the American Southwest before 1830.* Norman: University of Oklahoma Press, 1930.

———, ed. *A Traveler in Indian Territory: The Journal of Ethan Allen Hitchcock, Late Major-General in the United States Army.* Cedar Rapids, Mich.: Torch Press, 1930.

Foshee, Andrew. "The Political Economy of the Southern Agrarian Tradition." *Modern Age* (Spring 1983): 161–70.

Foster, George. *Culture and Conquest.* Chicago: Quadrangle Books, 1960.

Foster, Stephen William. *The Past Is Another Country: Representation, Historical Consciousness, and Resistance in the Blue Ridge.* Berkeley: University of California Press, 1988.

Fowler, Melvin. *Cahokia: Ancient Capital of the Midwest.* Boston: Addison-Wesley Modules in Anthropology, No. 48, 1974.

Fox, John, Jr. *The Trail of the Lonesome Pine.* New York: Scribner's, 1908.

Franklin, W. Neil. "Virginia and the Cherokee Indian Trade, 1673–1752." *East Tennessee Historical Society Publications* 4 (1932): 3–21.

Fraser, Walter J., and Winfred B. Moore. *From the Old South to the New: Essays on the Transitional South.* Westport, Conn.: Greenwood Press, 1981.

French, Benjamin F., ed. *Historical Collections of Louisiana.* Vol. 4. New York: Wiley and Putnam, 1846–53.

French, Capt. Christopher. "Journal of an Expedition to South Carolina." *Journal of Cherokee Studies* 2 (Summer 1977): 275–96.

French, Laurence, and Jim Hornbuckle, eds. *The Cherokee Perspective: Written by Eastern Cherokees.* Boone, N.C.: Appalachian Consortium Press, 1981.

Fries, Adelaide L., et al., eds. *The Records of the Moravians in North Carolina.* 11 vols. Raleigh: North Carolina Historical Commission, 1922–69.

Friis, Herman R. "A Series of Population Maps of the Colonies and the United States, 1625–1790." *Geographic Review* 30 (1940): 463–70.

Frome, Michael. *Strangers in High Places: The Story of the Great Smoky Mountains.* Garden City, N.Y.: Doubleday and Company, 1966.

Fromm, Roger W. "The Migration and Settlement of Pennsylvania Germans in Maryland, Virginia and North Carolina and Their Effects on the Landscape." *Pennsylvania Folklife* 37 (Autumn 1987): 39–40.

Frost, William. "Our Contemporary Ancestors in the Southern Mountains." *Atlantic Monthly* (March 1899): 311–19.

Gallman, Robert. "Self-Sufficiency in the Cotton Economy of the Antebellum South." In William N. Parker, ed., *The Structure of the Cotton Economy of the Antebellum South.* Washington, D.C.: Agriculture History Society, 1970.

Garretson, Martin S. *A Short History of the American Bison.* New York: American Bison Society, 1927.

Gaston, Kay Baker. *Emma Bell Miles*. Signal Mountain, Tenn.: Walden's Ridge Historical Association, 1985.

Gates, Paul W. *Agriculture and the Civil War.* New York: Alfred A. Knopf, 1965.

Gaventa, John. *Power and Powerlessness: Quiescence and Rebellion in an Appalachian Valley.* Chicago: University of Chicago Press, 1980.

———. "Property, Coal, and Theft." In Helen Lewis, Linda Johnson, and Dan Askins, eds., *Colonialism in Modern America: The Appalachian Case.* Boone, N.C.: Appalachian Consortium Press, 1978, 141–59.

Geertz, Clifford. *The Interpretation of Cultures.* New York: Basic Books, 1973.

Georgia Humanities Council. *The New Georgia Guide.* Athens: University of Georgia Press, 1996.

Gersmehl, Phil. "Factors Leading to Mountaintop Grazing in the Southern Appalachians." *Southeastern Geographer* 10 (April 1970): 67–72.

Giddens, Anthony. *Central Problems in Social Theory: Action, Structure, and Contradiction in Social Analysis.* Berkeley: University of California Press, 1979.

Giddings, N. J. *Untitled Report on Chestnut Blight in West Virginia.* Harrisburg: Pennsylvania Chestnut Blight Conference, 1912.

Gilbert, Bil. *God Gave Us This Country: Tekamthi and the First American Civil War.* New York: Atheneum, 1989.

Gildrie, Richard P. "Towards an Environmental History of Tennessee." *Tennessee Historical Quarterly* (1994): 42–51.

Gilmore, Melvin. *Uses of Plants by the Indians of the Missouri River Region.* Lincoln: University of Nebraska Press, 1977.

Gilmore, William J. *Reading Becomes a Necessity of Life: Material and Cultural Life in Rural New England, 1780–1835.* Knoxville: University of Tennessee Press, 1989.

Ginns, Patsy Moore. *Snowbird Gravy and Dishpan Pie: Mountain People Recall.* Chapel Hill: University of North Carolina Press, 1982.

Gipson, Lawrence. *The British Empire before the American Revolution.* New York: Alfred Knopf, 1939.

Glacken, Clarence J. *Traces on the Rhodian Shore: Nature and Culture in Western Thought.* Berkeley: University of California Press, 1967.

Glassie, Henry. "The Appalachian Log Cabin." *Mountain Life and Work* 39 (1965): 5–14.

———. "The Old Barns of Appalachia." *Mountain Life and Work* 40 (Summer 1965): 21–30.

———. *Pattern in Material Folk Culture of the Eastern United States.* Philadelphia: University of Pennsylvania Press, 1968.

———. "The Types of the Southern Mountain Cabin." In Jan Harold Brunward, ed., *The Study of American Folklore.* New York: W. W. Norton and Company, 1978.

Gold, Raymond. *Ranching, Mining, and the Human Impact of Natural Resource Development.* New Brunswick, N.J.: Transaction Books, 1985.

Goldfield, David R. *Promised Land: The South since 1945.* Arlington Heights, Ill.: Harlan Davidson, 1987.

Goldstone, Jack. "Ideology, Cultural Frameworks, and the Process of Revolution." *Theory and Society* 20 (1991): 405–53.

Goodwin, Gary C. *Cherokees in Transition: A Study of Changing Culture and Environment prior to 1775.* Chicago: University of Chicago, Department of Geography, 1977.

Goodwyn, Lawrence. *The Populist Moment: A Short History of the Agrarian Revolt in America.* New York: Oxford University Press, 1978.

Gordon, C. H. "Notes on the Geology of the Cove Areas of East Tennessee." *Science* 51 (May 1920): 492–93.

Govan, Gilbert E., and James Livingood. *The Chattanooga Country, 1540–1962: From Tomahawks to TVA.* Chapel Hill: University of North Carolina Press, 1963.

Grant, Nancy L. *TVA and Black Americans: Planning for the Status Quo.* Philadelphia: Temple University Press, 1989.

Graves, Henry S. "The South's Forestry and Water Resources." *American Forests* 21 (1915): 370–85.

Gray, Cecil Lewis. *History of Agriculture in the Southern United States to 1860.* Vols. 1 and 2. Gloucester, Mass.: Peter Smith, 1958.

Gray, L. C. "Economic Conditions and Tendencies in the Southern Appalachians as Indicated by the Cooperative Survey." *Mountain Life and Work* 9 (July 1933): 7–12.

Great Smoky Mountains Natural History Association. *Flowering Plants of the Great Smokies.* Gatlinburg, Tenn.: Great Smoky Mountains Natural History Association, n.d.

Green, Evarts, and Virginia D. Harrington. *American Population before the Federal Census of 1790.* New York: Columbia University Press, 1932.

Green, Fletcher. "Democracy in the Old South." In George Brown Tindall, ed., *The Pursuit of Southern History.* Baton Rouge: Louisiana State University Press, 1964.

Green, Michael D. *The Politics of Indian Removal: Creek Government and Society in Crisis.* Lincoln: University of Nebraska Press, 1982.

Griffin, James B. "Eastern North American Archaeology: A Summary." *Science* 156 (1967): 175–91.

———. *The Fort Ancient Aspect: Its Cultural and Chronological Position in Mississippi Valley Archaeology.* Ann Arbor: University of Michigan, Museum of Anthropology Anthropological Papers No. 28, 1966.

Guess, William G. *County Government in Colonial North Carolina.* James Sprunt Historical Publications, Vol. 11, No. 1. Chapel Hill: University of North Carolina Press, 1911.

Gutman, Herbert G. "Work, Culture, and Society in Industrializing America, 1815–1919." *American Historical Review* 78 (June 1973): 531–88.

Guyot, Arnold. "On the Appalachian Mountain System." *American Journal of Science and Art* 31 (1861): 157–87.

Hahn, Steven. "Capitalism and Southern History: The Nineteenth Century." *Social Concept* 6 (December 1991): 52–65.

———. *The Roots of Southern Populism.* New Haven, Conn.: Yale University Press, 1982.

———. "The Unmaking of the Southern Yeomanry." In Steven Hahn and Jonathon Prude, eds., *The Countryside in the Age of Capitalist Transformation: Essays in the Social His-*

tory of Rural America. Chapel Hill: University of North Carolina Press, 1985, 179–203.

Hahn, Steven, and Jonathon Prude, eds. *The Countryside in the Age of Capitalist Transformation: Essays in the Social History of Rural America*. Chapel Hill: University of North Carolina Press, 1985.

Haines, Francis. *The Buffalo*. New York: Thomas Y. Cromwell, 1970.

Hall, Bob. *Environmental Politics: Lessons from the Grassroots*. Durham, N.C.: Institute for Southern Studies, 1988.

Hall, Jacquelyn, et al. *Like a Family: The Making of a Southern Cotton Mill World*. Chapel Hill: University of North Carolina Press, 1987.

Hall, Peter, ed. *Von Thünen's Isolated State*. Oxford: Pergamon Press, 1966.

Hall, Thomas D. "Incorporation in the World-System: Toward a Critique." *American Sociological Review* 51 (June 1986): 390–420.

———. "Peripheries, Regions of Refuge, and Nonstate Societies: Towards a Theory of Reactive Social Change." *Social Science Quarterly* 64 (1983): 582–97.

Hall, William L. "To Remake the Appalachians: A New Order in the Mountains That Is Founded on Forestry." *World's Work* 28 (July 1914): 321–38.

Hally, David J. "The Chiefdom of Coosa." In Charles Hudson and Carmen Chaves Tesser, eds., *The Forgotten Centuries: Indians and Europeans in the American South, 1521–1704*. Athens: University of Georgia Press, 1994, 227–29.

Hally, David J., and James B. Langford. *Mississippi Period Archaeology of the Georgia Ridge and Valley Province*. Athens: University of Georgia Laboratory of Archaeology, 1988.

Hamel, Paul B., and Mary U. Chiltoskey. *Cherokee Plants: A 400 Year History*. Sylva, N.C.: Herald Publishing Company, 1975.

Hamer, Philip M. *Tennessee: A History, 1673–1932*. Vol. 1. New York: American Historical Society, 1933.

Hamilton, Earl J. "What the New World Economy Gave the Old." In Fredi Chiappelli, ed., *First Images of America: The Impact of the New World on the Old*. 2 vols. Berkeley: University of California Press, 1976, 2: 853–84.

Handley, James. *Scottish Farming in the Eighteenth Century*. London: Faber and Faber, 1953.

Hann, John H. *Apalachee: The Land between the Rivers*. Gainesville: University of Florida Press, 1988.

———. "Demographic Patterns and Changes in Mid-Seventeenth-Century Timucua and Apalachee." *Florida Historical Quarterly* 64 (Fall 1986): 371–92.

Hanna, Charles. *The Wilderness Trail*. New York: AMS Press, 1971.

Haragan, Patricia Dalton. *Weeds of Kentucky and Adjacent States*. Lexington: University Press of Kentucky, 1991.

Hardeman, Nicholas P. *Shucks, Shocks, and Hominy Blocks: Corn as a Way of Life in Pioneer America*. Baton Rouge: Louisiana State University Press, 1981.

Hargrove, Erwin C., and Paul K. Conkin. *TVA: Fifty Years of Grass-Roots Bureaucracy*. Urbana: University of Illinois Press, 1983.

Harley, J. B. "Deconstructing the Map." *Cartographica* 26 (Summer 1989): 1–20.

Harney, Will Wallace. "A Strange Land and Peculiar People." *Lippincott's Magazine* 12 (October 1873): 429–38.

Harper, Jared Vincent. "The Adoption and Use of the Horse among Southeastern Indians." *Tennessee Anthropologist* 5 (Spring 1980): 27–35.

Harris, Francis Lantham. *Lawson's History of North Carolina*. London, 1714. Reprint, Richmond, Va.: Garrett and Massie, 1952.

Harshaw, Lou. *The Gold of Dahlonega: The First Major Gold Rush in North America*. Asheville, N.C.: Hexagon Company, 1976.

Hart, John Fraser. "Land Rotation in Appalachia." *Geographical Review* 67 (April 1977): 148–66.

———. "The Spread of the Frontier and the Growth of Population." *Geoscience and Man* 5 (June 1974): 73–81.

Harvey, David. *The Condition of Postmodernity: An Inquiry into the Origins of Cultural Change*. London: Basil Blackwell, 1989.

Hasse, Larry. "Water Mills in the South: Rural Institutions Working against Modernism." *Agricultural History* 58 (July 1984): 280–95.

Hatley, Thomas. "Cherokee Women Farmers Hold Their Ground." In Robert Mitchell, ed., *Appalachian Frontiers: Settlement, Society and Development in the Preindustrial Era*. Lexington: University of Kentucky Press, 1991, 37–51.

———. *Dividing Paths: Cherokees and South Carolinians through the Revolutionary Era*. New York: Oxford University Press, 1995.

Hawkins, Nyoka. "Building Community through Grassroots Democracy." *Local Voices* 10 (February–March 1993): 5–8.

Hay, Robert. "Toward a Theory of Sense of Place." *Trumpeter* 5, no. 4 (Fall 1988): 159–64.

Hays, W. J. "Notes on the Range of Some of the Animals in America at the Time of the Arrival of the White Man." *American Naturalist* 5 (1871): 387–92.

Headden, Harmon C., and Damon Headden. *Conservation of Wildlife and Forests in Tennessee*. Kingsport, Tenn.: Southern Publishers, 1936.

Heiser, Charles B., Jr. *Seed to Civilization: The Story of Man's Food*. New York: W. H. Freeman Company, 1973.

Hemperly, Marion. *Historic Indian Trails of Georgia*. Athens: Garden Club of Georgia, 1989.

Henderson, A. Gwyn, ed. *Fort Ancient Cultural Dynamics in the Middle Ohio Valley*. Madison, Wis.: Prehistory Press, 1992.

Henderson, A. Gwyn, and Christopher Turnbow. "Previous Fort Ancient Chronologies." In A. Gywn Henderson, ed., *Fort Ancient Cultural Dynamics in the Middle Ohio Valley*. Madison, Wis.: Prehistory Press, 1992, 9–15.

Henretta, James A. "Families and Farms: Mentalité in Pre-Industrial America." *William and Mary Quarterly* 35 (January 1978): 3–32.

Henri, Floretta. *The Southern Indians and Benjamin Hawkins, 1796–1816*. Norman: University of Oklahoma Press, 1986.

Hepting, George H. "Death of the American Chestnut." *Journal of Forest History* (July 1974): 61–67.

Herndon, Melvin G. "Indian Agriculture in the Southern Colonies." *North Carolina Historical Review* 44 (1967): 283–97.

Hewatt, Alexander. *An Historical Account of the Rise and Progress of the Colonies of South Carolina and Georgia.* Vol. 2. London, 1779.

Hewes, Leslie. "Cultural Fault Line in the Cherokee County." *Economic Geography* 19 (1942): 136–42.

Hildreth, S. P. "Wild Turkeys in the Kanawha Valley." *American Journal of Science* 29 (1836): 83–90.

Hill, Sarah H. "Weaving History: Cherokee Baskets from the Springplace Mission." *William and Mary Quarterly* 53 (January 1996): 115–35.

———. *Weaving New Worlds: An Ecological History of Southeastern Cherokee Women and Their Basketry.* Chapel Hill: University of North Carolina Press, 1997.

Hilldrup, Robert Leroy. "The Salt Supply of North Carolina during the American Revolution." *North Carolina Historical Review* 22 (October 1945): 393–415.

Hilliard, Samuel B. *Atlas of Antebellum Agriculture.* Baton Rouge: Louisiana State University Press, 1986.

———. *Hog Meat and Hoe Cake: Food Supply in the Old South, 1840–1860.* Carbondale: Southern Illinois University Press, 1972.

———. "An Introduction to Land Survey Systems in the Southeast." *West Georgia Studies in the Social Sciences* 12 (June 1973): 1–15.

"The Historical News: State of Tennessee, Anderson, Campbell, Knox, Morgan, and Scott Counties." *Southern Historical News* 10, no. 39 (February 1990): 1–20.

Hobhouse, Henry. *Seeds of Change: Five Plants that Transformed Mankind.* London: Sidwick and Jackson, 1985.

Hoffman, Alfred. "The Mountaineer in Industry." *Mountain Life and Work* 5 (January 1930): 2–7.

Holloway, Joseph. *Africanisms in American Culture.* Bloomington: Indiana University Press, 1990.

Holm, Le Roy G. *The World's Worst Weeds: Distribution and Biology.* Honolulu: University of Hawaii Press for the East-West Center, 1977.

Holmes, William F. "Whitecapping in Late Nineteenth-Century Georgia." In Walter Fraser and Winfred Moore, eds., *From the Old South to the New: Essays on the Transitional South.* Westport, Conn.: Greenwood Press, 1981, 121–32.

Hooker, Richard J., ed. *The Carolina Backcountry on the Eve of the Revolution: The Journal and Other Writings of Charles Woodsmason.* Chapel Hill: University of North Carolina Press, 1953.

Hopkins, James Franklin. *A History of the Hemp Industry in Kentucky.* Lexington: University of Kentucky Press, 1951.

Horigan, Stephen. *Nature and Culture in Western Discourses.* London: Routledge, 1988.

Horn, Stanley F. *This Fascinating Lumber Business.* New York: Bobbs-Merrill, 1943.

Horwitz, Elinor Lander. *Mountain People, Mountain Crafts.* Philadelphia: J. B. Lippincott, 1974.

Hoskins, Katherine B. *Anderson County.* Memphis: Memphis State University Press, 1979.

Houston, R. A., and I. D. Whyte. *Scottish Society, 1500–1800*. Cambridge: Cambridge University Press, 1989.

Hsiung, David C. "Geographic Determinism and Possibilism: Interpretations of the Appalachian Environment and Culture in the Last Century." *Journal of the Appalachian Studies Association* 4 (1992): 14–23.

———. "How Isolated Was Appalachia?: Upper East Tennessee, 1780–1835." *Appalachian Journal* 16 (Summer 1989): 336–49.

———. *Two Worlds in the Tennessee Mountains: Exploring the Origins of Appalachian Stereotypes*. Lexington: University Press of Kentucky, 1997.

Hudgins, Andrew. *After the Lost War*. Boston: Houghton Mifflin Company, 1988.

Hudson, Charles. "The Hernando de Soto Expedition." In Charles Hudson and Carmen Chaves Tesser, eds., *The Forgotten Centuries: Indians and Europeans in the American South, 1521–1704*. Athens: University of Georgia Press, 1994, 74–122.

———. *The Juan Pardo Expeditions: Explorations of the Carolinas and Tennessee, 1566–1568*. Washington, D.C.: Smithsonian Institution Press, 1990.

———. "Juan Pardo's Excursion beyond Chiaha." *Tennessee Anthropologist* 12 (1987): 74–87.

———. *Knights of Spain, Warriors of the Sun*. Athens: University of Georgia Press, 1997.

———. *The Southeastern Indians*. Knoxville: University of Tennessee Press, 1976.

———. "A Spanish-Coosa Alliance in Sixteenth Century North Georgia." *Georgia Historical Quarterly* 62 (1988): 599–626.

———. "An Unknown South: Spanish Explorers and Southeastern Chiefdoms." In George Sabo and William Schneider, eds., *Visions and Revisions: Ethnohistoric Perspectives on Southern Cultures*. Proceedings of the Southern Anthropological Society, No. 20. Athens: University of Georgia Press, 1987, 6–24.

———, ed. *Black Drink: A Native American Tea*. Athens: University of Georgia Press, 1979.

Hudson, Charles, Marvin Smith, and Chester DePratter. "The Hernando de Soto Expedition: From Apalachee to Chiaha." *Southeastern Archaelogy* 3 (1984): 65–77.

Hudson, Charles, Marvin T. Smith, Chester B. DePratter, and Emila Kelley. "The Tristan de Luna Expedition, 1599–1561." *Southeastern Archaeology* 8 (1989): 31–45.

Hudson, Charles, Marvin Smith, David Hally, Richard Polhemus, and Chester DePratter. "Coosa: A Chiefdom in the Sixteenth-Century Southeastern United States." *American Antiquity* 4 (1985): 723–37.

Hudson, Charles, and Carmen Chaves Tesser, eds. *The Forgotten Centuries: Indians and Europeans in the American South, 1521–1704*. Athens: University of Georgia Press, 1994.

Hufford, Mary. "Weathering the Storm: Cultural Survival in an Appalachian Valley." In Harvard Ayers, ed., *An Appalachian Tragedy: Air Pollution and Tree Death in the Eastern Forests of North America*. San Francisco: Sierra Club Books, 1998, 147–59.

Hughes, J. Donald. *Ecology in Ancient Civilizations*. Albuquerque: University of New Mexico Press, 1975.

Hughes, Ralph H. "Fire Ecology of Canebrakes." *Proceedings of the Tall Timbers Fire Ecology Conference* 5 (1966): 149–57.

Hulbert, Archer B. *The Paths of Inland Commerce: A Chronicle of Trails, Roads, and Waterways.* New Haven, Conn.: Yale University Press, 1920.

Humphrey, Richard A. "Religion and Place in Southern Appalachia." In Patricia D. Beaver and Burton L. Purrington, eds., *Cultural Adaptation to Mountain Environments.* Athens: University of Georgia Press, 1984.

Hunt, Raymond F. "The Pactolus Ironworks." *Tennessee Historical Quarterly* 25 (1966): 176–96.

Hurst, Thomas, ed. *Columbian Consequences.* Vol. 2, *Archaeological and Historical Perspectives on the Spanish Borderlands East.* Washington, D.C.: Smithsonian Institution Press, 1990.

Hurt, Douglas R. *Indian Agriculture in America.* Lawrence: University of Kansas Press, 1987.

Imlay, Gilbert. *A Topographical Description of the Western Territory of North America.* 3rd ed. London, 1797.

Inscoe, John. "Appalachian Otherness, Real and Perceived." In Georgia Humanities Council, *The New Georgia Guide.* Athens: University of Georgia Press, 1996.

———. "Mountain Masters: Slaveholding in Western North Carolina." *North Carolina Historical Review* 41 (April 1984): 143–73.

———. *Mountain Masters, Slavery, and the Sectional Crisis in Western North Carolina.* Knoxville: University of Tennessee Press, 1989.

Institute for Southern Studies. *Who Owns North Carolina?: Part 1: Ownership.* Durham, N.C.: Institute for Southern Studies, 1988.

Irwin, John Rice. *Baskets and Basket Makers in Southern Appalachia.* Exton, Pa.: Schiffer Publishing Company, 1982.

———. *Alex Stewart, Portrait of a Pioneer.* Atglen, Pa.: Schiffer Press, 1985.

Jackson, Laura E. *Mountain Treasures at Risk: The Future of the Southern Appalachian National Forests.* Washington, D.C.: Wilderness Society, 1989.

Jackson, Peter. *Maps of Meaning: An Introduction to Cultural Geography.* Winchester, Mass.: Unwin Hyman, 1989.

Jakle, John A. "Salt on the Ohio Valley Frontier, 1770–1820." *Annals of the Association of American Geographers* 59 (1969): 689–703.

Jefferson, Thomas. *Notes on the State of Virginia.* New York: Harper, 1964.

———. *Thomas Jefferson's Garden Book, 1766–1824.* New York: American Philosophical Society, 1944.

Jeffries, Richard. *The Gamekeeper at Home: Sketches of Natural History and Rural Life.* London: Smith, Elder and Company, 1878.

Jenkins, Gary C. "The Mining of Alum Cave." *East Tennessee Historical Society Publications* 60 (1988): 81–85.

Jillson, Williard Rouse. "Geology of Eastern Kentucky Soils." *Mountain Life and Work* 4 (October 1928): 11–13.

Johnson, Amandus. *The Swedes of the Delaware, 1638–1664.* Philadelphia: Lenape Press, 1914.

———. *The Swedish Settlements of the Delaware.* Vols. 1 and 2. Philadelphia: University of Pennsylvania Press, 1911.

Johnson, E. A. "Effects of Farm Woodland Grazing on Watershed Values in the Southern Appalachian Mountains." *Journal of Forestry* 50 (January 1952): 109–13.

Johnson, Walter Adams. "Elk—The Last of the Big-Game Herds." *Country Life in America* 8 (1905): 506–11.

Johnstone, William C. "The Kentucky Coffeetree." *Filson Club Quarterly* 51 (April 1977): 190–201.

Jolley, Harley E. *Southern Appalachian Forests: The Last Fifty Years.* In Barry Buxton and Malinda Crutchfield, eds., *The Great Forest: An Appalachian Story.* Boone, N.C.: Appalachian Consortium Press, 1985, 23–28.

Jones, Alwyn. "Social Symbiosis: A Gaian Critique of Contemporary Social Theory." *The Ecologist* 20 (May–June 1990): 108–13.

Jones, Loyal. "Appalachian Values." In Robert Higgs and Ambrose Manning, eds., *Voices from the Hills.* Boone, N.C.: Appalachian Consortium Press, 1975.

Jordan, James. "An Ambivalent Relationship: Dog and Human in the Folk Culture of the Rural South." *Appalachian Journal* 27 (1975): 238–48.

Jordan, Terry. *Trails to Texas: Southern Roots of Western Cattle Ranching.* Lincoln: University of Nebraska Press, 1981.

Jordan, Terry, and Matti Kaups. *The American Backwoods Frontier: An Ethnic and Ecological Interpretation.* Baltimore, Md.: Johns Hopkins University Press, 1989.

Joyner, Charles. *Down by the Riverside: A South Carolina Slave Community.* Urbana: University of Illinois Press, 1984.

Kahn, Si. *The Forest Service and Appalachia.* New York: John Hay Whitney Foundation, 1974.

Kains, M. G. *Ginseng: Its Cultivation, Harvesting, Marketing and Market Value, with a Short Account of Its History and Botany.* New York: Orange Judd Company, 1902.

Kammen, Michael. *Selvages and Biases: The Fabric of History in American Culture.* Ithaca, N.Y.: Cornell University Press, 1987.

Kegley, F. B. *Kegley's Virginia Frontiers: The Beginning of the Southwest: The Roanoke of Colonial Days, 1740–1783.* Roanoke, Va.: Stone Press, 1938.

Keith, Arthur. "Topography and Geology of the Southern Mountains." *Mountain Life and Work* 4 (October 1928): 22–28.

Kelley, Michael. "Scientist Showing New Interest in Ancient Folk Remedies." *Knoxville News-Sentinel,* 28 November 1991: B2.

Kellner, Douglas. "The Postmodern Turn: Positions, Problems, and Prospects." In George Ritzer, ed., *Frontiers of Social Theory.* New York: Columbia University Press, 1990, 255–85.

Kellogg, R. S. "Development of Cut-Over Lands." *Southern Lumberman,* 21 December 1912: 99–101.

———. "Future of the Appalachian Forests." *Southern Lumberman,* 21 December 1907: 54–55.

Kennamer, John Robert. *History of Jackson County, Alabama.* Scottsboro, Ala.: Jackson County Historical Association, 1993.

Kennedy, N. Brent. *The Melungeons: The Resurrection of a Proud People.* Macon, Ga.: Mercer University Press, 1995.

Kephart, Horace. "Horace Kephart by Himself." *North Carolina Library Bulletin* 5 (June 1922): 49–52.

———. *Our Southern Highlanders.* 1922. Reprint, Knoxville: University of Tennessee Press, 1976.

Kercheval, Samuel. *A History of the Valley of Virginia.* Woodstock, Va.: J. Gatewood, 1850.

Kern, Stephen. *The Culture of Time and Space, 1880–1918.* Cambridge, Mass.: Harvard University Press, 1983.

Killebrew, Joseph Buckner. *Introduction to the Resources of Tennessee.* Nashville: Tavel, Eastman and Howell, 1874.

Kimbrough, David. *Taking up Serpents: Snake Handlers of Eastern Kentucky.* Chapel Hill: University of North Carolina Press, 1995.

Kincaid, Robert. *The Wilderness Road.* New York: Bobbs-Merrill, 1947.

———. "The Wilderness Road in Tennessee." *East Tennessee Historical Society Publications* 20 (1948): 37–48.

King, Crawford. "Closing of the American Range: An Exploratory Study." *Journal of Southern History* 48 (February 1982): 53–70.

King, Duane H. "Long Island of the Holston: Sacred Cherokee Ground." *Journal of Cherokee Studies* 1 (1976): 113–27.

King, Philip B., and Arthur Stupka. "The Great Smoky Mountains." *Science Monthly* 3 (1950): 31–43.

King, Wayne. "Powder Horn Commemorating the Expedition against the Cherokees." *Journal of Cherokee Studies* 1 (1976): 23–40.

Kingsport Rotary Club. *Kingsport: The Planned Industrial City.* Kingsport, Tenn.: Kingsport Press, 1946.

Kirby, Jack Temple. "The Chapel Hill Regionalists and the Southern Landscape." In Valeria Gennaro Lerda and Tjebbe Westendorp, eds., *The United States South: Regionalism and Identity.* Estratto, Italy: Bibliotecha di Cultura, 1991, 1–39.

———. *Rural Worlds Lost: The American South, 1920–1960.* Baton Rouge: Louisiana State University Press, 1987.

Klink, Carl F., and James J. Talman, eds. *The Journal of Major John Norton, 1816.* Publications of the Champlain Society 46. Toronto: Champlain Society, 1979.

Kloppenburg, Jack. *First the Seed.* New York: Cambridge University Press, 1988.

Knepper, George W. *Travels in the Southland, 1822–1823: The Journal of Lucius Vernus Bierce.* Columbus: Ohio State University Press, 1966.

Knight, L. L. *Standard History of Georgia and Georgians.* Vol. 3. Chicago and New York, 1917.

Knox, John Ballenger. *The People of Tennessee: A Study of Population Trends.* Knoxville: University of Tennessee Press, 1949.

Kollmorgen, Walter M. "The Woodman's Assault on the Domain of the Cattleman." *Annals of the Association of American Geographers* 59 (1969): 215–39.

Kolodny, Annette. *The Land before Her: Fantasy and Experience of the American Frontiers, 1630–1860.* Chapel Hill: University of North Carolina Press, 1984.

Korp, Maureen. *The Sacred Geography of the American Mound Builders.* Lewiston, N.Y.: Edwin Mellen Press, 1990.

Krech, Shepard, III. *Indians, Animals, and the Fur Trade: A Critique of Keepers of the Game.* Athens: University of Georgia Press, 1981.

Kricher, John C. *A Field Guide to Eastern Forests.* Boston: Houghton Mifflin, 1988.

Kroeber, A. L. *Cultural and Natural Areas of Native North America.* Berkeley: University of California Press, 1963.

Kuhlman, E. G. "The Devastation of the American Chestnut by Blight." *Proceedings of the American Chestnut Symposium.* Morgantown: West Virginia University, 1978, 1–3.

Kunz, George Frederick. *Gems and Precious Stones of North America: A Popular Description of Their Occurrence, Value, History, Archaeology, and of the Collections in Which They Exist, Also a Chapter on Pearls and on Remarkable Foreign Gems Owned in the United States.* New York: Scientific Publishing Company, 1890.

Kunz, George Frederick, and Charles Stevenson. *The Book of the Pearl: The History, Art, Science, and Industry of the Queen of Gems.* New York: Century Company, 1908.

Kurry, Theodore W. "Iron and Settlement: The New York–New Jersey Highlands in the Eighteenth Century." *Geoscience and Man* 5 (June 1974): 7–23.

Lambert, Robert S. "Logging on the Little River, 1880–1940." *East Tennessee Historical Society Publications* 13 (1961): 350–63.

———. "Logging the Great Smokies, 1880–1930." *Tennessee Historical Quarterly* 20 (1961): 350–63.

———. "The Oconaluftee Valley, 1800–1860: A Study of Sources for Mountain History." *North Carolina Historical Review* 35 (October 1958): 421–23.

Lamont, Michele, and Robert Wuthnow. "Betwixt and Between: Recent Cultural Sociology in Europe and the United States." In George Ritzer, ed., *Frontiers of Social Theory.* New York: Columbia University Press, 1990, 255–85.

Lander, Arthur B. *A Guide to Kentucky Outdoors.* Hillsborough, N.C.: Menasha Ridge Press, 1978.

Lander, Ernest M. "The Iron Industry in Antebellum South Carolina." *Journal of Southern History* 20 (1954): 337–55.

Lanman, Charles. *Letters from the Allegheny Mountains.* New York: G. P. Putnam, 1849.

Larsen, Lawrence. *The Urban South: A History.* Lexington: University Press of Kentucky, 1990.

Laslett, Peter. *The World We Have Lost: England before the Industrial Age.* 2nd ed. New York: Scribner's, 1965.

Lefler, Hugh T., ed. *A New Voyage to Carolina.* London, 1709. Reprint, Chapel Hill: University of North Carolina Press, 1967.

Leibhardt, Barbara. "Interpretation and Causal Analysis: Theories in Environmental History." *Environmental Review* 12 (Spring 1988): 23–36.

Lemon, James T. "The Weakness of Place and Community in Early Pennsylvania." In James R. Gibson, ed., *European Settlement and Development in North America: Essays on Geographical Change in Honour and Memory of Andrew Hill Clark.* Toronto: University of Toronto Press, 1978.

Lenski, Gerhard, and Jean Lenski. *Human Societies.* New York: McGraw Hill, 1982.

Leong, Wai-Teng. "Culture and the State: Manufacturing Traditions for Tourism." *Critical Studies in Mass Communication* 6 (1989): 335–75.

Le Page du Pratz, Antoine. *The History of Louisiana.* London: T. Beckett, 1774.

Lesley, J. Peter. *The Iron Manufacturer's Guide to the Furnaces, Forges and Rolling Mills of the United States.* New York: J. Wiley, 1859.

Lewis, Helen, et al. *Colonialism in Modern America: The Appalachian Case.* Boone, N.C.: Appalachian Consortium Press, 1978.

Lewis, Johanna Miller. "Women Artisans in Backcountry North Carolina, 1753–1790." *North Carolina Historical Review* 68, no. 3 (July 1991): 214–36.

Lewis, Ronald L. *Coal, Iron, and Slaves: Industrial Slavery in Maryland and Virginia, 1715–1865.* Westport, Conn.: Greenwood Press, 1979.

———. "Railroads, Deforestation, and the Transformation of Agriculture in the West Virginia Back Counties, 1880–1920." In Mary Beth Pudup, Dwight Billings, and Altina Waller, eds., *Appalachia in the Making: The Mountain South in the Nineteenth Century.* Chapel Hill: University of North Carolina Press, 1995, 297–320.

———. *Transforming the Appalachian Countryside: Railroads, Deforestation, and Social Change in West Virginia, 1880–1920.* Chapel Hill: University of North Carolina Press, 1998.

Lewis, Thomas McDowell Nelson, and Madeline Kneberg. *Tribes that Slumber: Indian Times in the Tennessee Region.* Knoxville: University of Tennessee Press, 1956.

Leyburn, James G. *The Scotch-Irish: A Social History.* Chapel Hill: University of North Carolina Press, 1962.

"Life of the Raftsman." *Daily Times* (Chattanooga, Tenn.), 17 February 1902: 3.

Lindsay, Mary M., and Susan Power Bratton. "The Vegetation of Grassy Balds and Other High Elevation Disturbed Areas in the Great Smoky Mountains National Park." *Bulletin of the Torrey Botanical Club* 106 (October–December 1974): 264–75.

Lindstrom, Diane. "Southern Dependence upon Interregional Grain Supplies: A Review of the Trade Flows, 1840–1860." In W. N. Parker, ed., *The Structure of the Cotton Economy of the Antebellum South.* Washington, D.C.: Agriculture History Society, 1970, 101–13.

Livermore, Shaw. *Early American Land Companies: Their Influence on Corporate Development.* New York: Octagon Books, 1968.

"Local Officials Optimistic about Bear Creek Funding." *Scott County News* (Oneida, Tenn.), 28 September 1989: 1.

Logan, John H. *A History of the Upper Country of South Carolina from the Earliest Period to the Close of the War of Independence.* Charleston, S.C.: S. G. Courtney and Company, 1859.

Lopez, Barry. *The Rediscovery of North America.* Lexington: University of Kentucky Press, 1990.

Lovingood, Paul E., Jr., and Robert E. Reiman. *Emerging Patterns in the Southern Highlands: A Reference Atlas.* Vol. 2, *Agriculture.* Boone, N.C.: Appalachian Consortium Press, 1987.

Lowitt, Richard. "The TVA, 1933–45." In Erwin C. Hargrove and Paul Conkin, eds., *TVA: Fifty Years of Grass-Roots Bureaucracy.* Urbana: University of Illinois Press, 1983.

Luther, Edward T. *Our Restless Earth: The Geologic Regions of Tennessee.* Knoxville: Historical Commission/University of Tennessee Press, 1977.

Lytle, Andrew Nelson. *From Eden to Babylon: The Social and Political Essays of Andrew Nelson Lytle.* Washington, D.C.: Regnery Gateway, 1990.

MacCleery, Douglas W. *American Forests: A History of Resiliency and Recovery.* Durham, N.C.: Forest History Society, 1994.

MacKensie, Donald A. *Scottish Folk-Lore and Folk-Life: Studies in Race, Culture, and Tradition.* London, 1935.

Maclean, John P. *An Historical Account of the Settlements of Scotch Highlanders prior to the Peace of 1783.* Clearfield, 1997.

MacLean, Malcolm, and Christopher Carrell. *As an Fhearann/From the Land: A Century of Images of the Scottish Highlands.* Edinburgh and Glasgow: Mainstream Publishing, 1986.

MacLeish, William H. "1492 America: The Land Columbus Never Saw." *Smithsonian* 22 (November 1991): 34–48.

MacLysaght, Edward. *Irish Life in the Seventeenth Century.* Shannon: Irish University Press, 1969.

MacMaster, Richard K. "The Cattle Trade in Western Virginia, 1760–1830." In Robert D. Mitchell, ed., *Appalachian Frontiers: Settlement, Society, and Development in the Preindustrial Era.* Lexington: University of Kentucky Press, 1991.

"Madison et al. v. Ducktown Sulphur, Copper, and Iron Co., Limited. McGhee et al. v. Tennessee Copper Co. et al. Farner v. Tennessee Copper Co." Supreme Court of Tennessee, 26 November 1904. *Southwestern Reporter,* 658–67.

Malone, Henry F. *Cherokees of the Old South: A People in Transition.* Athens: University of Georgia Press, 1956.

Mancall, Peter C. *Deadly Medicine: Indians and Alcohol in Early America.* Ithaca, N.Y.: Cornell University Press, 1995.

———. *Valley of Opportunity: Economic Culture along the Upper Susquehanna, 1700–1800.* Ithaca, N.Y.: Cornell University Press, 1991.

Mann, Ralph "Mountains, Land, and Kin Networks: Burkes Garden, Virginia, in the 1840s and 1850s." *Journal of Southern History* 50 (1992): 411–34.

Mann, Susan Archer. *Agrarian Capitalism in Theory and Practice.* Chapel Hill: University of North Carolina Press, 1990.

Manning, Russ. *The Historic Cumberland Plateau: An Explorer's Guide.* Knoxville: University of Tennessee Press, 1993.

Marburg, Sandra. "Women and the Environment: Subsistence Paradigms, 1850–1950." *Environmental Review* 8 (Spring 1984): 7–22.

Mark, Alan F. "The Ecology of the Southern Appalachian Grass Balds." *Ecological Monographs* 23 (1958): 293–336.

Marks, Stuart A. *Southern Hunting in Black and White: Nature, History, Ritual in a Carolina Community.* Princeton, N.J.: Princeton University Press, 1991.

Markusen, Ann R. *Regions: The Economics and Politics of Territory.* Totoma, N.J.: Roman and Littlefield, 1987.

Martin, Joel W. *Sacred Revolt: The Muskogees' Struggle for a New World.* Boston: Beacon Press, 1991.

Marx, Leo. *The Machine in the Garden: Technology and the Pastoral Ideal in America.* New York: Oxford University Press, 1964.

Mather, Eugene Cotton, and James Fraser Hart. "Fences and Farms." *Geographical Review* 44 (April 1945): 201–23.

Matthews, M. Taylor. *Experience-Worlds of Mountain People: Institutional Efficiency in Appalachian Village and Hinterland Communities.* New York: Teachers College, Columbia University, 1937.

Matthiessen, Peter. *Wildlife in America.* New York: Viking, 1987.

Maxwell, Hu. "The Use and Abuse of Forests by Virginia Indians." *William and Mary College Quarterly Historical Magazine* 19 (October 1910): 73–103.

Mayer, John J., and I. Lehr Brisbin Jr. *Wild Pigs of the United States: Their History, Comparative Morphology, and Current Status.* Athens: University of Georgia Press, 1991.

McCain, Stacy, et al. "Vision of Conquest: 'It Was the Richest Land in the World.'" In Pierre-Rene Noth, ed., *Past-Times: From the Dawn of Time to de Soto.* Rome, Ga.: News Publishing Company, 1994.

McClane, A. J. *McClane's Field Guide to Freshwater Fishes of North America.* New York: Holt, Rinehart and Winston, 1965.

McCourt, Desmond. "Infield and Outfield in Ireland." *Economic History Review* 16 (July 1955): 369–78.

McCoy, Joseph G. *Cattle Trade of the West and Southwest.* 1874. Reprint, Readex Microprint, 1966.

McCoy, William J. "Recollections of an Early Fish Trap on the Holston River." *Tennessee Anthropologist* 5 (Fall 1980): 179–84.

McCuller, Bernice. *This Is Your Georgia.* Northpost, Ala.: American Southern Publishing Company, 1966.

McDaniel, Susie Blaylock. *The Official History of Catoosa County.* Dalton, Ga.: Gregory Printing and Office, 1956.

McDonald, Forrest, and Ellen Shapiro McDonald. "The Ethnic Origins of the American People, 1790." *William and Mary Quarterly* 37 (April 1980): 179–99.

McDonald, Forrest, and Grady McWhiney. "The Antebellum Southern Herdsman: A Reinterpretation." *Journal of Southern History* 41 (May 1975): 148–68.

McDonald, Michael J., and John Muldowny. *TVA and the Dispossessed.* Knoxville: University of Tennessee Press, 1982.

McEvoy, Arthur F. *The Fisherman's Problem: Ecology and Law in the California Fisheries, 1850–1980.* New York: Cambridge University Press, 1986.

McKensie, Roberta. "Appalachian Culture as a Reaction to Uneven Development: A World Systems Approach to Regionalism." *Journal of the Appalachian Studies Association* 1 (1989): 93–104.

McKenzie, Robert Tracy. "Wealth and Income: The Preindustrial Structure of East Tennessee in 1860." *Appalachian Journal* 21 (Spring 1994): 260–79.

McKinney, Gordon, Edward Cowan, Rodger Cunningham, Altina Waller, and David Hackett Fischer. "Culture Wars: David Hackett Fischer's *Albion's Seed.*" *Appalachian Journal* 19 (Winter 1992): 161–200.

McLoughlin, William Gerald. *The Cherokee Ghost Dance: Essays on the Southeastern Indians, 1789–1861.* Mercer, Ga.: Mercer University Press, 1984.

———. *Cherokee Renascence in the New Republic.* Princeton, N.J.: Princeton University Press, 1986.

McLoughlin, William Gerald, and Walter H. Conser. "The Cherokees in Transition: A Statistical Analysis of the Federal Cherokee Census of 1835." *Journal of American History* 64 (1977): 678–703.

McLuhan, T. C. *The Way of the Earth: Encounters with Nature in Ancient and Contemporary Thought.* New York: Simon and Schuster, 1994.

McMichael, Philip. *Settlers and the Agrarian Question.* New York: Cambridge University Press, 1984.

McPherson, John. *Brain Tan Buckskin.* Randolph, Kans.: Prairie Wolf, 1987.

———. *Making Meat I: The Primitive Bow and Arrow.* Randolph, Kans.: Prairie Wolf, 1987.

McWhiney, Grady. *Cracker Culture: Celtic Ways in the Old South.* University of Alabama Press, 1988.

McWhiney, Grady, and Forrest McDonald. "Celtic Origins of Southern Herding Practices." *Journal of Southern History* 51 (1985): 165–82.

Meigs, Return J. *A General Statistical Table for the Cherokee Nation.* Winston-Salem, N.C.: Moravian Archives, 1809.

Meining, D. W. *The Shaping of America: A Geographical Perspective on 500 Years of History.* Vol. 1. New Haven, Conn.: Yale University Press, 1986.

Mellos, Koula. *Perspectives on Ecology: A Critical Essay.* New York: St. Martin's Press, 1988.

"Memoirs of Andrew Gennett, Lumberman." *Chattooga Quarterly* (Summer 1997): 5–10.

Menius, Arthur. "James Bennith: Portrait of an Antebellum Yeoman." *North Carolina Historical Review* 58 (July 1981): 305–26.

Merchant, Carolyn. *The Death of Nature: Women, Ecology, and the Scientific Revolution.* San Francisco: Harper and Row, 1980.

———. *Ecological Revolutions: Nature, Gender, and Science in New England.* Chapel Hill: University of North Carolina Press, 1989.

———. "Gender and Environmental History." *Journal of American History* 76 (March 1990): 1117–21.

Meriwether, Margaret Babcock, ed. *The Carolinian Florist of Governor John Drayton of South Carolina, 1766–1822.* Columbia: University of South Carolina Press, 1943.

Meriwether, Robert. *The Expansion of South Carolina, 1729–1765.* Kingsport, Tenn.: Southern Publications, 1940.

Merrell, James. *The Indians' New World: Catawbas and Their Neighbors from European Contact through the Era of Removal.* Chapel Hill: University of North Carolina Press, 1991.

Merrens, H. Roy. *Colonial North Carolina in the Eighteenth Century.* Chapel Hill: University of North Carolina Press, 1964.

Merrill, Michael. "Cash Is Good to Eat." *Radical History Review* 3 (Winter 1977): 42–71.

Merritt, Frank. *Early History of Carter County, 1760–1861.* Knoxville, Tenn.: Archer and Smith Printing Company, 1950.

Metcalf, Haven. "The Chestnut Tree Blight: An Incurable Disease That Has Destroyed Dollars Worth of Trees." *Scientific American* (16 March 1912): 241–42.

Milanich, Jerald T., and Susan Milbrath, eds. *First Encounters: Spanish Explorations in the Caribbean and the United States, 1492–1570.* Gainesville: University of Florida Press, 1989.

Miller, Char, and Hal Rothman, eds. *Out of the Woods: Essays in Environmental History.* Pittsburgh: University of Pittsburgh Press, 1997.

Miller, Trevelyn Francis, ed. *The Photographic History of the Civil War.* Vols. 5 and 6. New York: Thomas Yoseloff, 1957.

Miller, Zell. "Southern Appalachia." *Georgia Wildlife: The Blue Ridge* 6 (1997): 80.

Mills, Stephanie. *In Service of the Wild: Restoring and Reinhabiting Damaged Land.* Boston: Beacon Press, 1995.

Milner, George. "Epidemic Disease in the Postcontact Southeast: A Reappraisal." *Midcontinental Journal of Archaeology* 5 (1980): 39–56.

———. "The Late Prehistoric Cahokia Cultural System of the Mississippi River Valley: Foundations, Florescence and Fragmentation." *Journal of World Prehistory* 4 (1990): 1–43.

Mintz, Sidney. *Sweetness and Power: The Place of Sugar in Modern History.* New York: Penguin Books, 1986.

Mitchell, Elisha P. *Diary of a Geological Tour in 1827 and 1828.* Chapel Hill: University of North Carolina Press, 1827.

Mitchell, Robert D. *Commercialism and the Frontier: Perspectives on the Early Shenandoah Valley.* Charlottesville: University of Virginia Press, 1977.

———, ed. *Appalachian Frontiers: Settlement, Society, and Development in the Preindustrial Era.* Lexington: University of Kentucky Press, 1991.

Mitchell, Robert D., and Paul A. Groves, eds. *North America: The Historical Geography of a Changing Continent.* Totowa, N.J.: Rowman and Littlefield, 1987.

Moerman, Daniel E. *Medicinal Plants of Native America. Research Reports in Ethnobotany,* Contribution 2. Ann Arbor: University of Michigan Department of Anthropology, 1986.

Moltmann, Gunter, ed. *Germans to America: 300 Years of Immigration, 1683–1983.* Stuttgart: Institute for Foreign Relations, 1982.

Montelius, Sigvard. "The Burning of Forest Land for the Cultivation of Crops: 'Svejebruk' in Central Sweden." *Geografiska Annaler* 35 (1953): 41–54.

Montell, William L. *Don't Go up Kettle Creek: Verbal Legacy of the Upper Cumberland.* Knoxville: University of Tennessee Press, 1983.

———. *The Saga of Coe Ridge.* Knoxville: University of Tennessee Press, 1970.

Moore, Tyrel G. "Economic Development in Appalachian Kentucky, 1800–1860." In Robert D. Mitchell, ed., *Appalachian Frontiers: Settlement, Society, and Development in the Preindustrial Era.* Lexington: University Press of Kentucky, 1991.

Moore, Wayne. "Damming the Valley." *Southern Exposure* 23 (Summer 1995): 34–35.

Morgan, Gwenda. "Community and Authority in the Eighteenth-Century South: Tidewater, Southside and Backcountry." *Journal of American Studies* 20 (December 1986): 435–48.

Morgan, John. "Difficulty in Obtaining Lumber in Antebellum Tennessee: Its Impact on House Construction Patterns." *Proceedings of the Fourth Conference on Appalachian Geography.* Athens, W.Va.: Geography Department, Concord College, 1988, 23–30.

———. *The Log House in East Tennessee.* Knoxville: University of Tennessee Press, 1990.

Morgan, Philip D. "Work and Culture: The Task System and the World of Lowcountry Blacks, 1700–1880." *William and Mary Quarterly* 39 (October 1982): 563–99.

Mosby, Henry, and Charles Handley. *The Wild Turkey in Virginia: Its Status, Life History, and Management.* Richmond, Va.: Commission of Game and Inland Fisheries of Virginia, 1943.

Muenscher, W. C. *Weeds.* New York: Macmillan, 1952.

Muir, John. *A Thousand Mile Walk to the Gulf.* Boston: Houghton Mifflin, 1916.

Murie, Olaus. *The Elk of North America.* Harrisburg, Pa.: Stackpole Company, 1951.

Murrill, W. A. "The Spread of the Chestnut Disease." *Journal of the New York Botanical Garden* 9 (1908): 23–30.

Myer, William E. *Indian Trails of the Southeast.* Nashville: Blue and Gray Press, 1971.

———. "Pearl Fisheries of Tennessee." *Tennessee Academy of Science, Transactions* 2 (January 1914): 19–25.

Myers, Steven L. "Wild Turkeys Roar Back from Near Extinction." *New York Times,* 24 November 1991: E5.

Nabhan, Gary Paul. *Enduring Seeds: Native American Agriculture and Wild Plant Conservation.* San Francisco: North Point Press, 1989.

Nabokov, Peter. *Native American Architecture.* New York: Oxford University Press, 1989.

Nash, Gerald D. *Creating the West: Historical Interpretations, 1980–1990.* Albuquerque: University of New Mexico Press, 1991.

Nash, Roderick Frazier. *The Rights of Nature: A History of Environmental Ethics.* Madison: University of Wisconsin Press, 1989.

———. *Wilderness and the American Mind.* New Haven, Conn.: Yale University Press, 1967.

Nash, Stephen. "The Blighted Chestnut." *National Parks* 62 (July–August 1988): 14–19.

Needleman, Carla. *The Work of Craft: An Inquiry into the Nature of Crafts and Craftsmanship.* New York: Alfred A. Knopf, 1979.

Neely, Sharlotte. *Snowbird Cherokees: People of Persistence.* Athens: University of Georgia Press, 1991.

Nelson, R. M., and G. F. Gravatt. "The Tannin Content of Dead Chestnut Trees." *Journal of the American Leather Chemical Assocation* 24 (1929): 479–99.

Newman, Robert D. "The Acceptance of European Domestic Animals by the Eighteenth Century Cherokee." *Tennessee Anthropologist* 4 (1979): 101–7.

———. "Euro-American Artifacts." In Gerald F. Schroedl, ed., *Overhill Archaeology.* Knoxville: University of Tennessee Department of Anthropology Report of Investigations 38, 1986.

News Publishing Company. *Past Times: Birth and Exile of the Cherokee Nation.* Rome, Ga.: News Publishing Company, 1990.

———. *Past Times: From the Dawn of Time to de Soto.* Rome, Ga.: News Publishing Company, 1994.

———. *Past Times: Tales of the Old-Timers.* Rome, Ga.: News Publishing Company, 1995.

Newton, Milton. "Cultural Preadaptation and the Upland South." *Geoscience and Man* 5 (June 1974): 143–54.

Niering, William A., and Nancy C. Olmstead. *The Audubon Society Field Guide to North American Wildflowers, Eastern Region.* New York: Alfred A. Knopf, 1979.

O'Dell, Ruth Webb. *Over the Misty Blue Hills: The Story of Cocke County, Tennessee.* Easley, S.C.: Southern Historical Press, 1982.

Odum, Eugene. *Fundamentals of Ecology.* Philadelphia: Saunders, 1975.

Odum, Howard W. *Southern Regions of the United States.* Chapel Hill: University of North Carolina Press, 1936.

Ogburn, Charlton. *The Southern Appalachians: A Wilderness Quest.* New York: William Morrow and Company, 1975.

Oldmixon, John. "From the History of the British Empire in America, by John Oldmixon, 1708." In Alexander Salley, ed., *Narratives of Early Carolina, 1650–1708.* New York: Charles Scribner's Sons, 1911, 317–73.

Olmsted, Frederick Law. *A Journey in the Backcountry, 1853–1854.* 1860. Reprint, New York: Ben Franklin, 1970.

Opie, John. "Where American History Began: Appalachia and the Small Independent Family Farm." *Proceedings of the Appalachian Studies Conference, 1980.* Boone, N.C.: East Tennessee State University/Appalachian Consortium Press, 1981, 58–67.

Opler, Paul A. "Insects of American Chestnut: Possible Importance and Conservation Concern." *Proceedings of the American Chestnut Symposium.* Morgantown: West Virginia University, 1978.

O'Toole, Thomas. "Culture and Development: Through Romantic Relativism into the Emerging Present." *Appalachian Journal* 6 (Summer 1979): 264–71.

Otto, John S. "The Decline of Forest Farming in Southern Appalachia." *Journal of Forest History* 27 (April 1983): 18–27.

———. "The Migration of the Southern Plain Folk: An Interdisciplinary Synthesis." *Journal of Southern History* 51 (1985): 183–200.

———. "Oral Tradition in the Southern Highlands." *Appalachian Journal* 9 (Fall 1981): 20–31.

———. *Southern Agriculture during the Civil War.* Westport, Conn.: Greenwood Press, 1994.

———. *The Southern Frontiers, 1607–1860: The Agricultural Evolution of the Colonial and Antebellum South.* New York: Greenwood Press, 1989.

Otto, John S., and Nain E. Anderson. "The Diffusion of Upland South Folk Culture, 1790–1840." *Southeastern Geographer* 22 (1982): 89–98.

———. "Slash-and-Burn Cultivation in the Highlands South: A Problem in Comparative Agriculture History." *Society for Comparative Study of Society and History* 24 (January 1982): 131–47.

Owsley, Frank L. "The Pattern of Migration and Settlement on the Southern Frontier." *Journal of Southern History* 2 (1945): 147–76.

———. *Plain Folk of the Old South.* Baton Rouge: Louisiana State University Press, 1949.

———. *The South: Old and New Frontiers.* Athens: University of Georgia Press, 1969.

Paredes, Anthony, and Kenneth Plante. "A Reexamination of Creek Indian Population Trends: 1738–1832." *American Indian Culture and Research Journal* 6 (Fall 1983): 3–28.

Parker, Lin. "Poke Sallit Festival." *Chattanooga News–Free Press,* 21 April 1991: C1.

Parker, William N., ed. *The Structure of the Cotton Economy of the Antebellum South.* Washington, D.C.: Agriculture History Society, 1970.

Parris, John. "Axes, Saws, Splashdams Long Vanished from Smokies." *Asheville Citizen,* 18 March 1991: 1B, 6B.

———. "Gopherwood, Both Rare, Beautiful." *Asheville Citizen-Times,* 24 September 1989: 5A.

———. "Sawing the Virgin Timber." *Asheville Citizen-Times,* 31 August 1980: 2A.

Passmore, John. *Man's Responsibility toward Nature: Ecological Problems and Western Tradition.* New York: Scribner's, 1974.

Paynter, Robert. *Models of Spatial Inequality: Settlement Patterns in Historical Archaeology.* New York: Academic Press, 1974.

"Pearl Fishing Has Vanished as Industry." *Knoxville Journal,* 26 April 1936: 1.

Peattie, Roderick. *Mountain Geography.* Cambridge, Mass.: Harvard University Press, 1936.

———, ed. *The Great Smokies and the Blue Ridge: The Story of the Southern Appalachians.* New York: Vanguard, 1943.

Peebles, Christopher S. "From History to Hermeneutics: The Place of Theory in the Later Prehistory of the Southeast." *Southeastern Archaeology* 9 (Summer 1990): 23–34.

Peet, J. Richard. "The Spatial Expansion of Commercial Agriculture in the Nineteenth Century: A von Thünen Interpretation." *Economic Geography* 45 (October 1969): 283–301.

———. "Von Thünen Theory and the Dynamics of Agriculture Expansion." *Explorations in Economic History* 8 (1971): 181–201.

Pendleton, William C. *History of Tazewell County and Southwest Virginia.* Richmond, Va.: W. C. Hill Printing Company, 1920.

Peregrine, Peter. "Prehistoric Chiefdoms on the American Midcontinent: A World System Based on Prestige Goods." In Christopher Chase-Dunn and Thomas D. Hall, eds., *Core/Periphery Relations in Precapitalist Worlds.* Boulder, Colo.: Westview Press, 1991.

Perkins, Elizabeth. "The Consumer Frontier: Household Consumption in Early Kentucky." *Journal of American History* (September 1991): 486–510.

Perlin, John. *A Forest Journey: The Role of Wood in the Development of Civilization.* Cambridge, Mass.: Harvard University Press, 1991.

Peterson, Lee Allen. *A Field Guide to the Edible Wild Plants of Eastern and Central North America.* Boston: Houghton Mifflin, 1977.

Peterson, Richard A., ed. "Five Constraints on the Production of Culture: Law, Technology, Market, Organizational Structure and Occupational Careers." *Journal of Popular Culture* 16, no. 2 (Fall 1982): 143–53.

———. *The Production of Culture.* Beverly Hills, Calif.: Sage Publications, 1976.

Pferd, William, III. *Dogs of the American Indians.* Fairfax, Va.: Denlinger's, 1987.

Phenis, Albert. "Southern Appalachian Forest Reserve: Its Practical Bearing upon the Country's Industrial and Commercial Development." *Manufacturers' Record* (25 June 1914): 41–43.

Phillips, Ulrich Bonnel. *A History of Transportation in the Eastern Cotton Belt to 1860*. New York: Columbia University Press, 1908.

Pillsbury, Richard. "The Europeanization of the Cherokee Settlement Landscape prior to Removal: A Georgia Case Study." *Geoscience and Man* 23 (1983): 59–69.

Pinkerton, John. *Voyages and Travels in All Parts of the World*. Vol. 13. London: Longman, Hurst, Ress, Orme and Brown, 1812.

Plummer, Gayther. "18th Century Forests in Georgia." *Bulletin of the Georgia Academy of Science* 33 (1975): 1–19.

Pomeroy, Kenneth B., and James G. Yoho. *North Carolina Lands: Ownership, Use, and Management of Forests and Related Lands*. Washington, D.C.: American Forestry Association, 1964.

Pope, John. *A Tour through the Southern and Western Territories of the United States North America, the Spanish Dominions on the Mississippi River, and the Floridas; the Countries of the Creek Nations; and Many Uninhabited Places*. New York: Charles L. Woodward, 1792. Reprint, 1888.

Porter, Albert. *County Government in Virginia: A Legislative History, 1607–1904*. New York: Columbia University Press, 1947.

Posey, Walter B. "Kentucky, 1790–1815: As Seen by Bishop Francis Asbury." *Filson Club Quarterly* 31 (Fall 1957): 333–47.

Pounds, Norman J. G. *Hearth and Home: A History of Material Culture*. Bloomington: Indiana University Press, 1989.

Powell, John Wesley. *Physiographic Regions of the United States*. National Geographic Monographs. Vol. 1. New York: American Books Company, 1985.

Pratt, J. H. "Good Roads and Lumbering." *Southern Lumberman*, 24 December 1910: 63–64.

Preston, Howard Lawrence. *Dirt Roads to Dixie: Accessibility and Modernization in the South, 1885–1935*. Knoxville: University of Tennessee Press, 1991.

Puckett, John L. *Foxfire Reconsidered: A Twenty-Year Experiment in Progressive Education*. Chicago: University of Chicago Press, 1989.

Pudup, Mary Beth. "Beyond the Traditional Mountain Subculture: A New Look at Pre-Industrial Appalachia." In Jim Lloyd and Anne Campbell, eds., *The Impact of Institutions in Appalachia*. Boone, N.C.: Appalachian Consortium Press, 1986.

———. "The Boundaries of Class in Preindustrial Appalachia." *Journal of Historical Geography* 15 (1989): 139–62.

———. "The Limits of Subsistence: Agriculture and Industry in Central Appalachia." *Agriculture History* 64 (Winter 1990): 61–89.

———. "Social Class and Economic Development in Southeast Kentucky, 1820–1880." In Robert D. Mitchell, ed., *Appalachian Frontiers: Settlement, Society and Development in the Predindustrial Era*. Lexington: University Press of Kentucky, 1991, 235–60.

Pudup, Mary Beth, Dwight Billings, and Altina Waller, eds. *Appalachia in the Making: The Mountain South in the Nineteenth Century*. Chapel Hill: University of North Carolina Press, 1995.

Purrington, Burton L. "The Status and Future of Archeology and Native American Studies in the Southern Appalachians." *Appalachian Journal* 5 (Autumn 1977): 40–54.

Pyne, Stephen J. *Fire in America: A Cultural History of Wildland and Rural Fire*. Princeton, N.J.: Princeton University Press, 1982.

———. "Indian Fires," *Natural History* 92 (1983): 6–11.

Raine, James Watt. *The Land of Saddle-Bags: A Study of the Mountain People of Appalachia*. New York: Council of Women of Home Missions and Missionary Education Movement of the United States and Canada, 1924.

Raitz, Karl B., and Richard Ulack. *Appalachia, a Regional Geography: Land, People, and Development*. Boulder, Colo.: Westview Press, 1984.

Ramsey, J. G. M. *Annals of Tennessee to the End of the 18th Century*. Philadelphia: Lippincott, Grambo and Company, 1853.

Ranck, George W. *Boonesborough*. Louisville, Ky.: Filson Club, 1901.

Randall, Henry S. *Sheep Husbandry in the South*. Philadelphia, 1848.

Ransom, Roger, and Richard Sutch. *One Kind of Freedom: The Economic Consequences of Emancipation*. New York: Cambridge University Press, 1977.

Rasnake, Roger Neil. *Domination and Cultural Resistance: Authority and Power among the Andean People*. Durham, N.C.: Duke University Press, 1988.

Raulston, J. Leonard, and James W. Livingood. *Sequatchie: A Story of the Southern Cumberlands*. Knoxville: University of Tennessee Press, 1974.

Reader, John. *Man on Earth*. Austin: University of Texas Press, 1988.

Ready, Milton. "Forgotten Sisters: Mountain Women in the South." *Journal of the Appalachian Studies Association* 3 (1991): 61–67.

Redfield, Robert. "The Folk Society." *American Journal of Sociology* 52 (1947): 293–308.

Redfield, Robert, Ralph Linton, and Melville Herskovits. "Memorandom for the Study of Acculturation." *American Anthropologist* 38 (1938): 149–52.

Reynolds, George P., ed. *Foxfire 10*. New York: Doubleday, 1993.

Reynolds, T. W. *The Southern Appalachian Region*. Vol. 2. Highlands, N.C.: T. W. Reynolds, 1966.

Rhoads, Samuel Nicholson. "Contributions to the Zoology of Tennessee." *Academy of Natural Sciences* 3 (1887): 387–96.

Rice, Otis. *The Allegheny Frontier: West Virginia Beginnings, 1730–1830*. Lexington: University Press of Kentucky, 1970.

Rifkin, Jeremy. *Biosphere Politics*. New York: Crown Books, 1991.

Rikoon, J. Sanford. *Threshing in the Midwest: A Study of Traditional Culture and Technological Change*. Bloomington: Indiana University Press, 1988.

Riley, Harvey. *The Mule: A Treatise on the Breeding, Training and Uses to Which He May Be Put*. New York: Dick and Fitzgerald Publishers, 1876.

Ritchie, Andrew Jackson. *Sketches of Rabun County History, 1819–1948*. Rabun, Ga.: Andrew Jackson Ritchie, 1959.

Robbins, Roy M. *Our Landed Heritage: The Public Domain, 1776–1970*. Lincoln: University of Nebraska Press, 1976.

Robertson, James Alexander, ed. *True Relation of the Hardships Suffered by Governor Hernando de Soto during the Discovery of the Province of Florida . . . Now Newly Set Forth by a Gentleman of Elvas*. 1540. 2 vols. Deland: Florida State Historical Society, 1933.

Robinson, W. Stitt. *The Southern Colonial Frontier, 1607–1763.* Albuquerque: University of New Mexico Press, 1979.

Roe, Frank Gilbert. *The North American Buffalo: A Critical Study of the Species in Its Wild State.* Toronto: University of Toronto Press, 1970.

Rogers, Anne. "The Great Forest: Prehistory." In Barry Buxton and Malinda Crutchfield, eds., *The Great Forest: An Appalachian Story.* Boone, N.C.: Appalachian Consortium Press, 1985.

Rogers, William B. *Report of the Geological Reconnaissance of the State of Virginia.* Philadelphia: Desilver, Thomas and Company, 1836.

Rogers, William Flinn. "Life in East Tennessee near the End of the Eighteenth Century." *East Tennessee Historical Society Publications* 1 (1929): 27–42.

Rogin, Michael Paul. *Fathers and Children: Andrew Jackson and the Subjugation of the American Indian.* New York: Knopf, 1975.

Rohrbough, Malcolm J. *The Trans-Appalachian Frontier: People, Societies, and Institutions.* Oxford: Oxford University Press, 1978.

Romans, Bernard. *A Concise Natural History of East and West Florida.* New Orleans: Pelican, 1961.

Roosevelt, Theodore. *Winning of the West.* 6 vols. New York: G. P. Putnam's Sons, 1889.

Rose, Albert Chatellier. *Historic American Roads: From Frontier Trails to Superhighways.* New York: Crown Publishers, 1976.

Rose, Dan. *Patterns of American Culture: Ethnography and Estrangement.* Philadelphia: University of Pennsylvania Press, 1984.

Ross, Anne. *The Pagan Celts.* Totowa, N.J.: Barnes and Noble, 1986.

Rossiter, W. S. *A Century of Population Growth, 1790–1900.* Baltimore, Md.: Genealogical Publishing Company, 1967.

Rostlund, Erhard. "The Geographic Range of Historic Bison in the Southeast." *Annals of the Association of American Geographers* 50 (1969): 395–407.

Rothrock, Mary. "Carolina Traders among the Overhill Cherokee, 1690–1760." *East Tennessee Historical Society Publications* 1 (1929): 3–18.

Rothrock, Mary U., ed. *The French Broad–Holston Country: A History of Knox County, Tennessee.* Knoxville: East Tennessee Historical Society, 1946.

Rouse, Parke, Jr. *The Great Wagon Road: From Philadelphia to the South.* New York: McGraw-Hill, 1978.

Rudolph, James L. "Earthlodges and Platform Mounds: Changing Public Architecture in the Southeastern United States." *Southeastern Archaeology* 3 (1984): 33–45.

Russ, Kurt, and Jefferson Chapman. *Archaeological Investigations at the Eighteenth Century Overhill Town of Milalquo.* Publications in Anthropology 36. Knoxville: Tennessee Valley Authority, 1983.

Russell, Emily. "Indian-Set Fires in the Forests of the Northeastern United States." *Ecology* 64 (1983): 78–88.

Russell, James M. *Atlanta, 1847–1890: City Building in the Old South and the New.* Baton Rouge: Louisiana State University Press, 1988.

Rutman, Darrett B. "Assessing the Little Communities of Early America." *William and Mary Quarterly* 43 (April 1986): 163–78.

Sabel, John G. "Trade and Development of Local Status and Rank in Dallas Society." *Tennessee Anthropologist* 3 (1978): 14–29.

Sabot, George, and William Schneider, eds. *Visions and Revisions: Ethnohistorical Perspectives on Southern Cultures.* Athens: University of Georgia Press, 1987.

Saikku, Mikko. "The Extinction of the Carolina Parakeet." *Environmental Review* 14, no. 3 (Fall 1990): 1–18.

Sale, Kirkpatrick. *The Conquest of Paradise: Christopher Columbus and the Columbian Legacy.* New York: Alfred A. Knopf, 1990.

———. *Dwellers in the Land: The Bioregional Vision.* San Francisco: Sierra Club Books, 1985.

Salstrom, Paul. "Agricultural Origins of Economic Dependency." In Robert D. Mitchell, ed., *Appalachian Frontiers: Settlement, Society and Development in the Predindustrial Era.* Lexington: University of Kentucky Press, 1991, 261–83.

———. *Appalachia's Path to Dependency: Rethinking a Region's Economic History, 1730–1940.* Lexington: University Press of Kentucky, 1994.

———. "Cash Is a Four-Letter Word." *Appalachian Journal* 16 (Spring 1989): 242–53.

———. "Subsistence Farming, Capitalism, and the Depression in West Virginia." *Appalachian Journal* 11 (Summer 1984): 384–94.

Sartrain, James Alfred. *History of Walker County, Georgia.* Vol. 1. Dalton, Ga.: A. J. Showalter Company, 1932.

Satz, Ronald N. *Tennessee's Indian Peoples: From White Contact to Removal, 1540–1840.* Knoxville: University of Tennessee Press, 1979.

Saucier, Roger T. "Current Thinking on Riverine Processes and Geologic History as Related to Human Settlement in the Southeast." *Geoscience and Man* 22 (May 1981): 7–18.

Sauer, Carl O. *The Early Spanish Main.* Berkeley: University of California Press, 1966.

———. *Land and Life.* Berkeley: University of California Press, 1963.

———. *Seventeenth Century North America.* Berkeley: Turtle Island, 1980.

———. *Sixteenth Century North America: The Land and the People as Seen by the Europeans.* Berkeley: University of California Press, 1971.

Saunders, William L., ed. *The Colonial Records of North Carolina, 1662–1776.* 10 vols. Raleigh, N.C.: Joseph Daniels, 1886.

Schaffer, Daniel. "Managing Water in the Tennessee Valley in the Post-War Period." *Environmental Review* 13 (Summer 1989): 1–16.

Schenck, Carl Alwin. *Birth of Forestry in America, Biltmore Forest School, 1898–1913.* Santa Cruz, Calif.: Forest History Society/Appalachian Consortium Press, 1974.

Schier, Sharon Pierce. *Dietz Family History.* Chattanooga, Tenn.: Sharon Pierce Schier, 1990.

Schlebecker, John T. "The World Metropolis and the History of American Agriculture." *Journal of Economic History* 20 (June 1960): 187–208.

Schlotterbeck, John T. "The 'Social Economy' of an Upper South Community: Orange and Greene Counties, Virginia, 1815–1860." In Orville Vernon Burton and Robert C. McMath Jr., eds., *Class, Conflict, and Consensus: Antebellum Southern Community Studies.* Westport, Conn.: Greenpress, 1982, 3–28.

Schmidt, Ronald G., and William S. Hooks. *Whistle over the Mountain: Timber, Track and Trails in the Tennessee Smokies.* Yellow Springs, Ohio: Graphicom Press, 1994.

Schnaiberg, Allan. *The Environment: From Surplus to Scarcity.* New York: Oxford University Press, 1980.

Schockel, B. H. "Changing Conditions in the Kentucky Mountains." *Scientific Monthly* 3 (August 1916): 115–18.

Schoepf, J. D. *Travels in the Confederation.* Vol. 1. Philadelphia: William J. Campbell, 1911.

Schorger, A. W. *The Wild Turkey.* Norman: University of Oklahoma Press, 1966.

Schroeder, Joan Vannorsdall. "First Union: The Melungeons Revisited." *Blue Ridge Country* (November–December 1997): 36–41.

Schroedl, Gerald, ed. *Overhill Cherokee Archaeology at Chota-Tanasee.* University of Tennessee Department of Anthropology Report Investigations 38. Knoxville: University of Tennessee Department of Anthropology, 1986.

Schroedl, Gerald F., and Clifford Boyd Jr. "Late Woodland Period Culture in East Tennessee." In Michael Nassaney and Charles Cobb, eds., *Stability, Transformation, and Variation: The Late Woodland Southeast.* New York: Plenum Press, 1991.

Schroedl, Gerald, Clifford Boyd Jr., and R. P. Stephen Davis Jr. "Explaining Mississippian Origins in East Tennessee." In Bruce D. Smith, ed., *The Mississippian Emergence.* Washington, D.C.: Smithsonian Institution Press, 1990, 175–95.

Schroedl, Gerald, and Kurt Russ. "An Introduction to the Ethnohistory and Archaeology of Chota and Tennessee." In Gerald Schroedl, ed., *Overhill Cherokee Archaeology at Chota-Tanasee.* University of Tennessee Department of Anthropology Report Investigations 38. Knoxville: University of Tennessee Department of Anthropology, 1986, 1–42.

Schwaab, Eugene, ed. *Travels in the Old South, Selected from Periodicals of the Time.* Lexington: University Press of Kentucky, 1973.

Schwartzman, Helen B. *Transformations: The Anthropology of Children's Play.* New York: Plenum Press, 1978.

Scott, Edward, comp. *Laws of the State of Tennessee.* Knoxville, Tenn.: Heiskell and Brown, 1821.

Scott, James G. *Domination and the Arts of Resistance.* New Haven, Conn.: Yale University Press, 1990.

Sears, John F. *Sacred Places: American Tourist Attractions in the Nineteenth Century.* Chicago: University of Chicago Press, 1989.

Sellers, Charles. *The Market Revolution and the Creation of Capitalism, 1815–1846.* New York: Oxford University Press, 1992.

Sellers, James L. "The Economic Incidence of the Civil War in the South." In Ralph Andreano, ed., *The Economic Impact of the American Civil War.* Cambridge, Mass.: Schenkman Publishing, 1962.

Semple, Ellen Churchill. "The Anglo-Saxons of the Kentucky Mountains: A Study in Anthropogeography." 1901. *Bulletin of the American Geographical Society* 42 (August 1910): 561–94.

———. *Influence of Geographic Environment on the Basis of Ratzel's System of Anthropo-Geography.* New York: Henry Holt, 1911.

Serpell, James. *In the Company of Animals: A Study of Human-Animal Relationships.* Oxford: Basil Blackwell, 1986.

Service, Elman R. *Origins of the State and Civilization*. New York: W. W. Norton, 1975.

Shadburn, Don L. *Cherokee Planters in Georgia, 1832–1838: Historical Essays on Eleven Counties in the Cherokee Nation of Georgia*. Vol. 2. Roswell, Ga.: W. H. Wolfe Associates, 1990.

Shammas, Carole. "How Self-Sufficient Was Early America?" *Journal of Interdisciplinary History* 13 (Autumn 1982): 247–72.

Shands, William E., and Robert G. Healey. *The Lands Nobody Wanted*. Washington, D.C.: Conservation Foundation, 1977.

Shanks, R. E. "Climate of the Great Smoky Mountains." *Ecology* 35 (1954): 354–61.

Shapiro, Henry David. "America and the Idea of America: The Problem of the Persisting Frontier." In J. W. Williamson, ed., *An Appalachian Symposium: Essays in Honor of Cratis D. Williams*. Boone, N.C.: Appalachian State University Press, 1977, 43–55.

————. *Appalachia on Our Mind: The Southern Mountains in the American Consciousness, 1870–1920*. Chapel Hill: University of North Carolina Press, 1977.

Shea, John P. "Our Pappies Burned the Woods." *American Forests* 46 (April 1940): 159–62.

Shelford, Victor E. *The Ecology of North America*. Urbana: University of Illinois Press, 1963.

Shields, Randolph. *The Cades Cove Story*. Gatlinburg, Tenn.: Great Smoky Mountains Natural History Association, 1977.

Shipp, Bernard. *The History of Hernando de Soto and Florida from 1512 to 1538*. Philadelphia, 1881.

Shiva, Vandana. "Resources." In Wolfgang Sachs, ed., *The Development Dictionary: A Guide to Knowledge as Power*. London: Zed Books, 1992.

Shulman, Steven F. "The Lumber Industry of the Upper Cumberland Valley." *Tennessee Historical Quarterly* 32 (1973): 255–64.

Shumate, Claude. "Monthly Column of the American Treeing Feist Association." *Full Cry* (December 1982): 56–57.

Silcox, F. A., W. C. Lowdermilk, and Morris L. Cooke. "The Scientific Aspects of Flood Control." *Science* 84, no. 3 (October 1936): 5–16.

Silver, Timothy. *A New Face on the Countryside: Indians, Colonists, and Slaves in South Atlantic Forests, 1500–1800*. New York: Cambridge University Press, 1990.

Simmons, Morgan. "Owners New, Ghosts Old at Charit Creek: Lodge Reborn in Big South Fork." *Knoxville News-Sentinel*, 1 October 1989: C14.

Simon, Richard M. "Regions and Social Relations: A Research Note." *Appalachian Journal* 7 (1983–84): 23–31.

Simpson, Daniel L. "A Comparison of Pisgah Plant Food Remains from the Warren Wilson Site with Related Archaeological Complexes and Records of the Historic Evidence." In David G. Moore, assembler, *The Conference of Cherokee Prehistory*. Swannanoa, N.C.: Warren Wilson College, 1986.

Sloan, Verna Mae. *How We Talked*. Pippa Passes, Ky.: Pippa Passes Printing, 1982.

Sloane, Eric. *Our Vanishing Landscape*. New York: Wilfred Funk, 1955.

Slotkins, Richard. *The Fatal Environment: The Myth of the Frontier in the Age of Industrialization, 1800–1890*. New York: Atheneum, 1985.

Smith, Betty Anderson. "Distribution of Eighteenth Century Cherokee Settlements." In Duane King, ed., *The Cherokee Nation: A Troubled History*. Knoxville: University of Tennessee Press, 1979, 46–60.

Smith, Bruce D., ed. *The Mississippian Emergence*. Washington, D.C.: Smithsonian Institution Press, 1990.

———. "Research on the Origins of Mississippian Chiefdoms in Eastern North America." In Bruce Smith, ed., *The Mississippian Emergence*. Washington, D.C.: Smithsonian Institution Press, 1990.

———. "The Role of *Chenopodium* As a Domesticate in Pre-Maize Garden Systems of the Eastern United States." *Southeastern Archaeologist* (1985): 51–72.

———. "Variation in Mississippian Settlement Patterns." In Bruce Smith, ed., *Mississippian Settlement Patterns*. New York: Academic Press, 1978, 479–503.

———, ed. *Mississippian Settlement Patterns*. New York: Academic Press, 1978.

Smith, Daniel Blake. "The Study of Family in Early America: Trends, Problems, and Prospects." *William and Mary Quarterly* 39 (1982): 3–28.

Smith, Henry Nash. *Virgin Land: The American West as Symbol and Myth*. New York: Vintage Books, 1957.

Smith, J. Gray. *A Brief Historical, Statistical, and Descriptive Review of East Tennessee, United States of America: Developing Its Immense Agricultural, Mining, and Manufacturing Advantages, with Remarks to Emigrants*. London: J. Leath, 1842.

Smith, James F. *The Cherokee Land Lottery*. New York: Harper and Brothers, 1838.

Smith, John. *Advertisements of the Inexperienced Planters of New England or Anywhere*. Vol. 3. Boston: Massachusetts Historical Society Collection, 1833.

Smith, Marvin T. *Archaeology of Aboriginal Culture Change in the Interior Southeast: Depopulation during the Early Historic Period*. Gainesville: University of Florida Press, 1987.

———. "Indian Response to European Contact: The Coose Example." In Jerald T. Milanich and Susan Milbrath, eds., *First Encounters: Spanish Explorations in the Caribbean and the United States, 1492–1570*. Gainesville: University of Florida Press, 1989.

Smith, Marvin T., and David J. Hally. "Chiefly Behavior: Evidence from Sixteenth Century Spanish Accounts." In Alex W. Barker and Timithy R. Pauketat, eds., *Lords of the Southeast: Social Inequality and the Native Elites of Southeastern North America*. Archaeological Papers of the American Anthropological Association No. 3, 1992.

Smith, Richard M., ed. *Land, Kinship, and Life-Cycle*. Cambridge: Cambridge University Press, 1988.

Smith, Thomas, and John O. Choules. *The Origin and History of Missions Compiled and Arranged from Authentic Documents*. Boston: Gould, Kendall and Lincoln, 1837.

Smout, T. C., ed. *Scottish Woodland History*. Edinburgh: Scottish Cultural Press, 1997.

Smyth, J. F. D. *A Tour of the United States of America*. London: G. Robinson, 1784.

Soltow, Lee. "Land Equality on the Frontier." *Social Science History* 5, no. 3 (Summer 1981): 275–91.

Sondley, A. *Asheville and Buncombe County*. Asheville, N.C.: Citizen Company, 1930.

Southern Arts Federation. *Cumberland Music Tour* (March–April 1988): 1–25. Atlanta: Southern Arts Federation.

Sparks, Jared, ed. *Lives of Daniel Boone and Benjamin Lincoln.* Vol. 13. Boston: Library of American Biography, Second Series, 1847.

"Special Report: Shear Madness." *U.S. News and World Report,* 11 August 1997: n.p.

Speck, Frank G. *Gourds of the Southeastern Indians.* Boston: New England Gourd Society, 1941.

Speer, Jean Haskell. "Culture as Barter." *Appalachian Journal* 10 (Summer 1983): 366–71.

Spicer, Edward H. "Persistent Cultural Systems." *Science* 174 (1971): 795–800.

Spongberg, Stephen A. *A Reunion of Trees: The Discovery of Exotic Plants and Their Introduction into North American and European Landscapes.* Cambridge, Mass.: Harvard University Press, 1990.

Spruill, Julia Cherry. *Life and Work in the Southern Colonies.* New York: Russell and Russell, 1969.

Stanley, L. Lawrence. *A Rough Road in a Good Land.* Cashiers, N.C.: Lawrence Stanley, 1971.

Stannard, David E. *American Holocaust: Columbus and the Conquest of the New World.* New York: Oxford University Press, 1992.

Starobin, Robert S. *Industrial Slavery in the Old South.* New York: Oxford University Press, 1970.

Steele, William O. *The Cherokee Crown of Tannassy.* Winston-Salem, N.C.: John F. Blair, 1977.

Steen, Harold K. *The U.S. Forest Service: A History.* Seattle: University of Washington Press, 1976.

Stephenson, John B. "Eskimos, Scots, and Appalachians: Thoughts on Ethnicity, Energy, and Organization." In Merle Black and John Shelton Reed, eds., *Perspectives on the American South.* Vol. 1. New York: Gordon and Breach Science Publishers, 1985, 217–25.

Steward, Julian, and Louis Faron. *Native Peoples of South America.* New York: McGraw Hill, 1959.

Stilgoe, John R. *Common Landscape of America, 1500–1845.* New Haven, Conn.: Yale University Press, 1982.

Stolzenburg, William. "The Mussels' Message." *Nature Conservancy* (November–December 1992): 17–23.

Stuart, George E. "Etowah: A Southeast Village in 1491." *National Geographic* 180 (October 1991): 54–67.

Stupka, Arthur. *Notes on the Birds of the Great Smoky Mountains National Park.* Knoxville: University of Tennessee Press, 1963.

Summers, Lreis P. *History of Southwest Virginia, 1746–1786.* Richmond, Va.: J. L. Hill Printing Company, 1903.

Surrey, N. M. *The Commerce of Louisiana during the French Regime, 1699–1763.* New York: Columbia University Press, 1916.

Sutton, Ann, and Myron Sutton. *Eastern Forests.* Audubon Nature Series Guides. New York: Alfred A. Knopf, 1985.

Swank, James Moore. *History of the Manufacture of Iron in All Ages, and Particularly in the United States from Colonial Times to 1891.* Philadelphia: American Iron and Steel Association, 1892.

Swanson, Bill. "History, Culture, and Nature." *Trumpeter: Journal of Ecosophy* 8 (Fall 1991): 164–69.

Swanson, Robert E. *A Field Guide to the Trees and Shrubs of the Southern Appalachians.* Baltimore, Md.: Johns Hopkins University Press, 1994.

Swanton, John. "The Kaskinamo Indians and Their Neighbors." *American Anthropologist* 32 (1930): 405–13.

Tate, Luke E. *History of Pickens County, Georgia.* Atlanta: Walter W. Brown, 1935.

Taylor, Joe Gray. *Eating, Drinking, and Visiting in the South: An Informal History.* Baton Rouge: Louisiana State University Press, 1982.

Taylor, Rosser H. "Fertilizers and Farming in the Southeast, 1840–1950: Part I, 1840–1900." *North Carolina Historical Review* 30 (July 1953): 305–28.

————. "Fertilizers and Farming in the Southeast, 1840–1950: Part II, 1900–1950." *North Carolina Historical Review* 30 (October 1953): 483–523.

Theodorson, George, and Achilles G. Theodorson. *A Modern Dictionary of Sociology.* New York: Barnes and Noble, 1969.

Thomas, Jean. *Big Sandy.* New York: Henry Holt, 1940.

Thomas, Keith. *Man and the Natural World: A History of the Modern Sensibility.* New York: Pantheon, 1983.

Thompson, Kathleen, ed. *Touching Home: A Collection of History and Folklore from the Copper Basin, Fannin County Area.* Orlando, Fla.: Daniels Publishers, 1976.

Thompson, Kenneth. "Wilderness and Health in the Nineteenth Century." *Journal of Historical Geography* 2 (February 1976): 145–61.

Thompson, Samuel H. *The Highlanders of the South.* New York: Eaton and Mains, 1910.

Thorndale, William, and William Dollarhide. *Map Guide to the U.S. Federal Censuses, 1790–1920.* Baltimore, Md.: Genealogical Publishing Company, 1987.

Thornton, Russell. *American Indian Holocaust and Survival.* Norman: University of Oklahoma Press, 1987.

————. *The Cherokees: A Population History.* Lincoln: University of Nebraska Press, 1990.

Thorpe, Daniel B. "Assimilation in North Carolina's Moravian Community." *Journal of Southern History* 52 (1986): 19–42.

————. *The Moravian Community in Colonial North Carolina: Pluralism on the Southern Frontier.* Knoxville: University of Tennessee Press, 1990.

Thrower, Norman J. W. *Maps and Man: An Examination of Cartography in Relation to Culture and Civilization.* Englewood Cliffs, N.J.: Prentice Hall, 1972.

Thwaites, Reuben Gold, ed. *Travels West of the Alleghanies Made in 1773–96 by André Michaux; in 1802 by F. A. Michaux; and in 1803 by Thaddeus Mason Harris, M.A.* Notes, Introduction, and Index by Reuben Gold Thwaites. (Separate publication from *Early Western Travels, 1748–1846,* in which series appeared as vol. 3.) Cleveland: Arthur H. Clark Company, 1904.

Tober, James A. *Who Owns Wildlife?: The Political Economy of Conservation in Nineteenth-Century America.* Westport, Conn.: Greenwood Press, 1981.

Tonnies, Ferdinand. *Fundamental Concepts of Sociology: Gemeinschaft and Gesellschaft.* New York: American Book Company, 1940.

Touchstone, Thomas W., and Judith E. Touchstone. *Stone Treasures.* Rome, Ga.: Print Shop, 1983.

Tracy, E. C. *The Life of Jeremiah Evarts.* Boston: Crocker and Brewster, 1845.

Trent, Emma Deane Smith. *East Tennessee's Lore of Yesteryear.* Whitesburg, Tenn.: Emma Deane Smith Trent, 1987.

Troost, Gerard. *Fifth Geological Report.* Nashville, Tenn.: J. George Harris, 1840.

Trout, Ed. *Historic Buildings of the Smokies.* Gatlinburg, Tenn.: Great Smoky Mountains Natural History Association, 1995.

Truett, Randle Bond. *Trade and Travel around the Southern Appalachians before 1830.* Chapel Hill: University of North Carolina Press, 1935.

Tryon, Rolla Milton. *Household Manufactures in the United States, 1640–1860.* Chicago: University of Chicago Press, 1917.

Tucker, William. *Progress and Privilege: America in the Age of Environmentalism.* Garden City, N.Y.: Anchor Press/Doubleday, 1982.

Tunnard, Christopher, and Boris Pushkarev. *Man-Made America: Chaos or Control?* New Haven, Conn.: Yale University Press, 1963.

Turner, Frederick Jackson. *Frontier and Section: Selected Essays of Frederick Jackson Turner.* Englewood Cliffs, N.J.: Prentice-Hall, 1961.

———. *Rise of the New West, 1819–1829.* New York: Collier Books, 1962.

———. "The Significance of the Frontier in American History." *American Historical Association, Annual Report,* 1893.

Turner, William H. "Black Appalachians." In Charles Reagan Wilson and William Ferris, eds., *Encyclopedia of Southern Culture.* Chapel Hill, N.C.: University of North Carolina Press, 1989, 139–42.

Turner, William H., and Edward J. Cabbell, eds. *Blacks in Appalachia.* Lexington: University Press of Kentucky, 1985.

Ulack, Richard, and Karl Raitz. "Appalachia: A Comparison of the Cognitive and Appalachian Regional Commission Regions." *Southeastern Geographer* 21 (1981): 40–53.

———. "Perceptions of Appalachia." *Environment and Behavior* 14 (1982): 725–52.

Urry, John, ed. *Place, Policy and Politics: Do Localities Matter?* Winchester, Mass.: Unwin Hyman, 1990.

Usner, Daniel H. "American Indians on the Cotton Frontier: Changing Economic Relations with Citizens and Slaves in the Mississippi Territory." *Journal of American History* 72 (September 1985): 297–324.

Vanberg, Bert. *On Norwegian Ways.* Minneapolis: Dillon Press, 1974.

Vance, Rupert B. *Human Geography of the South.* Chapel Hill: University of North Carolina Press, 1935.

van der Donck, Adriaen. "A Description of the New Netherlands." *Collection of the New York Historical Society* 1 (1841). Reprint, Syracuse, N.Y.: Syracuse University Press, 1968.

Van Doren, Mark, ed. *The Travels of William Bartram.* 1791. Reprint, New York: Dover Publications, 1955.

Van Every, Dale. *Ark of Empire: The American Frontier, 1784–1803.* New York: William Morrow, 1963.

Van Noppen, Ina Woestemeyer, and John J. Van Noppen. "The Genesis of Forestry in the Southern Appalachians: A Brief History." *Appalachian Journal* 1 (Autumn 1972): 63–71.

———. *Western North Carolina since the Civil War.* Boone, N.C.: Appalachian Consortium Press, 1973.

Verhoeff, Mary. *The Kentucky Mountains, Transportation and Commerce, 1750–1911: A Study in the Economic History of a Coal Field.* Filson Club Publication, Vol. 1, No. 26. Louisville, Ky.: Filson Club, 1911.

———. *The Kentucky River Navigation.* Filson Club Publication, No. 28. Louisville, Ky.: Filson Club, 1917.

Viazzo, Pier Paolo. *Upland Communities: Environment, Population and Social Structure in the Alps since the Sixteenth Century.* Cambridge: Cambridge University Press, 1989.

Vincent, George E. "A Retarded Frontier." *American Journal of Sociology* 4 (1989): 1–20.

Viola, Herman. *After Columbus: The Smithsonian Chronicle of the North American Indians.* New York: Orion Books, 1990.

Viola, Herman, and Carolyn Margolis, eds. *Seeds of Change: A Quincentennial Commemoration.* Washington, D.C.: Smithsonian Institution Press, 1991.

Vlach, John Michael. "African Influences." In Charles Reagan Wilson and William Ferris, eds., *Encyclopedia of Southern Culture.* Chapel Hill: University of North Carolina Press, 1989, 139.

Wagenen, Jared. *The Golden Age of Homespun.* Ithaca, N.Y.: Cornell University Press, 1953.

Wagner, Mark. "The Introduction and Early Use of African Plants in the New World." *Tennessee Anthropologist* 6 (Fall 1981): 112–23.

Walker, H. G., and W. G. Haag, eds. *Man and Cultural Heritage.* Vol. 5, *Geoscience and Man.* Baton Rouge: Louisiana State University Press, 1974.

Walker, Laurence C. *The Southern Forest: A Chronicle.* Austin: University of Texas Press, 1991.

Walker, Robert Sparks. *Torchlight to the Cherokees: The Brainerd Mission.* New York: Macmillan Company, 1931.

Wallach, Bret. "The Slighted Mountains of Upper East Tennessee." *Annals of the Association of American Geographers* 71 (1981): 359–72.

Wallerstein, Immanuel. *The Capitalist World-Economy.* Cambridge: Cambridge University Press, 1979.

———. *The Modern World System.* Vol. 1, *Capitalist Agriculture and the Origins of the European Economy in the Sixteenth Century.* New York: Academic Press, 1974.

———. *The Modern World System.* Vol. 2, *Mercantilism and the Consolidation of the European World Economy, 1600–1750.* New York: Academic Press, 1980.

———. *The Modern World System.* Vol. 3, *The Second Era of Great Expansion of the Capitalist World Economy, 1730–1840s.* New York: Academic Press, 1989.

Walls, David S. "Internal Colony or Internal Periphery?" In Helen Lewis et al., *Colonialism in Modern America: The Appalachian Case.* Boone, N.C.: Appalachian Consortium Press, 1978, 319–49.

———. "On the Naming of Appalachia." In J. W. Williamson, ed., *An Appalachian Symposium: Essays in Honor of Cratis D. Williams.* Boone, N.C.: Appalachian State University Press, 1977, 56–75.

Walpole, Matthew R. "The Closing of the Open Range in Watauga County, North Carolina." *Appalachian Journal* (Summer 1989): 321–35.

Walton, George E. *Mineral Springs of the United States and Canada.* New York: D. Appleton and Company, 1874.

Waselkov, Gregory A. "Lamhatty's Map." *Southern Exposure* 16 (Summer 1988): 23–29.

———. "Seventeenth-Century Trade in the Colonial Southeast." *Southeastern Archaeology* 8, no. 2 (1989): 117–33.

Watkins, Charles. "Culture and Rumors of Culture." *Appalachian Journal* 12, no. 2 (1985): 147–54.

Wauchope, Robert. *Archaeological Survey of Northern Georgia.* Salt Lake City: Memoirs of the Society for American Archaeology, 1966.

Weals,Vic. *Last Train to Elkmont.* Knoxville, Tenn.: Olden Press, 1991.

Weatherford, Jack. *Indian Givers: How the Indians of the Americas Transformed the World.* New York: Crown Publishers, 1988.

———. *Native Roots: How the Indians Enriched America.* New York: Crown Publishers, 1991.

Webb, W. B. "Retrospect of the Lumber Industry in Eastern Kentucky: Story of Fifty Years of Progress." *Southern Lumberman,* 22 December 1923: 178G–78I.

Weber, David. *The Taos Trappers: The Fur Trade in the Far Southwest, 1540–1846.* Norman: University of Oklahoma Press, 1971.

Weiman, David F. "Farmers and the Market in Antebellum America: A View from the Georgia Upcountry." *Journal of Economic History* 47 (September 1987): 627–47.

Weiner, Annette, and Jane Schneider, eds. *Cloth and Human Experience.* Washington, D.C.: Smithsonian Press, 1989.

Weingartner, Paul J., Dwight Billings, and Kathleen Blee. "Agriculture in Preindustrial Appalachia: Subsistence Farming in Beech Creek, 1850–1880." *Journal of the Appalachian Studies Association* 1 (1989): 70–80.

Weller, Jack E. *Yesterday's People: Life in Contemporary Appalachia.* Lexington: University of Kentucky Press, 1965.

Wells, Ann Harwell. "A Checklist of Tennessee Maps, 1820–1830." *Tennessee Historical Quarterly* 43 (Fall 1984): 209–28.

———. "Early Maps of Tennessee, 1794–1799." *Tennessee Historical Society* 35 (Summer 1976): 123–37.

Wells, Robin F. "Castoreum and Steel Traps in Eastern North America." *American Anthropologist* 74 (1972): 475–86.

———. "More on Castoreum and Steel Traps in Eastern North America." *American Anthropologist* 77 (1975): 600–17.

Western and Atlantic Railroad. *Annual Reports of the Western and Atlantic Railroad, 1850–1860.* Milledgeville, Ga.: Western and Atlantic Railroad, 1850–60.

Whaples, Robert. "A Quantitative History of the Journal of Economic History and the Cliometric Revolution." *Journal of Economic History* 51 (June 1991): 289–302.

Wheeler, David. "Where There Be Mountains, There Be Chestnuts." *Katuah Journal* 21 (Fall 1988): 3–5.

Wheeler, Lester R. "Changes in the Dietary Habits of Remote Mountain People since 1900." *Journal of the Tennessee Academy of Science* 10 (1935): 167–74.

———. "A Study of the Remote Mountain People of the Tennessee Valley." *Journal of the Tennessee Academy of Science* 9 (January 1935): 33–36.

Wheeler, William B., and Michael J. McDonald. *TVA and the Tellico Dam, 1936–1979: A Bureaucratic Crisis in Post-Industrial America.* Knoxville: University of Tennessee Press, 1986.

Whetstone, Jeff. "When the Valley Became a Lake: Portrait of Watauga." *Southern Exposure* 23 (Summer 1995): 31–32.

Whisnant, David. *All That Is Native and Fine.* Chapel Hill: University of North Carolina Press, 1983.

———. *Modernizing the Mountaineer: People, Power, and Planning in Appalachia.* New York: Burt Franklin, 1980.

White, George. *Historical Collections of Georgia.* New York: Pudney and Russell, 1855.

White, Richard. "Environmental History, Ecology, and Meaning." *Journal of American History* 76 (March 1990): 1111–16.

———. *"It's Your Misfortune and None of My Own": A History of the American West.* Norman: University of Oklahoma Press, 1991.

———. *Middle Ground: Indians, Empires, and Republics in the Great Lakes Region, 1650–1815.* New York: Cambridge University Press, 1991.

———. *The Roots of Dependency: Subsistence, Environment, and Social Change among the Choctaws, Pawnees, and Navajos.* Lincoln: University of Nebraska Press, 1983.

White, Robert H. *Tennessee: Its Growth and Progress.* Nashville, Tenn.: Robert H. White, 1947.

Whittington, G. "Field Systems of Scotland." In Alan R. H. Baker and Robin A. Butlin, eds., *Studies of Field Systems in the British Isles.* Cambridge: Cambridge University Press, 1973.

Whyte, Ian. *Agriculture and Society in Seventeenth Century Scotland.* Edinburgh: John Donald, 1979.

———. "Infield-Outfield Farming on a Seventeenth-Century Scottish Estate." *Journal of Historical Geography* 5 (Fall 1979): 391–401.

Widmer, Randolph J. "The Structure of Southeastern Chiefdoms." In Charles Hudson and Carmen Chaves Tesser, eds., *The Forgotten Centuries: Indians and Europeans in the American South, 1521–1704.* Athens: University of Georgia Press, 1994.

Wigginton, Eliot, ed. *The Foxfire Book.* Garden City, N.Y.: Doubleday, 1972.

Wilhelm, Eugene J. "Animal Drives in the Southern Highlands." *Mountain Life and Work* 42 (Summer 1966): 6–11.

———. "Cultural Heritage of the Blue Ridge." *Mountain Life and Work* 41 (Summer 1965): 16–20.

Williams, Buzz. "The Chattooga Watershed's Cultural Heritage." *Chattooga Quarterly* (Summer 1997): 11–14, 21.

———. "Early Logging in the Chattooga Country." *Chattooga Quarterly* (Winter 1995): 5–14.

Williams, David. *The Georgia Gold Rush: Twenty-Niners, Cherokees, and Gold Fever*. Columbia: University of South Carolina Press, 1993.

———. "Georgia's Forgotten Miners: African-Americans and the Georgia Land Rush." *Georgia Historical Quarterly* 75 (Spring 1991): 76–89.

Williams, John Alexander. "Counting Yesterday's People." *Journal of Appalachian Studies* 2 (Spring 1996): 3–27.

Williams, Michael Ann. *Great Smoky Mountains Folklife*. Jackson: University of Mississippi Press, 1995.

———. *Homeplace: The Social Use and Meaning of the Folk Dwelling in Southwestern North Carolina*. Athens: University of Georgia Press, 1991.

———. "Pride and Prejudice: The Appalachian Boxed House in Southwestern North Carolina." *Winterthur Portfolio* 25 (Winter 1990): 217–30.

Williams, Samuel Cole. "Colonel Joseph William's Battalion in Christian's Campaign." *Tennessee Historical Magazine* 9 (1925–26): 100–14.

———. *Dawn of Tennessee Valley and Tennessee History*. Johnson City, Tenn.: Watauga Press, 1937.

———. "Early Iron Works in the Tennessee Country." *Tennessee Historical Quarterly* 6 (1947): 39–46.

———. *History of the Lost State of Franklin*. Johnson City, Tenn.: Watauga Press, 1924.

———. "Report of the Journey of the Brethren Abraham Steiner and Frederick C. de Schweinitz to the Cherokees and the Cumberland Settlements." 1799. In Samuel Cole Williams, ed., *Early Travels in the Tennessee Country, 1540–1800*. Johnson City, Tenn.: Watauga Press, 1928.

———. "Stephen Holston and Holston River." *East Tennessee Historical Society Publications* 8 (1936): 24–27.

———, ed. *Adair's History of the American Indians*. Johnson City, Tenn.: Watauga Press, 1930.

———. *Early Travels in the Tennessee Country, 1540–1800*. Johnson City, Tenn.: Watauga Press, 1928.

———. *Lieutenant Henry Timberlake's Memoirs, 1756–1765*. Johnson City, Tenn.: Watauga Press, 1927.

Williamson, J. W., ed. *An Appalachian Symposium: Essays in Honor of Cratis D. Williams*. Boone, N.C.: Appalachian State University Press, 1977.

Wilson, Alexander. *The Culture of Nature: North American Landscape from Disney to the Exxon Valdez*. New York: Basil Blackwell, 1992.

Wilson, Charles Reagan, and William Ferris. *Encyclopedia of Southern Culture*. Chapel Hill: University of North Carolina Press, 1989.

Wilson, Darlene. "Multicultural Mayhem and Murder in Virginia's Backcountry: The Case of Pierre-François Tubeuf, 1792–1795." *Journal of Appalachian Studies* 4, no. 1 (Spring 1998): 57–86.

Wilms, Douglas. "Agrarian Progress in the Cherokee Nation Prior to Removal." *Studies in the Social Sciences, West Georgia College* 16 (1977): 1–16.

———. "Cherokee Land Use in Georgia before Removal." In William Anderson, ed., *Chero-kee Removal Before and After*. Athens: University of Georgia Press, 1991.

Wing, Elizabeth S. "Evidences for the Impact of Traditional Spanish Animal Uses in Parts of the New World." In Juliet Clutton-Brock, ed., *The Walking Larder: Patterns of Domesti-cation, Pastoralism, and Predation*. London: Unwin Hyman, 1989, 72–79.

Winters, Donald. "'Plain Folk' of the Old South Reexamined: Economic Democracy in Ten-nessee." *Journal of Southern History* 53 (November 1987): 565–85.

Witthoft, John. "Cherokee Indian Use of Potherbs." *Journal of Cherokee Studies* 2 (1977): 250–55.

W. M. Ritter Lumber Company. *The Romance of Appalachian Hardwood Lumber: Golden Anniversary, 1890–1940*. Richmond, Va.: Garrett and Massie, 1940.

Wolch, Jennifer, and Michael Dear. *The Power of Geography: How Territory Shapes Social Life*. Boston: Unwin Hyman, 1989.

Wolfe, Margaret R. *Kingsport, Tennessee: A Planned American City*. Lexington: University Press of Kentucky, 1987.

Wood, Denis. *The Power of Maps*. New York: Guilford Press, 1992.

Wood, Peter. "Re-Counting the Past." *Southern Exposure* 16 (Summer 1988): 30–37.

Wood, Peter, Gregory Waselkov, and M. Thomas Hatley. *Powhatan's Mantle: Indians in the Colonial Southeast*. Lincoln: University of Nebraska Press, 1989.

Woodward, Henry. "A Faithful Relation of My Westoe Voiage, by Henry Woodward, 1674." In Alexander Salley, ed., *Narratives of Early Carolina, 1650–1708*. New York: Charles Scribner's Sons, 1911, 126–34.

Worster, Donald. *Nature's Economy: The Roots of Ecology*. San Francisco: Sierra Club Books, 1974.

———. "Transformations of the Earth: Toward an Agroecological Perspective in History." *Journal of American History* 76 (March 1990): 1087–106.

———. *The Wealth of Nature: Environmental History and the Ecological Imagination*. New York: Oxford University Press, 1993.

———, ed. *The Ends of the Earth: Perspectives on Modern Environmental History*. Cam-bridge: Cambridge University Press, 1988.

Wright, J. Leitch, Jr. *The Only Land They Knew: The Tragic Story of the American Indian in the Old South*. New York: Free Press, 1981.

Wright, Louis B., ed. *The Prose Works of William Byrd of Westover: Narratives of a Colonial Virginian*. Cambridge, Mass.: Harvard University Press, 1966.

Wright, Wade H. *History of the Georgia Power Company, 1855–1956*. Atlanta: Georgia Power Company, 1957.

Yeadon, David. *Hidden Corners of the Mid-Atlantic States*. New York: Funk and Wagnalls, 1977.

Young, Chester Raymond. "Observance of Old Christmas in Southern Appalachia." In J. W. Williamson, ed., *An Appalachian Symposium: Essays in Honor of Cratis D. Williams*. Boone, N.C.: Appalachian State University Press, 1977.

Young, Mary Sery. "Pets." In Charles Reagan Wilson and William Ferris, eds., *The Encyclo-pedia of Southern Culture*. Chapel Hill: University of North Carolina Press, 1989, 1233–35.

Zeigler, Wilbur, and Ben Grosscup. *The Heart of the Alleghenies*. Raleigh, N.C.: A. Williams and Company, 1883.

Znaniecki, Florian. *Cultural Sciences, Their Origin and Development*. Urbana: University of Illinois Press, 1963.

Theses, Dissertations, and Manuscripts

Arends, Ernesto. "Vegetation Patterns a Half Century Following the Chestnut Blight in the Great Smoky Mountains National Park." Master's thesis, University of Tennessee, Knoxville, 1981.

Baden, William W. "A Dynamic Model of Stability and Change in Mississippian Agricultural Systems." Ph.D. dissertation, University of Tennessee, Knoxville, 1987.

Baker, Christopher. "East Tennessee Agriculture Production and the Antebellum U.S. Cotton Trade: The Food Supply of the Cotton South in the World System." Manuscript, Department of Sociology, University of Tennessee, Knoxville, 1989.

————. "East Tennessee within the World-Economy, 1790–1850." Master's thesis, University of Tennessee, Knoxville, 1991.

Banks, William H. "Ethnobotany of the Cherokee Indians." Master's thesis, University of Tennessee, Knoxville, 1953.

Bays, Brad Alan. "The Historical Geography of Cattle Herding among the Cherokee Indians, 1761–1861." Master's thesis, University of Tennessee, Knoxville, 1991.

Black, Ellen Engelman. "A Study of the Diffusion of Culture in a Relatively Isolated Mountain Community." Ph.D. dissertation, University of Chicago, 1928.

Booth, Fred D. "The Watauga Settlements of the Appalachian Frontier." Master's thesis, East Tennessee State University, Johnson City, 1978.

Broida, Mary O'Neal. "Maize in Kentucky Fort Ancient Diets: An Analysis of Carbon Isotope Ratios in Human Bone." Master's thesis, University of Kentucky, Lexington, 1983.

Brown, Margaret Lynn. "Power, Privilege, and Tourism: A Revision of the Great Smoky Mountains National Park Story." Master's thesis, University of Kentucky, Lexington, 1990.

————. "Smoky Mountain Story: Human Values and Environmental Transformation in a Southern Bioregion, 1900–1950." Ph.D. dissertation, University of Kentucky, Lexington, 1995.

Brown, Margaret Lynn, and Donald Edward Davis. "Trail History Notebook." Great Smoky Mountains Natural History Association, Gatlinburg, Tenn., 1992.

Bruhn, Ellen. "Vegetational Succession on Three Grassy Balds of the Great Smoky Mountains." Master's thesis, University of Tennessee, Knoxville, 1964.

Bryan, Charles Faulkner. "The Civil War in East Tennessee: A Social, Political, and Economic Study." Ph.D. dissertation, University of Tennessee, Knoxville, 1978.

Cabrera, Juan Marquez. Letters from Governor Juan Marquez Cabrera in Secretaría de Estado, File 7620, No. 14. Microfilm at Special Collections, Western Carolina University, Cullowhee, N.C.

Cappon, Lester Jesse. "History of the Southern Iron Industry to the Close of the Civil War." Ph.D. dissertation, Harvard University, 1928.

Carter, Michael. "Religious Congregations in Organizational Perspective: The Appalachian

Case." Manuscript, 1990 Carlyle Marney Lecture, 30 October, Carson-Newman College, Jefferson City, Tenn.

Case, Earl C. "The Valley of East Tennessee: The Adjustment of Industry to the Natural Environment." Ph.D. dissertation, University of Chicago, 1925.

Champion Fiber Company. "An Industrial Forest Policy in Western North Carolina." Vertical files, Great Smoky Mountains National Park Archives, Sugarlands Visitor Center, Gatlinburg, Tenn., 1927.

Cochrane, Gavin. Letter to British Crown, 1766, Box 4, file 12. Robert S. Davis Collection, Georgia Department of Archives and History, Atlanta.

Crawford, Martin. "Wealth, Slaveholding and Power in the Southern Mountains: Ashe County, North Carolina in 1860–1861." Paper presented to the annual meeting of the Appalachian Studies Conference, Appalachian State University, Boone, N.C., 1986.

Cridlebaugh, Patricia. "American Indian and Euro-American Impact upon Holocene Vegetation in the Lower Little Tennessee River Valley, East Tennessee." Ph.D. dissertation, University of Tennessee, Knoxville, 1984.

Davis, Donald E. "Logging History Facts." Manuscript, Great Smoky Mountains Natural History Association, Sugarlands Visitor Center, Great Smoky Mountains National Park, 1993.

———. "The Politics of Wilderness Preservation: A Sociological Analysis of 'Uninhabited' Landscapes." Paper presented to the annual meeting of the Southern Sociological Society, Louisville, Ky., 1990.

———. "Where There Be Mountains: Environmental and Cultural Change in the Appalachian South, 1500–1800." Ph.D. dissertation, University of Tennessee, Knoxville, 1993.

———. "Wilderness Preservation: The Appalachian Case." Paper presented to the annual meeting of the Appalachian Studies Conference, Berea College, Berea, Ky., 1991.

Davis, Mattie Boggs. "Last Will and Testament." 5 June 1932. In author's possession.

Derthick, Lawrence G. "The Indian Boundary Line in the Southern District of British North America, 1763–1779." Master's thesis, University of Tennessee, Knoxville, 1930.

Draper, Lyman C. The Draper Collection of Historical Manuscripts. 4B, 57J. State Historical Society of Wisconsin, Madison, 1929.

Dunaway, Wilma. "In Search of a Development Model for the Southern Mountains: Moving Appalachian Studies beyond Internal Colonialism." Manuscript, Department of Sociology, University of Tennessee, Knoxville, n.d.

———. "Southern Appalachia's People without History: The Role of Black Slaves and White Croppers in the Region's Antebellum Economy." Paper presented to the annual meeting of the Social Science History Association, November 1989.

Dyer, Delce. "The Farmstead Yards at Cades Cove: Restoration and Management Alternatives for the Domestic Landscape of the Southern Appalachian Mountains." Master's thesis, University of Georgia, Athens, 1988.

Eller, Ronald D. "Miner, Millhands, and Mountaineers: The Modernization of the Appalachian South, 1880–1930." Ph.D. dissertation, University of North Carolina, Chapel Hill, 1979.

Ford, Thomas B. "An Analysis of Anglo-American/Cherokee Culture Contact during the

Federal Period, the Hiwassee Tract, Eastern Tennessee." Master's thesis, University of Tennessee, Knoxville, 1982.

Freudenburg, William R., Scott Frickel, and Robert Gramling. "The Sociocultural Definition of 'Natural' Resources: Learning to Think like a Mountain." Paper presented at the Stone Symposium of the Society for the Study of Symbolic Interaction, Knoxville, Tenn., 1993.

Gersmehl, Phil. "A Geographic Approach to a Vegetation Problem: The Case of the Southern Appalachian Grassy Balds." Ph.D. dissertation, University of Georgia, Athens, 1970.

Gilbert, V. C. "Vegetation of the Grassy Balds of the Great Smoky Mountains National Park." Master's thesis, University of Tennessee, Knoxville, 1954.

Gump, Lucy. "Half Pints to Horse Shoes: Meeting the Needs of a Growing Nineteenth Century Appalachian Frontier." Paper presented at the Appalachian Studies Conference, East Tennessee State University, Johnson City, 1993.

————. "Possessions and Patterns of Living in Washington County, Tennessee, 1771–1796." Master's thesis, East Tennessee State University, Johnson City, 1989.

Hagy, James W. "Castle's Woods: Frontier Virginia Settlement, 1769–1799." Master's thesis, East Tennessee State University, Johnson City, 1966.

Hall, Thomas. "The Effects of Incorporation into the World System on Ethnic Persistence: The American Conquest of the Southwest." Paper presented at the annual meeting of the American Sociological Association, San Francisco, September 1992.

Harly, Mary Parker. "Georgia Indian Trade in the Trustee Period, 1733–1852." Master's thesis, University of Georgia, Athens, 1935.

Helkamp, Richard. "Biosocial Organization and Change in East Tennessee, Late Woodland and Mississippian." Ph.D. dissertation, Purdue University, LaFayette, Ind., 1985.

Hersh, Alan. "The Development of the Iron Industry in East Tennessee." Master's thesis, University of Tennessee, Knoxville, 1958.

Hill, James M. "Wildlife Value of *Castanea dentata* Past and Present, the Historical Decline of the Chestnut, and Its Future Use in Restoration of Natural Areas." Manuscript, Randolph Macon College, Lynchburg, Va., 1993.

Hopcroft, Rosemary. "Field Systems and Development in Late Medieval England and France." Paper presented at the 85th annual meeting of the American Sociological Association, Washington, D.C., 11–15 August 1990.

Hoskins, Katherine B. "Anderson County, Historical Sketches." Clinton, Tenn.: Katherine Hoskins, n.d.

Hsiung, David C. "Isolation and Integration in Upper East Tennessee, 1785–1860." Ph.D. dissertation, University of Michigan, 1991.

Johnson, H. H., to William H. Thomas, 13 May 1853. William Holland Thomas Papers, Duke University, Durham, N.C.

Jones, Michael Owen. "Chairmaking in Appalachia: A Study in Style and Creative Imagination in American Folk Art." Ph.D. dissertation, Indiana University, 1970.

Kephart, Horace. "Origin of Place Names in the Great Smoky Mountains." Kephart Collection, Great Smoky Mountains National Park Archives, Sugarlands Visitor Center, Gatlinburg, Tenn., n.d.

————. "Report on Appalachian Mountain Nomenclature to North Carolina Park Commission." Vertical file, "Place Names," Great Smoky Mountains National Park Archives, January 1931, 1.

Kuentzel, Walter F. "The Myth of Wilderness." Paper presented at the annual meeting of the Southern Sociological Society, Norfolk, Va., 15 April 1989.

Matvey, Joseph J. "Central Appalachia: Distortions in Development, 1750–1986." Ph.D. dissertation, University of Pittsburgh, 1987.

McCammon, Samuel. "Diary of Samuel McCammon, 1846–1854." McClung Collection, Lawson McGhee Library, University of Tennessee, Knoxville.

McCann, Eugene J. "Mapping Appalachia: Prospects and Problems in Using Maps to Study Economic Development in Eastern Kentucky." Paper submitted to the Appalachian Studies Association, Carl A. Ross Appalachian Student Paper Competition, 15 January 1995.

McClure, Virginia Clay. "The Settlement of the Kentucky Appalachian Highlands." Ph.D. dissertation, University of Kentucky, Lexington, 1933.

McCracken, H. Weaver. "Comparison of Forest Cover prior to and following Disturbance in Two Areas of the Great Smoky Mountains National Park." Master's thesis, University of Tennessee, Knoxville, 1978.

McFarland, Robert E. "Head for the Mountains: Slavery and Nature in North Alabama." Paper presented at the Eighth Biennial Conference of the American Society for Environmental History, Las Vegas, Nev., 1995.

———. "Of Time and the River: Economy, People, and Environment in the Tennessee Valley, 1500–1990." Ph.D. dissertation, University of Alabama, Tuscaloosa, 1997.

Messick, Rob. "Old Growth Communities in the Grandfather District of Pisgah National Forest." Manuscript, Forest History Society, Durham, N.C., November 1997.

Moore, Tyrel G. "An Historical Geography of Economic Development in Appalachian Kentucky, 1800–1930." Ph.D. dissertation, University of Tennessee, Knoxville, 1984.

Mount, S. G. R., to William H. Thomas, 5 April 1853. William Holland Thomas Papers, Duke University, Durham, N.C.

Nave, Robert Tipton. "A History of the Iron Industry in Carter County to 1860." Master's thesis, East Tennessee State University, Johnson City, 1953.

Nelson, Robert Lynn. "Planters and Hill People: Competing Agroecologies in Virginia's Blue Ridge Mountains, 1770–1860." Paper presented to the Conference of the American Society for Environmental History, Las Vegas, Nev., March 1995.

Norburn, Martha Elizabeth. "The Influence of the Physiographic Features of Western North Carolina on the Settlement and Development of the Region." Ph.D. dissertation, University of North Carolina, Chapel Hill, 1932.

Peregrine, Peter. "The Evolution of Mississippian Societies in the American Midcontinent from a World-System Perspective." Ph.D. dissertation, Purdue University, West Lafayette, Ind., 1990.

Puckett, James M. "The Scotch-Irish Emigration: The Great Wagon Road/The Settlement of Upper Georgia, etc." Vertical files, Sugarlands Visitor Center, Great Smoky Mountains National Park, n.d.

Pyle, Charlotte. "Vegetation Disturbance History of the Great Smoky Mountains National Park." Manuscript, Uplands Laboratory, Gatlinburg, Tenn., 1985.

Reedy, Dennis E. "The W. M. Ritter Family History Book." Vertical files, Forest History Society, Durham, N.C., n.d.

Robbins, Louise Marie. "The Identification of the Prehistoric Shawnee Indians—The Description of the Population of the Fort Ancient Aspect." Ph.D. dissertation, Indiana University, Bloomington, 1968.

Rollins, Leonard H. "The Tennessee River as a Trade Route and Its Economic Relation to the Economic Development of East Tennessee." Master's thesis, University of Tennessee, Knoxville, 1928.

Rose, Jennifer. "A Rose Is a Rose Is a Rose." Family history of Rose Lumber Company, Knoxville, Tenn., 8 December 1992. In author's possession.

Salstrom, Paul. "The Subsistence-Barter-and-Borrow System in Southern Appalachia's Traditional Life." Paper presented at the Appalachian Studies Conference, East Tennessee State University, Johnson City, 1988.

Schenk, Carl A. "The Biltmore Story." Manuscript, vertical files, Forest History Society, Durham, N.C., 1895.

Schulman, Steven A. "Logging in the Upper Cumberland River Valley: A Folk History." Master's thesis, Western Kentucky University, Bowling Green, 1973.

Seeber, Raymond Clifford. "A History of Anderson County, Tennessee." Master's thesis, University of Tennessee, Knoxville, 1928.

Shapiro, Henry David. "A Strange Land and Peculiar People: The Discovery of Appalachia, 1870–1920." Ph.D. dissertation, Rutgers University, New Brunswick, N.J., 1966.

Sheldon, Elisabeth S. "Introduction of the Peach to the Southeastern United States." Paper presented at the annual meeting of the Society for Economic Botany, St. Louis, Mo., 1978.

Smith, James L. "Historical Geography of the Southern Charcoal Iron Industry, 1800–1860." Ph.D. dissertation, University of Tennessee, Knoxville, 1982.

Stotik, Jeffrey. "The Political Economy of Appalachia: A Critique and Synthesis of Radical Approaches to Underdevelopment." Master's thesis, University of Tennessee, Knoxville, 1990.

Wagner, Gail Elaine. "Uses of Plants by the Fort Ancient Indians." Ph.D. dissertation, Washington University, St. Louis, Mo., 1987.

Watson, Judge. "The Economic and Cultural Development of Eastern Kentucky from 1900 to the Present." Ph.D. dissertation, Indiana University, Bloomington, 1963.

Western Carolina Lumber and Timber Association. "Report of Committee Appointed by Western Carolina Lumber and Timber Association." Manuscript, Forest History Society, Durham, N.C., 25 July 1925.

Wilburn, H. C. "The Indian Gap Trail." Archives, Great Smoky Mountains National Park, Gatlinburg, Tenn., n.d.

Williams, J. Mark. "The Joe-Bell Site: Seventeenth-Century Lifeways on the Oconee River." Ph.D. dissertation, University of Georgia, Athens, 1984.

Wilms, Douglas C. "Cherokee Land Use in Georgia, 1800–1838." Ph.D. dissertation, University of Georgia, Athens, 1973.

Government Documents

Alldredge, Haden J. *A History of Navigation on the Tennessee River System: An Interpretation of the Economic Influence of This River System on the Tennessee Valley.* Washington, D.C.: U.S. Government Printing Office, 1937.

Appalachian Regional Commission. *Appalachia: A Reference Book.* Washington, D.C.: Appalachian Regional Commission, 1979.

Arnold, J. H. *Ways of Making Southern Mountain Farms More Productive.* USDA Farmers' Bulletin No. 905. Washington, D.C.: U.S. Government Printing Office, 1918.

Ashe, William W. "Chestnut in Tennessee." *Forest Studies in Tennessee, Bulletin 10.* Nashville: Baird-Ward Company, 1912.

———. *Preliminary Report of the Inland Waterways Commission.* 60th Cong., 1st sess., Senate Document 325, 1908.

Ayres, Horace B., and William W. Ashe. *The Southern Appalachian Forests.* Department of the Interior, U.S. Geological Survey, Series H, Professional Paper No. 37. Washington, D.C., 1905.

Bent, Arthur Cleveland. *Life Histories of North American Gallinacous Birds: Orders Galliformes and Colubiformes.* Washington, D.C.: Smithsonian Institution/U.S. Natural History Bulletin No. 162, 1932.

Brown, George. *History of Tennessee Wildlife Conservation Laws.* Nashville: Wildlife Resources Agency, n.d.

Buttrick, P. L. *Chestnut in North Carolina.* North Carolina Geological and Economic Survey, Economic Paper No. 56. Raleigh: North Carolina Geological and Economic Survey, 1925, 1–10.

Chapman, Jefferson. *Archaeological Investigations at the Eighteenth Century Overhill Town of Milch.* Publications in Anthropology 36. Knoxville: Tennessee Valley Authority, 1983.

Commissioner of Corporations. *Report of the Commissioner of Corporations on the Lumber Industry.* Part 1, *Standing Timber, February 13, 1911.* Washington, D.C.: U.S. Government Printing Office, 1911.

Culbertson, Nicole. *Status and History of the Mountain Lion in the Great Smoky Mountains National Park.* U.S. Department of the Interior, National Park Service, n.d.

Delcourt, Paul, and Hazel Delcourt. "Late-Quaternary Paleoecology of the Appalachian Ranges Natural Region." In H. R. DeSelm, ed., *Potential Natural Landmarks of the Appalachian Ranges Natural Region Ecological Report.* Washington, D.C.: National Park Service.

DeVivo, Michael S. "Indian Use of Fire and Land Clearance in the Southern Appalachians." In Stephen C. Nodvin and Thomas A. Waldrop, eds., *Fire and the Environment: Ecological and Cultural Perspectives: Proceedings of an International Symposium.* USDA, Forest Service. Asheville, N.C.: Southeastern Forest Experiment Station, 1991.

Dykeman, Wilma, and Jim Stokely. *Highland Homeland: The People of the Great Smokies.* Washington, D.C.: U.S. Department of the Interior, 1978.

Frothingham, E. H. *The Present Stand of Chestnut in North Carolina and in the Southern Appalachians.* Geological and Economic Survey, Economic Paper No. 56. Raleigh: North Carolina Geological and Economic Survey, 1925, 11–17.

———. *Timber Growing and Logging Practices in the Southern Appalachian Region.* USDA Technical Bulletin No. 250. Washington, D.C.: U.S. Government Printing Office, 1931.

Geological Survey of Kentucky. *Reports of Progress.* Frankfort: State of Kentucky, 1878.

Georgia Department of Archives and History. Moravian Mission diaries, Murray County, Ga. Vol. 1, 1800–18. Atlanta: Georgia Department of Archives and History.

Georgia Department of Natural Resources. "The Vann House." n.d.

Glenn, Leonidas Chalmers. *Denudation and Erosion in the Southern Appalachian Region and the Monongahela Basin.* U.S. Geological Survey, Professional Paper No. 72, 1911.

Goodwin, O. C. "Eight Decades of Forestry Firsts: A History of Forestry in North Carolina, 1889–1969." Raleigh: North Carolina Forest Service, n.d.

Gravatt, G. F. *Chestnut Blight.* USDA Farmers' Bulletin No. 1641. Washington, D.C.: U.S. Government Printing Office, 1930.

———. *The Chestnut Blight in North Carolina.* Geological and Economic Survey, Economic Paper No. 56. Raleigh: North Carolina Geological and Economic Survey, 1925, 18–24.

Great Smoky Mountains National Park. "Nununyi, the Kituhwas, or Mountain Indians and the State of North Carolina." Vertical files, Great Smoky Mountains National Park Archives, Gatlinburg, Tenn., n.d.

———. "Stone Walls, Cairns and Old Roads." Cultural Resources Section, Resources Management Plan, Great Smoky Mountains National Park, Sugarlands Visitor Center, Gatlinburg, Tenn., 1986.

Hall, William L. *The Waning Hardwood Supply and the Appalachian Forests.* USDA, Forest Service, Circular 116, 1907.

Harper, V. L., Bernard Frank, and W. E. McQuilkin. "Forest Practices and Productivity." In USDA, *Yearbook of Agriculture 1957.* Washington, D.C.: U.S. Government Printing Office, 1958, 732–39.

Haseltine, R. H. *Iron Ore Deposits of Georgia.* Geological Survey of Georgia, Bulletin No. 41. Atlanta: Stein Printing Company, 1924.

Holmes, J. S. "Forest Conditions in Western North Carolina." Geological and Economic Survey, Economic Paper No. 23. Raleigh: North Carolina Geological and Economic Survey, 1911, 79–81.

———. *Forest Fires in North Carolina during 1912.* Geological and Economic Survey, Economic Paper No. 33. Raleigh: North Carolina Geological and Economic Survey, 1913.

———. *Forest Fires in North Carolina during 1918, 1919, and 1920.* Geological and Economic Survey, Economic Paper No. 51. Raleigh: North Carolina Geological and Economic Survey, 1921, 1–75.

Hornaday, William Temple. *The Extermination of the American Bison.* Washington, D.C.: U.S. Government Printing Office, 1889.

Hufford, Mary. *One Space, Many Places: Folklife and Land Use in New Jersey's Pinelands*

National Reserve. Report and Recommendations to the New Jersey Pinelands Commission for Cultural Conservation in the Pinelands National Reserve. Washington, D.C.: Library of Congress/American Folklife Center, 1986.

Kentucky Geological Survey. *The Eastern Coal Field; Comprising Eight Reports on the Resources of Some of the Counties Located in the Eastern Coal Field.* Frankfort, 1884.

Leighton, M. O., M. R. Hall, and R. H. Bolster. *Relation of the Southern Appalachian Mountains to the Development of Water Power.* USDA, Forest Service, Circular No. 144, 1908.

Leighton, M. O., and A. H. Horton. *Relation of the Southern Appalachian Mountains to Inland Water Navigation.* USDA, Forest Service, Circular No. 144, 1908.

Mather, William Williams. "Report of the Geological Reconnaissance of Kentucky, Made in 1838." *Kentucky Senate Journal.* Frankfort: State of Kentucky, 1839.

McCallie, S. W. *Report on the Fossil Iron Ores of Georgia.* Geological Survey of Georgia, Bulletin No. 17. Atlanta: Stein Printing Company, 1908.

Modelski, Andrew M. *Railroad Maps of the United States: A Selective Annotated Bibliography of Original 19th Century Maps in the Geography and Map Division of the Library of Congress.* Washington, D.C.: Library of Congress, 1975.

Mooney, James. "Myths of the Cherokees." In *Nineteenth Annual Report of the Bureau of American Ethnology, 1897–98.* Washington, D.C.: U.S. Government Printing Office, 1900.

———. "The Sacred Formulas of the Cherokees." In *Seventh Annual Report of the Bureau of American Ethnology, 1885–86.* Washington, D.C.: U.S. Government Printing Office, 1891.

Mosby, Henry, and Charles Handley. *The Wild Turkey in Virginia: Its Status, Life History and Management.* Richmond: Commission of Game and Inland Fisheries of Virginia, 1943.

Myers, William. *Indian Trails of the Southeast. Forty-Second Annual Report of the Bureau of American Ethnology, 1924–1926.* Washington, D.C.: U.S. Government Printing Office, 1928.

President's Commission on Coal. *Coal Data Book.* Washington, D.C.: U.S. Government Printing Office, 1980.

Quinn, David, and Alison Quinn, eds. *The First Colonists.* Raleigh: North Carolina Department of Cultural Resources, 1982.

Quinn, Edythe Ann. *History of the Little Tennessee River Valley.* Knoxville: Tennessee Valley Authority, Cultural Resources Program, 1992.

Rau, Charles. *Ancient Trade in North America.* Report of the Smithsonian Institution for 1872. Washington, D.C.: Smithsonian Institution, 1873.

Roosevelt, Theodore. *Message from the President of the United States Transmitting a Report of the Secretary of Agriculture in Relation to the Forest, Rivers, and Mountains of the Southern Appalachian Region.* 1901. Washington, D.C.: U.S. Government Printing Office, 1902.

Seerey, Daniel F. *Small Sawmills: Their Equipment, Construction, and Operation.* USDA, Bulletin No. 718. Washington, D.C.: U.S. Government Printing Office, 1918.

Southern Appalachian Man and the Biosphere Cooperative. *The Southern Appalachian As-*

sessment Social/Cultural/Economic Technical Report. Report 4 of 5. Atlanta: USDA, Forest Service, Southern Region, 1996.

———. *The Southern Appalachian Assessment Summary Report.* Report 1 of 5. Atlanta: USDA, Forest Service, Southern Region, 1996.

———. *The Southern Appalachian Assessment Terrestrial Technical Report.* Report 5 of 5. Atlanta: USDA, Forest Service, Southern Region, 1996.

Statutes at Large of South Carolina. 4 vols. Columbia, S.C.: Republican Print Company, State Printers, 1873–75.

Supreme Court of Tennessee. *Madison et al. v. Ducktown, Sulphur, Copper and Iron, Ltd.* Tennessee Supreme Court, Nashville, 26 November 1904.

Swanton, John R. *Final Report of the United States de Soto Expedition Commission.* 76th Cong., 1st sess., H. Doc. 71. Washington, D.C.: U.S. Government Printing Office, 1939.

———. *Social Organization and Social Use of the Indians of the Creek Confederacy.* 42nd Report of the Bureau of American Ethnology. Washington, D.C.: U.S. Government Printing Office, 1928.

Switzer, J. A. *The Larger Undeveloped Water-Powers of Tennessee.* State Geological Survey, Bulletin No. 20. Washington, D.C.: U.S. Geological Survey, 1918.

Tennessee Department of Conservation, Division of Forestry. *Management Plan for Prentice Cooper State Forest, 1989–1999.* Nashville: Tennessee Department of Conservation, 1989.

Tennessee Valley Authority. *The Chickamauga Project.* Technical Report No. 6. General Correspondence, 1940–45. East Point Records Center, Atlanta.

———. Division of Reservoir Properties. Record Group 142. General Correspondence, 1940–45. East Point Records Center, Atlanta.

———. *The First Fifty Years: Changed Land, Changed Lives.* State of the Environment in the Tennessee Valley. Chattanooga/Knoxville: Tennessee Valley Authority, 1983.

Tennessee Wildlife Resources Agency. *History of Tennessee Wildlife Conservation Laws.* Nashville: Tennessee Wildlife Resources Agency, n.d.

———. *A Strategic Plan for Wildlife Resources Management for the 1990s.* Nashville: Tennessee Wildlife Resources Agency, 1991.

Troost, Gerald. *Fifth Geological Report of the State of Tennessee.* Nashville: State of Tennessee, 1840.

United States de Soto Expedition Commission. *Final Report of the United States de Soto Expedition Commission.* Washington, D.C.: U.S. Government Printing Office, 1939.

U.S. Bureau of the Census. *Agriculture of the United States in 1860.* Washington, D.C.: U.S. Government Printing Office, 1864.

———. *Population of the United States in 1860.* Washington, D.C.: U.S. Government Printing Office, 1864.

———. *Fourth Census of the United States* (1820). Manufacturing Schedules.

———. *Sixth Census of the United States* (1840). Population, Manufacturing, and Agriculture Schedules.

———. *Seventh Census of the United States* (1850). Population, Manufacturing, and Agriculture Schedules.

————. *Eighth Census of the United States* (1860). Population, Manufacturing, and Agriculture Schedules.

————. *Twelfth Census of the United States* (1900). Population Schedules.

————. *Thirteenth Census of the United States* (1910). Population Schedules.

————. *Fourteenth Census of the United States* (1920). Population Schedules.

U.S. Department of Agriculture (USDA). *Deterioration of Chestnuts in the Southern Appalachians.* Technical Bulletin No. 257. Washington, D.C.: U.S. Department of Agriculture, 1931.

————. *Draft Environmental Impact Statement: Land and Resource Management Plan, Cherokee National Forest.* Forest Service, Southern Region, 1984.

————. *Draft Land and Resource Management Plan, Cherokee National Forest.* Forest Service, Southern Region, 1984.

————. *Economic and Social Problems and Conditions of the Southern Appalachians.* Miscellaneous Publications No. 205. Washington, D.C.: U.S. Government Printing Office, 1935.

————. *Field Operations of the Bureau of Soils.* Fifteenth Report. Washington, D.C.: U.S. Government Printing Office, 1913.

————. *Forest Rangeland Birds of the United States: Natural History and Habitat Use.* Forest Service, Agriculture Handbook 688, 1991.

————. *Iron Ore Mining in Northwest Georgia.* Forest Service, Chattahoochee-Oconee National Forests, 1985.

————. "July Field Program." Forest Service, 1914.

————. *Mountaineers and Rangers: A History of Federal Forest Management in the Southern Appalachians, 1900–1981.* Forest Service History Series, No. 380. Washington, D.C.: U.S. Department of Agriculture, 1983.

————. *The National Forests and Purchase Units of Region Eight.* Region 8 Report. Regional Office, Atlanta, 1955.

————. *Proceedings of the American Chestnut Symposium, Morgantown, West Virginia, 1978.* Northeastern Forest Experiment Station. Morgantown: West Virginia University Books, 1978.

————. *Timber Growing Practices in the Southern Appalachian Region.* Washington, D.C.: U.S. Department of Agriculture, 1931.

————. *Weeks Act of March 1, 1911.* Forest Service Manual. Washington, D.C.: U.S. Government Printing Office, 1978.

U.S. Department of Labor. *U.S. Wages and Hours of Labor in the Lumber, Millwork, and Furniture Industries.* Washington, D.C.: U.S. Government Printing Office, 1913.

U.S. Department of the Interior. *Furnishing Study: Walker Sisters Complex.* Historic Structures Report, part 2. Office of Archeological and Historic Preservation, 1969.

U.S. House of Representatives. *Report 1514 on H.R. 365.* 60th Cong., 1st sess., 1908.

U.S. Tariff Commission. *Broomcorn.* Report to the President on Investigation No. TEA-I-12 under Section 301(b) of the Trade Expansion Act of 1962. Washington, D.C.: Tariff Commission, 1968.

van Dersal, William R. *Native Woody Plants of the United States: Their Erosion-Control and*

Wildlife Values. USDA, Miscellaneous Publications No. 303. Washington, D.C.: U.S. Government Printing Office, 1938.

West Virginia Board of Agriculture. *Second Biennial Report of the West Virginia State Board of Agriculture for the Years 1893 and 1894.* Charleston, W.Va.: Moses W. Donally, 1894.

Wilburn, H. C. "Indian Gap Trail." Vertical files, Great Smoky Mountains National Park, Sugarlands Visitor Center, Gatlinburg, Tenn., n.d.

Works Project Administration. *Tennessee, a Guide to the State.* New York: Hastings House, 1939.

Zon, Raphael. *Chestnut in Southern Maryland.* USDA, Bureau of Forestry Bulletin No. 58. Washington, D.C.: U.S. Government Printing Office, 1904.

Journals

Garden and Forest 5 (1892)

Manufacturers' Record, 8 April 1892, 17 August 1894, 7 December 1894, 31 October 1901, 1 September 1905, 20 January 1910, 13 July 1911

Southern Cultivator 1 (1843), 3 (1845), 11 (1853), 54 (1896)

Southern Lumberman, 18 January 1908, 21 March 1908, 14 August 1909, 10 August 1910, 3 September 1910, 29 March 1913

Newspapers

Asheville Citizen-Times
Charleston Gazette
Chattanooga News
Cherokee Phoenix
Clinton Gazette
Daily Times
East Tennessean
Knoxville Journal
Knoxville News-Sentinel
Knoxville Register
Madisonville Patriot
Maryville Times
Nashville Banner-Advertiser
Rugbeian
Scott County News
Southern Historical News
Southwestern Reporter

Interviews and Oral Histories

Brackin, Raymer. Interview by Weaver McCracken, 1978. Transcript in Weaver McCracken Collection, Vol. 15, Great Smoky Mountains National Park.

Cagle, Winfred. Interview by William Weaver, 1973. Transcript in William Weaver Collection, vertical files, Great Smoky Mountains National Park.

Capps, Frank. Interview by author, 22 June 1990. Powell, Tenn.

Cole, Walter. Interview by Charles Grossman, 1965. Transcript in Oral History Collection, Great Smoky Mountains National Park Archives, Sugarlands Visitor Center, Gatlinburg, Tenn.

Diehl, Carl. Interview by author, 30 May 1991. Knoxville, Tenn.

Ethridge, Robbie. Interview by author, 18 September 1996. University of Georgia, Department of Anthropology.

Gump, Lucy. Interview by author, 23 March 1992. Johnson City, Tenn.

Hannah, Mark. Interviews of Tom Alexander, Uncle Thomas, Garfield Jenkins, summer 1969. Transcript in Oral History Collection, Great Smoky Mountains National Park Archives, Sugarlands Visitor Center, Gatlinburg, Tenn.

Hudson, Charles. Interview by author, 5 May 1995. Athens, Ga.

Manning, Mrs. Birgie and Johnny. Interview by Glenn Cardwell, 22 April 1980. Everts Cove, Sevier County, Tenn.

Newman, Fred. Interview by Jane Whitney, 1973. Transcript in Oral History Collection, Great Smoky Mountains National Park Archives, Sugarlands Visitor Center, Gatlinburg, Tenn.

Riggs, Brett. Interview by author, 12 February 1992. Knoxville, Tenn.

Robertson, Reuben. Interview by Jerry Mander, 1959. Vertical files, Forest History Society, Durham, N.C.

Sloan, Verna Mae. Interview by author, 12 June 1998. Hindman, Ky.

Thompson, Arnold. Interview by Weaver McCracken. Vertical files, Great Smoky Mountains National Park.

Wachacha, Maggie. Interview by Lois Calonehuskie, Earl Davis, and Tom Hill. Fading Voices Oral History Collection; transcript also in *Journal of Cherokee Studies* (1989).

Warren, Arthor. Interview by author, 10 March 1992. Ellijay, Ga.

Woody, Paul. Interview by Katherine Manscill, 1973. Transcript in Oral History Collection, Great Smoky Mountains National Park Archives, Sugarlands Visitor Center, Gatlinburg,

INDEX

Barrett, William, 201

Bartram, William, 4, 14, 44, 48, 54, 69, 71, 75, 77, 112, 223 (n. 67)

Bays, Brad Alan, 74, 75

beans, 14, 15, 17, 19, 22, 34, 38, 47, 50, 51, 60, 73, 81, 87, 100, 126, 142, 204, 209

beavers, 39, 40, 60, 63–66, 68, 69, 76, 78, 80, 90, 97, 115, 203, 207

Beech Creek (Kentucky), 140, 141

beechnuts, 25, 113. See also mast

beeswax, 77, 78, 121, 143

Biosphere Politics, ix

bison, 38, 39, 40, 53–55, 69, 111, 203. See also buffalo

black bears, 16, 31, 61, 115, 175

Black Drink, 48

Blount County (Tennessee), 97, 101, 125, 140, 148, 180

Blue Ridge mountains, 3, 4, 6, 8, 12, 13, 20, 23, 25, 32, 42, 44, 72, 77, 85, 87, 88, 97, 100, 103, 109, 130, 131, 135, 139, 142, 143, 145, 149, 155, 164, 165, 167, 168, 171, 181, 192

Board of Indian Commissioners, 64

Bookchin, Murray, x

Book of the Pearl, The, 33, 189, 190

Boone, Daniel, 96, 97

Bowron, James, 163, 164

boxed houses, 197

Braun, Lucy, 213

Brown, Margaret Lynn, xvi

buckwheat, 142, 143

buffalo, 16, 53–55, 60, 67, 73, 78, 79, 91, 111, 112, 155, 207. See also bison

Buncombe County (North Carolina), 29, 131, 143, 149, 179

Buncumbe Turnpike, 128

Burkes Gardens, 112

Burra Burra Copper Company, 158

butter, 14, 72, 75, 81, 111, 120, 132, 143

Cabrera, Juan Marquez, 39

caciques, 17, 21, 22–23, 33

Cades Cove, 101; bloomery forge in, 148; settlement of, 125–26

Campbell, John C., 6, 7, 89

Canby, Henry, 174

Cane Brake (North Carolina), 13

canebrakes, 11, 16, 27, 29, 71, 72, 75, 77, 78, 89, 97, 101, 120. See also river cane

Caribbean Islands, 46

Carolina parakeet, 15

Carter County (Tennessee), 149, 151, 152

Carter Ironworks, 152

cash markets, 136, 138, 145, 158

Castle's Wood (Virginia), 93, 96, 110

castor beans, 46, 52

cattle, 40, 46, 51, 62, 63, 68, 71–77, 79, 84, 89, 99–102, 108, 110, 111, 113, 117, 118, 126, 130–34, 136, 137, 139, 145, 146, 155, 158, 168, 174, 179, 198, 203, 207, 209. See also livestock

Caudill, Harry, 41, 193

Champion Fiber Company, 176

charcoal production, 129, 147–48; environmental impacts of, 149–51, 156, 157, 164

Chattahoochee National Forest, 153, 174

Cherokee Appalachia, 4–5, 57, 62, 79. See also Cherokees

Cherokee County (North Carolina), 131, 150

Cherokee Nation, 8, 66, 67, 84, 85, 128

Cherokee Rose, 120

Cherokees, 4, 5, 7, 24, 29, 39, 40, 44, 45, 48, 49, 52, 53, 59–81, 83–90, 95, 96, 102, 106, 107, 118, 122, 128, 156, 195, 202–11; mythology of, 61; place-names, 5, 83

Chiaha, 14–15, 23; location of, 14

Chickasaws, 59

Civil War, 50, 146, 242 (n. 123); effects on iron industry, 153; environmental effects of, 160; mussel consumption during, 190; saltpeter, 156–57

Clay County (Kentucky), 155; manufacturing in, 155

Clay County (North Carolina), 178
Cleland, Charles, xv
Clelland, Donald, xv
Clendening, Carl, 165
Clinchfield Railroad, 176
Clinchfield Timber Corporation, 176
Cole, William, 197
Conasoga, 13
Coosa, 15, 17, 18, 21–23, 27, 43, 48, 76
Cope, Dorie, 177
Copper Basin, 157; mining in, 157–59,
    204–05
core/periphery, 208, 209
corn, 14, 17, 19, 24, 27, 34, 49, 55, 60, 73,
    74, 84, 86–88, 99, 100, 108, 110, 114,
    125, 127, 131–33, 136–44, 146, 147,
    152, 160, 177, 203, 204, 209, 218 (n.
    34); corn cultivation, 28, 30, 31; corn rights,
    94; cornshuckings, 137–38; harvest home
    celebrations, 138; surpluses, 43, 139, 141
cowpeas, 46, 50–52, 55
Crackers (Georgia), 68, 131, 134
cranberries, 13
Crane, Verner, 40, 66
Crawley, David, 63
Creek Confederacy, 24, 45
Creeks, 24, 45, 47, 59, 67, 75, 106
Cronon, William, x
Crosby, Alfred, x, 43
cultural ecology, 5
Cumberland Plateau, 4, 8, 16, 17, 20, 32,
    68, 72, 96, 97, 103, 106, 108, 111, 114,
    115, 121, 123, 126, 127, 130, 131, 135,
    137, 144, 146, 149, 154, 164, 166, 176,
    178, 179, 181, 185, 186, 192, 193, 204,
    207, 213
Cumberland Valley, 15, 20
Cumming, William, 3

dams, in southern Appalachia, 182–92;
    Apalachia Dam, 184; Blue Ridge Dam,
    184; Cheoah Dam, 184; Cherokee
    Dam, 184, 186; Chickamauga Dam, 186;

Fontana Dam, 184; Hales Bar, 182;
    Hiwassee Dam, 184; Norris Dam, 184,
    186, 191; Watauga Dam, 184, 186, 192;
    Wilson Dam, 183, 190
Daniel Boone National Forest, 174
Davis, James, 94, 126
Davis, Janie Ross, 8
Davis, Mattie Boggs, 126
de Ayllón, Lucas Vázquez, 42
de Biedma, Hernandez, 11
deculturation, 45–46
deer, 22, 27, 31, 32, 38–40, 60–69, 72, 73,
    77–79, 88, 91, 108, 109, 111–13, 155,
    175, 176, 194, 203, 206, 207, 245 (n. 48)
deforestation, 34, 53, 165, 180; antebellum,
    146–47; caused by cattle, 77; caused by
    iron industry, 148–54; on frontier, 105–
    7; due to palisade construction, 30–31;
    timber industry's role in, 167–70, 175–
    76, 179–82
de la Vega, Garcilasco, 11, 42
de Luna, Tristán, 23, 37, 43, 48
Demeré, Captain Paul, 86
de Schweinitz, Frederick, 29, 48, 75, 103,
    117
de Soto, Hernando, 11–19, 25, 26, 29, 31,
    33, 42, 43, 76, 89, 206, 209
Dickerson County (Virginia), 178
Dickson-Mason Lumber Company, 176
disease, 42–43; communicable,
    42; epidemic, 42–43, 53, 85;
    European-introduced, 42; influence
    on social and cultural evolution, 44;
    smallpox, 42, 43
dogs, 25–26; feists, 25–26, 115; as pets and
    hunting animals, 25, 26, 115; Plott
    hounds, 115
Doherty, Cornelious, 66, 67
Donelson, John, 54, 111
Dragging Canoe (Chief), 88–89, 210
Drooker, Penelope Ballard, 17, 45
drovers, 100, 111, 130–33
Duke of the Cumberlands, 163

Dunaway, Wilma, 208
Dunn, Durwood, 138
du Pratz, Le Page, 50

earthen mounds, 19, 21, 33, 44, 110, 220 (n. 26)
Eastern Continental Divide, 4
East Tennessee Land Company, 150
Eller, Ronald, xvi
English, influence of, 22, 33, 38, 40, 47, 50–52, 54, 62–64, 70, 71, 73, 76, 83, 94, 97–100, 102, 104–7, 110, 111, 117, 118, 120, 121, 134, 138, 164, 203, 204
English clover, 117
environmental history, xi; 211–14
Ergood, Bruce, 7
Estill Furnace (Kentucky), 150
Etowah Furnace (Georgia), 151
Europeans, xi, 11, 12, 21, 44, 51, 62–64, 68, 79, 96, 97, 111, 117, 121, 202–4
Evarts, Jeremiah, 128

Fannin County (Georgia), 106, 136, 139, 158, 159, 172, 179
Featherstonhaugh, G. W., 4–5, 129
fences, 90, 104, 107, 195, 204; paling, 109; split-rail; 108–9, 197; stone, 109–10
Finney, John H., 169
fire, 22, 28–31, 33, 54, 85, 106, 113, 137, 147, 148, 154, 155, 157, 167–70, 186, 197; phlogiston, 29. *See also* woods burning
fish, 15, 32, 33, 60, 63, 69, 174, 179, 185–92, 194, 198, 204; fish traps, 158, 186–88, 204, 206
Fisher, David Hackett, 83, 98, 202
flooding, 69, 140, 151, 153, 168, 170, 171, 175, 182, 183, 188, 190, 205, 212; due to logging, 169–71, 175
Floyd County (Kentucky), 167, 185
folk ballads, 99
folkways, 197, 202

forests. *See* old-growth timber
Ford, Thomas R., 7
Foreign Hardwood Log Company, 176
Fort Ancient (Indians), 17, 20, 21, 23, 25, 27, 33, 44, 45, 54
Fort Loudon, 86
Foundation on Economic Trends, ix
Franklin, State of, 8, 97, 98
French, in southern Appalachia, 4, 8, 60, 71, 85, 94, 203
French and Indian War, 87, 93, 94, 103
French Broad River. *See* rivers
freshwater eels, 32, 191
freshwater pearls, 33–34, 219 (n. 54); pearl industry, 188–91
frontier, 4, 6, 14, 39, 40, 50, 62, 63, 66, 68, 76, 86, 88–90, 93, 94, 97, 99–101, 105–11, 130, 142, 150, 152, 154, 178, 179, 202, 207–9; definition of, 125, 236 (n. 1); subsistence practices, 114
fur trade, 5, 39, 62–64, 67–69, 78, 96, 203, 206, 208, 224 (n. 18)

Garden and Forest, 167
Gaventa, John, xv
Gennett Land and Lumber Company, 172
Gennett purchase, 172
Gentleman of Elvas, 11–13, 42
Georgia, 6, 7, 12, 15, 17–18, 20, 21, 37, 38, 39, 40, 41, 45, 47, 48, 49, 55, 59, 60, 65, 67, 69, 74, 75, 76, 80, 82–83, 86, 106, 112, 118, 128, 132, 135, 139, 142, 143, 146, 151, 152, 153, 155–56, 157–59, 171, 172, 173, 174, 176, 177, 179, 183, 184, 189, 192, 193, 205, 206
Georgia Gazette, The, 67
Georgia Pomological Society, 82
Georgia Railway and Power, 183, 186
Germans, influence of, 97, 102–4, 109
Giardina, Denise, x
Giles County (Virginia), 145
Gilmer County (Georgia), 172

National Forest Reservation Commission,
168, 173
Native Americans. *See* Cherokees;
Mississippians
Nelson, Robert Lynn, 138
New World: subsistence practices in, 11, 26,
46, 47, 49, 64, 100, 115, 126, 138
Norris, George W., 184
North Carolina, 7, 12, 13, 20, 23, 25, 29, 38,
41, 43, 44, 47, 48, 51, 54, 59, 60, 63, 68,
70, 72, 80, 82, 86, 87, 89, 94, 95, 96, 101,
103, 108, 112, 113, 115, 125, 127, 128,
130, 131, 135, 137, 142, 143, 144, 148,
149, 150, 155, 164, 165, 167, 168, 170,
171, 172–75, 181, 192, 193, 194, 195,
196, 197, 204, 212. *See also* Blue Ridge
Mountains

Ochlockonee River, 3
Odum, Eugene, 15
okra, 46, 52, 160
old-growth timber, 11, 16, 60, 89, 123, 164,
212
Old World crops, 46–52, 204, 206
Oliver, John W., 101, 125
Olmsted, Frederick Law, 131, 133, 143
Organic Administration Act, 169
Ortmann, A. E., 190–91
Overhill Cherokees, 45, 49, 59, 60, 63, 72,
86, 88

paddlefish, 32, 188, 191
Paintsville Lake, 185
palisades, 19, 22, 30, 31, 34
Pardo, Juan, 37, 41, 209
passenger pigeons, 31
Patton, Col. James, 93–94
peaches, 46–49, 51, 52, 55, 76, 202, 205,
208. *See also* Indian peach
pearl industry, 188–91. *See also* freshwater
pearls
Perry County (Kentucky), 145
Pinchot, Gifford, 168, 171, 175, 179, 194

Pisgah National Forest, 173–74, 178
Plott hound, 115
pokeweed, 80, 135
Polk County Copper Company, 158
pork, 72, 76, 110, 136, 154, 195. *See also*
hogs
potassium nitrate, 156
poultry, 63, 126, 136, 141, 204, 209
Powell, John Wesley, 6, 7
privet, 116, 119, 133
Pudup, Mary Beth, 126
pumpkins, 81, 100, 142, 204, 209

Qualla Cherokees, 44, 79–80, 221 (n. 29)
quillback, 32, 33, 191

Rabun County (Georgia), 143, 177, 179,
186; sheep raising in, 135
raccoons, 108, 115
Raitz, Karl, xvi
ramps, 80
Ranjel, Rodrigo, 11, 14, 18
rats, 119, 140, 177; European, 119
Ratzel, Frederick, 201
red foxes, 119
Red River Iron Region, 150
Revolutionary War, 49, 75, 88, 90, 95;
pension lists, 98
Ridge and Valley, 14, 15, 20, 75, 115, 130,
131, 134, 137, 142, 144–45, 192, 205;
deforestation in, 146
Rifkin, Jeremy, ix
Riggs, Brent, xv, 49
river bottoms, 6, 15, 17, 27, 33, 69, 72, 126,
134, 141, 203; meander-belt, 15, 203
river cane, 12, 15, 17, 29, 34, 44, 60, 71, 72,
78, 83, 133, 186, 217 (n. 6). *See also*
canebrakes
rivers: 34, 186–87, 189, 191–92;
Apalachicola, 38; Big Sandy, 20, 44,
45, 127, 166; Chattahoochee, 88, 174;
Chattooga, 3, 59, 83, 183; Clinch, 23,
32, 95, 166, 184, 189, 191; Coosa, 17, 18,

sturgeon, 32, 191

subsistence. *See* New World, subsistence practices in

sugar maple, 12, 16, 81, 144

Sumter National Forest, 174

swamp rabbit, 72, 226 (n. 52)

Swannanoa Gap (North Carolina), 12

swans, 32, 111

Swanton, John, 24, 40

Swedes: influence of, 102, 105, 223 (n. 51)

sweet potatoes, 46, 49–52, 55, 87, 139, 160, 202, 205, 222 (n. 48)

syncretism, cultural, 209–11, 250 (n. 10)

Talbot, William, 4

Tallulah Falls, 183, 185

Tallulah Falls Conservation Association, 185

Tamahittans, 39, 40

tanning industry, 196

taverns, 99, 128

Taylor, James W., 5

Tellico Blockhouse, 48, 75

Tennessee, 6, 8, 13, 14, 15, 20, 22, 29, 30, 33, 38, 45, 47, 48, 54, 59, 60, 63, 71, 72, 75, 84, 86, 87, 88, 89, 94, 95, 97, 98, 101, 103, 110, 111, 112, 114, 117, 121, 125, 126, 127, 128, 129, 130–31, 132, 134, 135, 136, 137, 139, 140, 142, 144, 145, 146, 148, 149, 150, 151, 152, 153, 154, 156, 157, 158, 159, 163, 164, 165, 166, 167, 171, 172, 173, 174, 176, 178, 180, 183, 184, 186, 187, 188, 189, 191–92, 193, 194, 195, 197, 204, 205

Tennessee River, 8, 23, 32, 44, 94, 183, 189, 190, 247 (n. 71). *See also* rivers

Tennessee Timber, Coal and Iron Company, 176

Tennessee Valley, 6, 15, 22, 23, 40, 55, 73, 74, 75, 84, 88, 93, 95–97, 110, 115, 125, 128, 130, 183, 184, 191

Tennessee Valley Authority, 8, 183–85, 186, 191

thermal belts, 81

Thompson, Peter G., 176

Tidewater region, 98

timber production, 167, 170, 172, 175, 180; effects on population, 177–78. *See also* logging; old-growth timber

Timberlake, Henry, 60, 71

timothy grass, 117, 118

Toa, 12

Toqua, 30, 48

transhumance: in Blue Ridge Mountains, 100–101; in British Isles, 100, 107

Transylvania County (North Carolina), 13

Treaty of Hard Labor, 95

Turner, Frederick Jackson, 125, 130, 155

turtles, 32, 61

Twelfth of July celebration, 99

Unaka National Forest, 174, 178

Unaka Timber Company, 167

Union County (Georgia), 172; Gennett purchase in, 172, 177

U.S. Fish and Wildlife Service, 194

Van Buren, Jarvis, 82–83

Vanderbilt, George, 175, 179

Vann, Joseph, 48, 49

Virginia, 7, 13, 23, 32–33, 42, 59, 61, 65, 66, 67, 68, 80, 81, 87, 88, 93, 94, 95, 96, 98, 103, 108, 111, 112, 117, 130, 134, 135, 139, 142, 143, 144, 145, 155, 166, 174, 176, 178, 189, 191, 195, 204

Virginia Indian Company, 65

von Thünen, Johann, 207–8

Walker, Dr. Thomas, 94

Wallace, Sam, 7

Wallerstein, Immanuel, 138

Walls, David, 3

Ward, Nancy, 75

Waselkov, Gregory, 39

Washington County (Tennessee), 110

watermelons, 46, 47, 51, 52, 223 (n. 62)

Weeks Act (1911), 171–73

West Virginia, 7, 17, 20, 23, 44, 49, 68, 87, 95, 107, 112, 114, 127, 128, 146, 147, 164, 166, 167, 171, 174, 177, 185, 195, 213

wheat, 46, 84, 99, 100, 108, 125, 127, 132, 139, 142, 143, 146, 147, 152, 160, 197

whiskey making, 99, 140, 141

Wiggan, Eleazor, 63

Wilderness Road, 97, 163

Wilderness Trail, 96

wild turkeys, 26, 27, 38, 60, 73, 77, 79, 111, 113–15, 139, 144, 175, 194; feathers, 78

William M. Ritter Lumber Company, 176

Williams, Samuel Cole, 97, 98, 148

Williamsburg (Virginia), 52, 64, 70

Wilson, James, 170

Wise County (Virginia), 178

woods burning, 14, 22, 28–31, 54, 74, 86, 100, 105–8, 155, 157, 174, 187, 193, 223 (n. 67). *See also* fire

Woodsmason, Charles, 115

Woodward, Henry, 4

wool, 53, 134–36, 143, 238 (n. 41); coloring agents, 135. *See also* sheep

world systems theory, 208, 209, 249 (n. 6)

Worster, Donald, x

Xuala, 23

yams, 46, 49

Zeigler, Wilbur, 5